What Happened to the Southern Baptist Convention?

A Memoir of the Controversy

What Happened to the Southern Baptist Convention?

A Memoir of the Controversy

by
Grady C. Cothen

Smyth & Helwys Publishing
Macon, Georgia

ISBN   1-880837-30-7 paperback
1-880837-26-9 hardcover

What Happened to the Southern Baptist Convention?
A Memoir of the Controversy

Grady C. Cothen

Copyright © 1993
Smyth & Helwys Publishing, Inc.
Macon, Georgia

Printed in the United States of America.

The paper used in this publication meets the minimum
requirements of American Standard for Information
Sciences—Permanence of paper for Printed Library Materials,
ANSI Z39.48–1984.

Library of Congress Cataloging-in-Publication Data

Cothen, Grady C.
What happened to the southern baptist convention?
a memoir of the controversy / by Grady C. Cothen
xii+382pp.   6x9" (15x23cm.)
ISBN 1-880837-30-7 (alk. paper)
1. Southern Baptist Convention—History—20th century.
2. Baptists—United States—History—20th century.
3. Fundamentalism—History.   I. Title.   II. Title: Southern Baptist
Convention controversy.   III. Title: Controversy.
BX6462.3.C67 1993
286'.132'09048—dc20   93—4908
                                                                CIP

With Appreciation
for
Grady Jr. and Leila
Carole and Hugh
Mary and Ken

Contents

Preface

The almost total disruption of the largest non-Catholic denomination in America has occurred in the last decade and a half. From a well-organized and cooperative body deeply involved in missions and education, it has moved toward fragmentation. Its institutions and agencies have suffered near catastrophic disruption. Emphasis has shifted from co-operative endeavor to the discussion of schism. In a large measure growth has been interrupted, financial goals go unmet, and institutional disruption has reached to almost every corner of the Southern Baptist Convention.

For forty years, the convention was my spiritual home. I participated in its activities beginning in the local congregation, the regional association of churches, the state convention bodies and the national convention. I was a pastor, a state Executive Secretary, a university president, a seminary president and president of the national publishing house. Life was totally involved with being a Southern Baptist.

The controversy represented for me and thousands of others a personal catastrophe, not because of any loss of status but because of the loss of a way of life. Thus, this memoir.

This is an attempt to chronicle what is known about what happened more than an investigation of all the antecedent culture and sociology. The emphasis is on the changes produced by the conflict within the structure and functions of the denomination. It seems necessary to trace the events, large and small, in some detail in order to feel sweep of change. The changes are more drastic than appear on the surface and an understanding of the inner workings of the denomination is necessary to present an accurate picture.

Access to many persons, documents and facets of the conflict was available. While other good accounts of the controversy have been written, none had the personal perspective that seemed desirable in documenting the development and results of the problems. The personal element, of course, probably obscures some elements from a clear view.

This memoir is based on interviews with most of the important leaders of both sides of the conflict. Many of these people I have known for many years. Massive documents from interested persons, agencies, board members and archives have been accumulated and studied. The Baptist Press and other news releases have furnished an historical and chronological framework for organizing the study.

Perhaps it is best to admit from the beginning that I have not told all I know. Some incidents do not contain all of the inside information I have had available. The welfare of persons and institutions have played a serious role in my choice of material. At the same time, I have tried to present a true picture of the various situations.

The interpretations and conclusions are my own, unless otherwise stated. They come from my understanding of what went on and the results produced.

During the years since the controversy burst on the national scene in 1979, the nature of being a Southern Baptist has been redefined. The character of the denomination has been radically changed with the resultant redefinition of the nature of our fellowship. An attempt is made in this work to trace this revolution.

On Calling People Names

Concerning the use of names in this work, it is not easy to chose those that are both descriptive and acceptable. The press, without much success, tried several combinations such as fundamental-conservatives and moderate-conservatives. The leaders of the invasion preferred to be called conservatives and called the rest liberals. Finally, because of the cumbersome usages, the most conservative called themselves con-servatives and the others sometimes moderates and sometimes liberals. The moderates frequently called the others fundamentalists, which many of them strongly resented. This use of names is important because whole careers have risen or fallen because of the side of the conflict chosen.

In this work, the movement that swept over the Southern Baptist Convention will be called fundamentalism. The term and reasons for it are described at length in Chapter 4. By any scholarly definition of the term "fundamentalist", the movement qualified for the name.

On occasion, the name of rightists is assigned to the movement participants and centrists to the so-called moderates.

Though the movement was fundamentalist in its program and orientation, not all of those who joined its cause or voted its line are true fundamentalists. Many of the people who supported the movement by votes were and are conservative Christians who had honest convictions about what ought to be done, many without malice toward others. It is not possible to identify who all of these are and at any given point in the last twelve years, some have shifted from one side to another depending on the issue.

For those who do not like to be called fundamentalists, there are many others who do not like to be called moderates or liberals. In this volume, the movement will be identified and described with no intent to catagorize individuals except the obvious leaders who positioned themselves. When the term "fundamentalists" is used, the intention is to describe the movement and the actions the movement caused. This of necessity includes those persons who helped make these decisions.

I have tried to let the words and actions of the participants tell their story with a minimum of adjectives. In retrospect, some of the evidence cited seems to me to be in the "horrendous" category, and I have reexamined some of it to see if the facts are there. In my judgment, they are.

There has been far too much material to use all of it. There remains to be done intensive research into many aspects of the controversy in the SBC. Several doctoral dissertations will likely come from the conflict. It is evident now that sources are being closed to research, history is being rewritten or at least restated. and the news released sometimes seems to be skewed. More and more Baptist meetings are being held behind closed doors and decisions are being made in caucuses without official standing. Individuals are being silenced and the future of such investigations is cloudy.

Acknowledgments

Lilly Endowment vice president Fred Hofhienz first made inquiry about such a study. The Endowment made this study possible by a grant that permitted the travel and necessary research. It could not have been done without this gracious assistance. James Wind of the Endowment was most helpful in evaluating the concept and securing the grant.

Samford University in Birmingham, Alabama acted as fiscal agent handling the detailed accounting and disbursing functions. Provost William Hull made this possible. Dennis Simms, Controller of the University, and his staff have been very helpful and always courteous.

I am indebted to the Advisory Committee who helped me to formulate and outline the study. Their contribution was limited only by my time and health constraints. The committee consisted of: William

Hull, Provost of Samford University, Bill Leonard, formerly professor of Church History, Southern Baptist Theological Seminary and now head of the Religion Department of Samford University; Glenn Miller, formerly of Southeastern Baptist Theological Seminary, now professor of Church History, Bangor Theological Seminary; Carolyn Weatherford Crumpler, former Executive Director of Woman's Missionary Union, now a pastor's wife; and Christa Klein, consultant to Lilly Endowment, seminary professor and pastor's wife.

Each in a special way gave me a pointer or suggestion or attitude or question that pointed up some aspect of the work. To them all, I extend hearty thanks. Any shortcomings are mine, not theirs.

When the need arose, Hugh Westbrook, Chairman of the Board of Hospice, Inc. in Miami, Florida made additional funds available. This substantial gift allowed some additional investigation to be performed that made the task easier and more complete.

My wife, Bettye, has watched the process with interest and cooperated in every way, including doing without my presence sometimes when she needed me.

I have talked to many of the principal participants in the drama. Many of them have been cooperative and open in their responses. Many persons in places of responsibility have talked with me at some length and sometimes at some risk to themselves. I have tried to be careful with their confidences and honest with their answers. A few could not or would not talk freely because of constraints placed on them by position or instruction.

I am indebted to Albert McClellan of Nashville for his "Theses" and hours of conversation. He has shared generously of his time and learning while undergoing great personal physical stress.

Many persons have offered documents and information of one variety or other. Some of this I would never have found on my own and some is hidden from the world at large. They have offered insights into problems that were vital to understanding the larger picture.

To all these and to those of whom I will think when this is done, I extend my grateful thanks. You have made a long road easier.

All royalties to the author from this book will be given to Baptist causes.

Grady C. Cothen

Chapter One

Classic Confrontation

"In The Beginning. . . ."[1]

The Houston Astrodome was packed with nearly 50,000 people, many scrambling for a seat. The atmosphere was alive with anticipation and excitement. Baptists—Southern variety—had come to launch formally their greatest mission effort in history. It has often been said since that it was the most ambitious such attempt in evangelical history. They were happy to be there and to be a part of such an impossible effort. It was June 13, 1979.

This was the night in the middle of the convention meeting set aside for the launching of Bold Mission thrust—an attempt to take the gospel to every person in the world by the year A. D. 2000. Rationally, many recognized it was impossible, but most agreed that it should be tried. This night was the culmination of years of planning, meeting, conferring, exhorting, and financing—and even of a conference at the White House with Southern Baptist President Jimmy Carter.

Cliff Barrows of the Billy Graham staff led an 8000 voice choir in singing "The Lord's Prayer." Baker James Cauthen, president of the Foreign Mission Board, reminded the audience that they had been given the Great Commission by Christ and pled for support of the missionaries who were to be sent to the far places. He appealed for the appointed missionaries to come down to the playing field and for at least one other Baptist willing to support them with money and prayers to come with them. The throng holding hands in rows almost covered the playing field.

Billy Graham urged the audience to "turn the world upside down for Christ." He issued a call for volunteers to "go where God wants you to go, and do what he wants you to do." More that 1200 persons responded to the spirited appeal. The high moments of the Bold Mission launch had

---

[1]Genesis 1:1.

come and Baptists seemed ready to give it their best effort. They left moved, happy, and sobered by the challenge that was a part of who they were. This challenge was different, though, since they had never undertaken such a staggering assignment.

This movement had begun three years before when a Missions Challenge Committee led by Tulsan Warren Hultgren had made fifteen recommendations that urged the convention to do that which they claimed to believe. The essence of this organization of Baptists was cooperation in the proclamation of the gospel. This was its stated purpose from the first day when the convention came into existence in 1845. Many other activities had been added across the years, but this was the genius and guiding principle of the loosely knit churches that had sent their representatives to this meeting in large numbers.

The committee report began by emphasizing the need to let every person in the world hear the gospel in the next 25 years. Along with this basic premise, there was a call to make the local congregation central in the effort, that a complex integration of the programs of all the organized entities be undertaken to support the effort. This included the Foreign Mission Board, Home Mission Board, Sunday School Board, the six seminaries, and all the commissions. In addition to all this, there were financial plans for implementation, the seminaries were encouraged to cooperate in every way, and various suggestions were given to assure coordinated efforts. One of the important features of the effort was a provision that the mission boards create as many ways for short-term involvement of as many lay persons as possible. This aspect of the movement had been strongly addressed by President Jimmy Carter with SBC leaders in the White House.

By 1977, plans were advancing rapidly to undergird the world-wide effort. At the convention that year, detailed plans were presented for the cooperation of five agencies in mission education, looking toward lay participation in the short and long terms, and in financing the effort. It was recommended and passed that 5000 individuals and churches be enlisted to secure and fund 5000 volunteers who would go to mission sites around the world for one or two year terms. It was hoped that 100,000 shorter term persons would undertake some special task in the movement.

By 1978, agencies, churches and individuals were getting into the spirit of the effort. Five-year cycles were established with unusual goals set for performance, for example 5800 church-type missions were set as a goal for the first cycle. 1000 career missionaries were to be added to the HMB and FMB. Each church was urged to enlarge its financial base by fifteen per cent annually and double its Cooperative Program (state and national unified cooperative mission budget) giving.

Specific and detailed plans were advanced to help the churches get ready for this unusual undertaking. Emphasis was placed on Bible study, enlarged Sunday schools were planned, renewed dedication to personal spiritual development was called for, and every entity in the state conventions and the SBC were called on to give prominence in every meeting to this united effort.

This rehearsal represents only a small fraction of the planning and effort dedicated to Bold Mission Thrust. By 1979, all the seminaries (six) were fully involved, as were many of the colleges and universities (more than fifty). Southern Baptists at the time were about six percent of the population of the United States, but had about twenty percent of all the theological students in the nation in our seminaries. Enthusiasm for Bold Mission was growing by 1979.

Massive efforts were made at every level to enlist the support of every Southern Baptist in the country. In the state conventions, in the district associations, and in the churches programs were dedicated to the promotion of the effort and provided extensive information to as many persons as possible. Special promotional meetings were held all over the country. Lay persons began to volunteer for short-term mission projects. Churches began raising their level of giving to the national mission funds. Professional volunteers were increasing and the mission boards began to call for yet more money to fund the growing effort. There had never been anything like this in the SBC before and it began to gain momentum. Since the convention had no authority over churches or individuals, this was an outstanding achievement.

The denomination was possessed of strong capable leadership in almost every major post on the national level. Though the executive leaders of the Foreign Mission Board, the Radio-Television Commission, and the Executive Committee of the SBC all retired as the effort was launched, they and others had prepared well, and the great effort moved on without discernable hitch. Their replacements and other executives not long on the scene brought new vigor and determination to see Bold Mission Thrust succeed.

Prior to 1979, there had been no major theological difficulty since the controversy over the new Broadman Commentary had reached its height in 1970–1971. This commentary had produced a flurry of theological disagreement that lasted for several years. There had been a conscious effort since then not to muddy the Baptist waters, with many feeling that this mission endeavor was worthy of the best that could be given to it. The seminary faculties seemed to go out of their way to avoid problems. The Sunday School Board—the source of many differences of opinion—had a period of nearly ten years without a major controversy.

The people were ready. The agencies were fully supportive of BMT, the laity were buying into the effort in large numbers, and financial support was increasing. Mission volunteers were coming to the mission boards in large numbers. The colleges, universities, and seminaries had more mission volunteers than ever. By 1979, the Foreign Mission Board had 2912 missionaries under appointment. The Home Mission Board had 2805 missionaries spread across all fifty states. The Sunday School Board distributed more that 12,600,000 periodicals to thousands of churches, with millions of pieces of supportive materials of almost infinite variety. The seminaries in 1978–1979 enrolled 10,945 students.

A book full of information is available on the state of the denomination that fateful day in 1979. Much of it was good to very good and signaled a new approach to an old task with new enthusiasm for sharing the gospel. Almost all was in readiness for the acceleration of the cumbersome machinery of the largest non-catholic denomination in America. It was beginning to move in new ways with new levels of cooperation in every area of denominational life. All of this was the result of good will, cooperation for the common good, and commitment to a common goal.

The leadership was encouraged, thinking that all was as well as it ever is in a structure wholly dependent on cooperation without any form of ecclesiastical control.

But there was *ANOTHER AGENDA.*

Another Agenda

On Tuesday afternoon of this same week, June 12, 1979, there had been six persons nominated for president of the convention. Some of them were well-known and long-time servants of the denomination, including Robert Naylor, popular former president of Southwestern Seminary. Of just over 12,000 votes cast, Adrian Rogers pastor of Bellevue Baptist Church, Memphis received 6129 (51.36 percent) on the first ballot! Few there knew the long-range ramifications of this seemingly routine election. After all, who was president made little difference —usually—in the direction of the convention. This time, it would make a lot of difference. He was to become the first of a long line of presidents elected by reactionary forces.

This election was the culmination of a long and tedious process set in motion by many forces. That the turning point in SBC history came at this moment was the result of the work of many persons led by Appeals Court Judge Paul Pressler from Houston and Paige Patterson, president of Criswell Center for Biblical Studies, Dallas. Pressler reputedly came from a wealthy Texas family who had strong ties to the George Bush family and others of affluence and political clout. He was a graduate of Phillips Exeter Academy of Exeter, New Hampshire, Princeton University, and the University of Texas Law School.

Paul Pressler has said that he identified theological liberalism as far back as his days at Exeter. He was surrounded with it at Princeton. While at Princeton, he organized a group of conservative students and led them into a church that was not Baptist. With his return to Houston, he continued his pattern of finding theological liberalism. He often told the story of Baylor students whom he had taught in Sunday School bringing him their text books from Baylor University, the largest of the Baptist universities. He says that he was appalled at what they were being taught in religion classes at the university.

By the 1960s he was involved in trying to enlist help to make at least one of the seminaries of the Southern Baptist convention "conservative." He and a group of Texas laymen had chosen New Orleans Baptist Theological Seminary as their choice. He had worked at some length with president Leo Eddleman to secure the conservatism he felt desirable. When I became president in 1970, it was not many months before he called me to inquire if I would cooperate with them to create and maintain a Southern Baptist seminary that would fit his understanding of theological conservativism. In return, the seminary would receive funds from a private foundation with which he had influence. I refused the initial $10,000 offer since I knew of the rising tide of controversy surrounding the seminary partially because of these events.

Then there was the matter of the trustee system that had worked well in the convention for a hundred years. The system was arranged so that a Southern Baptist school must not come under the control of an outside group, whatever their motives.

Paige Patterson, who was to play a major role in the developing problems, was the son of a very conservative former executive director of the Baptist General Convention of Texas. He was a graduate of New Orleans Seminary. He was known as an avid conservative theologically and had contested theology with the seminary faculty.

Back at the convention meeting in Houston, the Judge reportedly sat high in a sky-box overlooking the convention floor calling the signals for his organization. Southern Baptists were getting their first look at an organized take-over attempt in 134 years. The judge was bringing to bear on the convention his own ideas of what it should be. This was the emergence of the tip of the political iceberg that had been years in the making.

From the outset of its public emergence, the methodology of the Pressler group was under scrutiny and criticism. The obviously organized attempt to elect a president was a new phenomenon. Of course, there had been minor political actions before on behalf of others who had served as president. These efforts usually consisted of a few phone calls or letters. Sometimes an alumni group would get together to try to elect one of their own. There were a few failed attempts to promote someone for president with public relations campaigns. One had a biographical film extolling the greatness of a candidate (he was defeated). There were other rather obvious and unsuccessful efforts at self-glorification. These brought laughter, disgust, or some votes—according to the effectiveness of the effort. But by and large, there had never been an organized effort to control the election of the president. Most thought the office honorary, and few had any real fears of what would be done regardless of who was elected.

But this time, it was all different.

Judge Pressler was and is a skilled politician. He understood the requirements necessary for controlling the election of a president of the Southern Baptist Convention. He set out to accomplish the objective. He talked incessantly to anyone he could get to listen about getting "conservative" Baptists to the convention in large numbers to vote for a "conservative" president.

Perhaps more importantly, he thought he had discovered a way to take complete control of the convention over a period of eight to twelve years. The president of the convention appointed the Committee on Committees. The Committee on Committees nominated the Committee on Boards (now Committee on Nominations). The Committee on Boards nominated all the members of the boards of trustees of all the agencies of the convention. Simply then, if the right president could be elected, in a few years all the agencies would be controlled by trustees whose appointment was dictated by the power structure in control.

Pressler gave an interview to Gary North in 1985 or 1986. It came to be known as the "Firestorm Chats." In the interview, he said that he had been studying these matters for more than twenty years. This would place the beginnings on his part back to at least 1965. He said in the same interview that he was an observer during a controversy over a book by Ralph Elliot, a professor at Midwestern Baptist Theological Seminary. He also studied the Broadman Commentary controversy that raged over doctrinal disputes about the commentary. At the time of those conflicts, he had never been to a meeting of the Southern Baptist Convention. In the interview with North he described in detail the mechanisms to be understood and utilized in controlling the convention through the election of presidents who agreed with his philosophy.

When asked by North, the interviewer on the Firestorm Chat, whether he had a model, he replied that he did not. He knew (1) how to get the people out to vote their own personal convictions and (2) how to work within the system to change it. When asked how he got the people out, he said that he started speaking and Paige Patterson started speaking. They were trying to convince the people that the liberals were in charge of the convention. He quoted from books and speeches "written by liberals" to the people "all over the country." He said that in 1978, in one trip from Houston for six days, he spoke at least six or seven times a day and probably spoke fifty times during those six days. (Between January and June, 1985 he said that he spoke over 200 times in sixteen states.)

As a result of all this and a lot more, Pressler said in the above mentioned interview, that in the Houston convention in 1979, there were six candidates for president of the convention. Some of them were very conservative, but all "our" people supported Adrian Rogers. Adrian Rogers was elected with over fifty percent on the first ballot, which had never happened in a six-man race before.[2]

This interview is startling in its clarity about the methods used and the results. When asked what Adrian Rogers, the new president, did to indicate that the beginning of the war was now going in his direction, Pressler replied that Adrian appointed an absolutely superb Committee on Committees and an absolutely superb Committee on Resolutions, and the other appointments he made were very good. But those are the two crucial committees. Practically, this meant that the take-over group got the nominations they wanted in the first year of the organized effort.

Through a Glass, Darkly

When the 1979 convention meeting is examined in detail, it is obvious that a lot more of the intended direction was exposed than was generally known or understood. Many matters (some of which had come up before) that were to become major issues were introduced to the convention in the form of motions or resolutions.

A motion was made requiring doctrinal positions of officers. It failed.

A motion was made that all appointments . . . of the mission boards refuse to "recognize the ordination of women as being scriptural truth held by Baptists." It failed.

One resolution called for disavowing the Baptist Joint Committee as the spokesman of the convention to the government. It failed but was a taste of things to come.

One resolution supported public schools. It passed.

Abortion was center stage in a discussion on another resolution.

On the other side of the fence, resolutions or motions were passed disavowing political activity in the election of the officers of the convention. Judge Pressler thought it necessary to reply as a point of personal privilege since he and others thought it was directed at him. A motion was passed to have a study of reported voting irregularities investigated. Some thought that others voted more than one ballot and children too young to understand what was going on were reported to be

---

[2]Gary North Interview with Paul Pressler, "Strategies for Overwhelming Liberalism," Firestorm Chats, Dominion Tapes, Fort Worth or Institute of Christian Economics, Tyler, Texas, 1986.

voting with adult supervision.

The seminaries had been under increasing attack for liberalism, a charge that remained largely unspecified. Specific complaints were often drawn from problems several years old. During this water-shed convention meeting, a resolution was hotly debated that called on those who had concerns to observe the procedures for dealing with such issues set forth in the constitution and bylaws of the convention.

In the same meeting, the program statements for the seminaries were changed, and they were instructed to maintain high academic standards. They were to verify the educational quality "through participation in appropriate accrediting agencies such as regional accrediting agencies . . . [and] the Association of Theological schools." Even this would be challenged in years to come.

Still another resolution on doctrinal integrity in the seminaries was introduced and finally ruled out of order since it had been dealt with in another doctrinal resolution.

Creedalism and priesthood of believers were also discussed.[3]

Clearly, many of the issues that would haunt the Baptist fellowship for years were laid out in one form or another that first year of the declared war. Notice was being served on those in leadership positions that the preferred issues were being staked out and that trouble was brewing. The intent of the new movement can now be discerned in the events of that week in 1979. They were not so clear then.

We did not recognize the arrival of a developing fundamentalist mind-set and a set of fundamentalist leaders who would wield vast influence over the body politic.

Long-time Baptist leaders saw these events in a variety of ways. No one knew the full significance of the obvious change of attitude by many toward the affairs of the denomination. Some thought there was simply a swing of the pendulum. Others thought that it was serious but that there was not much that the Pressler group could do. Others thought that discerning people would see the light pretty soon and the ship would return to a straight course.

No one was aware that this was the beginning of a major fundamentalist movement. They had never seen such a movement before, did not believe that it was that serious, and were unprepared to deal with

---

[3]*SBC Annual*, Nashville, 1979.

it. They were confident that Christians did not do such things as organize to elect a president and control a denomination. There were boards of trustees with established written procedures in place to correct any genuine problems, and these had been used many times before. Perhaps the most serious misreading of the situation was in the idea that if the people were told the truth and had adequate opportunity for discussion and deliberation, they would ultimately come out in support of the traditional Southern Baptist positions. In this case, "ultimately" was a long time away.

Few denominational executives and seminary administrators realized the scope of the continuing misrepresentation of the problems in the seminaries. All of them had heard the general and nebulous charges of "liberalism." A liberal as defined by Paul Pressler was anyone "who believes that the Bible can contain errors." Few realized that more and more honest people were beginning to believe the oft repeated charge and what was now the party line that the seminaries were full of liberal professors. The few problems that did exist were magnified and the proper procedures for correcting them were ignored. The seminaries would become the center of the problems for years to come. They were in a poor position to defend themselves, since to many uneducated Baptists, they had always been suspect.

Few denominational executives realized the strong anti-establishment mood of many Baptists—and of the entire country. In the years to come, one got the feeling from the wild accusations and general unrest that all incumbents in the organizations of the denomination should be thrown out. Few realized that the fundamentalist attack on the agency executives would be so severe. Often the people were led to believe that executives had to go in order for a new age to be born. The avowed determination to change the constituency of the trustees of all the agencies was also aimed at ridding the convention of its principal leadership.

It was not yet clear the the central battles would be fought over the nature of scripture. Generally Southern Baptists believe in the inspiration and authority of scripture. There have always been differences as to how God inspired the Bible. But Baptists will always vote for the Bible. Within a very short time, the issue of "inerrancy" came to the fore and has remained there through the years. The issue basically had to do with the differences in the accounts of various historical events, the accuracy of observations about scientific matters, whether books of the Bible bearing the name of a person were actually written by them, and a variety of technical issues that have little to do with the spiritual message of the Bible. (The nature of these problems are discussed at length in chapter 5.)

The fact that the people on the two developing sides of the issue were in the main very close together on their understanding of scripture was minimized and often deliberately ignored and sometimes misrepresented. Fundamentalist leaders early on staked out the position that theirs was the only position that was orthodox. In future confrontations, then, it was only requisite that the motions and resolutions for denominational action be formulated in such a way as to magnify the importance, veracity, and authority of the Bible. The vote to verify an orthodox faith in scripture would be forthcoming.

There was another early misunderstanding on the part of the traditional leadership and many others. They did not recognize that the conflict was so formulated that there was no negotiating room on any issue. The fundamentalists proceeded from the inerrancy stance, and any compromise on their part was unthinkable. To negotiate was to give in to heresy (from their perspective, defined as any view that did not agree with their position). While they became consummate politicians, they did not know or did not subscribe to the theory that "politics is the art of the possible." Early in the controversy, they adamantly refused to acknowledge that their view did not take into account the diversity that had characterized Southern Baptists from the beginning. It became obvious very soon that there was no intention of trying to find a meeting of minds on the issues they raised. This was the case, in spite of the often repeated assertion that the "moderates" (anyone who disagreed) would not sit down and discuss the issues.

In fact, discussions were held from time to time with small groups (sometimes inappropriate groups), but they ended in frustration since one side had no ground to give. For the fundamentalists, the statement that "there are some things I will not compromise on" became the declaration of choice when final decisions had to be made.

Theology or Control

In the years that followed, an argument over the nature of the controversy developed and continued. The fundamentalists insisted that the conflict was over theology. Others saw it as a struggle for power. A major mistake of the moderates was the failure to see that for the fundamentalists the issue was really theological. Most moderate leaders contended for years that the struggle was all about power, and it certainly was about power. Many moderates had the understanding that the fundamentalists were accusing them of drifting too far to the left theologically, so they must change the system to save the denomination. Their illustrations of liberalism did follow this line. Moderate leaders did not believe this to be true and, thus, denied that the conflict was theological.

The real truth about the matter, however, was that this was an attempt to force on the Southern Baptist convention a fundamentalist mind-set and make it the norm for all decisions in matters of faith, polity, philosophy, and theology. From this stance, the issue was surely theological. Nothing less than a total exchange of a fundamentalist theology for the long-ascendant centrist theology would satisfy the fundamentalist leaders and their supporters. From the outset, it sounded like the old saying, "East is east and west is west and ne'er the twain shall meet."[4]

It is certain that we saw "through the glass darkly."

In retrospect, it is surprising that centrist leadership did not see the handwriting on the walls. An examination of the events surrounding the 1979 meeting of the convention casts a clear light on what was going on.

A quick look at some events that year recorded by Baptist Press will reveal a pattern that was to obtain for years to come. The strategy of the fundamentalists was carefully thought out and orchestrated masterfully.

In April, 1979 a Knoxville, Tennessee, interim pastor sent out 4000 copies of a two-page indictment of a sentence in a Sunday School quarterly that contained an obvious error.

In May, Paige Patterson—the Pressler confidant and partner—confirmed to the press that there had been meetings in fifteen states to discuss the issues before the convention—namely the reliability of scripture—and to discuss ways to elect leadership committed to inerrancy.[5]

Two weeks later, the seminary presidents attempted to refute the inflated charges of liberalism in the schools. Each of them affirmed

---

[4]Fundamentalism is discussed at length in Chapter 3.
[5]Baptist Press, 9 May 1979.

personal faith in the reliability of scripture. They told the meeting and press that they would continue their tradition of helping Southern Baptists to continue as a "Bible-centered people, firmly believing and striving to practice what the Bible teaches." They further affirmed that in each of the six seminaries, faculty persons had pledged their allegiance to the doctrinal statement, *The Baptist Faith and Message*.[6]

The calendar of events keyed to the future unfolded in the next three days of that convention meeting. On June 1, 1979, just days before the convention meeting started, W. A. Criswell, pastor of the First Baptist Church in Dallas (the largest SBC church), said that he and James Robison, fiery evangelist, would hold fifteen to twenty conferences during the next year aimed at affirming the Bible as the authoritative Word of God. The seminary presidents promptly volunteered to speak at these meetings. The press did not confirm that this offer was accepted.[7]

It was Adrian Rogers who fired the opening salvo in the conference of pastors just before the convention convened. He was pastor of Bellevue Baptist Church in Memphis, the largest of the churches east of the Mississippi river.He criticized liberalism, which he said was taking over the Baptist colleges, seminaries, and denominational agencies. He attacked the press for supporting the agencies he criticized.

On that same day, in the meeting of the Pastor's Conference attended by thousands, Criswell strongly and emotionally endorsed Rogers for president of the convention. Rogers had said that he was still praying over the matter.

Later in the day, James Robison made a scathing attack on the seminaries and colleges as seedbeds of liberalism and urged the election of a president who would clean up the situation.

On the same day, Harold Lindsell, sometime Southern Baptist and the author of a controversial book, *The Battle For The Bible*, appeared at a news conference. After his problems at Fuller Seminary, he had now come to the rescue of Southern Baptists. He thoroughly excoriated the "liberals" and called for their exclusion. Duke McCall, president of Southern Baptist Theological Seminary answered him and tried to deal with the charges.[8]

---

[6]Baptist Press, 23 May 1979.
[7]Baptist Press, 1 June 1979.
[8]Baptist Press, 11 June 1979.

The Executive Committee of the convention, meeting in pre-convention session, used the opportunity to hear appeals from its chairman, Brooks Wester, and Duke McCall and others to avoid schism.

On Monday, June 11, SBC president Jimmy Allen used the meeting of the Women's Missionary Union as a platform to plead for unity in the convention.

Interestingly, future stars of the fundamentalist movement were prominent in the Pastor's Conference that week. James Draper was elected as its president. Jerry Vines preached in a prominent spot on the program. Charles Stanley, pastor in Atlanta made a patriotic appeal, decrying socialism and communism as well as immorality, drugs, pornography, and governmental red tape. All three of these men were in subsequent years elected president of the convention.[9]

On the opening day of the convention, President Jimmy Allen pleaded with the messengers to refuse to be divided. He said, "As I perceive it, we are being pressed by good and sincere people right now to alter our agenda from Bold Mission Thrust. We must resist that temptation."[10]

It was that afternoon that Adrian Rogers was elected President over five other candidates on the first ballot. As a matter of fact, due to his popularity as a preacher, he would probably have been elected whether the Pressler-Patterson coalition supported him or not.

At his press conference, he declared that "the presidency of the Southern Baptist convention does mean that certain people feel certain ways or a certain man would not be elected, but that doesn't mean he has control of the convention." He pledged his complete support for the emphasis on Bold Mission thrust. He said that he would head no witch hunt but favored an investigation of the seminaries by a "balanced committee." He said that he would try to be president of all Southern Baptists. He disavowed any debt to the Pressler-Patterson faction. He also stated that he did not agree to be nominated for president until after 2:30 A. M. in a prayer meeting the night before the nomination.[11]

Reaction to Roger's election varied from exaltation to bitter disappointment. Most of the reaction was cautious or rejoicing depending

[9]Baptist Press, 12 June 1979.
[10]Baptist Press, 12 June 1979.
[11]Baptist Press, 12 June 1979.

on the individuals. Most centrist leadership, still not understanding the extent of the revolution, displayed little emotion, and most practiced Christian reserve.

In an impromptu press conference, Judge Pressler "denied planning, strategizing or implementing any organized effort to elect Adrian Rogers." He admitted participating in a dinner meeting attended by 400 conservatives where an "advisory sampling of opinion" was taken to reflect to the three individuals under consideration. He asserted that "simply the conservatives are communicating with each other for the first time." He said that when he returned to Houston after a vacation with an ailing son, "Conservatives will continue to do what others have done: communicate.[12]

Interestingly, Pressler probably was not a legal messenger to the convention. He said that he was an "honorary" member of the Bellaire Church but was a member of First Baptist Church. The Bellaire Church elected him as a messenger. There is no provision in the constitution of the convention for such a person to be recognized as a messenger.

As one might expect, these carryings on were not appreciated by those who had given their lives to the building of the convention. Porter Routh, for more than 25 years the chief executive officer of the Executive Committee of the convention, declared on the final day of the meeting that the concerns over the seminaries should be heard. But he added, "I am concerned about the methodology of a secular political machine used at the convention this year. I don't believe this is the way God would have us move in the future."

Routh's successor, Harold Bennett, affirmed his own commitment to inerrancy of scripture and admitted to having had lunch earlier in the year with Criswell, Patterson, and Pressler. Had he known of their activities, he said that he probably would not have done so.[13]

The same press report said that the registration secretary of the convention promised an intensive investigation into alleged irregularities in voting procedures during the election of the president. Since the Rogers' majority was only 163 votes, some thought the outcome was in question. Some churches had more than the legal limit—ten—messengers. Some messengers registered twice, and some pastors registered for all ten

---

[12]Baptist Press, 13 June 1979.
[13]Baptist Press 14 June 1979.

of their messengers—a practice since disallowed. One pastor registered for himself, his wife, and four children. Under questioning by another pastor, he admitted that the children were out at the KOA campground and not at the convention. Another pastor told of watching a man mark eleven ballots in the presidential election and turn in all of them.

On Thursday morning, the body erupted into controversy over a resolution decrying overt political activity in the selection of convention officers. The body passed the resolution after a short but acrimonious debate. Pressler said after the meeting,

> I'm against power politics, but I'm for greater participation of laymen in the convention. I'm absolutely appalled by the reaction that it is wrong to encourage more participation of laymen in the convention. All we did was to inform other Baptists about the problems of parking and transportation, and suggest that some churches might want to form transportation pools and more than one church come in buses or cars.[14]

Newly elected president Rogers met with the editors of the 34 state Baptist papers after the meeting. A wide variety of subjects was discussed. BP reported that "several of the state Baptist newspapers have been at odds with the 'conservative coalition' that helped propel Rogers into office on the first ballot." One of them said that he feared Roger's greatest problem would be his former association with non-Southern Baptist convention-owned and operated agencies. Rogers replied that he would continue to support Mid-America Baptist Theological Seminary, which was adjacent to his church in Memphis. He had served as a trustee of Luther Rice seminary in Jacksonville, Florida. He was reported to have said that he did not object to the Florida school awarding a doctorate to a student who might have come straight from high school. "You pay for what you get." He reiterated his belief that the SBC seminaries had professors who do not believe in the inerrancy of the Bible.

In listing his goals, the new president said he wanted to be heard, to listen, and to help distill the issues; he wanted to communicate that a man who believes the Bible is not an ogre; he wanted to set the tone of evangelism and missions for Bold Mission Thrust; he would not appoint

---

[14]Pressler, as quoted by Baptist Press, 14 June 1979.

a person to anything who does not believe the Bible is inerrant.[15] This was probably the first time that a single doctrinal position would become the criterion for all appointed and elected officials of the convention.

On the last day, the convention affirmed its confidence in its seminaries.

The convention rejected the barring of ordained women from appointment by the mission boards. The mind-set of the fundamentalists related to women in ministry was not yet dominant. This matter would arise again and again for years.

The Stage Is Set

In these few pages, much if not most of the ground to be covered in the next twelve years is clearly visible. The glaring incongruities can be traced. The constant contradictions are clearly illustrated. The fundamentalist mindset is revealed. The moderates were clearly unprepared for what happened and for what was to come. The pastor's conference would be used again and again as the pep rally before the business of the convention. Organized opposition to the established leadership would surface frequently. Those who were opposed to the movement saw catastrophe, while the other a side saw a "return" to biblical faith.

The moderates were to be shorn increasingly of any future influence in the agencies because no fundamentalist president would appoint anyone to a committee who was not an inerrantist. It was of no consequence that the two groups were really very close together in their views of scripture.

It is ironic that at the very meeting where the open conflict took form and substance, the "liberals" were leading in launching the most ambitious effort in evangelical history to bring the gospel of Christ to the world. In truth, there probably were not a dozen true theological liberals in the entire meeting.

It is also interesting to note that the moderate leadership that had led for the life of the convention had no part in the Pastor's Conference, which had been under control of the fundamentalists for years. The

---

[15]Baptist Press, 14 June 1979.

fundamentalists who found the moderates so objectionable were in the Astrodome launching of the mission effort in large numbers.

Herein contained in "Classic Confrontation" is a fair microcosm of the next twelve turbulent years.

The Way It Was

It was the best of times, it was the worst of times;
It was the age of wisdom, it was the age of foolishness,
It was the epoch of belief, it was the epoch of incredulity;
It was the season of light, it was the season of darkness;
It was the spring of hope, it was the winter of despair.[16]

W. C. Fields of the Baptist Press observed, "We confuse the cultural dimensions of Southern religion with the religious dimensions of Southern culture."[17] He also noted that "Irenaeus, one of the early church fathers, described this kind of excess of zeal, [He was speaking of Baptist zealots who have a messianic complex] as 'irreligious solicitude' for the things of God."[18]

---

[16]Charles Dickens, *The Tale of Two Cities*, as quoted by W. C. Fields in "The Road to 2000 A.D."

[17]W. C. Fields, "The Road to 2000 A. D.," 2.

[18]Ibid.

Chapter Two

Roots

"The Pit From Which We Are Digged. . . ."[1]

To understand the nature of Southern Baptist problems, it is helpful to look at the cultural background of its people.

The name "Southern Baptist Convention" was well chosen. The convention was made up of a body of Christians who were distinctly southerners from the beginning. The churches fashioned a denomination in 1845 that was born of the trauma of the South. It was conceived in the shadow of the coming national catastrophe over slavery. There were other issues in its beginning, but the determinative factors were shaped by that tragedy. The refusal of The Triennial Convention (which was a co-operative effort of many Baptists) to appoint slave holders as missionaries was the triggering mechanism that brought the religious struggle to a definitive decision.

The Southern Heritage

Southern Baptists would be in every way "southern." They were a part of the culture that dominated the South for a hundred years. Their churches and schools bore the marks of sectionalism and shared in the problems of the culture that were produced by human bondage. The convention grew and later prospered in a society that had great difficulty moving beyond the regionalism forced on them by the uncivil conflict. The churches often reflected the mindset created out of the pride of being "southern."

The convention was hardly born when it was inundated by the war. From the beginning, it struggled with providing for the elementary needs

---

[1] Isaiah 51:1.

of the churches. Its earliest effort at publication of Bible study materials failed, partly because of the chaotic society in which it tried to function. The first attempt to found a theological seminary was interrupted by the war between the states and was not revived until after the war was over. The mission efforts of the fledgling body—the reason for its existence—languished for years in spite of having a number one priority. There was simply little money available, few candidates for mission work, and the minds of the people were on other things.

In spite of all these problems, the convention began to coalesce into viable model of cooperative work. The meetings that resumed after the war were small, made up of the better educated and more sophisticated of the ministers and some laity. After a few years of searching, they came to believe that they had discovered in the "convention system" a way to function as a democratic body. Completely voluntary cooperation became the wave of the future for Baptists. There would be many starts and stops in various phases of the operation. For a hundred years the convention worked its way through a myriad of problems and refined its organizations and functions.

All of this went on in a society whose distinctive characteristics in some ways threatened the existence of the body while strengthening it in other ways. The Southern Baptist Convention struggled and then flourished in the South.

For the first century of the convention's distincive existence, the South was rural. The population was relatively scattered. Urbanization would not come to the South as it had the North for a long time. This meant that most of the churches would be in open country and in small villages. It also meant that with the Baptist zeal, there would be lots of them. Many would be "quarter-time," meaning that public worship would be held once a month. "Half-time" churches held services on alternate Sundays. This meant that a pastor could serve more than one church as two or more of these small churches formed a "field" and called the same pastor. Many of the smaller churches met on Sunday afternoons, and the pastor would come from a morning service elsewhere. As late as the 1930s, one Mississippi pastor served an even dozen such churches, using every night of the week for worship somewhere.

This South was agricultural in its basic orientation. Much of its wealth before the war had been in land and slaves. It was the supplier of much of the nation's cotton, corn, and other agricultural products. Slavery had shaped the economic life of the region. By the end of the war, the South had lost its economic base and most of its wealth.

Dr. Wayne Flynt, longtime head of the History Department of Auburn University and specialist in southern history and religion, said, "By the end of the war, the South had begun a downward economic mobility for longer than any other area in U. S. history."[2] The number one problem of the South is illustrated by this comment—it was poverty. The economic base that had produced goods and services was no longer available. Flynt suggests that southern society in the last half of the nineteenth century was chaotic and capricious. The people were less sure of themselves and were unsettled in an insecure world. Nature was capricious and the agricultural economy was dependent on nature.

The blacks were uneducated, repressed, poor, and in every way disadvantaged. The total disruption of the way of life in the South left the region socially and economically backward. The industrial revolution skipped the South, and there was little migration into the region. The great influx of foreign population that brought cultural cross-fertilization and a diverse labor force to the North reached the South on a much smaller scale.

Thus, the people in the South were more homogeneous than the rest of the country. In many ways, the South was repudiated by the economic and cultural leadership of the country. Almost until the time of the second world war, southerners seemed to live in relative isolation from the forces that were shaping the country. Further, the region was largely captive to the trio of trouble: poverty and rural and agricultural limitations.

Religion in the South

Dr. Flynt has suggested that

Southerners lived closer to nature than most and tended to look for original causes. They tended to omit the intermediate steps. They saw rain coming from God instead of clouds. Drought was seen as God withholding His blessings instead of weather systems and cold fronts, and babies were gifts from God and not just the result of natural procreation.

---

[2] Wayne Flynt, personal conversation, 6 June 1991.

This closeness to and dependence on nature helped in fashioning the nature of the religious experience of the people. There were no solutions in government. Unions did not exist for them. Business was owned by the few, and institutions so frequent in modern life were not there.

The whole nature of life tended to drive the people to God. The southern problems and culture became the seedbeds in which Southern Baptists with their biblical faith grew and finally flourished. Their success was almost paralleled by Methodists and to a lesser degree Presbyterians. The explosion of the charismatic movements were yet to come. But to be southern almost required being religious.

Dr. David E. Harrell, the Breeden Eminent Scholar in the Humanities of Auburn University and long time student of southern religion, in commenting on the school systems of the South, said "The school system was actually almost a Protestant parochial system."[3] His point was that the systems in most places in the South were dominated by non-Catholics, largely Baptists, Methodists, and Presbyterians. In my own schools in the twenties and thirties, it was common to read the Bible, have prayer, and sometimes have the visiting evangelist from one of the churches to speak to the students. In our town, all teachers were Christians of one variety or another. When we moved to the third largest city in our state, a town of about 25,000 people, the schools were not so overtly controlled by Christians, but traditional Judeo-Christian values were openly espoused.

Parochial schools were almost all Catholic, and there were not many of them in our state. Southern Baptists supported the public school system in fact and by resolutions adopted in the convention sessions until very recent years.

For many years the politics of the South were dominated by the Democratic Party. It was the party of the South and the preserver of traditional values. It was seen as the party of the whites, of order, of the poor, and a natural product of the South. My grandfather used to say with some pride, "I would vote for the devil if he was on the Democratic ticket." As late as the 1930s, Flynt says that 75 percent of southerners voted for Franklin D. Roosevelt. The Republican Party was seen as the party of the North, blacks, wealth, chaos, and change.

It is Flynt's thesis that this has reversed itself now, and the Democratic Party is seen as the party of blacks, liberal causes, social

---

[3]David E. Harrell, personal conversation, 6 June 1991.

revolution, change, chaos, and radicalism. The Republican Party is now seen as the Democratic Party used to be.

As Flynt states,

> Southern Baptists are a mirror image of the white South. The Southern Baptist conflict is a model of the changes in the white south. It is difficult now to distinguish between Southern Baptist leadership and the right wing of the Republican Party.[4]

It is Flynt's conclusion that much of the present turmoil in the convention is the result of similar turmoil in the society generally.

Flynt continued with the need of southerners for authoritarianism. The southern culture was suited to hierarchal values. These value systems had developed over the years. Men were superior to women, whites over blacks, government over the citizen, employer over employee. He sees the reassertion of hierarchal values in the Southern Baptist Convention as more important in the "conservative resurgence" than theology.

In this culture that was unique to the South, religion had been developing out of step with the rest of the country in confronting modernity—or modernism as it was called by some religionists. Generally, Dr. Harrell says that the South encountered the issues of modernity from 50 to 75 years after the North. Such issues as higher criticism, the historical-critical method, and Darwinism brought crisis to the North long before they became major problems in the South.

The better educated and more urbane pastors and teachers had long known that these issues existed. Some of them had struggled with solutions and accommodations long before they became issues with the laity. The general population often did not confront these problems—if it did at all—until after World War II.

Flynt suggests that "Southernness begins to end at the end of World War II." The conservative society of the South began to confront modernity. The war brought wide-spread travel to southerners and brought many non-southerners to the South. Immigration to the Sun Belt began in earnest several years after the war. Alien ideas and religions invaded the land that had been controlled by Protestants. Urbanization began to accelerate with the rapid development of large sophisticated cities.

---

[4]Wayne Flynt, personal conversation.

The economy of the South rapidly improved and in some places rivaled that of the North. The glut of communication, with information available to most every citizen, began to homogenize the society. Regionalism soon began to break down before the onslaught of all these forces.

The South was going through many of the cultural changes after the war that the North had experienced in part as far back as the turn of the century. When a conservative society confronts modernity, it becomes increasingly uncomfortable. Some of its people adjust to new circumstances. Some opt to try to preserve the old. Modernity challenges in many ways.

It was destabilizing to southern society. All kinds of new issues—or reformulations of old issues—had to be be confronted. The South was now faced with the new issues related to race, the radical changes in the school systems, the place of women in the society, church-state problems, and the loss of control of various aspects of life. One of the more radical aspects of change was the rather sudden and dramatic increase of pluralism in many areas of life. Whole value systems were challenged.

Life had become much more complicated. It was confusing. There were new values, new choices, and new conflicts. The old guidelines were no longer accepted, and norms were suddenly not those long held dear. On this point Harrell commented,

> Modernity says things aren't simple any more. The preeminent intellectual dilemma of our time is that modernity tended to destroy absolutes and created a relativistic intellectual world in which nobody is very comfortable. And there is a basic need in human nature to know answers.

These brief analyses foreshadow coming Southern Baptist conflicts.

Ministers in the South

Before World War II, Southern Baptists were often outside the power structure and the circles of influence. Almost as a contradiction, they were frequently a strong "peoples" influence in the society.

One of the differences between them and other evangelicals was that Baptists believed that ordination was the responsibility of the local congregation, not the denomination or the clergy. Baptists ordained large numbers of uneducated and bivocational ministers. Contrary to the position of Methodists, Episcopalians, and Presbyterians, there usually was an adequate number of clergy for the many part time churches. Pastoral care was important and came in the form of visitation in the homes when people were sick, had new babies, or got married, and other special events. Pastors were close to their people if they were living up to the expectations of the congregations. Harrell remarked in discussing these matters: "The genius of Southern Baptists was in their close touch with the common people." In fact, they were the copmmon people. They did seem to find ways of meeting the needs of their people.

All of this seemed Southern to the core and a part not only of the religious community but of the very culture itself. Southerners before World War II were not yet preoccupied with the struggles of the fundamentalists in the North. Evangelism and missions were the bread and butter of the Baptists in the South. There was considerable resistance to any changes that would alter the status quo.

In 1942, California churches asked for permission to cooperate with the convention and thus be recognized as authentic Southern Baptist churches. The committee appointed to study the matter was opposed to the admission of these congregations and had no report ready for the convention meeting. A motion made from the floor to admit them to cooperative status was passed by the rank and file messengers over the protest of the establishment. This was to mark the beginning of the expansion of the convention until it had representative congregations in all fifty states within a relatively few years. Change was coming.

In spite of the preceding analyses, there was not a monolithic SBC at all, particularly as far as the ministry was concerned. There was what Dr. Flynt called "a bifurcation that had been there all the while." He was talking of the striking differences in the clergy and some of the laity.

Southern Baptists had always produced some scholarly, erudite, and informed ministers. These men knew about the issues that had divided the faithful in the North and would soon divide those in the South. They had studied the languages of the scriptures, systematic theology, and other disciplines that equipped them to confront the issues of the day. They were familiar with the problems of biblical criticism, the social issues facing the nation, and the nature of Darwinism.

On the other hand, a vast number of the ministers had little or no for-mal theological training. Usually, but not always, they were pastors of rural or small-town congregations. Many were bivocational pastors who made their living farming, clerking, laboring, or selling and did their pastoral work on the weekends and Wednesday night. Many of them were highly effective at what they did and furnished solid leadership to the smaller congregations. They were often good students of the English Bible, and some were very effective preachers and personal evangelists.

Both these groups have always been there in the Southern Baptist fellowship. How much substantive interaction there was depended on the local circumstances. As the more urbane middle class grew and its clergy continued control of the denominational mechanisms, the distance between the groups sometimes tended to grow. The uneducated and bivocational preachers did not have the influence and leadership positions of their better prepared counterparts. Their points of possible problem multiplied. Often the educated were suspect to their less fortunate colleagues, and the reverse was also true.

One of Dr. Flynt's doctoral candidates at Auburn read all of the doctoral dissertations written at the Southern Baptist Theological Seminary from 1895 to 1925. He reached the conclusion that the often repeated charge was true that the seminary did, indeed, turn out doctoral graduates who had been influenced by German rationalism and theology. He also concluded, however, that these graduates used the tools of higher learning to defend the faith! In their dissertations they used philology, archeology, and other disciplines to deny theological liberalism and defend orthodoxy.

It is clear in any competent study of Southern Baptists that central places of leadership were in the hands of the more urbane and educated leaders. This is a predictable state of things, human nature being what it is. It is equally true that these centrists never had a sense of exclusiveness in the denomination. They were in the main possessed of a true willingness to include all the faithful. Indeed, they worked at securing massive support for missions and the denominational organizations. It is true that while trying to include all, the leadership posts usually went to the more sophisticated. It is not clear what the outcome would have been had the less fortunate clergy been in the ascendancy.

A Following People

While we recognize the leadership of the educated and more sophisticated, we should also note that in denominational affairs from the beginning, most of the Baptists were a "following people." Therein is a base of much of the present problem in the convention. Most of the people are middle of the roaders and generally follow the ascendant leadership so long as they feel that it is headed in the right direction. There have always been times of rebellion and conflict, and at times the conflicts have been severe. But the characteristic of followship is both the strength and failure of the denomination.

Dr. Harrell suggests that from about 1890 to 1965, the moderate leaders showed the ability to divert the energies of the denomination from the growing problems to evangelism and missions. The rise of astute fundamentalist leaders immersed in the societal flux created increasing problems. These people were unwilling to settle for the centrist theology that had dominated the convention from the beginning.

With the growth of true diversity in the constituency, the rapid development of mass communications, and the rise of religious media super-stars, the trauma increased. The basic changes in the Bible belt previously discussed and those that followed created a fertile field for dissent from the old theology and the demand for a new. From 1979, the problems would grow exponentially.

By the end of World War II, the changes in all aspects of the southern culture were accelerating. Southern Baptists were no different from the rest of the society, except that they clung to the conservative theology that had been their heritage from the beginning. From time to time, the occasional differences were widely publicized. The secular press took increasing notice of this body that was the largest non-Catholic religious group in the country. Baptists helped considerably with this dissemination of information by the creation of Baptist Press. This communication network was tied into the total denominational structure that included more than thirty state-owned and state-controlled Baptist papers, most of which published weekly. Regular information was provided to the public media.

In the 1950s the three older seminaries were flourishing, and demands rose from the West, the Midwest, and the Southeast for schools that would be closer to the constituency. The established seminaries at Louisville, Fort Worth, and New Orleans filled up dramatically, and new schools were established in Kansas City and Wake Forest, North Carolina. The Golden Gate Seminary begun by California Baptists was adopted by the national body.

As the cooperating state bodies developed, the convention was adopting the radically different problems of the newer states, together with what was often a different kind of constituency. The convention was not only becoming a national entity but was becoming heterogeneous. The homogeneity of a hundred years was giving way.

Further, the South was being invaded by a host of other religious groups including the Buddhists, who by the 1980s set up a temple in Nashville in an abandoned Baptist church building. The Sun Belt was attracting a wide variety of industries, businesses, and military establishments, and small factories were springing up in small towns across the South. With all this came all kinds of people with all kinds of religions and no religion at all.

Baptist enclaves were discovering that they were no longer the dominant force in the community, and the challenges were hard to face in many places. Religious pluralism soon became a problem in managing the many phases of community life. The schools were no longer to be the exclusive province of the Protestants. With the coming of the pluralistic population, new demands were made on the governmental units, the school boards, and the society at large.

The religious arguments faced and disposed of in the North many years before had now come to the South in ways not faced before. As Drs. Flynt and Harrell would probably put it, "The South and Southern Baptists were confronting modernity."

Albert McClellan, long time convention leader and Program Planning Secretary for the Executive Committee described part of the same phenomenon:

> From the 1940s, the sudden transition of Southern Baptist life from (a) rural consciousness to suburban consciousness, and from (b) part time to full time churches, created a vital new ferment that provided opportunities for foment. The transition to urban consciousness and the movement to full time churches rapidly accelerated following World War II, and was companion to the rise of the Great Fundamentalist Takeover Controversy of the Southern Baptist Convention.[5]

---

[5]Albert McClellan, "Theses Concerning The Great Fundamentalist Takeover Controversy Of the 1980s, A Traditional Baptist View." 1991, unpublished.

The Tap Root

In addition to and interwoven with the denomination's "southernness" and the revolutionary changes within it was another complicated and divisive cultural and religious phenomenon—fundamentalism.

For much of the nineteenth century and almost half of the twentieth, the open confrontations about fundamentalism were largely in the North, but the roots of cultural and religious fundamentalism grew deep in the spiritual soil of the South. Fundamentalism flourished before the Civil War principally in the North in various forms and sometimes disguises. After the war, it was reinvigorated by a new but old set of concerns.

> It (fundamentalism) was a movement among American "evangelical" Christians, people professing complete confidence in the Bible and pre-occupied with the message of God's salvation of sinners through the death of Jesus Christ.[6]

Thus, George M. Marsden describes the early base of fundamentalism.

This simple definition of the early movement highlights one of the problems of later controversies. Almost all of the Baptists would fall into this early category, then and now, and most would deny being fundamentalists. Many Baptists, however, would reject the theological and social barnacles that would adhere to the modern versions.

In discussing the movement, Marsden commented that "the fundamentalists most alarming experience was that of finding themselves living in a culture that by the 1920s was openly turning away from God." He quotes H. L. Menchen as saying, "Christianity may be defined briefly as that part of the world in which, if any man stands up in public and solemnly swears that he is a Christian, all his auditors will laugh."

The comment highlights the growing controversy between Christianity and the philosophical materialism. This confrontation fits

---

[6]George M. Marsden, *Fundamentalism and American Culture*," (New York: Oxford University Press, 1980). I am endebted to Marsden for much of this discussion. Further notes will be identified by "Marsden."

well into the analyses of Flynt and Harrell when they define the Baptist problem as a belated confrontation with modernity.

It is not surprizing that Christians would be concerned with such basic challenges to their faith. It follows, as Marsden asserts, that

> militant opposition to modernism was what most clearly set off fundamentalism from a number of closely related traditions such as evangelicalism, revivalism, pietism . . . the millenarianism . . . Baptist traditionalism and other denominational orthodoxies.[7]

Marsden continues by saying that two early types of interpretation of fundamentalism prevailed. One was to see fundamentalism as essentially the extreme and agonized defense of a dying way of life. The other was highlighted by Ernest Sandeen and saw fundamentalism as the outgrowth of the "millenarian" movement concerning the interpretation of Biblical prophecies. The Bible teachers who led in this direction, according to Sandeen, "acquired from conservative Presbyterians at Princeton Theological Seminary the newly defined dogma that the Bible was 'inerrant' in every detail. Millenariansism, however was primary."[8] Militant opposition to modernism was a recurring theme.

Distinctive emphases finally characterized fundamentalism according to Marsden. Four are listed as especially important to the movement. They are dispensational premillennialism, the holiness movement and its implications for social reform, efforts to defend the faith, and views of Christianity's relationship to culture.

These early fundamentalists had a tendency to identify at times with the establishment and sometimes with the outsiders. Early on, having been a part of the religious establishment of evangelicalism, fundamentalism took on the role of "a beleagured minority with strong sectarian or separatist tendencies." Out of its revivalist and pietist heritage, the movement adopted tendencies "toward individualistic, culture-denying,soul-rescuing Christianity."

Still another early characteristic, according to Marsden, was the tension between trust and distrust of the intellect. This tension involved a strong ambivalence toward culture. This conflict not only existed in the

---

[7]Ibid.,,, 4.
[8]Ibid., 4–5.

early part of this century but was to spawn confusing and contradictory pronouncements and actions in the SBC problems.

Marsden said,

> This early fundamentalism was a mosaic of divergent and sometimes contradictory traditions and tendencies that could never be totally integrated. Sometimes its advocates were backward looking and reactionary, at other times there were imaginative innovators. On some occasions they appeared militant and divisive; on others they were warm and irenic. At times they seemed ready to forsake the whole world over a point of doctrine; at other times they appeared heedless of tradition in their zeal to win converts. Sometimes they were optimistic patriots; sometimes they were prophets shaking from their feet the dust of a doomed civilization.[9]

Of particular interest to the present Baptist controversy are such items as the anti-Masonic movement of fundamentalists active before the Civil War and reborn in the last third of the nineteenth century. In the nineteenth century, the idea that the United States was a Christian nation was the subject of a crusade, and an effort was made to change the Constitution to recognize Christianity. At the same time efforts were made to pass laws establishing the Sabbath, prohibition, outlawing secret lodges, justice to Indians, abolition of the Electoral College, and the election of the President by popular vote of the people.

Much of the fundamentalist movement and associated arguments were more of a northern phenonmenon than southern until World War II. In one sense, even Baptists in the North were late comers to the discussions. Yet, according to Marsden, Northen Baptist and Northern Presbyterian controversies contributed significantly to the development of interdenominational fundamentalism.

Baptists then, as now, were a diverse group. They came from a Calvinist tradition yet had a strong emphasis on doctrinal freedom. They held an individualistic view of the church and a continuing affirmation of the individual right to personal religious freedom. Calvinism and Arminianism co-existed, sometimes in the same person and sometimes in peace.

---

[9]Ibid., 43.

From this freedom of conscience and lack of ecclesiastical authority came a variety of views of scripture. The seminaries in the north played a large part in a new approach to views of scripture. They brought to the discussion new approaches to the study of scripture including what came to be called the historical-critical method. For many years, differences in understanding of the nature of scripture was not a test of fellowship among Baptists.

The views of A. H. Strong on the nature of scripture became another factor that bore on subsequent Southern Baptist problems. He rejected the idea that scripture was inerrant. His *Systematic Theology* was to have considerable influence in years to come among Southern Baptists. His concept of authority in religion—Jesus Christ himself—would be repeated by E. Y. Mullins in the 1925 Baptist Faith and Message. These two views, Christ as final authority and scripture only, were to become two main streams of understanding in the SBC that would cause serious differences in the conflicts of the last half of the twentieth century.

In discussing the cultural crisis, Marsden said:

> An overwhelming atmosphere of crisis gripped America during the immediate postwar (World War I) period. The year of 1919 especially was characterized by a series of real as well as imagined terrors...There was alarm over rapidly deteriorating moral standards and a deep suspicion of foreign influence. The immediate reaction was to focus on the sinister implications of the strikes and terrorism and to rechannel the enormous emotional force of wartime patriotism against a different foreign enemy—Bolshevism. . . . It seemed as though the people needed an enemy, one that could account for the disruptions on the home front.[10]

This same kind of response occured in the Southern Baptist Convention during and after the Vietnam War.

Within a few years of the end of the World War I, northern fundamentalists and liberals were at each other's throats. Such thinkers as Shailer Mathews of the Chicago Divinity School added fuel to the theological fire. Mathews asserted that ideas and beliefs are not mirrors of external reality but products of the mind shaped by natural

---

[10]Ibid., 153.

evolutionary and cultural developments. Thus, religion was not based on static or standardized objective knowledge of God, but rather could best be understood as a social or historical development. Thus, he thought, the Bible was not a source of facts or true propositions about God, but "a trustworthy record of a developing experience of God which nourishes our faith." He defined Modernism as "the use of scientific, historical, and social method in understanding and applying evangelical Christianity to the needs of living persons."[11] This was an harbinger of the modern discussion of the use of the historical-critical method of Bible study.

Before the second World War, as has been noted,the confrontations over these problems were still largely confined to the North. Marsden observes,

> In the South generally, religious conservatism was directly tied to cultural conservatism in ways that differed from the North. The preservation of evangelical religion went hand-in-hand with the preservation of the Southern way of life. Their Northern counterparts had experienced the secularization of a society once dominated by evangelical thought. In the South, however evangelicalism was still a virtually unchallenged establishment. Southerners had made stringent efforts to keep their religion intact since the Civil War, as evidenced by the late nineteenth-century prosecutions of several professors for heresy.[12]

Historians often note that a distinguishing characteristic of the early models of fundamentalism was militancy. It would make its mark in bold strokes on the controversies of the last half of the twentieth century.

An additional note is needed concerning the content of fundamentalism. Premillennialism, with its ideas of a cataclysmic conclusion to the world order, still dominated the eschatological thought, but there remained a lingering belief that God's kingdom could, indeed, be found in America itself. Here again is the forerunner of the strong modern emphasis on the idea of Christian America.

In summary, this sketchy review of some of the emphases of early fundamentalism suggests deep roots for the modern controversy. Points

---

[11]Ibid, 176.
[12]Ibid, 179.

of contention rampant a half century and more ago elsewhere now are the focus of the controversy in the SBC. Evolution and creationism furnish the battle grounds for many present-day battles. The nature of the scripture and its relationship to modern science, the relationship of revelation and reason, the problems of supernaturalism and the miraculous all contribute to the present discussion. (The Southern Baptist brand of fundamentalism is discussed in Chapter Four.)

A Destabilized Society

The 1950s witnessed an unprecedented growth and strengthening of the Southern Baptist Convention and thousands of its churches. New churches were organized in large numbers, and many of the older ones experienced renewal. In many ways, this decade was the zenith of the organized life of Southern Baptists. The colleges and seminaries in the main grew rapidly. The state and national organizations were developing in unparalleled ways. Missions and evangelism were the cohesive forces. The Sunday School Board launched new ventures and Sunday schools grew rapidly. The people were employed, and church was the focal point of many lives. One could almost think the golden era had arrived.

A centrist moderate theology was dominant, at least on the visible levels. There were occasional skirmishes over some real or imagined problem, but in the main, peace and prosperity reigned. Leadership on the national and state levels consisted of middle of the road people who were anxious to build bigger and better service organizations and churches. Followship was good, alien forces had not yet gained a significant foothold. The cloud on the horizon, the size of a man's hand, was far off and largely unnoticed.

As the decade ended, the seas began to be choppy. Within five years or less, the world in which Southern Baptists were born and nurtured began to show cracks that would turn into chasms.

The Civil Rights Movement

As the civil rights movement began to gather steam, it concentrated on the South, where much of the problem lay. By the early 1960s, it was organized and led by the charismatic Martin Luther King, Jr. His tactic of non-violent civil disobedience was a stroke of genius. It was the only strategy that would work, given the emotional nature of the conflict. Anything else would have filled the streets with guns and blood.

The streets of Birmingham, Memphis, Atlanta, Selma, and Little Rock filled with carefully indoctrinated blacks. The protests gained national attention immediately and had the support of multitudes of people all over the land. Sometimes the authorities dedicated to segregation attacked the protesters with dogs and truncheons. This intensified the conflict and gained valuable support for the protesters. Civil disobedience that acknowledged the necessity for paying a penal price was a new phenomenon for America, and thousands of blacks and whites were carted off to jail. Within days or hours they were released and returned to the protest marches.

Such tactics raised serious questions for religious leaders and followers. Many sensitive whites recognized the basic rights of the blacks but were placed in a difficult position by the massive resistance to the laws on the books. Blacks showed up on Sunday morning at the First Baptist Churches in dozens of cities, demanding admittance. Many southerners could not abide this and quickly made their feelings known. The pastors were between two irresistible forces.

The deacons of the church where I was pastor at the time argued over the decision to admit blacks to the worship services until one O'clock in the morning. Finally, I demanded that they be admitted. Then the argument turned on whether to require them to sit in the balcony. They finally agreed that they should be seated anywhere there was a seat. It was a small skirmish but a harbinger of things to come. I departed shortly, but the battle went on for years, finally contributing to a schism in the church and decimating its fellowship and work.

A number of states actually had laws that forbade blacks and whites sitting together in the same room. Some whites fled to that retreat, and it became a focus of real problem to some segments of society. Dr. George Cross, long time president of the University of Oklahoma, told me of the incident of admitting the first black to the university. The law forbade the student to be seated in the classroom with whites. The state legislature, the university's financial watchdog, was watching closely. Cross was determined to devise a way to admit the student. He moved the class to a room that was adjoined by another one separated only by a small elevation. He placed a token cord between the two rooms, seated the black, and proceeded with education under very difficult conditions. This kind of problem occurred in many places, often frustrating efforts at solution.

The more tolerant whites were often at odds with others as to the rights or tactics or intention of blacks. Multitudes of white churches were thrown into turmoil. Good will was sacrificed, and fellowship was disturbed. Pastors were fired, institutions were disrupted, and many individuals who tried to support the movement were actually persecuted.

Attention began to turn away from the traditional emphases and concentrate on the problems produced in the churches by societal upheaval. Issues a century old were revived, and the long festering inflammation erupted anew. A new sense of unease appeared everywhere, and outright rage in some places forced a new approach to the biggest social issue the South had ever faced. The more fundamentalist the orientation, the more enraged and disoriented certain segments of the society became. A way of life was dying.

It should be said that there was a reservoir of good will in many places for the rights of the blacks. It should also be said that had it not been for the calming influence of the biblical doctrines long taught, there would have been a lot more bloodshed than there was. Once the federal civil rights laws were in place to protect the Black citizens, some of the overt hostility gradually began to die or be hidden. Churches everywhere, in time, began to admit blacks, not as a political statement, but as an expression of the conviction that God loves everyone. This was not, or course, universally true, but the situation changed rather rapidly given the hundred year history of segregation.

Recent studies have shown that the Southern Baptist Convention is now perhaps the most integrated of the major denominations, with many black churches accepted for cooperation and thousands of churches with black members. One is forced to the conclusion that the civil rights movement profoundly affected the mood of the country and denomination and contributed at least indirectly to the present conflict.

The Vietnam War

The nation in the 1960s became mired in what became the most controversial military involvement in our history. During the early 1960s, there was considerable general support for the Vietnam conflict. As the war escalated during the Johnson administration, more and more resistance began to be shown. As time went on and casualties increased dramatically, resistance by students and a multitude of others became vigorous and sometimes violent. What unity there had been in the beginning was soon shattered. The country divided into those groups called the "hawks" and the "doves." The older World War II generation, with memories of another war not too old, tended to be more visibly patriotic, and many were hawks. Patriotism became the issue to many, and thus the war was supported whether it was right or wrong. Most often it seemed that the young—especially those who might have to serve—were against the war.

The problems were exacerbated by the exemption of college students from military service until their graduation. The burden was thrust onto the disadvantaged, the poor, and blacks. Riots in the streets were common, and some of them lasted for days. Student unrest erupted, sometimes violently. The large universities with their heterogeneous populations became the locus of constant confrontations.

The University of California at Berkeley became the synonym for violence and conflict. At Kent State University, the National Guard killed four students in an attempt to restore calm to the campus. This set off a new round of confrontations. Buildings were burned on campuses, administrators were held hostage, class work was sometimes shut down, and the societal disruption grew by huge leaps. Faculty members often joined in the disruption and encouraged students to rebel. Priests sometimes led demonstrations and seemed to vie with blacks to see who could get arrested the most times.

As the colleges became focal points for the conflagration, the war hysteria grew. More and more "causes" used the educational institutions as recruiting offices for their efforts. With the colleges and other institutions in figurative flames, if not literal, the society seemed to be coming unglued. Everyone seemed to have to choose sides. Students were afraid of the draft. The educators with divided loyalties were afraid of the disintegration of educational functions. The government was trying to fight and win an unpopular war. The society was divided as never before, and the churches were often confused as to their place in this unprecedented time of national division.

During the last half of the sixties, I was a college president. Our students, in the main, came from conservative homes, mostly Baptist. We had little disruption because of the kind of students we had. They were constantly urged to join in one kind or another of disturbance. Their good sense prevented any serious confrontation. But they were in most ways sympathetic to the dissent that was displayed in other places.

The governor of the state on one occasion called all the college presidents in the state to the governor' mansion. He told us that the state investigative service had uncovered a plot to put a recruiter on every campus in the state to recruit students to commit violent acts on the campuses. It was never known which of the many disruptive organizations was responsible. The governor arranged for concentrations of state troopers to be on duty just outside the campuses to aid in quelling riots. With elaborate precautions visible, only the two largest state universities had confrontations, and they were relatively minor. This story illustrates the tensions and anxieties present in a broad spectrum of the society.

With the death of the students at Kent State University, even mild mannered students felt the necessity "to do something." On our campus, the students without authorization lowered the flag to half staff. The blue collar workers, led by the maintainance staff, immediately raised it to the top of the flagstaff. The students immediately tried to lower it again. As was usually the case, when things got sticky, someone called for the president. The workers threatened violence, and the students held their ground. When I arrived, there they stood facing each other down. By that time the Oklahoma wind had reached forty miles an hour, and the flag was being shredded. I thought I remembered that when a storm approached the flag was to be lowered. I decreed that this was the usual procedure and lowered the flag and took it in! Of course, the workers were warned not to assume jurisdiction of the flag, and the students were told that this was not their perogative. Such was the tension of the times.

Pastors and sometimes churches protested vigorously any student conduct they felt to be unchristian. Some of the young refused military service, angering all the hawks and those who thought the responsibility must be assumed even if the war was unpopular. As the pressure built, thousands of the young fled to Canada to escape the draft. Others, with no idea of ministerial service, went to theological schools to accomplish the same end. Many other conscientious young people were torn between a sense of loyalty to country and law and the popular tide of the time. This was an era of of challenge to authority on every front in the society.

It was not until the late 1970s that then President Jimmy Carter offered amnesty to those who fled to Canada and some of the divisions began to heal.

The Sexual Revolution

The social expressions of the time were doubly disturbing to the South with its recent roots in the remains of Puritanism and its own brand of fundamentalism. Its particular type of piety simply could not dominate the society rising out of the ruins in the streets.

The generation gave rise to the hippies, yippies, and the flower children. In appearance, they often were a scrubby lot. The men were usually bearded—a rarity at the time—often dirty and unkempt. The women were not pictures of southern gentility. This was a part of a generation dedicated to the free expression of any form of revolt against the authority of the society.

The symbol of the era seemed to be "free love." The sexual revolution came to the American society from a generation of the young that was completely out of tune with authority. Yankelovitch, Skelly, and White was a well known firm specializing in sociological studies. Their study of a decade of changes in social values, called Monitor, said of this era that was followed by the "me" generation: "There are relatively few forms of self-expression that are not tolerated today by our society." Ten years after the flower children came on the scene, Monitor would say, "The new sexual morality—a system of values that disassociates sex from marriage—continues to be more and more acceptable." By the late 1970s, Monitor would record that 54 percent of the American people believed it was acceptable for an unmarried couple to live together if they cared for each other. More than half the population would not fault a single woman who decided to have a child if she could support the child. More than 60 percent of the population thought it was acceptable for college students to live together. It was this same generation that would cause it to be said of their children by an observant university professor: "The students simply don't have the same view of sex as the Baptists." Colleges were beseiged with demands for coed dormitories, and they were soon to become the order of the day in public institutions. The results of all these things were devastating to the traditional nuclear family.

Southern Christians, and Southern Baptists fundamentalists in particular, were outraged at these developments and were largely ineffective in trying to do anything significant about them.

Still another phenomenon came on to the scene that would curiously effect the controversy, the society, and the fundamentalist movement. During the 1970s and 1980s, a number of influential preachers began to accumulate vast radio and television audiences. The Baptists in this movement were, in the main, independent and very conservative. As their audiences increased and cable systems came into vogue, their number multiplied and their influence grew. The Baptist public often grew enchanted with their ideas and some of the preachers. By the 1970s the young Baptist aspirants saw the potential of using show business techniques. Many new efforts were made to duplicate the success of the Jerry Falwells and the Charles Stanleys. Most failed, but the efforts and dreams continued.

Albert McClellan made a study in 1981 for one of the seminaries on the popularity of certain preachers. His study showed that Jerry Falwell was the most influential preacher among Baptists in 18 states. This startling fact highlighted a phenomenon that would contribute to the problems in the denomination. Falwell was not a Southern Baptist and had no sympathy at the time for the convention and its people—except that they were probably his most loyal supporters financially. The point of view they got from their preacher on television was a Moral Majority, fundamentalist, non-denominational, and right wing political stance. Hardline fundamentalism drew massive support, and its significance was not lost on the dissenters within the SBC.

With the coming of the television preacher stars, there came also to the people a kind of worship that was not like that in their churches. The television broadcasts could be edited, the glitches removed, and a compact, tightly organized half-hour or hour "show" presented. It was almost "instant religion," somewhat like instant potatoes. As these techniques became more sophisticated, more and more entertaining and spectacular presentations were made. Some showed elaborate Florida tropical scenes or had waterfalls. Some were musical extravaganzas featuring celebrities, sports stars, some very attractive women elaborately costumed, or whatever else could be thought of to encourage viewing. Many semi-spectaculars soon were being displayed in numbers of congregations. Rock music moved into the churches and took hold as the baby boomers grew up, and deafening sound systems were often the order of the day. Sometimes there was emotional response to the presentation that was often attributed to the work of the Lord.

The descendants of the Charleston Tradition had a hard time with this and often resented the applause that soon became not only an accepted but expected practice. The SBC Pastor's Conference became a show place for the displaying of celebrities' piety. It is an interesting sight to see a woman singer—much in the limelight because of her opposition to homosexuality—dressed in white march with preacher escorts down the aisle with the spotlights focusing on her and her escorts. The convention meetings had their own spectaculars, and rock music thundered through the halls—"Christian rock," of course.

These things were not lost on the more imaginative Southern Baptist pastors, and variations began to show up on Sunday morning in a lot of churches. In visiting churches in the last few years, I have witnessed many semi-spectaculars in a number of different kinds of congregations. It is interesting that some of the most fundamentalist of the pastors quickly adopted the techniques of the influences that were threatening their world.

A Fractured Society

From all of this, it is easy to understand that when the pietists, the fundamentalists, and conservative Christians were seeing a lot of their world disappearing, they reacted vigorously. The conservative forces had "lost" the civil rights battle. The Vietnam War had brought shame to some, fear to others, and anger and sorrow to all. Patriotism had been challenged on the deepest level. Civil religion had suffered a serious setback. The sexual revolution produced near panic among many conservative churches. The hippies and their ilk became symbols of a disintegrating society. The southern heritage was being destroyed, and the South had lost control of its own society. These losses were not easy to swallow.

For conservative ministers (almost all Southern Baptists ministers were) the gap between their Bible-based sermons and the actions on the streets widened. The world for which Christians prayed and worked was retreating further and further away. The children of Christians were thrust into the middle of a societal struggle for which they were often ill equipped. What their parents and the church stood for and the peer influence they met outside the home were on a violent collision course. The societal struggle came home with them every night, and the results were sometimes tragic and always disturbing. No matter how hard the conservatives resisted, the world would not be halted, so the conflict came to the homes and churches.

The sense of unease and the disappointment in the radical revolution that swept the nation created an intense desire among conservative Christians to do something. Fundamentalists with premillenial convictions did not seem to be able to decide whether to abandon hope for the world or spend their lives trying to save it. It was evident that usual methods would not work.

Perhaps it was frustration, perhaps sincere determination, or perhaps it was sheer anger, but whatever the cause, fundamentalists immediately began to focus on the problems of the denomination. Close at hand was an object that could be attacked and a place where changes could be made. As the family changed and the colleges and seminaries were filled with the youth who grew up during the national upheaval, the calls began to be heard to rid the denomination of liberal influences.

During the mid-1960s, a prominent Florida pastor approached me to see whether I would join a group dedicated to ridding the seminaries of "liberals." After listening to his pitch, I asked the inevitable: "What is your definition of a liberal?" The matter was dropped, and I never heard from him again, but the idea was beginning to generate some support.

James L. Sullivan, my predecessor at the Sunday School Board, tells of a retiring trustee from the Board who told him that as soon as they could find a cause, a campaign would begin to rid the denomination of liberals. Not long after these events, Paul Pressler began his efforts to influence New Orleans Seminary for the conservatives—at a time when it was about as conservative as it could be.

Early in the beginnings of organized denominational conflict, the fundamentalists organized a Premillenial Fellowship that met in conjunction with the annual convention meeting. The centrists organized the E. Y. Mullins fellowship for the sponsoring of conservative, but progressive, ideas. Neither lasted very long since the boiling point had not been reached. After a while, The Baptist Faith and Message Fellowship was organized. It sponsored its own journal, which castigated denominational leadership and the seminaries particularly. Out of this effort would grow at least two other papers as each in time lost its credibility.

While cause and effect are difficult to establish in social and religious movements, there is considerable evidence that the fractured society had a profound influence on the Southern Baptist Convention.

A Prophecy

In 1967, I was the president of Oklahoma Baptist University. That year a few students organized their own magazine, secured the authorization of the publishing board of the school and proceded to upset half of the state. They published their magazine, "The Pluralist," when the spirit moved them—irregularly. This kind of activity had been going on at the school since its beginning, though usually without the blessing of the publication board.

On the front of one issue, they had a picture of a coed in a bathing suit with a "hippie" companion standing in front of what appeared to be a communion table. Inside the issue was an article criticizing one of the state's prominent pastors for something or other. (He laughed at their comments but is today a leader in the fundamentalist movement.) Another article vigorously attacked Falls Creek, the state Baptist youth assembly, widely known for its tremendous crowds, great music, and constant conflicts over dress codes and mixed swimming.

A group of pastors in Oklahoma City was enraged by the students' impertinence. At a pastor's conference meeting on a Monday, they excoriated the university and its president for allowing such disgraceful goings on. On the next day, they sent a delegation to see me. They brought with them an unexpected United Press International reporter. In an instant, I had to decide whether to permit him to sit in the meeting. I agreed to the coverage, hoping for a square deal for the students and myself. The committee demanded that I punish the students for their "ungodly" conduct by expelling them from the university. I agreed to speak the next Monday at their meeting but made no promises. The next morning, *The Daily Oklahoman*, the state's leading newspaper, carried a banner headline and article excoriating the preachers. On the following Monday, the room was packed with the pastors and visitors. They declared an executive session and excluded the press that waited just outside the door.

I explained that these were students to whom we were to minister and give an education. They were Baptists and had a right to their religious opinions and were Americans with the right of free speech. Their sin was immaturity, from which some tend to recover, and they had broken no university regulation or law. The demand was made that they be dismissed from school immediately. I refused. The demand was made that they be punished. I refused to comment on any punishment or other action.

Some were mollified, and some were furious that students would criticize a popular pastor and the state conference program. The press outside wanted to know what I would do to students. I refused comment on the grounds that this was a university and personal matter. The problem was that I was a Baptist who did not agree with the students, but they were Baptists who had a right to their own views. I certainly did not agree with the fundamentalists who stirred up the furor, and so I took no action against the students.

Interestingly, one of the pastors who demanded the dismissal of the students soon was in my office pleading that his own son not be dismissed for public drunkenness, which was a violation of university regulations and the laws of Oklahoma. He was not dismissed, and later he graduated. His father later thanked me for ministering to his son.

This was the baptism by fire over nothing of significance that introduced me to militant fundamentalism out of control. It was a prophecy of things to come.

Chapter Three

What Is
a Southern Baptist?

"My Manner of Life. . . ."[1]

Southern Baptists are radically different in matters of ecclesiology from other evangelicals. Their ideas about the nature of the church, polity, rights of individuals, and the absence of ecclesiastical authority compound the confusion of the controversy.

At this point, it is requisite to ask, what is a Southern Baptist? The obvious and possibly only answer is that a Southern Baptist is a member of a Southern Baptist church. This opens a wide arena for discussion and controversy. Almost anyone can get into many Southern Baptist churches. The single requirement is a public profession of faith in Jesus Christ and baptism by immersion. The overwhelming number of the churches require no subscription to a creedal statement of any kind. An individual church is the sole judge of its practices, although it may be excluded from the local association of churches if it gets too far out of line. Even then, this does not usually interfere with its relationship to the state convention or the national body, and there is no ecclesiastical authority to prevent the church from calling itself a Southern Baptist church. There is no such thing as "The Southern Baptist Church" since the national body disclaims such a title or reality.

There has been no body of dogma to which a Baptist must subscribe nor any official definition of a Southern Baptist. Years ago when the controversy was heating up, I tried to get a dialogue going nationally on the definition of a Southern Baptist. It was my hope that such a discussion

---

[1]Acts 26:4.

would bring an awareness of the wide diversity of opinion on a variety of matters relating to the controversy. In the fall of 1981, I spoke in five or six state conventions on the subject of What is A Southern Baptist? I wrote related articles in one of our periodicals that reached every pastor. A number of addresses were made to groups of leaders with the suggestion that this become a matter of discussion so that the emerging leadership and others might become acquainted with the problems of the course toward disaster. The attempt met apparent complete indifference.

The official documents of the SBC do not furnish a definition of a Southern Baptist. The constitution of the convention says,

> The Convention shall consist of messengers who are members of missionary Baptist churches cooperating with the Convention as follows: 1. One (1) messenger from each church which is in friendly cooperation with this Convention and sympathetic with its purposes and work and has during the fiscal year preceding been a bona fide contributor to the Convention's work.

The constitution then continues to set out how "each such church" qualifies for more than one messenger. A church may have an additional messenger for every two hundred fifty members or "for each $250.00 paid to the work of the Convention during the fiscal year preceding the annual meeting." The constitution also states the SBC's purpose:

> It is the purpose of the Convention to provide a general organization for Baptists in the United States and its territories for the promotion of Christian missions at home and abroad and any other objects such as Christian education, benevolent enterprises, and social services which it may deem proper and advisable for the furtherance of the Kingdon of God.

While there is no definition of a Southern Baptist, *The Baptist Faith and Message*, a confessional statement adopted by the convention in 1963, indicates broad doctrinal agreement on many basic issues. It was not intended to be binding on any one and was not designed as a creed. Since the growth in intensity of the controversy, the statement has been interpreted often as a binding document setting forth "the Baptist faith."

Further, some have insisted in the last few years that certain theological positions cannot be tolerated and the holder remain in fellowship with the denomination. Toleration is not a Baptist idea. Freedom has been the watchword of Baptists.

Fundamentalist presidents of the convention in recent years have insisted that no one who is not an inerrantist can serve on any committee or board of trustees of any agency. There is no precedent for any such position in Southern Baptist life. Baptists on a national level have traditionally not been a creedal people and have had no definitions that were exclusive or inclusive.

The introduction of organized fundamentalism as a creedal requirement not only has no precedent in Baptist documents and practice but thrusts the entire body of theology into controversy. The practices, traditions, and commonly accepted understandings—admittedly a slim base for a denomination—came now to be reconsidered, debated, and attacked. Our very lack of creedal positions became a weakness. New creedal positions would be adopted foreign to historic practice with little base in traditional life.

This all went to the heart of a basic Baptist tenet: the priesthood of all believers. This doctrine holds that any believer is competent to approach and deal with God without no need for any intercessor whether it be a church or a priest. The idea requires equality of members in the church. The heart of the matter is that Jesus Christ himself is the authority for a Baptist and that the believer is guided in his understanding of that authority by Holy Scripture and the witness of the Holy Spirit.

The fundamentalist position was a curious distortion of that basic doctrine. They apparently believed that the freedom inherent in the idea of the priesthood of the believer should give way to the assumption that leadership had the right to mobilize the votes to make their consciences binding on others. This idea is hotly denied, but the actions of the convention and subsequent applications by officers and administrators tends to support the assertion.

What Is The Southern Baptist Convention?

The convention (meeting) actually exists for the three days it meets formally. Thus, it actually consists of the representatives (called "messengers") of the churches. They are elected by the churches, who normally do not instruct them, and they are free to vote their own convictions. Thus, they are not called "delegates."

The convention carries on its business through a trustee system whose members are elected at the annual meeting. Each agency has its own board of trustees and elects its own officers and employs its own staff. The trustees report through the executives usually to the next meeting of the convention.

No one actually knows in any given year how many cooperating churches there are until they make a report of their activities to the local association of churches—if they choose to do so. This report is called the Uniform Church Letter and contains questions about membership, Sunday School enrollment and attendance, financial contributions to the church, and the church's contribution to the various denominational mission and educational programs. This letter and gifts to the programs constitute the church as "a church in friendly cooperation" with the convention and, thus, a Southern Baptist church listed in the denominational records.

From the view of other Christians, the SBC was and is an ecclesiastical nightmare.

The Democratic Process

Add to this confusion on a national level the democracy of every unit of Baptist life. The local congregations are independent and autonomous. No outside entity has any control over the local congregation. It can ordain whom it pleases and baptize whom it pleases, both of which are usually recognized by other congregations. The congregation is constituted of individuals who theoretically are following their conscience as enlightened by the Holy Spirit and Holy Scripture. Each baptized member has an equal voice and vote in the affairs of the congregation. To be sure, many are influenced by the pastor, the deacons, the Sunday School teacher, or friends. But the vote counts in the business meeting, and the rule of democracy obtains. Sometimes this process is manipulated, as it has been in recent years on a national level. Yet, democracy is the method of congregational decision making.

The congregation decides whether it will become a cooperating church related to the local regional association of churches. If it decides to do so, and it usually does, it is voted into the cooperating fellowship of the Association. It is usually called a "member church," though actually it is the messengers that are members of the association. The only authority the Association has related to a given church is whether it will "seat the messengers" from that church. It has no further power related to its cooperating churches. The business of the association, like that of the churches, is determined by democratic vote in annual session. The Association has its own agenda of cooperative projects in its local area with emphasis on such things as ethnic, prison, student and other ministries.

The state conventions—now about 37 strong, some representing areas of sparse Baptist population—operate in the same democratic fashion as the churches and associations. The churches, not the associations, send their messengers to the state meeting. The states have their own agenda. There are colleges and universities, specialized state mission projects, the promotion and development of church organizations, hospitals, a foundation for the solicitation and management of endowment and other special funds, and such other cooperative ministries as the state feels are desirable. The states have their own system of trustees to manage these enterprises between sessions of the state conventions. The state bodies have no authority or jurisdiction over the associations or the churches. The entire system depends on trust, cooperation for common ends, and fidelity of performance by the persons elected to head these endeavors.

The democratic processes extending to the now massive meeting of the Southern Baptist Convention have until recently served well. For many years the national body was actually a deliberative body that afforded the opportunity for the messengers to debate in a limited way the various issues that arose. As it grew from a few thousand to more than forty thousand in some politically charged sessions, this luxury gradually faded so far as true discussion and debate were concerned. At all levels, the democratic processes that made possible this ecclesiastical monstrosity could be and have been manipulated. Yet, for more than a hundred years the convention process worked rather well. It was based on trust. Most people believed that whoever was elected to office or achieved a place of influence or prominence would proceed to work for the best interests of the institution involved and within the framework of accepted Christian practice.

In recent years the trust level has been destroyed by charge and counter-charge. Partisan politics became the usual order of procedure. People with ulterior motives and an organization to back them could make a farce of the processes. This seems inherent in democratic processes.

Many Kinds of Baptists

In these churches and organizations of the churches, many kinds of Baptists have always existed. A major concept held in common has traditonally been the idea of the priesthood of all believers. The premise of the priesthood of believers is based on the idea of freedom under God for the individual and its corollary of responsibility. This means that there has been a wide variety of opinions on many subjects. It has been said often that where there are two Baptists, you will have three opinions.

Until recently there have been no creedal norms for the individuals or churches. There were few, if any, official "Southern Baptist Positions" on any subject. The nearest thing to one would be the regulations of a local association of churches on some matter related to admitting messengers from the churches.

Some now interpret the resolutions of the national body as official positions. These are beginning to be used as "mandates" by some of the agency boards of trustees and executives. This practice is problematic as operating procedure since these positions change from year to year, sometimes radically. Further, these statements are never binding on anyone except those agencies who so interpret them. Occasionally, instructions are issued to an agency, which usually adheres to them. Further, it is usually recognized that resolutions represent only those present and voting in a given meeting. They have no authority over the state bodies, the local associations, the churches, or individual Baptists.

As one would expect in such an organization, there is a wide range of opinion on any subject. Various parts of the country have their own emphases, interpretations, or responses to any theological issue or denominational program. These variant Baptists begin from different perspectives with different backgrounds and different points of view. While there have been homogenizing influences, the variations have been many and the results have been interesting.

Roots

Dr. Walter Shurden of Mercer University has presented a formulation of Baptist roots that has been widely quoted and appreciated. Published in *Baptist History and Heritage* in April, 1981, the study was entitled, "The Southern Baptist Synthesis: Is It Cracking?" It gives a good deal of insight into the variant roots of Southern Baptists. It shows that during the eighteenth and nineteenth centuries at least four distinct traditions among Baptists in the South contributed to the Southern Baptist synthesis.

The Charleston Tradition

The tradition rose out of First Baptist Church in Charleston, South Carolina. It began with William Screven and was perfected in the ministry of Richard Furman. It was rooted in the Particular Baptists of England, who were rooted in English Calvinistic Puritanism. From this background came the two central affirmations of Charleston. One was the centrality of the religious experience, and the second was the sole authority of Holy Scripture. This tradition, personified in Richard Furman, can be summarized in one word, ORDER. Charleston provided theological order. The Charleston Association adopted the Philadelphia Confession of Faith, which was Calvinistic in character. The confession became a kind of consensus in Baptist theology. It was not conceived or used as a creedal statement. The association adopted "A Summary of Church Discipline" that magnified the independence of the local churches but called for cooperation. This became the key to Southern Baptist connectionalism in the denomination. Thus came ecclesiological order.

This tradition represented a style of worship that was ordered and stately and aimed at pleasing God and not entertaining people. The ordinances were important. So came liturgical order. A final contribution of the Charleston group was ministerial order. They believed in an educated ministry. The first educational fund promoted and supported by Baptists in America was born in the Charleston Association in 1755. From this pro-educational sentiment were born Baptist colleges: Furman, Georgetown, Richmond, Wake Forest, and Mississippi College.

Shurden sums up the Charleston Tradition: "In brief, the Charleston Tradition consisted of pietistic Puritanism, Calvinistic confessionalism, quasi-connectionalism, church liturgics, and a commitment to an educated ministry. . . . The word for Charleston is ORDER."[2]

---

[2]Walter B. Shurden, "The Southern Baptist Synthesis: Is It Cracking?" *Baptist History*

The Sandy Creek Tradition

The second word in the Southern Baptist synthesis is ARDOR. This strain came from the Sandy Creek tradition where the people were Separate Baptists. These fiery frontier folk migrated to the South and settled in Sandy Creek, North Carolina, in 1755. They came out of New England revivalism possessed of an ardor that expressed itself in individualism, congregationalism, biblicism, and egalitarianism. They had a dedication to freedom unparalleled in Baptist history. They wanted to evangelize everyone who crossed their path and brooked no interference from government or church. They emphasized the local church, were suspicious of the association, had little to do with confessions of faith, and wanted freedom of the individual conscience.

These Baptists were revivalistic, emotional, and deeply pietistic. Their praise of God took the form of reaching people with the gospel. They were charismatic. Conversion and the call to preach were internal and experiential; preaching was not a matter of professional choice. Ministerial education was discouraged. It was said of their patriarch, Shubal Stearnes:

> His voice was musical and strong, which he managed is such a manner,
> as one while to make soft impressions of the heart, and fetch tears from
> the eyes in a mechanical way; and anon to shake the nerves, and to
> throw the animal system into tumults and perturbations.[3]

Their ecclesiology was ruggedly independent, the probable beginning of the later Landmark movement. Their background in New England Congregationalism made them wary of confessions of faith becoming creeds and creeds becoming substitutes for the Word of God. They were not systematic theologians, being sometimes Calvinistic, sometimes Arminian.

Shurden summarizes:

> The Sandy Creek Tradition consisted of revivalistic experientialism,
> anti-confessionalsim, exaggerated localism, fierce libertarianism, and a

---

and Heritage 16:2 (9 April, 1981): 4.
    [3]Ibid., 5.

commitment to personal evangelism. . . . If you marry a semi-presbyterian from Charleston to a semi-pentecostal from Sandy Creek, you will get a whole host of Southern Baptists spreading all over the Southland.[4]

As these two groups began to come to together, you have the basis of the synthesis that formed the SBC. Within about fifty years, more than a thousand congregations could be traced back to the Sandy Creek church.

The Georgia Tradition

From W. B. Johnson and I. T. Tichenor came the principal contributions to this tradition. It is summed up in two ideas of Johnson: one in the Southern Baptist Convention constitution, which he had in his pocket when he arrived at the organizational meeting and the second in the Public Address, which was written to explain the new organization. The basic ideas that would have far-reaching effect were denominationalism and sectionalism.

Sectionalism had to do principally with slavery. The convention said that the issues were not theological that split them from their long-time partners in the Triennial Convention. Regionalism seemed inevitable given the issues they faced. Cooperative denominationalism marked a new kind of denominational structure—more connectional, centralized, and more cooperative. They confessed in their Address that they constructed no new theology. It would be eighty years before they adopted a confessional statement. They were building a plan for cooperative effort in missions and evangelism. Cooperation was the method to achieve larger goals than possible before. Missions was the motive.

The Tennessee Tradition

The Tennessee tradition had as its central figure J. R. Graves. His contribution was Landmarkism, which Shurden called a "questionable honor." Its emphasis was on local church successionism, the exclusive validity of Baptist churches, Baptist ministers, and Baptist ordinances.

---

[4]Ibid., 6.

Much of our anti-ecumenism and sectarianism can be traced to the Tennessee Tradition. As the new conventions were formed in various non-southern states, many of the issues raised by this tradition were contested over and over. Some contention continues over these issues until this day.

The Texas Tradition

Shurden wrote these observations in 1980. They are still pertinent to the controversy in the convention. Since that time, at least three other Baptist leaders have added another Tradition—*the Texas Tradition*. This discussion began to focus publicly about 1989. Different observers describe it differently. Leon McBeth, historian of Southwestern Seminary—whose book on the Sunday School Board's history was later destroyed—perhaps sums up the Texas Tradition best.[5] He wrote in *Baptist History and Heritage* in January 1991 that Southwestern Seminary was the major institutional expression of the Texas tradition, B. H. Carroll was the primary architect, L. R. Scarborough was its most fervent evangelist, and George W. Truett was its primary pastoral role model.[6]

McBeth states that this formulation of Baptist life rose partly in response to the frontier environment. The Mexican government's exclusion of all but the Catholic Church in early Texas furnished another fashioning influence. The Anglo insistence upon religious freedom to worship contributed to the conflict that led to Texan independence. The flood of immigrants from other states and several countries intensified the conflicts with the Indians and Mexicans. In this environment people tended to become more intense, more aggressive, more conservative. McBeth commented, "I sometimes think that Texas Baptists have absorbed some of the qualities of the Jalapena pepper, so common in that region; a few of these 'Jalapena Baptists' can flavor the Baptist bowl, but too many of them in one place can bring tears to your eyes."[7]

Texas Baptists seemed to absorb the spirit of conquest that followed the founding of the Republic. The militant spirit, intensified by the social and political environment, helped to form a distinctive kind of Southern

---

[5]Leon McBeth, "The Texas Tradition: A Study in Baptist Regionalism (Part I)," *Baptist History and Heritage* 26:2 (January 1991): 37–47. Part II follows on pages 48-57.

[6]Ibid., 38.

[7]Ibid., 39-40.

Baptists in the Southwest. As the immigrants came, they brought with them the conflicts of other places, which took on a peculiarly Texas flavor. McBeth wrote, "A. H. Newman concluded that 'A large proportion of the Baptists of the Southwest were so perverse in doctrine and so unamiable in spirit that Baptist growth was retarded.'" The conflict between progressive missionary Baptists and repressive fundamentalists continued to shape the spirit of Texas Baptists. McBeth continued,

> Texas has from the first nurtured opposite kinds of Baptists. The narrow, rigid, intolerant spirit of Daniel Parker has erupted from time to time; we see it in Martinism, Haydenism, Crawfordism, and above all in Norrisism. But at the same time, Texas has nurtured constructive, cooperative, and progressive Baptists.[8]

B. H. Carroll, "rarely uncertain about anything," quickly became "the John Wayne of Texas Baptists." He was influential in the Whitsitt controversy that swept Texas and some of the rest of the convention territory. Whitsitt was president of Southern Baptist Seminary. He denied the Landmark tenet of direct successionism of Baptist churches, declaring that it could not be demonstrated historically. The new scientific historical method used by Whitsitt was to become an ongoing source of controversy. McBeth commented, "Whitsitt's fate was played out in Louisville, but it was determined in Waco," Carroll's hometown.

McBeth summarized the Texas Tradition in his second paper in the same publication. "At least three major features distinguish this segment of Baptist life: intense conservatism, fervent evangelism, and a spirit of independence."[9] In the present SBC controversy, all these attitudes are adequately represented. Texas is divided on controversial matters today perhaps as much as any other state.

Albert McClellan insists that there is at least one other tradition that helped shape Southern Baptists—the Virginia Tradition. Perhaps still others could be identified, but it is enough to indicate at this point that there were many different kinds of Baptists in the milieu called the Southern Baptist Convention. It is a wonder that they could ever be

---

[8]Ibid., 41.
[9]Ibid., 48.

unified on any subject for 130 years. The story is not yet fully told.

Cultural Diversity

The history of cultural diversity is almost as checkered as the traditions discussed above. From earliest days, for example, the First Baptist Church of Nashville had slave members. Many of the old South congregations not only had slave members but provided special areas for seating them. This did not last long after the Civil War in most places. In some churches, there was a core of educated, sometimes sophisticated, members. These sat alongside and served with equally uneducated, unsophisticated members. Sometimes there was social distance between them and sometimes little was apparent. The wealthy and the economically deprived often were members of the same congregation. In the Olivet Baptist Church in Oklahoma City where I served for more than eleven years, it was difficult to determine the social class to which the various members belonged. In other churches, the class distinctions are immediately obvious and objectionable.

Southernness, with all of its gentility or lack of it, was and is still a factor in some congregations. Many have been slow to adopt the language and folkways of the modern era. In the present controversy, one sometimes wonders whether the fundamentalists are trying to preserve the old ways or The Old Way. The social niceties of the old South obviously do not fit the modern scheme of things. The baby boomers and the established leadership in the older churches often have a hard time mixing.

Since World War II, social and cultural diversity has grown at an accelerated rate. Pluralism of every variety has impacted the culture of the South in ways never known before in the area. The coming of other economic forces has altered the financial world and feminized the work place. The religious pluralism mentioned before has caused an unease in many places that has been difficult to define and has produced drastic reactions in some situations.

The boomer generation has often developed an altogether different reaction to the religious establishment from that of their parents. They are looking for church situations that meet the needs of their families, often with little attention to the name on the church sign. The basketball league or the day care center may be more important than theological discussions. In the work place, the emphases will reflect similar changes.

Company loyalty and denominational loyalty both seem to be fading.

Matters of authority are creating their own problems. The highly individualistic young, raised in the "me" generation, often do not take kindly to the authoritarian patterns of the old South. The impacts on the business, social, and religious worlds are sometimes difficult to define or explain. In the same society, many of the less advantaged educationally or economically are seeking at church an authoritarian voice that says, "This is the way, walk ye in it." The presence of such authoritarianism and individualism in the same church furnishes a very volatile mixture.

Theological Tributaries

In addition to these traditions, reference must be made to many differing theological understandings. The "Church Fathers" of Southern Baptists are many and sometimes colorfully different. They run the gamut from dignified and saintly George Truett to the flamboyant and fractious Frank Norris, from the scholarly E. Y. Mullins with his *Axioms of Religion* to the unscholarly but profoundly influential J. R. Graves (born a Vermont Yankee). They span the spectrum from A. H. Strong to Walter Rauschenbusch (not Southern Baptists). Add B. H. Carroll and W. T. Conner and you get the flavor of Texas and its vitality. These and a dozen more left giant-sized footprints in the, then, unset Baptist concrete.

In illustrating the theological diversity, Southern Baptists never really decided whether they were Calvinists or Armenians. Timothy George gives the doctrines of Calvin as summarized at the Dutch Reformed Synod of Dort (1618–1619) in five major assertions:

(1) the decrees of election and reprobation are absolute and unconditional, (2) the scope of the atonement is restricted to the elect, although the death of Christ is sufficient to expiate the sins of the whole world; (3) because of the fall human beings are totally incapable of any saving good apart from the regenerating work of the Holy spirit; (4) God's call is effectual and hence His grace cannot be ultimately thwarted by human resistance; (5) those whom God calls and regenerates He also keeps so that they do not totally nor finally fall

from faith and grace.[10]

James Spivey in the same volume says that B. H. Carroll was a fundamentalist and a Calvinist in tune with the New Hampshire Confession of Faith. He avowed that from eternity God unconditionally elected some for salvation. The non-elected were not given grace sufficient for salvation. James Leo Garrett says of the Texas stalwart W.T. Connor that in his Calvinism he clearly taught only two (election and perseverance) of the five points of the Dort Synod. J. P. Boyce, a founding father of Southern Seminary, clearly affirmed all five points of the Synod of Dorts in his Abstracts. Still others, like E. Y. Mullins, emphasized individual freedom and priesthood. So the greats of Baptist life had differing views of the basic possible theological positions. Certainly not all the students of these great Baptist divines subscribed to all the tenets of Calvin or Arminius. Nancy Ammerman has called attention to the fact that John Smyth, an early Baptist forebear, introduced his congregation to *Arminian* theology. He, unlike the Puritans, insisted that though God may have known the destiny of each individual from the beginning, the atoning redeeming work of Christ was available to all. This view is still widely accepted.[11]

George M. Marsden summarized the variance in Baptist theology:

> In America, the Baptists had long been a coalition of diverse elements. On the one hand they had a confessional Calvinist tradition; yet at the same time they had an a strong emphasis on doctrinal freedom. Calvinism was strong in the seventeenth-century Puritan origins of the American movement and also in the important eighteenth-century separation of New England Baptists from Congregationalism after the Great Awakening. Baptists, however, had an individualistic view of the church as a voluntary association of individuals who had experienced conversion. The Calvinist confessionalism was qualified by opposition to ecclesiastical centralization and vigorous affirmation of the individual right to theological freedom. Moreover, the emphasis on conversion in the pietist camp, and especially in nineteenth-century frontier revivalism, reinforced Arminian doctrines which emphasized human freedom of choice

---

[10]Timothy George and David Dockery, eds., *Baptist Theologians* (Nashville: Broadman, 1990) 89–90.

[11]Nancy Tatom Ammerman, *Baptist Battles*, (New Brunswick, NJ: Rutgers University Press, 1990) 20.

and were, as much as Calvinism, a venerable part of the diverse Baptist heritage.[12]

This last citation probably sums up the true situation among Southern Baptists theologically. It is important, however, to the present controversy to look at the position of the various "Fathers" on the nature of scripture. The views of the leaders, particularly those involved in theological education, came to be heard again and again in all of the battles Baptists have had. The views of the leadership in the Southern Baptist Convention on the nature of scripture have been almost universally conservative. They were frequently stated differently, but the common denominator was biblical conservatism. A sizable number did not and do not subscribe to the present day understanding of inerrancy as interpreted by recent SBC leaders. Many of these earlier leaders would have little trouble with the Chicago Statement on Inerrancy[13] but would reject the call for the "perfect Bible" of the present leaders who either do not understand the Chicago statement or do not subscribe to it.

J. R. Graves of the Tennessee Tradition believed the plenary-verbal theory of inspiration of scripture. He wrote:

> There may be errors in the transcriptions of the ancient manuscripts; there may be errors in translation, and errors many in interpretation, but that the original scriptures are the words of the living God, He most explicitly declares them to be.[14]

This sounds like the basic argument of many modern fundamentalists.

J. P. Boyce said that he believed in the "perfect inspiration and absolute authority of the divine revelation." He referred to the Bible as infallible and endorsed the inerrantist views of colleague Basil Manly, Jr. Yet, he admitted the scriptural use of the language of appearance and observation to describe natural events, just as we do now refer to the rising and setting of the sun. He asserted that had the Bible been written in the

---

[12]*Fundamentalism and American Culture* (New York: Oxford University Press, 1980) 104–105.

[13]The Chicago Statement on Inerrancy is dealt with at length in Chapter 5.

[14]I am indebted to *Baptist Theologians*, edited by Timothy George and David Dockery (Nashville: Broadman, 1990) for information on the position of some Baptist theologians on Holy Scripture.

language of true modern science, it would have been rejected again and again as false.

Augustus H. Strong had a profound influence on many Southern Baptists. His *Systematic Theology* was used as a text book in SBC schools as far back as the 1920s and for years afterward. His view of scripture was not as succinctly stated as moderns would have liked. He apparently believed inspiration did not guarantee inerrancy in things not essential to the salvific purpose of scripture. He felt human errors in things historical should not detract from the perfect inspiration of scripture. Religious truth rather than inerrancy became Strong's definitive stance.

It was said of B. H. Carroll of Texas: "President Carroll, Bible in hand, standardized orthodoxy in Texas."He concluded that creationism and Darwinism were irreconcilable but thought that creation was not accomplished in a literal week. His view of atonement was that it was sacrificial, voluntary, penal, and certainly vicarious. He rejected the idea of a universal church, refused the idea of alien baptism, and practiced "close communion." His ideas of scripture would fit well with the present leadership of the convention. They seem to be his spiritual children on matters of scripture. He believed in verbal, plenary inspiration, and not just ideas but every word was inspired. As for "contradictions," he attributed these to his limited understanding. His influence and dogma would be influential for generations.

E. Y. Mullins was the Baptist "father" who brought some moderation and careful articulation to the theological perceptions of Southern Baptists. His *Axioms of Religion* furnished a sort of philosophical base supporting many Baptist assumptions. He was chairman of the committee that prepared the first statement of faith for the denomination in 1925. His basic understanding of authority for Baptists was that Jesus Christ is the authority in all matters religious. This idea was included in the first and the second statement called *The Baptist Faith and Message*:

> The Bible is the inspired interpretation of Christ which creates the possibility of his life being experienced today. Christ as the revealer of God and Redeemer of man is the seat of authority in religion and above and underneath and before the Bible. But the Bible is the authoritative

literature which leads us to Christ.[15]

H. H. Hobbs, who will laugh at my calling him a contemporary "father" has had vast influence in the modern scene in Southern Baptist life. He was chairman of the committee of state convention presidents that brought the Baptist Faith and Message statement to the convention in 1963. He has often said that it was never intended as a creed, though often that has been tried. Hobbs has had great respect for scholarship and relied on the "grammatic-historical" method in his own writings, though it would be unacceptable to him to follow the radical conclusions of Form Criticism. Yet, he has called himself an inerrantist because his faith is in a God who does not make errors. In spite of this identification, he would call himself a middle-of-the-road Baptist.

All of these citations have been given for the purpose of showing that there have been substantial differences among the leadership of Baptists about the exact nature of scripture. Yet, a careful examination of these views reveals a remarkable conservatism in the various views. All of these men, together with many more, have had a basically conservative view of scripture. Without exception, they have viewed it as the inspired Word of God, authoritative, and binding. All may be said to have had a "high view" of the nature of scripture. Yet there has been enough difference to trace some of the variations now being heard back to teachers and preachers of influence.

Diversity of Clergy

From all of the discussion above, it is easy to understand that there was a wide diversity in the makeup of the ministry in the denomination. Figures vary marginally depending on the study, but it is clear that slightly more than half of the pastors do not have theological degrees. The educational background varies from multiple doctorates down to almost nothing. With the independence of the churches and the nature of ordination, wide variety is assured. Some have commented across the years that some churches would ordain anyone who was feeling good.

---

[15]E. Y. Mullins, *Freedom and Authority in Religion* (Philadelphia: The Griffith & Roland Press, 1913), as quoted by Fisher Humphries in *Baptist Theologians*, 339.

Some of the clergy come from urbane and sophisticated families with every advantage made available to them. Some come from the opposite extremes of poverty and ignorance. Of course, most would fall somewhere between the extremes. Many of the Baptist colleges have good to excellent religion departments and furnish reasonably good educational backgrounds for those who do not go on to seminary. Rarely, however, do these institutions deal with the complicated and controversial issues that are the routine pursuits of the accredited theological seminary.

There is still a substantial number of bi-vocational ministers in the smaller churches in both the rural and small town areas and the newer congregations in the cities. This is particularly true of the areas outside the traditional South. Many of these are professional people with solid preparation in a non-theological discipline. Without these bi-vocational pastors, many congregations that are doing good work could not continue.

Generally, it would be a mistake to divide the clergy into categories such as rural-urban, educated or uneducated, sophisticated or not. It would be difficult to categorize them properly on any such arbitrary basis. There are all kinds of differences, some of which are pertinent to the present problems. It would be fair to say that generally the less well-educated and the less sophisticated were less equipped to confront the intellectual questions inherent in the controversy. This does not have to do with intellectual ability but familiarity with the problems and methodology essential for proper understanding of the issues involved. It would be a mistake also to equate a seminary degree with the sophistication required to deal with these problems. As my mother-in-law was wont to say, "Education just doesn't take on everyone."

It is also important to say that regardless of the equipment brought to the controversy by the clergy, the problems have not in the main been dealt with on an intellectual level. One of the major mistakes of the moderates was that they thought they could have dialogue with the fundamentalists on the issues. When none was forthcoming, the moderates were confused as to why it was not possible to sit down and talk these things over like reasonable people. The fundamentalists were sure that they had the truth and the answers and that dialogue that would produce a meeting of minds was to compromise. This they refused to do.

The diversity of the clergy contributed heavily to the problems of the convention.

Diversity of Emphases

With the diversity of the clergy, one would expect a wide variety of emphases in churches that glory in their freedom from ecclesiastical controls. With the diverse constituencies as plentiful as the diverse leaders, Southern Baptists experience many kinds of churches and worship. Some of the churches want a leadership oriented to pastoral care. Some want a strong pulpit ministry. Others are interested in a "full service" church. This is a new understanding of what a church should be. It goes with the "super church" era in which some congregations demand all kinds of activities designed to meet the needs of every member of the family and keep them all entertained.

A brochure from a church recently contained seven or eight pages of listings of basketball teams for all ages, specialized activities for every age group, skating, exercise classes, baseball teams for all ages, male and female, and various activities for singles, the aged, the youth and preschoolers. There was even a class in oriental martial arts! This same church listed a few outreach activities of a truly spiritual nature.

Some of the churches, led by pastors with special interests, emphasize the need for Christians to head peace movements. The more traditional churches are constantly emphasizing evangelism. Still others are strong on worship, sometimes liturgical in form. Some specialize in various missionary activities, both locally and even overseas. Many churches sent teams of laity who pay their own expenses overseas for short term activities. Some help construct church buildings wherever there is a need. Some emphasize disaster relief. Some are concerned about the social applications of the gospel in varied forms. Some emphasize pietism, especially when there are few genuine opportunities for evangelization.

With these illustrations of a multiplicity of interests and commitments, it is easy to see the roots of controversy.

The Influence of The Evangelicals

Our theologians are still arguing whether Southern Baptists are or have been Evangelicals. For many years, it is true that denominational leadership tried to keep the attention of the people on the programs and materials of the convention. Displays of materials other than those produced by the denomination were prohibited in the exhibit halls at public meetings, especially the annual convention meeting. There was a denominational entity serving every known need of the churches, and they were zealous if not jealous of the "monopoly" they enjoyed. Of course, there was no attempt to control what a church bought or used, but in many ways it was a closed shop. Others not of the immediate family but with evangelical orientation were not usually represented in the meetings.

Within the new generation of leadership, some were more comfortable in the evangelical fellowships than they were in the SBC. Some began to be used outside the convention and brought their counterparts into an increasing number of SBC meetings and activities. The introduction of strong and attractive personalities into pastor's conferences, conventions, evangelism conferences, and revivals opened up new avenues of fellowship and cross fertilization of ideas and practices.

The growing use of electronic media in religion furnished the opportunity to non-Baptist groups to infiltrate many phases of Baptist life. Across the South, many homes received more influential and persuasive instruction from the media, principally television, than from their local churches. In many places the most attractive presentations of religion and righteousness came from the media presentations of evangelicals who were not interested in denominationalism. It is almost certain that many of these broadcasters received their major support from Baptists.

The interest of the fundamentalists in the right wing political activities was stimulated by the Reagan candidacy. They were courted and won and, to a larger degree than ever before, participated in partisan politics. This won the attention of the politicians and the Moral Majority. Thus began a movement that was to shake the walls of the Baptist house and contribute in a significant way to the controversy. Ideas, programs, curriculum materials, and evangelical programs not Baptist in their orientation gained increasing popularity.

Thus the stage was set for the emergence of a new movement that would change the face of the Southern Baptist Convention.

We Are Different

When we moved to a new state after some time in retirement, a primary task was to find a church. The nearest Southern Baptist church was first in line for a visit. The church was what is usually called "charismatic."

The second visit was to another church near by. They had a rousing music performance that probably fit the needs of the rock and roll generation—but not mine.

The third visit was to a church marvelously located on a major thoroughfare in a metropolitan setting. My father would have been at home there in the 1930s.

The fourth visit was to a distant but interesting church that was by Baptist standards "high church." There were three pages of liturgy, robed ministers called "reverend," women and black deacons, and a high level of competence. There I think they worship—differently but genuinely.

The fifth visit was to a positively intriguing congregation that did not use the name Baptist in the church title. The church had an imaginative outreach program with many unusual facets. The pastor was refreshing and more than competent. It was not the traditional church but probably a prophet of things to come, and they made me want to be a part of a different approach to spreading the old gospel.

The sixth visit was to a "peoples'" church in the heart of an old downtown section of the city. The music was good, the church crowded, and the pastor a superb preacher.

There are many kinds of Baptists!

Chapter Four

Fundamentalism and Southern Baptists

"Voices and Thunders. . . ."[1]

The marriage of fundamentalists, Norrisites, moderates, and a few more or less liberals had lasted for 135 years. They had lived together, with only occasional fusses and sometimes verbal violence, united by a common understanding of what was valuable in the kingdom enterprise. There had been various levels of awareness of the vast diversity that existed in the Southern Baptist Convention. Many were obviously unaware that there were substantial differences in understanding of scripture. Nearly all used the language of Zion but sometimes meant different things by it. There were those who had a partial awareness, accepted what they understood and made little fuss over what they did not understand. There were others who understood much of the diversity and accepted the others as fellow Christians who had a right as Baptists to be whatever God led them to be.

There had always been periods of time when confrontations occurred over some item of orthodoxy, most often on the level of the local association of churches. Frequently these occurred over such things as the charismatic movement, the interpretation of baptism, or the Lord's Supper. These arguments were fairly common in the newer states with the variety of Baptists who had been transplanted to a new environment from the South. In the main, these differences were either settled or there was general but often unspoken agreement that the issue was not worthy of a schism. Frequently, where there was a spirit of brotherliness, the issue was settled around, "If eating meat offends my brother, I will eat no

---

[1] Revelation 16:18.

meat."[2] Christian charity smoothed over many honest differences of opinion on a multitude of subjects. Disputes on a national level, as we shall see, sometimes were not so easily solved.

Problems related to Ralph Elliot's *The Message Of Genesis* were to furnish basis for many complaints by Pressler and company.[3] The *Broadman Commentary* became a cause around which fundamentalist and other sympathies coalesced.[4] The basic problem in both these battles had to do with the interpretation of Genesis and whether the first eleven chapters were to be taken as literal history. In both cases, the argument had to do with the nature of scripture. Elliot, among other things, had challenged the story of Abraham's sacrifice of Isaac. The commentary raised the questions, as most such works do, as to whether the Genesis record was to be interpreted literally and whether Moses wrote all of the Penteteuch. Both works were a little strong for most Baptist appetites.

Both of these publications by Broadman Press (owned by the Sunday School Board) raised a furor. Editors across the SBC raised questions about Elliot, his writings, and teachings. The pastor of the First Baptist Church in Houston, K. Owen White, wrote a stinging article that received wide distribution called "Death In The Pot." He was subsequently elected president of the SBC in 1964—one of a number who would be elected to "save the convention." The matter followed established procedures and was finally handled by the trustees of Midwestern Seminary, where Elliot taught. Interestingly, Elliot was not discharged for heresy but for insubordination when he refused to stop the publishing of a second edition.

The *Broadman Commentary* matter was of the same general nature but became more complex in its resolution. The convention in 1969 passed a motion that said,

> Call the attention of agencies to the doctrinal statement framed after careful discussion in 1963 and vigorously urge elected trustees to be diligent in seeing that programs assigned them are carried out consistent with that statement and not contrary to it.[5]

---

[2] 1 Corinthians 8:13.
[3] *The Message of Genesis* (Nashville: Broadman, 1961).
[4] *The Broadman Bible Commentary*, vol. 1 (Nashville: Broadman, 1968).
[5] Baptist Press, 12 June 1969.

The SBC narrowly defeated a motion requiring writers and professors to sign doctrinal statements. The next month, The Sunday School Board instructed its employees to abide with the resolution of the convention.[6]

At the meeting of the Executive Committee in September 1969, W. A. Criswell, president of the convention, told the members that Baptists who did not believe the convention-adopted statement of faith should leave and go to another denomination. He asked how long the convention could stay together, saying: "There are among us liberals, conservatives, fundamentalists; open communionists, closed communionists, alien immersionists; persons who would emphasize the social application of the gospel; those who would emphasize evangelism." He later added, "in my humble judgment, I think we ought to take those articles of faith of 1925 and 1963 and say: 'this is what it is, being a Baptist. If you don't believe that, you are not a Baptist.'"[7] The next month he termed "liberals" "termites who would destroy the church." Shortly, he said he would not be serving a second term as president had it not been for criticism of his preaching and writing by "liberals."[8]

The rhetoric was heating up as numbers of editors printed his inflammatory language and editorialized against it. Just prior to the June convention in Denver, 1970, about 200 conservatives had an unofficial rump session to air grievances and plot strategy against liberalism in the convention. The prime issue was the *Broadman Commentary* and the activities of the Christian Life Commission. The Pastor's Conference again furnished a platform for blasting liberals. Carl Bates of Charlotte, North Carolina, was elected president. He promptly said that he had no specific program, for he saw his job primarily as a presiding officer and in appointing committees and other routine convention responsibilities. He refused to comment on the *Broadman Commentary* problem.[9]

During this meeting, a motion to recall the first volume of the commentary passed by an estimated five to two vote. Vigorous debate preceded this action, but conservatism prevailed. The convention refused to abolish the Christian Life Commission or fire its employees.[10]

---

[6]Baptist Press, 25 July 1969.
[7]Baptist Press, 23 September 1969.
[8]Baptist Press, 3 February 1970.
[9]Baptist Press, 2 June 1970.
[10]Baptist Press, 3 June 1970.

The commentary matter would occupy the attention of the Baptists for another two years. Frequent headlines announced the current attacks and answers. A new writer had to be chosen after the recall, and the convention voted to change writers by a margin of 382 votes out of nearly 5000 cast.[11] Sunday School Board trustees agreed to the convention decree in their next meeting. Clyde T. Francisco, a professor of Old Testament at Southern Seminary, was chosen to do the rewrite. In Philadelphia the next year, the convention rejected a motion "by overwhelming standing vote" to withdraw the entire twelve-volume commentary.[12]

The intensity of the feeling of some about this matter is revealed by an incident which occurred two or three years after the issue was settled by the convention. One fundamentalist ordered copies of the commentary from a London publisher who had a license to reprint and sell the volume in Europe. These copies were put on sale in a hotel near the meeting place of the convention and were used to claim that the Sunday School Board was still selling the withdrawn volume.

These national controversies were of a different genre from the present one. These were fought out in the press and in public meetings but produced very little of an organized political nature beyond the local associations and state conventions. In the main, they followed established procedures and were resolved finally by the responsible trustees in both cases. They did furnish ammunition for Pressler and Patterson for years to come. Further, they sensitized many Baptists to the obvious diversity in the positions of many of their fellow Baptists. They furnished a base for accusations against the Sunday School Board and the seminaries. For more than a decade after these matters were resolved, they were still used as evidence of a denomination going liberal.

In fairness, it should be said that there was certainly no organized attempt in the institutions of higher learning to lead the faithful away from their traditional conservatism about the Bible. An occasional "liberal" opinion from time to time did get published. Sometimes it was expressed by a youthful faculty member trying to "make a contribution." One basic problem was that Southern Baptists were coming late to the discussion about the nature of scripture that had been going on elsewhere

---

[11]Baptist Press, 3 June 1971.
[12]Baptist Press, 7 February 1972.

for decades. Of course, many of the pastors and teachers had been along this road years before and had remained conservative to the core in their understanding of the nature of scripture. It should be said also that from time to time, a school would elect a faculty member whose theology was outside the bounds of Southern Baptist thought. These problems usually were dealt with by the trustees of the institution, usually after someone or group had made an issue of the matter. Sometimes this was slow in coming because democracy is slow to act, and the brethren in charge were usually loath to judge and condemn.

This lack of an official inquisitional spirit seemed right to many and made it possible for the widely diverse group to live together with some periodic peace. Illustrations of the use of the system to correct problems related to theology, however, can be found in the histories of the seminaries and the Sunday School Board. On several occasions, faculty members who were outside generally accepted Baptist theology were disciplined or terminated.

When the issue of electing the president of the convention began to surface with the rise of Presslerism, it came as something of a shock to many. No one could remember the convention having a "liberal" president. The nearest thing to a liberal that anyone could remember was Congressman Brooks Hays of Arkansas. His sin was that he was in favor of equal rights for blacks and often said so. He was a Baptist but probably would not have claimed a theological system. Every president known to living man had been conservative theologically. Across the years, a number of them had been elected on a platform of keeping or making the convention conservative. Among them was R. G. Lee of Memphis as far back as 1948. Other champions of conservatism were K. Owen White of Houston, W. A. Criswell of Dallas, and Jaroy Weber of Texas. It should be noted, however, that every president in my lifetime (and others say from the beginning) had been conservative in his theology, and none of them tried to lead in any other direction.

How were these presidents and other leaders elected? Since the elections were to play such an important role in the future, it is likely worth the effort to discuss this matter further. There has been a great deal of talk about the "good ole boy" network controlling the convention. It is probably true that the convention affairs had been dominated by a hard-to-identify group who had "paid their dues." There was no artificial limit set as to who these people were, and no one actually knew who would grow into a leadership role. These were, in the main, people who had gradually become recognized for three or four qualities.

They almost universally had been persons who were recognized in their local association of churches as leaders. The pastors who held the majority of positions were usually effective pulpiteers. This seemed to be a requisite for leadership. Their church usually had been led to give generously (by comparison) to the denominational causes. They were cooperative with the brethren in the affairs of the association and the state convention. They were usually competent in the area for which they were chosen to lead. Often, they had become prominent locally by some especially outstanding contribution to the work.

With the exception of national, state convention, and associational officers, the system employed the use of a committee on nominations at almost every level of Baptist life. These committees nominated the trustees of the various agencies. It was natural for the members to name the most prominent, and often most capable, persons they knew. It was true also that they tended to name the persons they knew best. Once a person had achieved leadership in the local setting, it was customary for him to be named to a state or national responsibility. Some became fixtures on committees and boards because of the system. It often lost in the cracks some competent and dedicated people.

The system tended not to use those less than prominent or those who were less aggressive in leadership roles. It did tend to select the more competent leaders. There were flaws in the system, but it was a democratic procedure, and there were few attempts to control it for the benefit of any person or class. Those attempts did secure posts for an occasional individual and sometimes worked improperly. The system was never, to my knowledge, controlled by any organized group.

Cecil Sherman, pastor of the Broadway Baptist Church of Fort Worth and an early leader in resistance to the fundamentalists, wrote a brief review of some of the events of those early days. He said that he wrote it in response to a request from his daughter to explain to her what had happened. In the paper he wrote of the "old politic" of the SBC:

> Was there a politic in the SBC back in those innocent days? Yes. The politic was arranged. Those bureaucrats (denominational leaders) knew who loved and supported the SBC. They knew who gave the money. They knew those churches that sacrificed some of their own needs for the good of the SBC. They marked the preachers who led those

churches to that sacrifice. Editors were a part of that politic. The pastors who loved and supported the SBC plus the bureaucrats plus the editors made common cause to put before Southern Baptists the people who loved, cared about and gave themselves to the SBC. It was a sort of ecclesiastical "good ole boy" system. After describing the "old politic" let me say a word for it. I think it was not only "old politic," I think it was also a good politic. It was used in all the churches I have ever served. The people who love the church and attend the church three times a week and give sacrificially to the church have an inordinate influence in the church.[13]

While I would disagree with Sherman that the system was dominated by the bureaucrats, I would agree that this was the spirit of the system, and usually it worked well. While I was a bureaucrat for twenty-three years, I very seldom had any active input as to who my trustees were to be. I can remember only two or three instances in all those years. Some of the other bureaucrats seemed to have more access to the system than I had, but it seemed to me that they sought those opportunities by talking to the members of the nominating committees. In no case known to me was a committee member coerced into choosing someone to serve.

New Wine and Old Skins

After the 1979 meeting, it was becoming clear that something new was appearing in Southern Baptist life. Few if any really understood what it was, but clearly something was going on. On May 9, 1979, Paige Patterson had confirmed what was suspected by the establishment. He acknowledged that meetings had been held in at least 15 states in recent months to encourage messengers to attend the meeting of the SBC in Houston to elect a president "committed to biblical inerrancy."[14] He said that he and Houston appeals court judge Paul Pressler had attended many of the meetings. He denied that this represented a radical departure from usual procedure. The meetings had two purposes:

(1) to meet together with fellow Baptists who are greatly concerned

---

[13]Cecil Sherman, letter to his daughter, used by permission.
[14]Baptist Press, 9 May 1979.

about some things happening in the SBC . . . to help those in leadership to know what we feel . . . especially as it concerns the reliability of the Scriptures. (2) To discuss ways by which we might be able to secure the elected leadership of the convention from among those who we know are committed to biblical inerrancy.

Both Patterson and Pressler cited "liberal" teachings in Southern Baptist seminaries, especially Southern Seminary and Southeastern. They also criticized Wake Forest University and the University of Richmond.

On June 13, 1979, Pressler talked with the press and denied "planning, strategizing or implementing any organized effort to elect Adrian Rogers. Simply the conservatives are communicating with each other for the first time." They would continue to do so, he emphasized. The next day, Pressler again denied unconfirmed reports that he and others had encouraged local churches to bus messengers to the convention for the election and that some churches had more than the permissible ten messengers. He vowed,

> I'm against power politics, but I'm for greater participation of layman in the convention. I'm absolutely appalled by the reaction that it is wrong to encourage more participation in the convention. All we did was to inform other Baptists about the problem of parking and transportation, and suggest that some churches might want to form transportation pools and more than one church come in buses or cars.[15]

Lee Porter, Registration Secretary of the convention, was instructed to study any voting irregularities. When he reported an exhaustive study to the Executive Committee in September, he concluded that the irregularities were probably due to the nature of the system, which he called "sloppy." The only exception to that statement, he said involved the get-out-the-vote effort, which he described thusly:

> Approximately 200 churches with 150 to 1000 members located within 150 miles of Houston elected 6, 7, 8, 9, or 10 messengers. Most of those registered on Tuesday (the day of the presidential election). Through a sample survey, I have confirmed that many of these came in small vans or busses and that 83 percent attended only business sessions

---

[15]Baptist Press, 14 June 1979.

on Tuesday. The survey indicates that 71 percent of them also attended the Wednesday night service at the Astrodome. In my judgment, registration facts point to a 'get-out-the-vote'campaign.

He said there was no evidence of a massive busing of voters.
Baptist Press reported Porter's conclusions.

Porter said his investigation showed that reports of large numbers of discarded ballots at the SBC were true. [Porter said,] "One usher collected about 400 sets off the floor. Others turned in 30 to 40 sets in the registration booth. The clean-up crew showed me another large container of discarded ballots. Apparently, between 1000 and 2000 sets were thrown away after the Tuesday afternoon session."

This was the session in which the president was elected. He noted that at least 47 churches permitted only 10 messengers had more than that, including one with 22, one with 20, one with 16, two with 14, five with 13, eleven with 12 and twenty six with 11. The top five churches in that list were from Texas but not Houston. Twenty-eight of the 47 were from Texas.[16]

By 1990 in the New Orleans convention, more that 8000 people would register on Tuesday morning in time for the presidential election. 37,224 people voted in that election.[17] In the missions emphasis that night, the Super Dome would host less than 3000.

Whatever the facts about organizations and getting out the vote, in 1979 the convention was buzzing about the controversy. Every meeting during the ensuing year had its share of discussion about the problems, either on the program or in the halls. The first of the Criswell-Robison Bible conferences tried to avoid the controversy. Criswell declared that a positive note would be sounded and that "there is no spirit of divisiveness in me." The seminary presidents were not invited to speak, and every speaker, with possibly one exception, would later be a leader of the so-called conservative side.

The *Southern Baptist Journal*, the publication of the Baptist Faith and Message Fellowship, moved its headquarters to South Carolina, and the

---

[16]Baptist Press, 19 September 1979.
[17]*SBC Annual, 1990, 56.*

editor was changed. Russell Kammerling, brother-in-law of Paige Patterson, was named editor. He assured the press that there was no direct connection between the paper and the Criswell Center where the fundamentalist leader was president.

In April of 1980, BP headlined: "Patterson Group Seeks Long Range Control of SBC." The story said,

> Its goal is to determine who is elected SBC president for at least four consecutive years and maybe as many as 10, and through presidential committee appointments, try to control nomination of trustees of SBC agencies. . . . Paige Patterson, president of Criswell Center for Biblical Studies in Dallas, revealed the plan and made the charges in a meeting April 3 seeking lay volunteers to organize the effort. He reiterated them in an interview with the Baptist Standard, Texas Baptist newspaper, on April 14. . . . This year it was revealed at the meeting April 3 . . . that Pressler has organizations in all state conventions. He is attempting to enlist laymen in every association.

It was also reported that in the same meeting Pressler charged that "a very large contingency in significant denominational posts do not in fact believe that (inerrancy) any longer." He declined to name them or the professors who were charged with teaching false doctrine. The report also noted of Pressler that "emphatically he felt what he is doing is not divisive and should not be branded as 'politics.'" He told the meeting that "they could depend on Adrian Rogers (SBC President) naming a committee on committees sympathetic to their views."

Rogers said he knew nothing of the current political moves, dissociated himself with them and said that he was "amazed and mildly disappointed" at the news.[18] He had said that he would appoint only inerrantists to committees. Pressler would say years later in the interview with Gary North that became known as the "Firestorm Chat" that Roger's nominees were "absolutely superb."

Response was quick in coming. Duke McCall, long time president of Southern Baptist Theological Seminary, told participants at the annual meeting of the SBC Historical Commission: "If I did not believe in God, I would predict and bet on the dissolution of the Southern Baptist

---

[18]Baptist Press, 21 April 1980.

Convention in the 1980s." He warned the Southern Baptists not to think that it couldn't happen here. Many of our leaders think the "stability of the SBC is self-righting and that it always comes back, and that our leaders, once in places of power, become leaders representing the total fellowship."[19] This sort of returning balance had happened before as some of the more vocal brethren were elected to some office, only to discover that there was more to the story than they had known.

At this juncture in SBC history, many thought that the "pendulum" would swing back to the middle in time. Others recognized that for us this was a new phenomenon.

There was growing apprehension about the intentions of the Pressler-Patterson faction. Many believed that as soon as the word got around as to their intentions, the people would back off from any participation in such an effort. Others weren't so sure. Still others welcomed this attempt "to save the convention." Some of the most astute observers of convention affairs completely misunderstood the true state of affairs, thinking that if the matter was left alone it would go away. Most were simply unwilling to believe that Baptists would act like this.

As the time for the 1980 convention meeting approached, the rhetoric began to heat up. Some of us were trying to work behind the scenes to see if some reasonable accommodation could be made that would defuse a possible disaster. James Sullivan, recently president of the convention, and I talked about the leadership of the movement. It was decided that he, in company with two or three other former presidents, would talk to W. A. Criswell to see if he could dissuade Patterson from pursuing this political campaign. Sullivan did so. On May 8, 1980, Criswell said that his associate, Paige Patterson, would withdraw from the leadership of a movement aimed at electing presidents of the Southern Baptist Convention and controlling nominations of the trustees of SBC agencies. He praised Patterson's theological stance, but he said the methods used are "those of a different world" that Baptists traditionally disdain.

This prompted a meeting of leaders of the First Baptist Church, where Criswell was pastor and Patterson acted as an associate in addition to his duties at Criswell Center. Baptist Press said that while no formal vote was taken, the group was reportedly four to three in favor of Patterson withdrawing from his political involvement. Criswell said

---

[19]Baptist Press, 1 May 1980.

Patterson's future involvement would be "resolved" and Patterson "will be a part of the resolving. After a little while you will never hear of it again."[20] Criswell was wrong.

Six days later, Patterson would be in the headlines again. He had now become specific about "all those liberals" in the schools. Patterson, in response to an editorial in the Baptist Standard urging him to be specific about charges of liberalism, had named the following professors as "representative of the nature and extent of the problem." He named: E. Glenn Hinson, professor of church history, and Eric C. Rust, retired professor of Christian philosophy, both of Southern Seminary; G. Temp Sparkman, associate professor of religious education and church administration, Midwestern Seminary; Fisher H. Humphrys, associate professor of theology at New Orleans Seminary; C. W. Christian, professor of religion at Baylor University; Frank E. Eakin, professor of religion at the University of Richmond; and George L. Balentine, pastor of First Baptist Church, Augusta, Georgia.[21]

Patterson quoted fragments of various books and articles written by the seven. They reacted quickly and vigorously. Each explained the intent of the passages cited, saying that in the main they had been taken out of context. Hinson commented:

> Fundamentalism developed without any connection with Baptists as a reaction to the use of historical methods and some Baptists have been Fundamentalists. But being a Baptist and a Fundamentalist are not the same thing. In fact, some things about Fundamentalism are quite alien to our Baptist outlook.

He continued, "The Paige Patterson group represents the rabid right. They do not represent our Baptist position; in fact I see him standing opposed to it at very, very critical points."

Fisher Humphrys in response said, "Paige Patterson is deceiving Southern Baptists. He has not told the truth, the whole truth and nothing but the truth."

It was mandatory that I reply to some of the accusations that were made concerning three of these men who wrote for the Sunday School Board. It was my opinion after the examination of the materials that they

---

[20]Baptist Press, 9 May 1980.
[21]Baptist Press, 15 May 1980.

had in the main been misjudged. At a point or two some material was subject to misinterpretation and this had been done.

The timing of these events must have been chosen on purpose. By May 29, 1980, Baptist Press would herald, "SBC Aglow With Presidential Politics." Adrian Rogers had declared that he would not allow his nomination for the traditional second term. Speculation was rampant. One pastor of a small congregation in Knoxville, Tennessee, declared his candidacy in contrast to the usual SBC-style of politics that dictates that the job seek the person, not the person seek the job. Baptist Press said,

> With biblical inerrancy debate still a live issue, indications are that some sort of motion or resolution may come to the floor declaring that the Bible's original manuscripts were errorless "doctrinally, historically, philosophically and scientifically."

Of considerable importance were other potential topics. One was of special interest to church-state observers. United States Senator Jesse Helms was leading an effort to remove authority from the Supreme Court, via congressional action, to decide the constitutionality of prayer in the public schools. He would turn that over to the individual states. SBC president Rogers and other prominent evangelicals had supported Helms' attempt. The SBC had supported the Supreme Court decision on school prayer on the grounds that government sponsored prayer was unconstitutional and threatened the rights of minorities. The problem would be confusing and divisive for years.

Tower Grove Baptist Church in St. Louis on Sunday before the SBC met became the staging area for a presidential election in 1980. Jimmy Draper, pastor of First Baptist Church, Euless, Texas, told the congregation that they must not jeopardize their influence with internal battles. Less than an hour before, Paige Patterson had discussed inerrancy, decrying the position of those Southern Baptists who claim Jesus Christ rather than the Bible as their ultimate authority. While he said that evangelism and missions should be at the heart of Southern Baptist cooperative effort, all such endeavors are impossible without belief in inerrancy.[22]

Bailey Smith, pastor of First Southern Baptist Church, Del City,

---

[22]Baptist Press, 9 June 1980.

Oklahoma, was elected president on the first ballot over five opponents. Some of them were among the most gifted leaders in the convention. In the press conference that followed, he declared himself an inerrantist. He said, however, that he saw no need for reform in the SBC because most Southern Baptists believed in the inerrant word of God. He said that he was not part of any major effort to take control of the denomination, nor did he know of any ten-year plan to make the convention more conservative.[23]

The Baptist Faith and Message Fellowship had fallen on hard days and during convention week issued a statement that Russell Kammerling had been relieved of his duties as editor of the *Southern Baptist Journal*. The vote was nine to seven. He had been editor for six months. The dispute had begun when Bill Powell was relieved as editor. M. O. Owens of Gastonia, North Carolina,one of the founders, admitted that the organization had split. At least five directors resigned.[24] What this meant was unclear at the time and appeared to be the beginning of serious differences among the fundamentalists. Powell had used the paper to make virulent attacks on persons and institutions. No one with official responsibility in the convention had paid much attention to his excessive pronouncements. This was probably a mistake, since he helped the virus of doubt about the denomination to take hold.

In retrospect, it appears that the fundamentalist movement wished to disassociate itself from his extremes and set up a house organ that would be more in line with the will of the leaders. In any case, the *Southern Baptist Journal* shortly disappeared, and *The Advocate* was born, with Russell Kammerling as editor. For years, the staff refused to reveal the names of its directors. Headquarters for the movement appeared to move from the East to Texas.

In the wrapup statement about the 1980 convention, BP headlined it, "SBC Takes Sharp Right Turn in St. Louis." The story reported, "Messengers . . . continued their march toward the theological right." Fundamentalist candidate Bailey Smith was elected on the first ballot over five other candidates. Forty-six resolutions were proposed. An attempt was made to deny messenger status to most employees of SBC agencies, institutions, and state conventions. The fact of the presence of

---

[23]Baptist Press, 11 June 1980.
[24]Baptist Press, 12 June 1980.

employees in the convention sessions as messengers was of considerable concern to Paul Pressler. The moderate position of the convention on abortion was changed by a resolution forbidding abortion except "to save the life of the mother." Anti-ERA language was added from the floor.

A doctrinal integrity resolution expanded the theological "guidelines" to its agencies by exhorting the trustees

> to carefully preserve the doctrinal integrity of our institutions and to assure that seminaries and other institutions receiving our support only employ, and continue the employment of, faculty members and professional staff who believe in the divine inspiration of the whole Bible, infallibility of the original manuscripts, and that the Bible is truth without any mixture of error.[25]

One resolution failed that would have condemned "political bias" on the part of the editors of the Baptist newspapers.

Meanwhile, at Glorieta—one of the conference centers operated by the Sunday School Board—leaders announced that two or three times as many young people as last year were committing themselves to full-time Christian service. Bold Mission Thrust was still alive.

"Ye shall have one manner of law."[26]

The most amazing thing about these early days of the conflict is that most of the more moderate faction of the convention did not understand what was happening. Most of us who were in positions of great responsibility had more that we could do in the professional tasks that were ours. Increasingly, the fundamentalists convinced many of their followers that their denominational leaders were not trustworthy. There was an age and interest gap among the pastors. Many of the most able did not want to get involved in the arguments as they grew more serious. In the mid years of the controversy, it was impossible to get some of the pastors with best hope of winning to stand for office. A principal factor in the reluctance of many was the fact that generally Baptists abhorred

---

[25]*SBC Annual*, 1980.
[26] Leviticus 24:22.

political activity that tried to control some aspect of the denomination. Many of the more sensitive pastors wanted no part of such activities.

Something beyond our experience was going on. Perhaps our greatest handicap was the belief that this could not continue. Most held that the pendulum would swing. "Trust the Lord and tell the people" had long been a slogan for the moderates. It wasn't working. Why?

There had been distinct change in the direction of the convention. The cultural and educational differences had been there all the while, so why did they suddenly crystallize into open conflict? Why did the theological differences that had been there for more than a hundred years suddenly become important enough to divide the convention? Why did the "following clergy," who constituted most of the messengers in any convention meeting, abruptly change directions to follow extremism rather than our traditional middle-of-the-road positions? Why did the mindset of the messengers undergo such radical change so quickly?

Herein lies one of the principal contentions of the struggle. The fundamentalists held that the issue was theology. The centrists held that the issue was power. From their different perspectives, they were both right. It would take years for the centrists to recognize that the new leadership was in process of converting the theology of the SBC from a biblical understanding to a fundamentalist understanding. All the time, we thought they were complaining about a few teachers they wanted to fire. Many of the less involved great middle of the denomination came to believe that the fundamentalists were right in their criticisms and joined them in their efforts.

From the perspective of 1991, it is easy to see that the system had been used very skillfully to accomplish ends for which it was not intended. An astute politician had been studying it for years by his own admission. The framers of the constitution and by-Laws had had little fear that the system could be manipulated for ulterior motives. Porter Routh, longtime leader of the Executive Committee, told me a short time before his death that he had not believed the fundamentalists could take the convention. He and a host of others believed that after a while sanity would prevail and the brethren would restore order.

By 1981, it was beginning to look like there was a new force involved that would not be deterred. Some of the leaders had tried to avoid polarizing the constituency. I was one of them, though I had spoken to the issues in our meetings and had written a good deal about issues, not personalities. It was becoming clear that we were not being heard as the efforts of the fundamentalists gained momentum.

A movement was underway. An organization was being formed. Issues were being chosen, and division was called for by the leaders of the movement. The differences between us were being exploited and dramatized. Our emphasis in the past had been to stress our commonality, but now people were being forced to take sides. Historical perspectives were being skewed to fit the needs of the movement. For example, it was now being said that we historically had a theology that held us together. The common theology was there, but there were significant differences.

Apparently, the issues were being clarified and simplified. The best beginning for a Baptist was the Bible. Every pastor's conference on the national level became a pep rally for inerrancy. Every president elected from 1979 on emphasized inerrancy. Later subordinate issues would be added, such as abortion. Patterson would say years later that abortion would be as good for the movement as "the inerrancy thing." From the beginning, however, the central focus was on the nature of scripture.

The political structure was energized by politicians who saw and seized upon the differences among us. As the "troops" were mobilized for battle, the field was scripture. In truth, as has been confessed by several recent presidents, most Southern Baptists believed essentially the same thing about scripture. (This will be discussed at length in the chapter about inerrancy.) As the inerrancy issue was refined and simplified, it became a unifying force. This focus fit all the background and differences. It was easily "sloganized."

Each of the presidents since 1979 has emphasized that he would not appoint anyone to a committee who was not an inerrantists or a believer in a "perfect Bible." Thus, it is easy to see how this effort would result in agencies and seminaries controlled by fundamentalists within a decade. It has come to pass.

Additional but related descriptions of the chosen issues have been vocalized: "The liberal denomination is a dying denomination." "The seminaries are full of liberal professors." "We should not be required to pay for something we do not believe in." "We have to have a new kind of trustees to change the system."

This spirit of exclusiveness and negativism had been around all the time as an expression of a minority position. It was usually controlled by the brethren who had a larger vision of our nature and mission. The people with this mindset were usually not elected to prominent positions. When they were, they were usually set on the sidelines quickly. The new leadership seemed to have the mindset usually called "fundamentalist."

In reading the signs in the 1990s, it is easy to see that the SBC was being overrun by the juggernaut of organized and militant fundamentalism. There were skilled and dedicated leaders who played on the prejudices and convictions of multitudes of Southern Baptists. We had several problems.

First, there was a basic theological conviction among most of us that closely paralleled the 1920 definition of fundamentalists: "People professing complete confidence in the Bible and preoccupied with the message of God's salvation of sinners through the death of Jesus Christ." In other words, we were very much like those attacking the establishment in basic theology. By the standards of the so-called mainstream of Christianity, we were all fundamentalists.

Second, we did not recognize the distinctive differences between the new fundamentalism and traditional Southern Baptist positions.

Third, we did not understand sufficiently the nature of the new fundamentalism. Some restudy of the history of American evangelicalism would have been beneficial.

Fourth, it was difficult to believe that thousands of Baptists would join the attack on the denomination whose mission was to proclaim the gospel.

Fifth, many thousands of devoted Baptists thought it unchristian to engage in mortal combat over the control of the denomination.

It is perhaps worthwhile to repeat that we were being inundated with a new surge of a malignant form of fundamentalism while we thought we were being challenged to correct theological error in high places.

All of this and much of that which followed was strikingly similar to the problems experienced by the Lutheran Church, Missouri Synod almost exactly a decade before. John H. Tietjen wrote of their problems in *Memoirs In Exile*.[27] The methods, the issues of controversy, the uses of pressure, the unsubstantiated accusations, and many other points are so similar as to be shocking.

I spent considerable time trying to find a connection between the two. I finally determined that Paige Patterson and Robert Preus were friends.

---

[27](Minneapolis: Fortress Press, 1990).

Preus, himself a leading figure in the problems at Concordia Seminary, was a brother of J. A. O. Preus, who was a principal antagonist in the Lutheran controversy. Patterson and Robert Preus helped to found an international conference on inerrancy, according to Patterson.

The similarities are so striking it is worthwhile to mention a few.

(1) Political campaigns for church office were contrary to the traditions of the denominations.

(2) Early in both controversies, accusations against seminary faculty figured prominently.

(3) Inerrancy became the point of conflict early in the problems.

(4) Traditional views on the nature of scripture were said to be in conflict with historical-critical research.

(5) Both bodies had been held aloof from the mainstream of American religious life by a combination of forces.

(6) Acculturation and Americanization profoundly affected both.

(7) Curricular materials of the churches and Sunday schools brought into the denominations secular cultural methods.

(8) There were growing accusations of liberalism in the denominational structures.

(9) Organized efforts to control took hold in both groups, foreign to their traditions and history. Counter efforts were immediately undertaken.

(10) Leaders were elected promising theological house cleaning.

(11) Due process was ignored when inconvenient.

(12) Biblical principles of consideration for Christian brothers were ignored. Matthew 18:15 was a source of constant reference in the Lutheran body, though it seemed to be ignored by the accusers. It would be ignored as well as in the Baptist conflict.

(13) Special committees were utilized outside usual denominational procedures.

For sixty pages or so, Tietjen discusses the machinations that brought the downfall of the Missouri Synod, which sounds much like a Southern Baptist rehearsal. Fundamentalism was alive and well in the Missouri Synod, Lutheran Church.

What Is A Fundamentalist?

We Southern Baptists were being caught up in a movement, not necessarily theological, that was sweeping the world. The middle East was aflame with manifestations of the movement far more deadly than that which swept the United States. Iran, Iraq, Lebanon, Syria, and other less prominent countries were having their very existences threatened by various forms of violence related to political and religious fundamentalism. India continues to struggle with riots and deadly battles between Hindu and Moslem reactionaries. The resurgence of militancy in religion seemed to be rising around the world.

Changes in the nature of the societies of many countries brought severe and sometimes violent reaction in the religious realm. As value systems changed and folkways and mores followed suit, restless people resisted those changes, sometimes violently. Threats of poverty, hunger, and widespread violence caused global unrest and provoked marked responses whereever opportunity presented itself. This response often took the form of religious protest against changing ways or of demands for new ways.

In America, a fresh outbreak in fundamentalism swept over several major denominations including the Presbyterians, Episcopalians, and the Catholic Church, along with other lesser known groups. In several of these, the outbreak was militant.

In discussing the modern outbreak of fundamentalism in America, Marsden commented:

> One evidence of this persistent militancy was that the question of the inerrancy of Scripture was often an important battlefield within evangelicalism itself.
>
> In the early 1980s, however, a new and much larger fundamentalism suddenly awakened. . . . As followed World War I, a diffuse sense of crisis impelled bitter attacks on all sorts of modernism, now retitled "secular humanism." As in the 1920s, popular fundamentalist forays into politics signaled some abandonment of the strict separatism of the tradition. Once again fundamentalists seemed undecided as to whether they were living in Babylon or Israel. Rather than depicting themselves as the faithful remnant, their best-known representatives tagged themselves "the moral majority."
>
> Many themes and causes were the same as during the first fundamentalist era. The renewal of "a Christian America" was a frequent refrain. . . . Opposition to the teaching of biological evolution in public schools was revived as a major thrust. Other causes were new, such as the Christian school movement and fundamentalist opposition to the women's movement and abortion. The breakup of the family was

an important new symbol of the demise of the Christian heritage. Identification with secular nationalism and economic policies often was made with less qualification. One of the most persistent refrains, especially in the giant television ministries, was a gospel of personal success, reflecting the drift of evangelicalism generally away from Calvinist emphasis on depravity. . . . The imminent end of the age remained central to its message.[28]

These brief paragraphs describe rather precisely what was happening to the Southern Baptist Convention.

A brief review of the nature of fundamentalism will offer some additional insights to our problems. The modern developments in fundamentalism vary in significant ways from the original definition cited above.

Fundamentalism rose as a protest and defense against theological modernism. Its scholars sought to prove that biblical Christianity and modernism are incompatible. Edward Carnell, himself a former fundamentalist, commented on the nature of fundamentalism.

Fundamentalism is an extreme right element in Protestant orthodoxy. Orthodoxy is that branch of Christendom which limits the basis of its authority to the Bible. Fundamentalism draws its distinctiveness from its attempt to maintain status by negation. . . . When modernism decayed, therefore, fundamentalism lost its status. Neo-orthodoxy proved too complex for it to assess. . . . This is why fundamentalism is now a religious attitude rather than a religious movement. It is a highly ideological attitude. It is intransigent and inflexible; it expects conformity; it fears academic liberty.[29]

The word comes from the name *The Fundamentals*, twelve paperback volumes published from 1910 to 1915. The publication was the brainchild of a southern California millionaire and edited by Bible teachers and evangelists. George Marsden said that more than three million free individual volumes were mailed out to "every pastor, missionary,

---

[28]George Marsden, *Fundamentalism and American Culture* (New York: Oxford University Press, 1980) 228.

[29]Edward John Carnell, *A Handbook of Christian Theology* (New York: Meridian Books, n.d.) 142.

theological professor, Sunday school superintendent, and religious editor in the English-speaking world."[30]

The term "fundamentalist" was coined in 1920 and brought to mind the united front against modernism that was characterized in *The Fundamentals*. The principal thrust was a defense of the faith in the face of the various encroachments of modernity. Marsden continues his summation by saying that the overwhelming emphasis was on soul-saving, personal experience with little attention to ethical issues.

Bill Leonard, formerly a church history professor at the Southern Baptist Seminary, has given a descriptive account of the development of fundamentalism in America. He notes that Marsden defined fundamentalism as "a multifaceted movement which at its most basic level was 'organized opposition to modernism.'"[31] Citing a different assessment of fundamentalism by Stewart Cole, Leonard observed,

> It was the 1895 Niagara Conference, Cole believed, which established the "five-Points statement of doctrine" which became the basis for doctrinal unity among fundamentalists. These points included 1) biblical inerrancy, 2) the deity and virgin birth of Christ, 3) Christ's substitutionary atonement, 4) his bodily resurrection, and 5) second coming.[32]

Leonard also points out that Earnest Sandeen believed that it was millenarianism that gave "life and shape" to fundamentalism. When millenialism merged with the "Princeton Theology," the result was fundamentalism. "The Princeton theologians made biblical inerrancy one of the cardinal doctrines of Fundamentalism," according to Leonard. He also notes, "Sandeen writes that the doctrines of inerrancy 'did not exist in either Europe or America prior to its formulation in the last half of the nineteenth century.'"[33]

Leonard observes further,

> In a chapter on the "characteristics of the fundamentalists" Furniss gave credibility to numerous myths about the "typical" fundamentalist

---

[30]Marsden, *Fundamentalism and American Culture*, 118-19.

[31]Bill Leonard, "The Origin and Character of Fundamentalism," *Review & Expositor* 79:1 (Winter, 1982): 9.

[32]Ibid., 5.

[33]Ibid., 7-8.

mentality and personality. He described the devotees of Fundamentalism as manifesting an abiding fear of things modern, a yearning for certainty, a tendency toward violence in "thought and language, ignorance and egotism." These social and psychological traits became a ready method for characterizing all fundamentalists.[34]

Albert McClellan in his "Theses" characterized fundamentalism as follows.

What marks fundamentalism as fundamentalism is more than doctrines or doctrinal categories. It is best described as (a) temperament that includes both negativism and exclusiveness. Fundamentalists are constantly critical of Christians not precisely like themselves. They deny fellowship to others who do not use their exact words of doctrine and who refuse to accept their literal interpretations of Scripture.[35]

McClellan quotes Edward Carnell as saying fundamentalism has

cut itself off from the general stream of culture, philosophy, and ecclesiastical tradition. . . . It dismisses non-fundamentalist efforts as empty, futile and apostate. Its tests for Christian fellowship are so severe that divisions in the church are a sign of (its) virtue.

Carnell also said, "Fundamentalism is now a religious attitude rather than a religious movement. . . . It makes no allowance for the inconsistent, and thus partially valid, elements in other positions."[36]

McClellan continued,

Fundamentalism in its fervent quest for doctrinal purity appears to neg-lect a long list of New Testament teachings, notably, forgiveness, Jesus' willingness to use broken reeds and smoking flax in his kingdom, Paul's emphases on reconciliation in helping weak and slow believers, John's lessons on love, koinonia, and above all the New Testament's teaching that grace is ascendant over law. Fundamentalism's chief characteristics

---

[34]Ibid., 6.

[35]Albert McClellan, "Theses Concerning The Great SBC Takeover Controversy of the 1980s," 2.

[36]McClellan, 2.

are legalisms, exclusiveness, rancor, arrogance and pride.[37]

In "Thesis Number 9," McClellan comments on the popularizing of the fundamentalist temperament in Southern Baptist life.

> According to some descriptions of fundamentalism by certain of their national scholars (and by evangelical scholars), fundamentalists are famed for faultfinding and hairsplitting. Popularizing of this temperament led to the breaking down of the ancient barriers of respectful diversity, mutual understanding and forgiving tolerance in Southern Baptist life.

Leonard has given this summary characterization:

> By redefining orthodoxy and claiming to uphold it, fundamentalists set an agenda for all other groups in the church—conservatives, moderates, liberals, and interested bystanders. . . . The fundamentalist agenda provided for a theological system which aided the faithful in sorting out the more sophisticated theological issues of the "modern era." From biblicism to premillennialism, from Christology to eschatology, fundamentalists gave the believers a basic and easily constructed system of belief. The security of such a system then and now accounts for much of the popular response to the movement.[38]

It is clear now that the SBC contingent of fundamentalists were in the process of redefining orthodoxy. This was not so clear in 1979. By this redefinition, the agenda for the denomination was set for years to come.

The operative words in the Southern Baptist Convention brand of fundamentalism are attitude and temperament.

James T. Draper, Jr, who in 1983 would become the third president elected after the takeover, writing in 1973, said:

> Fundamentalism is the second of the two great heresies of our time. (Liberalism was the first.) In fact, Fundamentalism is more dangerous than Liberalism because everything is done in the name of the Lord. In the name of the Lord, the Fundamentalist (note the capital F again)

---

[37]Ibid.
[38]Leonard, 14.

condemns all who disagree with him. In the name of the Lord all is done, and great heresy is propagated across the land.

The Fundamentalist is any person who feels he has a corner on truth and the rest of the Christian world is groping in error. He is always dogmatic about his beliefs. He views his ideas about God, the world, and man to be as valid as what God had revealed. He uses the Bible as a club with which to beat people over the head, rather than a means of personal strength and a revealer of God. His approach is virtually always negative and condemning. . . . His entire life is a series of negatives which consume more and more of his energies until it becomes his whole approach. To the Fundamentalist, the test of fellowship is correct doctrine. . . . There is no room in his world for those who have a different persuasion. He feels threatened by diverse convictions and writes them off as sinister and heretical.

Draper commends the fundamentalist for his correct doctrine. He continues the discussion with a passage called "The Fundamentalist Condemned."

The Fundamentalist must be condemned first for his divisive spirit. . . . The Fundamentalist is sure that he is the only true follower of Jesus Christ. . . . The fundamentalist must be condemned for his bigotry. . . . The bigotry and prejudice of the Fundamentalist has set back the work of missions around the world at least fifty years.

He must also be condemned for his unfairness. He will never give anyone else a fair hearing. . . . The Fundamentalist stands condemned by his own dogma. He has a strange mixture of biblical truth and tradition and customs. Like the Pharisees in Jesus' day, he preaches tradition and custom with the same vigor and authority as he does the written Word of God. . . . [He] must also be condemned for his use of Scripture. His method is the "proof-text" method. He must be condemned because of his attitude toward the world. . . . He is condemned by the Spirit of the Word. . . . He seems to know little about love and compassion. . . . The Fundamentalist tactic is simple: hatred, bitterness, and condemnation of all whom they despise. . . . They direct their attack most often on other Christian leaders with whom they find disagreement.[39]

---

[39]James T. Draper, Jr., *The Church Christ Approves* (Nashville: Broadman, 1973).

Draper seems to have defined the movement of which he has been a part.

In evaluating fundamentalism in the Southern Baptist Convention, several things are important to remember. If the matter were limited to the doctrinal statements related to the basics of the Christian faith, hosts of "moderates" would agree with most of these statements. If in discussing inerrancy, the discussion would include the qualifications as described in The Chicago Statement on Inerrancy, many others would find agreement. In my judgment, the positions on the views of scripture are not nearly so far apart as people have been led to believe. Most of the moderates who would have problems with the Chicago Statement usually have a high view of scripture and accept it as the inspired authoritative Word of God. There are few true "liberals" in our circles when judged by their view of scripture. Several recent presidents of the convention have stated that the vast majority of our people are conservative in their view.

Unless there is more behind the intellectual scenes than is now evident, there is little to convince the thoughtful student of theology that the SBC brand of fundamentalism is a carefully integrated theological system. There is a serious lack of consideration of the ethics involved in its practical pronouncements and political acts. There is a serious gap between its pronouncements about the whole Bible being the Word of God and the practice of its obvious message of grace, love, fairness, and forgiveness.

Many writers, such as Richard Hofstader (who thought fundamentalists had status anxieties), Ernest Sandeen (who thought it impossible to call fundamentalism a genuine conservative tradition), and others (including even the reporter R. Gustav Niebur of The Wall Street Journal who thought Judge Pressler "combative") would agree that many if not all of these characteristics would be visible in the take-over movement.

After an examination of what others have said about fundamentalism, it appears that some characteristics as old as nineteenth-century evangelicalism and the 1920s brand of fundamentalism are alive and well in the SBC today.

At least the following characteristics have been evident in the attempt to control the Southern Baptist Convention:

1. Doctrinal rigidity—"This is the way, walk ye in it."
2. Religious exclusiveness—No one except inerrantists will be

appointed to any committee or board.

3. Militant attitude—"We are going for the jugular."

4. Defense of the faith posture—"We are bringing the convention back to its historical roots."

5. Negativism—campaign based on condemnation of real and supposed transgressions.

6. Legalism—setting of numerous rules and adoption of creedal statements and the requirement to use specific language.

7. Literalism—prone to literal interpretation of Scripture.

8. Ideological—uses preconceived assumptions in opposition to "liberalism."

9. Authoritarianism—imposition of majority opinion on agencies and institutions on insufficient grounds. The oft-repeated sentiment, "If you don't like what is going on, get out."

10. Inerrancy—the hallmark slogan of the movement.

11. Overtly political—Pressler, "I spoke probably fifty times during those (six) days."[40]

12. Premillenial—This is a characteristic of probably most of the leadership. It is the position predominantly heard.

13. It should also be said that there was within the fundamentalist group a solid body of biblical doctrine.

While each of these characteristics has appeared from time to time in Southern Baptist life, they have not been the dominant philosophy of our denominational life. While many of the participants do not like the name "fundamentalists" (and may not be themselves), the characteristics of the movement are clearly fundamentalistic.

The leaders must bear the onus of their own movement.

A Poem (?)

Believe as I believe, no more, no less;
That I am right, and no one else, confess;
Feel as I feel, think only as I think;
Eat what I eat, and drink but what I drink;
Look as I look, do always as I do;

---

[40]Paul Pressler, "Firestorm Chat," interview with Gary North.

And then, and only then, I'll fellowship with you.
That I am right, and always right, I know,
Because my own convictions tell me so;
And to be right is simply this—to be
Entirely and in all respects like me;
To deviate a hair's breath, or begin
To question, or to doubt, or hesitate, is sin.
I reverence the Bible if it be
Translated first, and then explained by me;
By churchly laws and customs I abide
If they with my opinion coincide;
All creeds and doctrines I concede divine,
Excepting those, of course, which disagree with mine."[41]

---

[41]Title unknown and author unknown. Quoted by Pat Nordman, *Florida Baptist Witness*, 12 August 1982.

Chapter Five

Inerrantists
Change the Guard

"And Overthrows Men Long Established. . . ."[1]

By 1981, the outlines of the campaign to take control of the Southern
Baptist Convention were emerging. Paige Patterson's description of the
effort given on April 3, 1980, and reiterated on April 14 to the press was
clear enough, but to many it was grandiose and improbable. A little more
than a year later, Paul Presser brought the campaign to the forefront of
Southern Baptist thinking by declaring in Lynchburg, Virginia that
"conservatives are 'going for the jugular' in their campaign to get control
of Southern Baptist institutions." He declared,

> We are going for having knowledgeable, Bible-centered, Christ-honoring
> trustees of all our institutions, who are not going to sit there like a
> bunch of dummies and rubber stamp everything that's presented to
> them, but who are going to inquire why this is being done, what is
> being taught, what is the finished product of our young people who
> come to our institutions, going to be. . . . The bottom line is trustees,
> not resolutions.[2]

In this meeting, he outlined how in three presidential elections (the
president usually served two years) the resultant trustees elected would
be 60 percent good and reliable. He emphasized that it would be
necessary to control eight more elections. Patterson urged churches to
budget money to send messengers to the convention. Pressler began in

---

[1]Job 12:19b, New International Version.
[2]Baptist Press, 19 September 1980.

this meeting to emphasize that the press was being unfair. This would continue for years and reach its zenith with the control of Baptist Press passing to the fundamentalist cause.

In this meeting, Patterson "deprecated the King James Version of the Bible as a 1611 translation 'by a bunch of Anglicans, most of whom were lost,' and cited 'tragic translations' in the King James Version."[3]

If there was any doubt about the nature of this effort, Pressler would clear it up in his interview with Gary North late in 1985 or early 1986. In this recorded interview, he expanded on the methodology used. He said that he had studied the system of the convention and had analyzied its strengths and weaknesses. He decided that 90 percent of the people were conservative. Messenger election thus became the important thing. He outlined the process of trustee selection and concluded that the way to win was to get out the people and elect a president who would appoint friendly committees. He commented that his "real traveling started early in '79."

To him, it was clear that the issue was a Bible without errors. Adrian Rogers, according to Pressler, was the first president with the viewpoint of how to effect change. He commented that the conservatives had supported Bailey Smith and James Draper and Charles Stanley, all of whom were elected in succession. In 1985, the largest convention ever had 45,000, registered messengers. This was a most significant "watershed convention."[4]

The movement now had a clear set of objectives, a news journal, an organization, and a platform—and would soon have the necessary "troops."

The Platform

The entire effort had begun with the often-repeated assertion that the seminaries were becoming liberal. Patterson had identified four professors—two at Southern Seminary, one at Midwestern, and one at New Orleans who were charged with being "liberal."[5] Accusations were made against two university professors. In the same release, he identified

---

[3]Ibid., 3.
[4]Interview with Gary North, transcription of tape.
[5]Baptist Press, 15 May 1980.

a pastor who was supposed to have written improper material for the Sunday School Board. Pressler would later make numerous charges against the seminaries and the Board.

The second plank in the platform was that inerrancy was the only proper view of scripture. Patterson said in the 1980 meeting at the Criswell Center where he outlined the campaign, "The issue still is truth—is the Bible in fact totally and completely true?"[6] When I asked Judge Pressler for his definition of liberal, he replied, "I would define a liberal as one who believes that the Bible does or can make error."[7] Both would later say that they did not demand the word inerrancy, but to others the concept was the same. This theme would return again and again in most if not all of the presidential elections in the future. It became the subject of a national conference to be held in 1987.

The third plank in the platform was the claim that conservatives had been as Pressler put it, "seriously under-represented on the boards, among teachers and bureaucrats."[8] This refrain would be taken up by many others who contended that they had been left out in the selections made by their peers. It is certain that many individuals had been left out—since there were under a thousand trustee posts for 14,500,000 Southern Baptists.

To claim that "conservatives" had been left out was an accusation of liberalism against many thousands who had served in the past and were serving then. To claim that many of the true fundamentalists had been left out was probably nearer the truth. The democratic system required nomination by peers.

My experience of 35 years of dealing with trustees might prove informative. In 1949, in the Oklahoma City convention, Dr. J. W. Storer of Tulsa was the Oklahoma member of the Committee on Boards. To my utter amazement—I was new in the state and only 28 years old—Dr. Storer nominated me to be a member of the Foreign Mission Board. I had only met Dr. Storer, and there was certainly no politics involved in that nomination. From that time until I retired in 1984, I cannot remember a single year that I was not a member of a state board or national board (sometimes both) or employed by one. For 35 years, I was closely related

---

[6]Baptist Press, 21 April 1980.
[7]Interview with author, 20 February 1991.
[8]Gary North Interview.

to boards of trustees. During that generation, I knew trustees, worked with them, and came to respect them as a group. Never, I repeat never, in those years was there a time when theologically conservative trustees did not control every one of those boards. Only occasionally was a "theological liberal" even a member.

Never was there an organized attempt to lead any entity away from biblical truth. Once or twice we had to deal with a problem called "liberal," but the trustees always stood solidly in the biblically conservative camp. From my observation over those years, I never saw any group of trustees of any other entity try to make anything "liberal."

I will be the first to admit that no one man should have served somewhere on a board every year for 35 years. I did none of the nominations of myself to the boards and never asked to be nominated to any one of them. I have asked numerous friends in the "good ole boy politic" mentioned by Sherman whether they knew of any attempt to steer the ship away from a biblical position. Unanimously they said that they had never witnessed such an attempt.

A very interesting study was made by Robert Dilday, Associate Editor of the *Religious Herald* of Virginia. His study showed that widely known fundamentalists served in significant spots in the years 1967–1978. These were the years that preceded the outbreak of the controversy. He names at least 29 well known persons who served, including second terms, in a total of 57 or 58 of the most important places in the convention. This included the presidency, four terms; the Committee on Committees (one of the most crucial spots) nine terms; Committee of Boards, six terms; Boards of Trustees, at least 19 persons not counting second terms. At least seven of those who are usually considered involved with or sympathetic to the movement served as President either before the beginning of the controversy or since. These include Criswell, Weber, Draper, Smith, Rogers, Vines and Chapman. All but Rogers served two terms and in two different times he has served three times. Some of these and several others were president of the Pastors' Conference, which was and is one of the crucial places for public exposure.

John Bisagno, pastor of First Baptist Church in Houston, protested that moderates had been appointed to positions since the controversy. Dilday, in computing the actual appointments, concluded that of the potential spots available in the years named by Bisagno, counting committees, trustees, and annual sermon selections there were 3830 possibilities. This would include second terms if any. So-called moderates occupied three-tenths of one percent of them.[9] This included one who has since declared that his sentiments have been with the fundamentalist movement from the beginning. While these data cannot be precise, since some seemed to have served only part of a second term or some other variation from the norm, they seem to be indicative of the true situation.

In McClellan's "Theses", he takes a slightly different tack from that given above concerning the causes of controversy. He lists inerrancy as the first issue and the interpretation of scripture as the second. He then proceeds to what are usually called polity issues. The third issue, he says is the equality and privileges of church members dealing with the issue of authority in the churches. The fourth issue is the democracy of the churches, dealing more specifically with the pastor as "ruler of the church," an idea propounded by the fundamentalists. The fifth issue is the priesthood of the believer, dealing with free souls with equal rights. A sixth related theological issue is the true meaning of religious liberty, dealing with the fundamentalist determination to change the historic meaning of the first amendment.[10]

In time, as needed, other issues were focused. Abortion became one of the criteria for being a seminary professor, according to some. One of the most volatile issues to be raised was the ordination of women to either the ministry or the diaconate. As the movement gained momentum, lobbying for tax money for Baptist schools became one of the issues that scandalized the more traditional Baptists. This was a depth to which Baptists had seldom descended! The pastor's role in the church began to divide churches, and hundreds of pastors were terminated for trying to rule the congregation or for "failure of communication."

The "Troops"

The people who made this effort successful are no monolithic mass of the uninformed. It would be a mistake to categorize them as

---

[9]Robert Dilday, Study of SBC Appointments, 1990, unpublished.

[10]Albert McClellan, "Theses Concerning The Great SBC Takeover Controversy of the 1980s," (1991) Unpublished.

educated/uneducated; small church/large church; rural/urban; bivocational/full-time professionals; seminary graduates/non-seminary graduates. Some of all these categories have been on both sides. The cry of liberalism to most Southern Baptists would attract attention from all kinds of people. Their history is full of illustrations of why. Previous controversies were usually about orthodoxy. The mere fact that they believed in the priesthood of the individual believer and democracy in church governance insured that.

Among those attracted to the fundamentalist side, often not knowing that it was fundamentalistic, was a large group of middle-of-the-roaders. These were sincere, concerned Baptists who were sometimes not aware of the nature of the argument or had not had access to adequate information about the issues. Some simply felt that the denomination needed a course correction. And Baptists will always vote for the Bible. These were often folk who followed the leadership that their peers had selected, trusting them to know and do what was right. It had been that way for more than a hundred years. They often did not believe that this was an organized effort to control the convention. They had heard all the accusations and assumed that where there is that much smoke there must by something wrong. Many were unequipped to pursue the matter for a variety of reasons, and many of them were uninterested in taking the trouble to know what was going on.

Most of these people would not like to be called fundamentalists— and, in fact, probably are not using the criteria cited above. They were motivated by honest concern. They loved the Southern Baptist Convention; it was home, and they didn't want anyone "messing with it." A sizable number of them have since seen the light but are not motivated to separate from the voting block since it is known to be "conservative."

Further, the moderates have not done a very good job of telling them what the true situation is. Early moderate efforts were sometimes extreme in statement and action, and the number alienated is still large.

The second group of adherents to the fundamentalist cause was a group of intelligent, educated opportunists with multiple motivations. Some of them honestly had concerns about some aspect of the denomination. Some of these apparently saw this movement as an opportunity to become spokesmen for a segment of their associates. Some saw it as a chance to achieve prominence in ways they had not been able to achieve. Some evidently saw the problems as an opportunity to put certain others down, all in the name of the Lord. Some were interested in the political implications for the convention in the movement.

It seems evident that some were interested in tying the convention to the right-wing national politics. They seem to have succeeded in a number of ways. Some were interested in changing the system within the convention by which elections were accomplished. Some saw an opportunity to seize leadership of a multi-billion dollar establishment that could be used for their ends. Some seemed to be on king-sized ego trips. Perhaps no one will ever know all the real motives for joining this movement that started for what the participants probably thought was a good purpose.

Then there was a group of true fundamentalists who needed to "defend the faith." They were much happier if they had an enemy who could be attacked with impunity. There was little penalty for attacking something as large and as far away as the SBC. They had little to lose since they had not been recognized as leaders before. Their understanding of the faith was such that anything outside the narrow confines of their experience was anathema. The desire to have others conform to their understanding seems to be inherent in the nature of fundamentalism. Given the multi-faceted background of the Southern Baptist Convention, it seemed inevitable that such an uprising would occur when there was sufficient strength to make it go.

Then, there were the disfranchised. Often, but not always, these came from smaller churches. Some were good and effective servants of the Lord who simply had never made it up the social, economic, or denominational ladder. Some of these were folk without college or, particularly, seminary training and were sensitive about their lack. Some were those who for a variety of reasons had not been accepted or recommended by their peers. Many such persons are known in our fellowship to have labored long and hard making real contributions to the corporate good but never achieving the recognition they wanted or deserved.

Then, there were those who were mad. Their anger was caused by any number of things from denominational leadership to their community problems. These tended to come from those disappointed by some event or circumstance in life over which they had little or no control. It may be that they could not get called to the church of their choice, or get elected to some post they wanted, or did not like the Director of Missions, or their church was growing smaller, or almost anything else that makes a person settle on anger as the expression of his problems.

There were also the power-hungry organizers and manipulators who wanted to participate in control of this monstrous organization. The Southern Baptist Convention was, at the beginning of the controversy, not only the largest non-Catholic Christian body in America, it was one of the most progressive. This was true only after a long history of struggle but it was beginning to mature in many ways. It was the sole body of evangelicals that was equipped numerically, financially, and organizationally to do what it was trying to do. The colleges, universities, seminaries, and a host of agencies for every known purpose represented a wealth of potential for good and God in the years ahead. To many this denomination was a great plum that needed plucking. To see the "good ole boys" in charge was more than some could bear. The anti-establishment feeling was strong in many places and furnished a ready fuel to be set on fire to achieve personal purposes.

By 1981, the terms of the conflict were being exposed. The moderates began to try to respond.

The "Moderates"

Many have felt that a major mistake of the "moderates" was to allow themselves to be stuck with that name. It was assigned by the fundamentalists, and it stuck. The name was a handicap in the war, but it also probably fit. This group was truly "moderate" in many reactions to the problems.

Organized opposition to the take-over was slow in coming. When it did, it was fragmented and tentative. This was an entirely different situation from any faced before. There was widespread difference of opinion about what was going on. Many responsible people did not believe that the situation was as serious as it was. Others thought that there was little the fundamentalists could do to the time-tested polity procedures of the convention.

Where were the leaders?

To many, the thought of participating in an organization designed to oppose another organization in the convention was repulsive. Overt political action with open conflict as the objective was so reprehensible that many intelligent and dedicated Baptist leaders refused to take part in the conflict. That situation still obtained in 1991. This naivete about the situation played a large part in the loss of the convention to regressive forces.

There were others who simply did not want to acknowledge that there was a serious conflict, and when forced to admit it, wanted no part in schism. After all, they had been taught cooperation all their lives and knew that any success the convention had enjoyed depended on cooperation of the largest number of people possible. Some saw the controversy as they would have seen it if it had been in their church. It spelled anger, conflict, confrontation, trouble, and alienation. This was not their way of life if it could be avoided, and in this case they thought it could be avoided.

As has been suggested before, many thought that this was a part of a cycle and what goes around comes around. To change the metaphor, they thought that the pendulum would swing back to the middle of the theological and political center after a period of noise and adjustment. Give it time, they were saying, and it will go away.

Further, the denomination offered no centralized authority to sponsor an organized effort to stay the movement. The democracy that had flourished in spite of its critics offered no firm base for sponsoring a resistance movement. The denominational bureaucracy generally opposed the movement, but there were several reasons why it could not be very effective in resisting.

There was an overriding understanding among the executives that their mission was to care for the institutions they presided over. This meant that as the movement spread, their first task was to try to shepherd their institution through the maze. The program assignments of the agencies were such that each was limited to a fairly well defined area of responsibilities. Several executives spoke out against some facet of the movement but were reluctant to engage in overt political activity to get out a vote large enough to do any good.

When after several years, some of the presidents began to propagandize against the movement, they were severely criticized, sometimes by both sides. The fundamentalists said that they did not want to pay the salaries of people to fight the will of the convention. After a convention action, an executive regardless of his personal opinions, was likely to have the feeling that his responsibility was to the larger body. In the face of continued pressure and agitation, together with the necessity for guarding his agency, most of the executives had their voices stilled. Newly empowered fundamentalist boards of trustees made certain that happened. More on that subject later.

In his "Theses," Albert McClellan makes a strong point that by the time the outlines of the controversy had been clearly drawn, the denominational executives had become helpless to do much. His idea is that over the last couple of decades, changes had taken place in the general operation of the denomination so that the executives were made almost faceless to large numbers of Baptists. In earlier years, the executives had sat on the convention platform and often participated in whatever business needed their guidance or participation. Later, they were moved off the platform to sit in front of it, and finally banished to a "pen" seventy-five feet from the platform. In later days, the fundamentalists, recognizing the potential from the executives and others, had forbidden anyone on the platform except committee members, officers, and program personnel. In the last years it has been virtually impossible for anyone to go onto the platform without permission of the president or his entourage. At least one president actually had bodyguards.

For most of its history, the Executive Committee (which functions as the convention ad interim) had sat, in its regular meetings, with the agency executives, along with the state executive directors and editors. Any other Baptist who wished to do so could attend and was almost always recognized to speak on an issue if he so desired. With the coming of a new building, visitors were separated from the Executive Committee members, but still participated in the discussions if they desired.

In the February meeting in 1991, the Executive Committee, now controlled by fundamentalists, discussed the termination of a century-old arrangement of trustees of the Foreign Mission Board and Home Mission Board. The presidents of the two institutions had no part at all in the discussion. Recently, there have been two motions presented in the Executive Committee to limit discussion to members only. They were defeated, but everybody got the idea, and another avenue of expression and deliberation had vanished.

Participation of executives in the deliberations in the annual convention meetings are now limited almost entirely to the affairs of their institutions during their formal presentation to the body once a year. McClellan said that the executives, the traditional leaders of the denomination, "became faceless to thousands of messengers and (were) lost in the crowd. . . . The SBC agency chief executive officers almost vanished from public view, especially from view in the annual conventions."[11]

The leaders of the Executive Committee during the 1960s and 1970s had led in the formulation of program statements for all the agencies. The design was to preclude infringement on the territory of other agencies by strong leaders and to provide for order in the distribution of assignments. In many ways it was a good step and contributed to the relative peace of my time as seminary president and publishing board president. Conflict between agencies was minimized. There was, however, another facet of this situation. It almost precluded any leader in the denomination from providing leadership in any area other than his particular responsibility. This was a severe handicap during the onset of the controversy and during the years since.

The state Executive Directors were in a position to do more than the national leadership. Had there been a solid front among them, and had they chosen to come to grips with the problem, more could have been done. Almost to a man, they felt the responsibility to spend their efforts keeping the mission funds flowing and the fellowship as strong as possible within the states. Their participation would have brought the controversy to the state level almost immediately. As it was, it would come, but more slowly. It should be realized that these were people who had spent their entire lives promoting missions and fellowship. It was hard to kick against the goad.

The strength of the democracy was becoming its enemy. There was no leader; there had been many leaders. Now the lack of dominant leadership became an Achilles' heel. Pastoral leadership was fragmented and on the moderate side was slow to materialize.

By the fall of 1980, a few of the bolder pastors, seeing the vacuum in the convention, began an effort to resist the takeover. On September 25, 1980, answering the call of Cecil Sherman, pastor of the First Baptist Church, Asheville, North Carolina, seventeen pastors from North Carolina, Kentucky, Texas, Tennessee, Virginia, and Georgia gathered in Gatlinburg, Tennessee. Sherman would later write,

> I gave my background with Paul (Pressler) and Paige (Patterson). I said
> these men should be "taken seriously." I went further and made what

---

[11]Ibid., Theses nos. 12 and 13.

sounds even now like a rash comment, "We are going to divide. The important thing is how we divide." Then I told those people we did not have long to do what we are going to do. I suggested we had about three to five years to "turn the convention around" if it were to be done.[12]

The persons present were prominent pastors, including one former president of the convention. The discussion centered on how to alert "mainline Southern Baptists" as to the danger facing them. They decided that if they could get 6000 votes for a moderate candidate in Los Angeles in 1981, they could probably elect a president. Sherman wrote, "We divided the states, set goals and began to call to mind people in each of the states who might be willing to help us." All this was in answer to an organized plan to take over the convention.

They were promptly dubbed "The Gatlinburg Gang." Sherman described what happened to the participants as follows.

> None of the people called to Gatlinburg by my letter knew exactly what could come of such a meeting. Some came out of courtesy to me; they had no stomach for politic and dropped out. Others stayed for a couple of years and slipped out. About half of the group has given strong and continued service for seven years. I cannot praise them enough. They received nothing for their work but trouble. We have lost everything that matters. Some have been marked for their participation and cut out of denominational life. They have paid. Their extra income has been reduced. They have found themselves described as "not believing the Bible." They have had outside engagements canceled. But they have stayed.[13]

These people felt that this was a matter of saving the delivery system of the gospel as Baptists understood it. This was theological to the core.

The criticism rained upon the group was biting and often ignored the realities they were facing. Many moderates at this relatively early stage of the conflict were equally incensed at this group of "presumptuous" pastors. Moderates were further divided over the methods to be used, and many thought that none at all should be used.

---

[12]Cecil Sherman, Historical Statement, written for his daughter, unpublished.
[13]Ibid, 52.

Various other efforts were made by different people over the next few years. The efforts were fragmented at best and frequently had little in the way of financial or organized support. Finally, after several years, a fragmented nationally based movement began that involved folk from over the convention. It involved various attempts by lay groups, Baptists Committed, Denominational Loyalists, and others to slow or change the direction of the fundamentalists. In places, these efforts were well organized and aimed at winning an election. None of these was to achieve great success. In 1981 in Los Angeles, the fundamentalist Bailey Smith defeated Abner McCall, who got 39.3 percent of the vote. In 1982, the moderate, Duke McCall, got 43.2 percent. In Pittsburgh in 1983, there was no moderate candidate. In Kansas City in 1984, the fundamentalist won over two moderate candidates on the first ballot. In 1985, the moderate got 45.6 percent of the vote. In 1986, the moderate got 46.5 percent, and in 1987 40 percent. In 1988, the moderate got 48.4 percent and in 1990 42 percent.

Moderates never found a charismatic leader for their cause until it was too late to overcome the incoming tide of fundamentalism. State and national organizations were formed, plans made, limited financial help secured, responsibilities assigned, and work performed. But they could not "get it all together." They were unwilling to engage in character assassination or half-truths, though their share of false rumors circulated. They were out organized, out talked, out financed, and out performed at every turn of the election wheel. The moderates, in the main, seemed basically unsuited to precinct politics. One of their problems was that they seemed to be "cursed with integrity."

Two Views

When I began this project, I asked two knowledgeable friends to give me their views of the reasons for the failures that produced the revolution.

Cecil Sims' view represents many years of observation of the SBC at all levels. He said in part:

My overall observation is that leadership at the SBC realm consistently refused to listen to small voices that repeatedly spoke up requesting recognition, pointing out weaknesses in the system, asking for privileges, requesting considerations for change, or pointing out areas of operation which were inconsistent with our Baptist way of life.[14]

Don McGregor, longtime editor of Baptist and secular papers gave his observations:

> One of the problems that I felt was paramount in the considerations of the fundamentalists was an elitist attitude on the part of those leading the moderates during the seventies.
>
> It is my opinion that we had made the Cooperative Program our creed. Everything revolved around that missions giving concept. . . . Churches were judged as to their loyalty according to their percentages given through the Cooperative Program.
>
> Some have referred to the cited elitist system as a "good ole boy network" I never called it that. In my consideration, those who were the central figures in the endeavors were first-class, high-caliber, dedicated, God-honoring people. Their mistakes were in the perceptions of the fundamentalists and not in actuality.
>
> The fundamentalists, however, were left out. . . . As the . . . Cooperative Program became a bigger and bigger taskmaster and the separation between the "ins" and the "outs" became wider and wider. . . . They wanted recognition but didn't want to have to pay the price to earn it.
>
> When the controversy began . . . they became easy targets for the fundamentalist leaders looking for the troops to fuel their takeover machinery.[15]

---

[14]Cecil Sims, Executive Director, Northwest Baptist Convention, 17 June 1991.
[15]Don McGregor, Editor Emeritus, *The Baptist Record*, 4 October 1990.

Chapter Six

The Conflict and Inerrancy

"Wars and Rumors of Wars. . . ."[1]

The denominational war was just beginning in 1980. It would have a multitude of incidental side effects that would profoundly affect the image of the Southern Baptist Convention. President Bailey Smith was barely in office in 1980 before a gaffe of monumental proportions was committed. He remarked in a sermon that God did not hear the prayers of a Jew. It is not certain what he meant, but the religious world erupted in a storm of protest. It was difficult to say whether Jews or Baptists were more upset. Protests poured in from all over the nation. He apologized and tried to explain what he meant, but the damage was done.

Rumors of deals made by fundamentalists with others related to the presidency were the order of the post-election day. In September 1980, Smith was asked if it were true that he had offered to Arizona pastor Richard Jackson, that if he would withdraw from the race in St. Louis, Smith would withdraw the next year in favor of him. Smith replied,

> There is so much that is strange about that, that would make me comment about others that I should not, that I cannot comment on that. I'm serious. I'm not trying to evade the question, because there is no truth to it that would be an embarrassment to me, but I might just involve some others that you have not mentioned for me to answer that question. Because a lot of phone calls were going on, you see. A lot of phone calls came to me, a lot went to Jackson, and, you know, there were a lot of suggestions given to a lot of us."

---

[1]Matthew 24:6.

Asked for a "yes or no," he refused to answer.[2] His comment was a masterpiece of confusion and evasion, but the answer seemed evident.

In this same press conference, President Smith said that no person or group controlled him or his presidency. He acknowledged his conservatism and said that he would appoint only conservative people to committees. He admitted that a person's stance on biblical inerrancy would be an influence on his appointments. In fairness, he did not seem to be interested in dismissing all those who disagreed with him, but his appointments to the significant committees would be the final testimony.

The Issue of Inerrancy

The convention meeting in St. Louis in June 1980 passed a resolution on doctrinal integrity. It said in part,

> Whereas, we acknowledge not only the right but the responsibility of this Convention to give explicit guidelines to the governing bodies of our various institutions, therefore be it Resolved: that the Southern Baptist Convention express its profound appreciation to the staff and faculty members of our seminaries and other institutions who have persistently and sacrificially taught the truth with love—enriching our appreciation for the Bible as God's Holy Word and enhancing our ministry in Christ's name and Be it further resolved, that we exhort the trustees of seminaries and other institutions affiliated with or supported by the Southern Baptist Convention to faithfully discharge their responsibility to carefully preserve the doctrinal integrity of our institutions and to assure employment of faculty members and professional staff who believe in the divine inspiration of the whole Bible, infallibility of the original manuscripts, and that the Bible is truth without any error.[3]

Two attempts to soften the resolution failed. Thus, the convention was setting a sure direction toward a fundamentalist interpretation of the nature of scripture. It became the basis of much controversy.

The Executive Committee of the SBC in its fall meeting in 1980 debated at length whether it should respond to the action of the

---

[2]Baptist Press, 24 September 1980.
[3]*SBC Annual* (1980) 51.

convention on the doctrinal resolution. It finally responded,

> Though the resolution on doctrinal integrity was not referred to the Executive Committee by the SBC, the Committee acknowledges the resolution as adopted by the Convention . . . and assures the convention that the professional staff of the Executive Committee over the years has accepted the Baptist Faith and Message as adopted in 1963.

President Smith was unhappy that the resolution did not include the word "infallible" since in his view that was the key word adopted by the Convention.[4] Others expressed publicly and privately their opinion that this was another step toward a creedal position long rejected by Southern Baptists.

On the same day, the Baptist Press released the story referred to previously about the meeting of the pastors in Gatlinburg to organize resistance to the fundamentalist take-over. Such actions and reactions would come frequently for years as the future of the convention was being debated and decided.

That November, the Georgia Baptist Convention requested that the Baptist Faith and Message Fellowship remove the words "Southern Baptist" from the name of their publication, *Southern Baptist Journal*. They declined to do so. In their reply, William A. Powell, Sr., editor of the publication, asked the Executive Committee of the Georgia Baptist Convention to instruct the editor of the *Christian Index* (Jack Harwell) to state in each issue of the publication that he denies that the Bible is the infallible word of God. In the 1979 meeting of the Georgia Convention, Harwell had survived an attempt to have him ousted over "liberal" views. This was a part of the movement that finally secured his dismissal. It was also a continuation of an effort to "elect a conservative as GBC president who will follow in the tracks of Adrian Rogers and Bailey Smith."[5]

The seminaries, the primary target of the fundamentalists, took notice of the convention's action on doctrinal integrity. Southeastern Seminary trustees at Wake Forest, North Carolina, adopted a statement to be included in their annual report to the convention. It read:

---

[4]Baptist Press, 3 October 1980.
[5]Baptist Press, 16 October 1980.

> The trustees . . . perceive their trusteeship as a sacred trust. We
> acknowledge the resolution . . . and assure the convention that this
> seminary employs, and continues employment of, personnel under the
> Lordship of Jesus Christ and in accordance with scriptural truths.

It listed 29 scripture references, identical to the list included in the Baptist
Faith Message statement adopted by the SBC in 1963. President Lolley
said the response was "within the context" of the statement, and added
the scriptures "speak to the matter of doctrinal integrity very adequately."

At Southwestern, trustees approved a resolution praising faculty and
administration and asked for at least an hour in the Los Angeles
convention in 1981 during which the seminaries could report to the
convention about their stewardship.

At Midwestern Seminary in Kansas City, trustees opted not to
respond. They felt they could not respond to generalized attacks and
thought that the critics should get to know the faculty and discover that
they were not liberals.

At New Orleans Seminary, the executive committee of the trustees
drafted "An Open Letter to Southern Baptists." Chairman Robert McGee
said,

> Our statement is not an effort to comply with the resolution. That would
> be impossible. Our statement is an effort to tell Southern Baptists that
> we are doctrinally and denominationally committed....that we haven't
> lost our moorings....The real question is not whether we believe the
> Bible, but whether we have faith in each other. We can quibble about
> terms, but if we have lost faith in each other, we cannot bridge the gap.

He continued, "The trustees took action to reinforce our doctrinal and
denominational commitment" before the Houston meeting of the SBC in
which doctrinal integrity emerged as a critical issue. "We have acted in
good faith toward the denomination," the statement says. "We believe
that our statement of faith as a seminary is explicit and adequate and the
administration and faculty have made a conscientious and faithful
response."

McGee said,

> We are trying to tell Southern Baptists we have not altered our course.
> We may be using words different from those of some other group, but

we believe our commitment to Scripture as the inspired word of God is as basic as it can be.

McGee placed the matter in perspective when he commented that the loss of faith in each other would be the deterrent to bridging the gap between the groups.

At both Southern Seminary at Louisville and Golden Gate Seminary in California, only executive committees met opting to delay action until the spring meetings of the trustees.

In Louisville, Kentucky, another group of pastors met and selected coordinators to get messengers from cooperating churches to the convention meeting in Los Angeles, June 9–11,1981. One of them said that they were operating without sponsorship or organization. "We represent nobody but ourselves, We are Baptists who love our denomination who want to see the work the Lord has so richly blessed continue."

In January of 1981, Walter Shurden, then dean of the School of Theology at Southern Baptist Theological Seminary told agency leaders that the controversy had in some ways been good for the denomination. The historian said,"The inerrancy controversy has sensitized all in the convention that we are a people of the Book and we must never forget it." He warned the executives that if Southern Baptists do not become sensitive to the politics of their convention they risk seeing the denomination's institutions taken over. He saw the most dangerous influence as the introduction of a

> highly organized, apparently well-funded political party who are going not only for the minds of the Southern Baptist people but for the machinery of the Southern Baptist Convention....while the rhetoric of the controversy has been the interpretation of Scriptures, the issue does not appear primarily to be biblical or theological. The issue appears to be—and has been for two years—political.

Shurden continued, "The very first action of the inerrancy advocates was to construct political organizations to see that the 'inerrancy' president was elected at the SBC." Since then, the politicizing has intensified, until last summer when the political issue was clarified with the announcement the inerrantists were "going for the jugular" of the convention. Shurden contended that inerrancy leader Paul Pressler is one of the first persons in the history of the Southern Baptist controversies to know what the jugular of the convention is. He is aware that to control the institutions of the SBC, you must control the boards of trustees.

The historian spelled out the strategy of the fundamentalists.

First, they turn out the votes at the annual meeting of the SBC even if they must bus people in. Second, they seek to elect an SBC president who they believe is committed to their goals. Third, their president appoints a committee on committees sensitive to their goals. Fourth, the committee on committees names a committee on boards sensitive to their goals. Fifth, the committee on boards nominates trustees who are sensitive to their goals. Sixth, they get the votes back out to make sure the committee on boards report is accepted. In no controversy in the history of the Southern Baptist Convention has the system been misused in this way.[6]

Shurden in a few sentences spelled out the precise mechanisms by which the convention was captured.

Bailey Smith, incumbent president of the convention, declared in January that he would seek a second term. He said his appointments to committees would be people

who have a commitment to evangelism and to missions who love the Word of God, but they also must be sold out to the goals and the system of the SBC. I do not want troublemakers on those committees. I will do my best to bring harmony and peace and I think that will be reflected in my nominations.[7]

Smith said that he would sit down with Pressler and Sherman, the leader of the "friends of the denomination" to discuss the nominations. Both said that they would meet with the president if he desired, but neither was optimistic about the outcome. He reiterated that he would be as fair as possible, appointing a cross section of Southern Baptists. [8]

---

[6]Baptist Press, 22 January 1981.
[7]Baptist Press, 23 January 1981.
[8]Baptist Press, 6 February 1981.

This sentiment would be repeated by most of the presidents through 1991. When the appointments were announced, they seldom included anyone except inerrantists.

Meanwhile, the "denominational loyalists"—the Sherman group— noted that Smith had promised to appoint "all kinds of Baptists" to the committees. If he did so, they would not present a candidate against him at the next convention. They were not interested in defeating Smith but in frustrating the Pressler-Patterson agenda.[9]

Smith opened conversations with Paul Pressler, the inerrantist and Cecil Sherman, the "denominational loyalist." He said that he told Pressler to be kind and not say hurtful things. He encouraged Pressler to disband his organization, but Pressler told Baptist Press, "There is no organization. There is communication between people of like belief, but no organization." Smith told Sherman again that all kinds of people would be appointed to committees and that he wanted to be a "unifier." In spite of these protestations, Smith told the press, "Since I believe in inerrancy, I will look for men who believe in that. . . . You would not expect a person who believes like I do to seek out men who do not believe in inerrancy."[10]

Paul Pressler, the leader of the inerrantist faction, outlined his role in the controversy in a speech in Charleston, West Virginia. He said, "My role is to say to people that we do have a problem. Second, it is to say that there is a solution to this problem and third, to motivate the people into activity." When asked if his understanding of the Bible was the only correct understanding, he replied, "We are not talking about the interpretation of Scripture. We are talking about what the Scripture is."[11] This turning of the question by giving an answer to a question not asked was to become a typical response to probing by the press.

Pressler's problems with the press were enunciated again when asked if the Baptist Press represents Southern Baptists. He said, "I certainly hope not." Pressler cited several uncomplimentary articles from various state papers. This would be a repetitive theme for years to come.

That the controversy over the control of the convention had not yet been won at all points was illustrated by a proposal that would have

---

[9]Baptist Press, 19 February 1981.
[10]Baptist Press, 20 February 1981.
[11]Baptist Press, 21 February 1981.

changed the bylaws. The bylaws stated that the president, "in conference with the vice presidents," shall appoint the committee on committees. This was the committee that nominated the Committee on Boards that nominated the the persons to serve on boards of trustees of agencies and institutions. The proposal was approved by the SBC Executive Committee in February 1981 to change the provision to read, "the committee on committees . . . shall be appointed by a committee composed of the president, as chairman, and the two vice presidents."

This was an obvious attempt to dilute the appointive powers of the president and, thus, secure a more balanced slate of appointments to the crucial committees. Interestingly, the former presidents who were available to discuss the matter, were divided—not on theological lines —but over the desirability of this solution. Some of them had used the vice presidents as a committee when their appointments were made, but Rogers opposed it as an attempt to stop the fundamentalist movement. Incumbent president Smith at first thought it was all right to distribute the power. He changed his mind after some consultation. The recommendation was defeated in the Los Angeles meeting, and the method of selection of the crucial committees remained unchanged.

There were repeated efforts from time to time to refine and delimit the fundamentalist line on the nature of scripture. In February, 1981, a group called the Committee To Promote Faith in the Bible held a meeting in Los Angeles. The reason the group held the meeting, its organizers said, was "to make people aware of the liberalism in the seminaries and what is being taught in them." According to one of its promoters, "The entire program was focused on the question of inerrancy in the Southern Baptist Convention."[12]

In the midst of all this, President Bailey Smith announced that he wanted to be a prophet and that the Los Angeles meeting of the convention in June, 1981, would be harmonious rather than controversial. He declared that he was committed to doing whatever he could to see that love and harmony prevailed at the meeting. He seemed genuinely interested in having the fellowship protected and the mission efforts enhanced. The relationship of these goals and the appointments he would shortly announce seemed to be lost on him.

---

[12]Baptist Press, 3 march 1981

Fuel was added to the fire in late March, 1981, when Robert Bratcher, a former Southern Baptist Missionary and translator of *Good News For Modern Man*, criticized biblical inerrancy. Bratcher stated,

> Only willful ignorance or intellectual dishonesty can account for the claim that the Bible is inerrant and infallible. To qualify this absurd claim by adding "with respect to the autographs (original manuscripts)" is a bit of sophistry, a specious attempt to justify a patent error.
>
> No truth-loving, God-respecting, Christ-honoring believer should be guilty of such heresy. To invest the Bible with the qualities of inerrancy and infallibility is to idolatrize it, to transform it into a false god.

His statement on inerrancy might not have attracted so much attention, but his comments on the nature of scripture did. He said,

> We are not bound by the letter of scripture, but by the spirit. Even words spoken by Jesus in Aramaic in the thirties of the first century and preserved in writing in Greek, 35 to 50 years later, do not necessarily wield compelling or authentic authority over us today. The locus of scriptural authority is not the words themselves. It is Jesus Christ as THE WORD of God who is the authority for us to be and to do.[13]

Bratcher, a graduate of Southern Baptist Seminary, did the cause little good with such a strong condemnation of inerrancy, and with his words, the argument gained new momentum. Bratcher who was an employee of the American Bible Society was shortly hunting a new job.

Bailey Smith went to Africa for the Foreign Mission Board and came home praising the work of the missionaries and saying that he planned to make Southern Baptists aware of the great investment they have in missions. He said that he would encourage his church to increase its giving to the Cooperative Program (the world mission fund) in the future. After he had seen that the money was well spent, his church increased its giving to missions from $50,000 to $150,000 that year, still a minute portion of its budget.

In April of 1981, Smith announced his appointments to the Committee on Committees. His appointees included his sister-in-law, six

---

[13]Baptist Press, 25 March 1981.

repeats from the 1980 committee and the wife of a 1980 member. The moderate faction was incensed. Smith declared, "It (the duplications) came as a surprise to me. I had no idea that there were repeats." He subsequently replaced the six repeaters.

The report of the Committee on Committees was reviewed carefully by a group of interested moderates. Cecil Sherman, a leader of the moderate wing responded. "I have examined carefully the Committee on Committees. I am truly disappointed. It is apparent that a narrow, provincial interest has been served." After a meeting with Smith in February, he said,

> I was led to believe that his appointments would reflect all parts of Southern Baptist life. We wanted to trust him. We were led to believe we could trust him. We tried to trust him. He said he wanted to unify us, but he hasn't. We are disappointed, but more than that, we are grieved and angered by his actions. He is serving a narrow, small set of people who have a creedal wish for the denomination.

Kenneth Chafin, long-time professor at two seminaries and pastor of the South Main Church in Houston, called the Committee on Committees

> an unbelievably unrepresentative committee, which in no way reflects the great diversity of Baptists. I like Bailey. He is an enjoyable human being, but I am not going to stand by and watch him turn this denomination over to a group of fundamentalists who neither built nor support it nor agree with its goals.[14]

Smith was shocked with the opposition.

Worse was to come. When the nominations of the Committee on Boards were released, ten persons eligible for second terms were bumped in favor of fundamentalist nominees. Several of these were prominent in Baptist life and included my wife, a one-term trustee of Golden Gate Seminary. These nominations were the product of the committee that Adrian Rogers had set in motion during his presidency. Bill Sherman, brother of Cecil, the leader of the opposition, immediately reacted. He said,

---

[14]Baptist Press, 23 April 1981.

The convention has fallen into the hands of ultra-conservatives and fundamentalists, many of whom are not graduates of our schools, who write for newspapers critical of who we are, give lip service to being Southern Baptists and do not support our work.

Some of the ousted trustees chose not to make an issue of the matter, including my wife. Others were incensed that the usual criteria for a second term—loyal service—were junked in favor of political appointments. Shortly, James A. Auchmuty, Jr., pastor of Shades Crest Baptist Church in Birmingham, said that he was "outraged" at being bumped from membership on the trustees of the Sunday School Board. He added, "I have been labeled both a heretic and a liar. In a reversal of the age-old maxim that a person is presumed innocent until proven guilty, I have had to, in fact, prove my innocence." The member of the committee from Alabama told Auchmuty that he had "made a personal, arbitrary decision not to recommend me for a second term in the interest of including others in leadership positions."[15] Auchmuty said that his theological integrity had been questioned with no opportunity to defend or explain himself. He promised to take the matter to the floor of the convention, since no other remedy was available. (Auchmuty was an excellent board member. He was knowledgeable and diligent in the discharge of his duties. There was no question during his service as to any departure from biblical faith. He was a trustee during much of my service as president of the Sunday School Board.)

The entire matter generated charge and counter charge and was interpreted by the committee members as an attack on Adrian Rogers who appointed the committee that nominated him. The system had seldom been used in this manner. It was customary for a member to serve a second term if attendance at and participation in the affairs of the Board had been satisfactory. The elimination of the ten was widely believed to be a part of the effort to pack the boards with inerrantists.

Auchmuty, along with my wife, was reinstated by the Committee on Boards before the convention met. On the floor of the convention after bitter debate, five others were substituted for the nominees of the committee. Adrian Rogers, immediate past president, argued for the committee report that would have given the posts to those subscribing to

---

[15]Baptist Press, 13 May 1981.

his point of view. The issue of electing inerrantists to boards was focused clearly, and notice was served that this would be the future course if the fundamentalist coalition could arrange it. They could. This was the last successful challenge of any substantial portion of a committee report naming trustees. Further efforts were made in later years, including a challenge of an entire report from the Committee on Boards. It failed. From June 1981, the fundamentalists would be in complete control of the nominating process.

In April, before the Los Angeles meeting in June, the press was predicting the issues to be faced:

> Among the controversial issues will be a proposed change in messenger qualification, the report of the committee on boards, which nominates trustees to the 20 SBC organizations, and the performance of those boards, agencies and institutions. Floating underneath nearly every issue to come before the estimated 8500 to 10,000 registered messengers is the question of doctrinal integrity, creedalism, biblical infallibility and inerrancy.
>
> Much of the controversy centers on one of the few powers a president has: appointments. Under SBC rules, a president can exert enormous influence through appointment of the committee on committees, which in turn nominates the committee on boards, which is charged with nominating trustees to govern the 20 SBC agencies.
>
> It is this power a faction of biblical inerrantists has focused on. Led by Paul Pressler, an appeals court judge in Houston, and Paige Patterson, president of Criswell Center for Biblical Studies in Dallas, the group says it aims to control the presidency and with it the appointment of trustees, particularly those of the six seminaries.[16]

During this era of history, there was much conversation and many motions brought to the convention to interpret the statement in *The Baptist Faith and Message* about scripture. The statement of faith was adopted in 1963 and in the portion on "The Scriptures" said,

> The Holy Bible was written by men divinely inspired and is the record of God's revelation of Himself to man. It is a perfect treasure of divine instruction. It has God for its author, salvation for its end, and truth,

---

[16]Baptist Press, 30 April 1981.

without any mixture of error, for its matter. . . . The criterion by which the Bible is to be interpreted is Jesus Christ.

This statement was not specific enough for many of the brethren. Repeated attempts were made across the years to interpret it to mean that scripture was "inerrant and infallible." To make such an interpretation an official act of the convention would create many of the problems that were now surfacing. Most Baptists were satisfied with the statement and refused from year to year to amend the wording. Historically, the convention had refused to codify statements of faith to give them controlling power. From the beginning, the scriptures have been our sole rule of faith and practice—"Sola Scriptura." In this regard, Martin Luther had led the way. Southern Baptists, however, had refused to spell out what it meant to be one. We now had a group of ultra-conservatives who were determined to adopt a creedal position that defined and limited the concept of being a Southern Baptist.

As the requirements for participation tightened up and more and more theological tests were devised, several of us editorialized against the movement. In May, 1981, before the meeting in June in Los Angeles, I wrote:

> When we test the nature of being a Baptist by the tenets of scripture, we are on safe ground. When the test of orthodoxy becomes the words of men about the Bible, we will have painted ourselves into a corner from which we cannot escape. . . . Our most serious crisis is whether we will adopt a further creedal interpretation that will alienate thousands even though they subscribe to the truth of the statement.[17]

In that article, I warned that charges and countercharges could widen differences to chasms and lead to irreconcilable polarizations.

These matters were of such concern to me and others that we felt some effort should be made to slow the creedal march. In discussion with Joe Ingram, the state Executive Director of Oklahoma, we agreed that he would talk to Bailey Smith, the SBC president who lived in his home town. Ingram talked to Smith, who agreed that the statement of faith did not need interpretation. He was of the opinion that further creedal pursuits

---

[17]*Facts and Trends* (Nashville: Baptist Sunday School Board, 1981) 6–8.

were not in the best interest of the SBC. He said as much in his presidential address in Los Angeles and helped slow down the movement. Unfortunately, the subsequent history of the convention shows that formal reinterpretation of the statement of faith is unnecessary for the purposes of the fundamentalists. The word and idea of inerrancy became so prominent that amending the statement of faith was not necessary.

The 1981 convention in Los Angeles proved to be rather quiet considering the issues it faced. Probably because of President Smith's statement regarding the problems of creedalism and because the issue was not precisely focused, the convention avoided a fight over the nature of the Bible. It corrected what was felt by many to be the mistake of the Committee on Boards by reelecting five of those bumped after a single term. Two others were renominated by a small committee of the larger group.

Smith was reelected over Abner McCall, former president of Baylor University, receiving about 60 percent of the vote. In his presidential address, he predicted a "great and joyful future" fulfilling the great commission of Christ. McCall acknowledged that he did not expect to defeat Smith but said that the vote for him showed a strong protest to the current trend of the SBC.

Smith, in his news conference after his election said that he did not believe that "we have sides" and that his election was not a victory for any side. He reiterated his statement that he did not believe that the SBC was headed toward creedalism and that the 1963 statement "is the strongest statement Southern Baptists need to make."

In retrospect, Smith tried to be conciliatory in his public statements, tried to defuse some of the more extreme language, and generally talked like a Baptist. The problem always crystallized around the appointments of the president to the important committees. His appointments in both terms as president followed the party line and systematically excluded anyone who did not agree with the inerrancy movement. This tack would be followed by his successors.

Almost immediately after the Los Angeles meeting, President Smith declared to the faithful, "The days of anger and hostility are over because Southern Baptists would rather win the world than fight each other. I think we are going to bury our hatchets, pick up our Bibles and go out and win the world."[18]

---

[18]Baptist Press, 29 June 1981.

The tenor of this address and others during his second year indicated that he thought that the controversy should cease and everybody carry on as they had before the argument or movement began. This theme would characterize some of his successors as well. The amazing and almost unbelievable thing about this point of view was that he and others thought that the disfranchised should simply accept the reorientation of the convention without protest. From his comments in public and private, it seems probable that he simply did not understand the radical nature of the fundamentalist movement. Nor did any of us.

Illustrative of the kind of things going on from time time was the effort of two fundamentalists to publicize a thesis of a master's degree student at Southern Seminary. It was written by Noel Hollyfield, Jr., "to see if he could determine degrees of 'Christian orthodoxy' among seminary students." According to the thesis, the results were "so skewed toward" orthodoxy that they could not be analyzed with normal tests. The thesis contained one conclusion that caused the fundamentalist's blood pressure to rise precipitously. Hollyfield discovered that "as higher education increased, orthodoxy decreased."[19] This finding was consistent with similar studies all over the world and was true of all faiths, according to the author. He further stated that age and number of years in a pastorate increased orthodoxy.

The two fundamentalists began circulation of the thesis in exchange for contributions to the ailing *Southern Baptist Journal*. Hollyfield protested, but the fundamentalists decreed, "It will take a court order" to stop the distribution of the thesis. To them, the thesis proved that Southern Seminary was teaching liberalism and apparently corrupting the students. This kind of disruptive and marginal conduct would continue spasmodically for years.

Indicative of the state of the convention and things to come, Paul Pressler met privately for an hour and a half with Harold Bennet, the new chief executive of the Southern Baptist Convention Executive Committee. Neither Pressler nor Harold Bennett would discuss extensively the conversation. Previously, Bennett had met with Bill and Cecil Sherman, leaders of the opposition to Pressler's political movement. Such a meeting would normally attract little attention. Two things made the meeting important. Pressler would later become an officer of the Executive

---

[19]Baptist Press, 23 July 1981.

Committee and, according to many, dominate its decisions. Secondly, Pressler used the opportunity to talk to Baptist Press.

"The conservative movement is seeking to restore our institutions to where rank and file Southern Baptists can have complete confidence in them," he said. "Only when we have confidence in what's being taught in our institutions can we effectively work together to meet a lost and needy world with the gospel of redemption." Concerning the 1982 convention, scheduled to meet in New Orleans, he said, "The 1982 convention is, fortunately, in the heartland of Southern Baptists. I hope it is extremely well attended. If it is well attended, we'll continue to see processes work to restore our convention to its historical biblical base." In an address to a local church in Nashville, he said that Southern Baptists are in a "life or death struggle for our denomination and for this book (Bible)."[20]

It was impossible then—and now—to find those persons who were "struggling" to discredit the Bible. Even those whom he accused of heresy were not agitating for a radical departure from the Bible, though some few viewed it differently. The entire "conservative movement" seemed to be based on the idea that there was a large number of seminary professors and denominational executives who were subverting the faith of the denomination in the Bible. This theory could not then or now be demonstrated.

The power structure of the SBC was being rapidly revised. Instead of elected leadership and the denominational agency leaders forming the vanguard, the direction was now being set by the small group of fundamentalist leaders, together with the presidents, who made appointments that were suitable to them. This situation would not change for more than a decade (and exists until this writing in August, 1991). The moderate faction would not regain dominance, and the fundamentalists openly celebrated "victory" while sometimes suggesting that those who did not agree with the direction could go elsewhere.

There had been little discussion of differences on a national level on the issue of inerrancy before the beginning of the fundamentalist movement. By now it was obvious to all that this was a winning issue since Baptists had demonstrated again that they would vote for the Bible, whenever and however the issue was presented.

---

[20]Baptist Press, 3 September 1981.

In June, 1982, before the New Orleans convention meeting, the Conference of Southern Baptist Evangelists held a marathon twelve-hour session "spiked with fiery preaching, boisterous singing and frequent calls for evangelists to 'stand by God's inerrant word.'"[21] Even the evangelists were concerned over who held the power in their independent organization. Their controversy over control was resolved by changing their bylaws transferring major responsibility from the conference's executive director to its elected officers. The press had noted charges made against President Freddie Gage of Fort Worth accusing him of manipulating the conference as a 'political machine' to garner support for conservative causes that centered on the issue of biblical inerrancy. Gage responded by vowing to "fight liberalism until all the blood is drained from my body. If you don't like Paige Patterson, then I don't want to be in the same conference with you." Three fundamentalist leaders, including Patterson, also spoke to the conference.

After forty years of attending Baptist meetings all over America and many foreign countries, I cannot remember a single meeting minimizing the importance or validity of the Bible. Suddenly we were confronted with a frantic defense of that which had not been questioned by the vast majority—to say nothing of being attacked. The charges that were made were largely about some writings or professor's statements that had more to do with interpretation than the nature of scripture.

It should be said in honesty, a few here and there differed from the majority of Baptists on the nature of scripture, but these folk were not propagandizing against the Bible in any way. In time, many would reject the description "inerrant." Some did so because they refused to be pushed into any theological pigeon hole. Some honestly felt that this was an inadequate or erroneous definition of scripture. Some rejected the label simply because they did not want to be associated with the fundamentalist mentality.

In August of 1982, Keith Parks, president of the Foreign Mission Board, tried to clarify some of the confusion. He said,

> Over emphasis on biblical authority is a heresy among Southern Baptists which is creating confusion and causing the denomination to stray from its purpose of missions. Any time anyone among us would pick any of

---

[21]Baptist Press, 17 June 1982.

our beliefs (such as) the authority of the Bible as sole rule for faith and practice and emphasize that to the point it is the only criterion that is chosen and nothing else matters—that is the only thing that makes you Christian or makes you Baptist—that's heresy.

He added that omitting such a belief about the Bible also is heresy. Parks, concerned that the convention was straying from its reason for existence commented,

Just as this Bold Mission Thrust was catching us up as Southern Baptists there began to move among us distractions about doctrinal integrity. We're beginning to try to focus on other truths to the neglect of our basic purpose and we will lose the blessing of God if we continue to do so. . . . There is confusion among us because some would have us believe that our identity, our characterizing principles, our unifying force is not in fact missions but something else.[22]

Frank Pollard, president of Golden Gate Seminary speaking in New Orleans in April of 1983, summed up the situation for many. Calling himself a fundamentalist, "if you don't capitalize the word and put the accent on the second syllable," Pollard said he had no problem declaring the Bible inerrant, infallible, and inspired.

When any Baptist institution causes young minds to doubt the Word of God, I believe it to be a tragedy which must be corrected.
    Like many of you I cannot side with the few who do not share those convictions about the Bible. Another great agony is that we cannot side with many who are calling themselves "inerrantists." In fact I do not believe inerrancy is all of the issue in our current division. a large part of the issue is integrity.

Pollard, according to Baptist Press, implied the integrity problem involved the spread of innuendo and false accusations. Tracing accusations of heresy, Pollard scheduled conferences with two of his former professors who were named as teaching specific heresies. He said that he learned the charges were untrue, and that no one accusing them had ever talked to them about these matters. He said,

---

[22]Baptist Press, 10 August 1982.

When I told that New Testament professor someone had said he didn't believe in the virgin birth, he shook his head and cried. . . . I fear there has been too much of this kind of slander. Broad general statements may sometimes contain a half truth, but if they are half true they are also half false.

He said there are several steps a Christian must take before he is biblically free to go public with a complaint. "If you really believe the Bible to be God's word you need to know it forbids you to slander anyone." He added, "Calling a Southern Baptist seminary professor 'liberal' is akin to calling a U. S. senator a 'communist.' His life's calling and ministry is at stake." He concluded, "Liberalism can kill a church or a denomination, but, an even greater warning for us is that a judgmental, negative spirit can kill a church or denomination also."[23]

By now it was clear that every issue and meeting would be haunted by the overarching determination of the fundamentalists to control the election of officers and members of boards who subscribed to their point of view. The focal point was biblical inerrancy.

What Is Inerrancy?

The nature of the argument over inerrancy deals with the basic problem of the veracity and reliability of the Bible. It should be noted that the acceptance of the Bible as the Word of God is an act of faith. That is to say that its authenticity is not subject to testing or proof by the so-called scientific method. There are, according to believers, many corroborating evidences that it is a totally unique book and reveals the mind of God concerning his revelation of himself to man. Further, believers hold that the Bible contains all that man needs to know to be rightly related to God. To the believer, the truths contained in the Bible are demonstrated to be true in every circumstance where demonstration is possible.

Let it be said again, however, these are statements of faith based on the act of faith involved in accepting the Bible as the Word of God. Many Southern Baptists recognize this elementary understanding as a part

---

[23]Baptist Press, 29 April 1983.

of their religious experience. When one subjects acts of faith to the judgments of the sciences and history, problems develop.

The non-scholar inerrantists generally claim absolute accuracy for the Bible in every statement that it makes. If it seems to contradict some known position of science or fact of history, or if the accounts of the same events do not coincide, explanation is sought in some "scribal inadvertency" or miscopied text or the problem is attributed to the understanding of the era of the writer.

The "errantists"—many of whom do not see these problems to be "errors"—being trained in scientific methodology, seek rational answers to the apparent difficulty. In most cases, these "problems" do not alter the faith of the believer in the validity of the revelation of scripture.

There is no single view of inerrancy acceptable to all inerrantists. This fact has been largely ignored during the present conflict.

The arguments related to inerrancy, widely variant in their descriptions, have plagued the denomination for years. Again it should be said that usually to the non-scholar inerrantist, the Bible was precisely accurate in all that it said and contained no misstatements or errors of fact in history or science. To the non-inerrantist, the problems were more complicated than that. This did not mean that one distrusted the spiritual truth of scripture.

But to the non-inerrantist, there were passages that in the light of modern knowledge and methodology gave problems of interpretation or obtaining precise information. For example, the New Testament frequently quotes the Old Testament according to its sense, not its precise wording. Parallel accounts of the same events do not track precisely. Numbers in some of the parallel Old Testament events vary from Kings to Chronicles. The language of scripture apparently was not designed to be scientifically precise, certainly not in keeping with the modern conclusions of science. These matters are described in the language and understanding of the writer's era. (If they had not been, scripture would have been impossible for the ancients to accept.)

Fisher Humphreys, in an address to the Conference on Inerrancy, calls attention to the Chicago Statement on Inerrancy. (This is arguably the best thought-out presentation of the doctrine to appear in recent years.) Humphreys refers to the fact that this statement lists ten items that do not negate inerrancy:

(1) lack of modern technical precision, (2) irregularities of grammar, (3) irregularities of spelling, (4) observational descriptions of nature, (5) reporting of falsehoods, (6) use of hyperbole, (7) use of rounded numbers, (8) topical arrangement of material, (9) variant selection of materials in parallel accounts, and (10) use of free citations.[24]

Basically, he is saying that many items that would be considered questionable by the scientifically trained of our day in any other document are said by the inerrantist not to negate inerrancy. When one agrees to the exceptions in the Chicago Statement, much of the genuine argument disappears.

In 1987, the presidents of the six SBC seminaries scheduled the conference just mentioned on Biblical Inerrancy, which met at the Ridgecrest Conference Center operated by the Sunday School Board. The best known available scholars—Baptists and others—on the nature of inerrancy and scripture were invited. Eleven major papers were presented, together with responses by a person who generally agreed and one who generally held another position from the basic premises of the paper. Seventeen additional presentations were made during seminar meetings. More than a thousand persons attended the conference.

Scholars who were not Southern Baptists included Robert Preus, president of Concordia Theological Seminary; Kenneth Kantzer, dean of the Christianity Today Institute and professor at Trinity Evangelical Divinity School; J. I. Packer, professor of systematic and historical theology at Regent College, Vancouver, Canada; Mark Noll, professor of historical and systematic theology at Regent College and senior editor of Christianity Today; and Millard J. Erickson, dean of Bethel Theological Seminary. More than thirty Southern Baptist scholars, professors, and pastors presented papers or responded to presentations.

The papers included discussions of the history, definition, and parameters of inerrancy, as well as problems related to inerrancy and the implications of biblical inerrancy. This conference had its proceedings preserved in a book called *The Proceedings of The Conference On Biblical Inerrancy.*

---

[24]*Proceedings of the Conference on Biblical Inerrancy* (Nashville: Broadman, 1987) 325.

The following discussion of the various aspects of inerrancy will draw heavily on this volume since it is felt that it represents the various views well and presents the matters from essentially the same context and time period.

Definition of Inerrancy

In his paper on What is Biblical Inerrancy, Clark H. Pinnock said, "You ought to be aware, if you are not, how little agreement there is among inerrantists about what biblical inerrancy actually means in practice."[25] He thus set the stage for what is essential to our purpose of showing that there are varying definitions of inerrancy and many applications.

Kenneth Kantzer in his notes to his address said:

The word inerrant derives from two Latin words meaning "not wandering" with "from the truth" to be supplied. The basic meaning in English and its cognates in other western European languages is "not wandering from the truth" or "truth without any mixture of error."[26]

Robert Preus defined inerrancy as follows:

In calling the sacred Scriptures inerrant we recognize in them (A), as words taught by the Holy Spirit (B), that quality which makes them overwhelmingly (C) reliable witnesses (D-E) to the words and deeds of the God who has in His inspired spokesmen and in His incarnate Son disclosed Himself to men for their salvation (F).[27]

He says in the next paragraph that the definition is very general.

Fisher Humphreys, then professor of theology at the New Orleans Seminary defined inerrancy as follows:

The word is negative; it means "without error." The meaning, however, is positive; it is an affirmation that everything that the Bible teaches, is

---

[25]Ibid., 75.
[26]Ibid., 119.
[27]Ibid., 47.

error free. . . . This includes its assertions in the fields of history and science as well as religion and spiritual matters.[28]

J. I. Packer gave a negative definition: "In any case inerrant is only a negative way of saying 'totally true and entirely trustworthy'."

Paige Patterson in the notes to his response to the presentation of Clark H. Pinnock said,

> Most inerrantists would agree with a simple definition like that of Paul Feinberg. "Inerrancy means that when all facts are known, the Scriptures in their original autographs and properly interpreted will be shown to be wholly true in everything that they affirm, whether that has to do with doctrine or morality or with the social, physical, or life sciences."[29]

David Dockery in an article published in various periodicals including *SBC Today* lists nine variations of inerrancy. In his book on *The Doctrine of The Bible*, he defines inerrancy as follows:

> Inerrancy means when all the facts are known, the Bible (in its autographs) properly interpreted in light of which culture and communication means had developed by the time of its composition will be shown to be completely true (and therefore not false) in all that it affirms to the degree of precision intended by the author's purpose, in all matters relating to God and his creation.[30]

In the same volume, Dockery lists six different views of inerrancy. The six views are as follows (omitting most of his discussion).

1. Naive Inerrancy assumes that God actually dictated the Bible to the writers.
2. Absolute Inerrancy seems to affirm the Bible is accurate and true in all matters and the writers intended to give a considerable amount of exact data in such matters.

---

[28]Ibid., 322–23.

[29]Ibid., 94. Feinberg, "Inerrancy," in *The Meaning of Inerrancy*, ed. Norman L. Geisler (Grand Rapids: Zondervan, 1979) 294.

[30]*Doctrine of the Bible* (Nashville: Convention Press, 1991) 89.

3. Balanced Inerrancy affirms that the Bible is completely true in all the Bible affirms to the degree of precision intended by the writer. This position regards scientific matters as phenomenal, that is they are reported as they appeared to the human writer, which perhaps may be different than the way they really are. It regards the historical matters as accurate, though sometimes in a very general way.

4. Limited Inerrancy maintains the Bible is inerrant in matters of salvation and ethics or faith and practice. Inspiration did not necessarily protect the biblical writers from misstatements in matters of science or history (empirical areas).

5. Functional Inerrancy contends that the Bible inerrantly accomplishes its purpose. It does not equate inerrancy with factuality. The purpose of the Bible is to reveal God and bring people into fellowship with him. To the degree that this is done, the Bible can be said to be inerrant.

6. Errant but authoritative is a view built on an encounter view of inspiration. It does not see the Bible as revelation, but as a pointer to a personal encounter with God. Questions of truth or falsity are of little concern.[31]

It is obvious from this brief recital of positions that there is wide variance in opinion on the nature of inerrancy. One or more of these definitions would include most Southern Baptists, including most "moderates."

When one considers the "qualifications" (those natters that limit) of inerrancy, the problem becomes more severe. As noted above in the definition of the various views, most leave some room for the problem passages that are difficult to explain. As noted previously, The Chicago Statement on Inerrancy lists ten classes of "qualifications" or problem areas that "do not negate inerrancy."

Robert Preus lists what he calls "Adjuncts To The Doctrine of Biblical Inerrancy" in his paper used at the Conference on Inerrancy.

1. Inerrancy does not imply verbal exactness of quotations (for example, the words of institution, the words on Jesus' cross). The New Testament ordinarily quotes the Old Testament according to its sense only. . . .

---

[31]Ibid., 86–87.

2. Inerrancy does not imply verbal or intentional agreement in parallel accounts of the same event.

3. Scripture is replete with figures of speech, for example, metonymy (Luke 16:29), personification (Matt 6:4), synecdoche (Luke 2:1), apostrophe, hyperbole (Matt 2:3). It should go without saying that figurative language is not errant language. To assert that Scripture, by rounding numbers and employing hyperbole, metaphors, and so forth is not concerned about precision of fact (and is therefore subject to error) is to misunderstand the intention of Biblical language. . . .

4. Scripture uses popular phrases and expressions of its day, for example bowels of mercy, four corners of the earth; Joseph is called the father of Christ. . . .

5. In describing the things of nature Scripture does not employ scientifically precise language, but describes and alludes to the things phenomenally as they appear to our senses; for example, the fixity of stellar constellations and the magnitude of the stars (Isa 13:10, Judg 5:20; Job 38:31; Amos 5:8; Job 9:9); the sun and moon as lights and the implication that the moon is larger than the stars (Gen 1:16). . . ;the sun as going around the fixed earth (Eccl 1:5; Matt 13:6; Eph 4:26). . . . Many things in the realm of nature are spoken of in poetic language. . . . In none of the above instances is inerrancy threatened or vitiated.

6. Certain alleged literary forms are not compatible either with the purpose of Scripture or with its inerrancy. For instance, in principle, strictly scientific, strictly historical, or salacious literary forms cannot be reconciled with the serious, practical theological purpose of Scripture.

7. Biblical historiography. (1) Some Biblical writers use and cite sources for their history. We must assume that the Biblical author by the way in which he cites sources believes that these sources speak the truth, that they are reliable sources; and therefore he follows them. . . . (2) Historical events are not described phenomenally as are the data of nature. (3) The historical genre employed by Scripture is apparently a unique form. As it cannot be judged according to the canons (whatever they may be) of modern scientific historiography, it cannot be judged by the mythological and legendary or even historical forms of ancient contemporary civilizations. . . . (4) Chronology and genealogies are not presented in Scripture in the full and orderly manner in which we might present a chronicle or family tree today. Scripture often spreads out time for the sake of symmetry or harmony. . . .

. . . .

10. Etymologies in Scripture are often according to sound and not (obviously) according to modern linguistic analysis. This fact does not affect inerrancy. The ancients are not thinking of etymologies in the modern sense.

11. The inerrancy and the authority of Scripture are inseparably related.

12. In approaching the Scripture as children of God who stand under the Scriptures, we shall do well to recall and observe two basic principles of our fathers: (1) Scripture is autopistos, that is to say, we are to believe its utterances simply because Scripture, the Word of God, makes these utterances (inerrancy is always to be accepted on faith!) and we are to believe without the need of any corroborating evidence. This applies to statements about God but also to to statements about events in history. (2) Scripture is anapodeiktos, that is, self authenticating. It brings its own demonstration, the demonstration of the Spirit and of power. Again no corroborating evidence for Biblical assertions is necessary or sought for. . . .[32]

When one considers all these qualifications, it appears often that what inerrantists call "qualifications" scientists or historians would call "errors" and many thoughtful theologians would call "problems." In the Southern Baptist controversy, very few, if any, of the theologians accused of heresy would say that these "problems" or "errors" had serious effect on the validity of the spiritual truths or authority of the Bible.

Fisher Humphreys, in his paper at the conference, commented on these "qualifications" of inerrancy:

The qualifications are frustrating to inerrantists and non-inerrantists for different reasons. Inerrantists feel frustrated because they believe that they have qualified inerrancy so carefully that no Bible-believing Christian ought any longer to resist inerrancy. On the other hand, non-inerrantists feel frustrated because they cannot see why they should be asked to accept a view which seems problematic, only to be forced to qualify it extensively in order to avoid problems which it unnecessarily created. Why not just bypass the problem and speak of the Bible as God's uniquely-inspired, trustworthy, authoritative revelation?[33]

---

[32]Ibid., 51-55.
[33]Ibid., 326.

Thus, it should be reiterated that the two sides have not been very far apart on the understanding of scripture. Had we followed the example of our Baptist Fathers, who knowing the differences and respecting them, lived together in relative peace, we might have done the same.

The Slippery Slope Theory

One of the principal arguments of some inerrantists is the "slippery slope" theory. James E. Carter described it:

> If one steps out on a slippery slope by admitting any error of any kind in the Bible the slide could carry that person to the bottom of the slippery slope with a complete denial of Christ. Or if error is found in any one statement of the Bible it creates a domino effect knocking down every belief until even the witness to the virgin birth or the bodily resurrection of Jesus could be doubted.[34]

In answer to this rationalistic conclusion, Mark Noll, in his discussion of the history of inerrancy, says,

> A modern history of Scripture does not, in my opinion, justify the famous slippery slope argument. That is, I do not feel that it is accurate to conclude that giving up traditional views of Scripture is the first mark of a slide into liberalism and unbelief.[35]

Fisher Humphreys, commenting on the Chicago Statement, said,

> Its appeal to the autographs also undermines its argument that to forfeit inerrancy is to put at risk the entire theology and mission of the church. For the church's theology and mission today cannot, of course, be guided by inerrant autographs which do not exist but only by existing texts and translations for which no claim of inerrancy is being made. This argument, which is sometimes called the slippery slide argument or the domino effect, can be employed properly only by inerrantists who affirm that we today have an inerrant text or translation. . . . The argument that only the possession of an inerrant bible can keep the

---

[34]Ibid., 28.
[35]Ibid., 21-22.

Church faithful, falters on the fact that the inerrant autographs no longer exist.[36]

The argument fails dramatically in the fellowship of the Southern Baptist Convention on a pragmatic basis. Many of the most devout and effective servants of Christ, Bible believers all, do not accept the inerrancy theory based on the lack of the autographs. They feel that the argument cannot be settled but have complete faith in the authenticity of the scriptures and their sure direction to mankind in all matters related to redemption, the nature of man and God, and the true nature of the gospel.

Many of these Baptists would readily accept the conclusion of the Chicago Statement in the section on "Transmission and Translation." It says in part,

> The Hebrew and Greek text appear to be amazingly well preserved, so that we are amply justified in affirming, with the Westminster Confession, a singular providence of God in this matter and in declaring that the authority of Scripture is in no way jeopardized by the fact that the copies we possess are not entirely error-free.

I do not know a Southern Baptist who does not recognize the authority of the Bible. The Southern Baptist Convention was not on the way to the "bottom of the slope" when the controversy over the nature of the Bible began, for it had certainly not deserted the authority of scripture. The convention was trying to launch its greatest missionary and evangelistic effort when the controversy burst full blown on the scene.

A Conundrum

Paige Patterson, president of Criswell Center For Biblical Studies, has been a principal leader in the fundamentalist movement in the Southern Baptist Convention. W. A. Criswell, pastor of the First Baptist Church in Dallas, has been a frequent critic of the "liberals" and "skunks" (his words) of the so-called moderate camp. Their criticism of the moderates has had to with their understanding of scripture. Both Criswell and

---

[36]Ibid., 327.

Patterson have repeatedly affirmed the inerrancy of the Bible. Patterson has frequently asked, "Is what the Bible says true or not?" They have further harshly criticized the historical-critical method of Bible study.

Patterson recently told a Dallas reporter that the controversy was not really about inerrancy but about Neo-Orthodoxy.

In 1979, Thomas Nelson published *The Criswell Study Bible.* Criswell is listed as the Editor. Patterson is listed as the Managing Editor. In the Foreword, Patterson says,

> The Criswell Study Bible represents the combined efforts of Dr. Criswell and a community of scholars gathered together at the Criswell Center for Biblical Studies. Twenty-one scholars profoundly committed to the basic theological posture which has been characteristic of Dr. Criswell have labored for more that four years, checking references, pursuing research, organizing material, and otherwise working with the pastor in the preparation of the materials which are a part of the explanatory notes in this Bible. The book which you hold in your hands is the blending of the thorough research with fifty years of preaching and pastoral care.[37]

In a number of places the volume questions the biblical text. In the King James translation, used by the study bible, Exodus 7:12 records, "For they cast down every man his rod, and they became serpents; but Aaron's rod swallowed up their rods." In the explanatory footnote, the statement is made: "Egyptian magicians had long ago mastered the art of inflicting a temporary paralysis on a cobra, making him appear stiff and rod-like. However, their 'rods' were swallowed up the 'rod of Aaron.'"[38] The obvious implication is that these were not rods at all but paralyzed snakes. Is the record accurate or not? The problem here is not a faulty translation or "scribal inadvertency."

In Exodus 7:17–19, the Lord said that he would smite the waters in the river and that they would be turned to blood. The fish would die, the river would stink, and the water would be undrinkable. Verses 19–20 read,

---

[37]*The Criswell Study Bible* (Nashville: Thomas Nelson, 1979).
[38]Ibid., 81.

And the Lord spake unto Moses, Say unto Aaron, "Take thy rod and stretch out thine hand upon the waters of Egypt, upon their streams, upon their rivers, and upon their ponds, and upon all their pools of water, that they may become blood; and that there may be blood throughout all the land of Egypt, both in vessels of wood, and in vessels of stone." And Moses and Aaron did so, as the Lord commanded; and he lifted up the rod, and smote the waters that were in the river, in the sight of Pharaoh, and in the sight of his servants; and all the waters that were in the river were turned to blood.

Verse 24 says, "And all the Egyptians digged round about the river for water to drink; for they could not drink of the water of the river." Notes in *The Criswell Study Bible* on 7:17-19 say,

The translation "blood" is accurate, but v. 24 indicates that drinking water could be obtained by digging around the banks of the river, which suggests that the 'blood' was filtered out by the sandy soil. This is not possible with literal blood. Thus, the word may suggest merely a change in color.[39]

The Bible says "blood." The notes say that to get potable water digging around the banks would not be possible with literal blood, and thus the change could be merely a change of color of the water. The basic question raised here is whether the Bible is telling the truth. Patterson says in an introductory passage entitled, "The Bible: a Book of Destiny": "The Bible's internal witness to its authority and divine authorship is unmistakable. The Bible claims in many places to be inerrant, i.e., without error."[40]

In one of the inerrantist's "qualifications" of inerrancy, *The Criswell Study Bible* attributes the discrepancy between numbers in 1 Chronicles 19:18 ("seven thousand men which fought in chariots, and forty thousand footmen") and 2 Samuel 10:18 ("the men of seven hundred chariots . . . and forty thousand horsemen") to rounded numbers and "transcriptional inadvertency."[41] The same kind of problem is dealt with in the note to 1 Chronicles 21:5 where the numbers do not agree with 2 Samuel 24:9.

---

[39]Ibid., 82.
[40]Ibid., xviii.
[41]Ibid., 508.

Scribal inadvertencies or similar problems are attributed in notes in many other places. Since the autographs are not available, explanations must be sought for "errors."

Matthew 2:23, reads, "And he came and dwelt in a city called Nazareth; that it might be fulfilled which was spoken by the prophets. He shall be called a Nazarene." The note in the study Bible says in part, "'Called a Nazarene' introduces an O. T. quotation . . . which does not exist in this precise form in any part of the O. T."

These passages are quoted at some length to indicate some of the kind of problems that inerrantists must deal with. Further they indicate that the authors of the notes recognize some of these problems and do not accept some presently available and precise biblical statements.

Patterson and Criswell—in spite of their recent statements— have both criticized the use of the historical—critical method of biblical analysis. The above quotations together with those that follow indicate extensive usage of the method in *The Criswell Study Bible.*

Genesis 7:11 says that Noah was 600 years old at the time of the flood. *The Criswell Study Bible* says, "Dating the flood and giving the age of Noah is impossible to do with any precision." The study Bible thus raises the question again as to whether available scripture is inerrant. The same sort of question may be asked in the treatment of the hair of Absalom, (p. 388), the dried up hand of Jeroboam, (p. 428), the double accounts of Saul's death (p. 370), and other places.

Textual problems are dealt with in the study Bible as they are in many modern commentaries—i.e., using the historical-critical methodology. (Other inerrantists also frequently criticize these efforts severely.) Illustrations of the use include: discussions related to the correct text in Matthew 5:22 (p. 1113), Judas' participation in the Lord's Supper in Luke 22:7-23 and John 13:26-30 (p. 1229), the correct text in John 5:3b,4, the correct meaning of "giants" in Genesis 6:4 and Deuteronomy 2:2, the correct text in Mark 16, and other matters.

The insistence upon an "inerrant" Bible, given the discussion above, could be considered a moot question. The "inadvertences," scribal errors in transmission of the text, rounded numbers, and other matters of the inerrantists are the "errors" or problems of scholars trained in modern science, history, and higher criticism. The inerrantists try to explain away the problems seen by others. The issue cannot be resolved because of the absence of the authority, the original autographs.

There is a line in Shakespeare that I cannot find that says, "Consistency, thou art as rare as a jewel in a swine's snout." (However, that may be a memory inadvertency!)

Chapter Seven

New Slants
on Old Issues

"New Things Do I. . . ."[1]

As time went by and the control of the fundamentalists grew more complete, issues under consideration by the country as well as the denomination became the focus of much discussion and agitation. As the fundamentalist mind-set was brought to bear on all these issues, the nature of the Southern Baptist Convention continued to change.

Matters of individual conscience, about which there had always been difference of opinion, now became matters for denominational pronouncement. There had always been resolutions presented to the annual meetings on a wide variety of subjects, and they were sometimes adopted and sometimes defeated. They were usually ignored by anyone who disagreed with them, and, after a spate of noise, they were forgotten by all except historians—and often by them. Matters of social conscience were now being called "theological" issues, and sometimes they were. The point of difference came to be that any resolution passed by the convention now, in the minds of some, became a matter of "mandate" to agencies, and sometimes to state conventions and local associations. Further, resolutions were being introduced and passed that related to the fundamentalist wish list. Many of these were reversals of former positions of the convention that no one had ever attempted to enforce, but the new positions were now treated as part of the mandate for change.

A look at some of these continuing problems is necessary in order to understand the nature of the changes taking place. Some of them were redefining what it meant to be a Southern Baptist.

---

[1]Isaiah 42:9.

Women in Ministry

For a hundred years and more the matter of ordination had been the sole province of the local congregation. For much of its history, the convention had some churches that ordained women to be deacons. Little was said about it, and nothing of significance came of it until the fundamentalist surge. The matter was brought to the fore when a few churches ordained women to the ministry. This precipitated the withdrawal of fellowship by some local associations from the church that ordained the women.

The First Baptist Church in Oklahoma City, one of the best known congregations in the convention, ordained three women as deacons. The Capitol Association, composed largely of churches in Oklahoma County, refused to seat the messengers from the church at the next annual meeting even though the church had not elected messengers to the meeting trying to avoid a confrontation. A year or so later,they were finally readmitted.

The Oklahoma convention withdrew an invitation to speak at its annual meeting from the pastor of the First Baptist Church in Nashville when that church ordained a woman as a deacon. Fundamentalists appeared to organize the effort in both cases.

The Home Mission Board of the national body employed a pastor and then discovered that his church had women deacons. He was promptly encouraged to offer his resignation. Larry Lewis, when elected as president of the Board in April, 1987, said,

> The convention has very emphatically and very explicitly expressed their feeling that they do not favor women serving in the role of pastors. So I do not feel that the Home Mission Board should implement a policy that would be contrary to the expressed will of the convention.[2]

He added,

> I personally never have been able to discover from scripture justification for the ordination of women, either as pastors or deacons. The biblical

---

[2]Baptist Press, 14 April 1987.

guidelines are very explicit that those who are ordained to lead the church in a pastoral role should be men.[3]

These incidents reveal a growing disposition to legislate whatever the particular prejudice dictated.

The Equal Rights Amendment to the United States Constitution was creating lively discussion in the country, and the convention was not immune. In the Los Angeles convention, a resolution was passed stating that the SBC "does not endorse the Equal Rights Amendment." The matter of women in church life would generate a great deal of heat for years.

In Coral Gables, Florida, the University Baptist Church licensed (usually a preliminary step toward ordination) a mother and daughter in what the press called "a history making action." It was believed to be the first mother-daughter licensing in the denomination. It caused a momentary surge of conversation and debate.

During this episode, Dr. Sarah Frances Anders, a sociologist at Louisiana College, commented that in the denomination,

> at least 175 women have been ordained. That many I have confirmed and there may be as many as 225. I am convinced that there are at least 200. But not more than a dozen of those women are in pastorates and half of those are co-pastoring with their husbands.

Most of the ordained women are in the chaplaincy or some sort of institutional service, and others are ministers of education or youth and a few are ministers of music, the professor said.[4]

In October, 1982, Ann Neil, a visiting professor at Southeastern Seminary urged female parity with men within the mission fields of the SBC. She noted that 54.4 percent of SBC missionaries are women and advocated full participation by women in all aspects of missionary work including staff positions of the convention's Foreign Mission Board. Married women who have the credentials and so choose may be appointed on the basis of specific work assignment. The trend, however, is still for women to be appointed under the broad category of 'home and church.'"[5]

---

[3]Ibid.
[4]Baptist Press, 25 August 1982.
[5]Baptist Press, 5 October 1982.

By May of 1983, the issue was of such significance that a group of women in church related vocations announced a pre-Southern Baptist Convention meeting in Pittsburgh to discuss matters related to their ministry. Anne Davis, a professor of social work at Southern Seminary, said that anyone was invited who is supportive of women in ministry roles and who wanted to affirm the call of women in church-related vocations. At that meeting an organization was formed by about 75 women and set a meeting for the following year. The adopted purpose statement was in part, to "provide support for the woman whose call from God defines her vocation as that of minister, or as that of woman in ministry within the Southern Baptist Convention, and to encourage and affirm her call to be a servant of God."[6]

In August of 1983, the Pine Bluff Baptist Church, Columbia, South Carolina, ordained Ester Tye Perkins and called her as interim pastor. She disavowed any interest in "Woman's Lib" or the ERA but defended her ordination. She said, "I do not see this ordination as involving manhood or womanhood, but servanthood. . . . As for women being liberated, Jesus Christ liberated me many years ago."[7]

In Chicago, the Metropolitan Baptist Association defeated a motion to exclude the messengers from the Cornell Baptist Church, which recently called a woman as pastor.

In Memphis, the Association refused to seat the messengers of a church that called Nancy Sehested as pastor.

In Nashville in November, 1983, historians recited the history of controversy surrounding women in ministry. Conflict over women's roles emerged in the early 1600s and intruded into the United States by mid 1700s. "The presence of women deacons is not something new in our denomination," said Lynn E. May, Executive of the Historical Commission. Leon McBeth, Church History professor at Southwestern Seminary, contributed:

> Baptists have not always been this uptight about the church roles of women. Minutes, diaries and literature show women have historically exercised leadership roles in the church. Women have testified, exhorted, led prayer meetings and preached.

---

[6]Baptist Press, 13 June 1983.
[7]Baptist Press, 18 August 1983.

He said that church minutes show some early churches in the South had elders and elderesses, deacons and deaconesses.[8]

The Southern Baptist Press Association meeting in Lake Buena Vista, Florida, was told, "It is likely that the single most important issue among Southern Baptists today is women in ministry." Sara Ann Hobbs, director of the missions division of the Baptist State Convention of North Carolina added that Southern Baptist churches are

> more culturally patterned than scripturally influenced in their organization. Churches today are more like corporate structures than the New Testament concept of shared ministry. We have adapted for effectiveness in organization the model of the industrial society.

At the convention meeting in Kansas City in June, 1984, a strongly-worded resolution opposing ordination of women was passed by a vote of 4793 to 3466. The resolution took the position that the Bible excludes women from pastoral leadership positions.[9]

This argument would go on unchecked and often uninformed.

Abortion

As society became more deeply involved in debating the Supreme Court decision on abortion (*Roe vs. Wade*), so did Southern Baptists. Traditionally, the SBC had adopted statements on abortion approving it only for reasons of rape, incest, or the health of the mother. Suddenly this was not enough. Fundamentalists began to say that if abortion was approved for these reasons, then it was easy for any reason to be accepted. This type of logic could create intellectual chaos for many issues.

In January of 1982, President Ronald Reagan, friend of some Southern Baptist leaders, reiterated his belief that abortion was the taking of human life and stated again his opposition to abortion even in cases of rape.[10] This statement seemed to give impetus among Baptists to the further qualification of acceptable reasons for abortion.

---

[8]Baptist Press, 1 October 1983.
[9]Baptist Press, 14 June 1984.
[10]Baptist Press, 20 January 1982.

In March of 1982, the Senate Judiciary Committee approved a proposed constitutional amendment that gave Congress and the states authority to regulate abortions. The vote was ten to seven, indicating the nature of the argument to come. Shortly afterward, the Supreme Court announced that it would review abortion laws in two states and a city in its next term. The Congress continued to haggle over various attempts to limit abortions. The Supreme Court heard arguments in November of 1982 amid much publicity and conflict. The Senate in November, 1983, defeated another move to attach anti-abortion legislation to a bill extending the life of the United States Civil Rights Commission.

The more the country and the right-wing of the Republican Party debated the abortion issue, the more it seemed to become the center of debate in the SBC. The overwhelming defeat of the Hatch Amendment in the Senate did little to slow the accelerating argument.

President Draper of the SBC, discussing common ground among Baptists (in spite of the controversy), used abortion as an illustration of magnifying the differences. He noted that the denomination

> has tended to emphasize the exceptions—rape, incest, deformity. But less than five percent of the abortions are for these causes. Ninety-five percent of the abortions are for convenience or birth-control. I think Southern Baptists ought to say that is wrong.[11]

At that juncture, probably most Southern Baptists would have agreed with him. The push by fundamentalists to eliminate the exceptions continued to cause friction.

In November of 1983, the South Carolina Baptist Convention voted to instruct the Baptist Hospital trustees to amend its policy to allow abortions only in cases of rape, incest, or when the mother's life is threatened. After lengthy study, the trustees adopted a policy stopping short of the instructions, saying, "Abortions are performed only, when in the professional judgment of the attending physician, they are medically necessary and comply with the staff regulation of the hospitals." Following debate, which consumed much of the afternoon session, the 1984 South Carolina convention messengers voted 758 to 565 to uphold the trustee's action.[12]

---

[11]Baptist Press, 21 February 1984.
[12]Baptist Press, 19 November 1984.

By February, 1985, Jerry Falwell, not a Southern Baptist, spoke at First Baptist Church of Dallas on abortion. He told the audience that momentum to protect unborn children was gaining so rapidly he expected to read headlines soon announcing, "Abortion outlawed in the United States." He predicted that "our beloved president" (Ronald Reagan) will appoint two to four new justices of the Supreme Court, and the issue will come before the Court.[13]

As the discussion heated up, Foy Valentine, Executive Director of the Christian Life Commission of the SBC, urged restraint. He called on Southern Baptists "to act with discernment, judgment, compassion, wisdom and courage" in dealing with the volatile issue of abortion. He reviewed the long history of debate about abortion and declared that the issue has been complicated further in recent years by overlapping political, social, and religious agendas. He said that scripture offers principles with which to deal with the issue but has no proof texts with which to smite opponents in the battle.[14]

The agencies were one by one dragged into the battle over abortion. Motivated by the 1984 SBC motion on abortion, the trustees of the Home Mission Board voted to appoint an ad hoc committee to discuss abortion alternatives. The board met with various laypersons and denominational professionals to brainstorm about ways to raise Southern Baptist awareness of the "world-wide abortion crisis" in light of the estimated 1.5 million abortions performed annually in America. They decided to encourage the teaching of Christian sex education in churches and to inform churches of abortion alternatives—ways they can become involved in constructive prevention of abortion.[15]

Gallup announced the results of a poll on abortion conducted in January of 1986. A higher proportion of Southern Baptists than Catholics opposed the Court's 1973 decision giving women a virtually unrestricted right to have abortions during the first three months of pregnancy. Results of the poll revealed Southern Baptists opposed the *Roe v. Wade* decision by a two to one margin (60% opposed, 31% favored). Among Catholics surveyed, 40 percent favored it, with 48 percent opposed.[16]

---

[13]Baptist Press, 21 February 1985.
[14]Baptist Press, 28 March 1985.
[15]Baptist Press, 5 June 1985.
[16]Baptist Press, 11 January 1986.

In June, 1986, fundamentalist leader Paige Patterson announced that his group expected to tie the hiring of denominational employees to their position on abortion, euthanasia, school prayer, and federal budget reduction. "We want an open, pro-life position in all of our institutions and agencies dealing with both abortion and euthanasia. We want to be pro-family, pro-prayer anywhere." Employees who would be required to agree with the Baptist elected leadership would include professors at the six Baptist seminaries, members of the Christian Life Commission, writers of literature published by the Sunday School Board, and employees of denominational hospitals and other agencies, Patterson said.

He said that he was encouraged by the sweeping mandate expressed in this year's convention. "We had reason to suspect that we were going to be able to do pretty much what we wanted, although not all within our camp were that optimistic." In commenting on the social agenda, he said, "The convention's actual posture is far more conservative than most of its (agency and seminary) leadership on social and moral issues." On abortion, Patterson said, "I THINK IT'LL GO OVER NEARLY AS WELL AS THE INERRANCY THING."[17]

The obvious cynicism and arrogance of the apparent assumption of the position of Baptist pope seemed to be lost on most Southern Baptists, even after the matter began to control the direction of the seminaries and agencies.

In this interview, Patterson highlighted two points that would occur again and again. He set up creedal positions for denominational employees. In discussing the necessary conformity of seminary professors, he outlined a position that years later would be heard from moderates, "We cannot be asked to pay for the teaching of a position diametrically opposed to our own," Patterson said. "I have a conscience problem with that."[18]

As it became clear that abortion was to be a major issue with the fundamentalist leadership, a conference was called by the Christian Life Commission to discuss alternatives. It was a diverse group of pastors, lay people, and denominational workers seeking a Christian solution to a difficult ethical issue on which there was not very much division. It was one more divisive issue on which the fundamentalist leadership had

---

[17]Brad Owens, *The Baptist Messenger* (Oklahoma)26 June 1986.
[18]Ibid., 4.

decided it must have its way, even if there was little controversy among the body. The consultation declared,

> Human life from conception is sacred and must be protected and nurtured in all its aspects. Abortion at any stage of pregnancy is ending human life and is a grave act with tragic spiritual, emotional, physical and social consequences. In those incidents in which this divine ideal is not fulfilled, there can be redemption in God's grace. Therefore:
> Let us speak forcefully and unequivocally against abortion on demand and with all vigor encourage alternatives to abortion.
> Let us pledge ourselves to be compassionate, aggressive agents of God's grace in nurturing human life and in taking God's grace to those caught in the tragedy of abortion.[19]

Commission chairman Lynn P. Clayton said, "If we pass this statement, we can stop fighting each other over exceptions and start fighting together against abortion." It was not to be.

Immediately, Paul D. Simmons, a Southern Baptist Seminary professor of ethics, defended the Supreme Court's decision in 1973 legalizing abortion. He spoke at a conference sponsored by Americans for Religious Liberty. Referring to what he called the "challenge from the Religious Right," Simmons said:

> Now we are testing whether those values should or can be preserved. A powerful coalition of religious and political interest groups has launched concerted efforts to return reproductive choice to the control of government. Ultraconservative religious groups and extremist political organizations have formed an alliance dedicated to the proposition that abortion is this nation's no. 1 moral problem and must be outlawed. They are determined to turn back the clock to an era of oppression and absolutism.[20]

Simmons had recently published a lengthy article in two Baptist papers setting forth his views on a proposed human life amendment to the United States Constitution. The trustees of Southern Seminary discussed whether the professor should be dismissed. The Academic Affairs

---

[19]*The Baptist Messenger*, 2 June 19.
[20]Baptist Press,, 2 June 1987.

Committee of the board concurred with seminary president Roy L. Honeycutt that there were no grounds for dismissal based on the seminary's Abstract of Principles. The full board agreed but expressed "concern with Dr. Simmons' position" and requested the president to "encourage him to moderate his public involvement in this issue."[21]

The president carried out the instructions of the Board of Trustees. The problem was still before the trustees in August of 1991. At least one member has vowed to try to get Simmons fired.[22] Once again, a minority view was threatened.

In the 1987 SBC meeting in St. Louis, a resolution passed without debate urging the convention's Christian Life Commission to continue expansion of services related to the sanctity of human life and to lobby for legislation to protect the lives of the unborn. Another resolution asked the United States Senate to pass the amendment that would prevent pro-life hospitals from being forced to perform abortions under provisions of the Civil Rights Restoration Act.[23]

At its semi-annual trustee meeting in February 1988, the Sunday School Board discussed the abortion problem for an hour. They debated whether to interrupt the regular sequence of Sunday school lessons with a dated lesson on the evils of abortion or to allow the churches the choice of an undated lesson that did not interrupt the sequence of regular Bible study. The president, Lloyd Elder, told the trustees that the studies of church reaction to turning aside from a series of Bible studies to occasional topics indicated that the churches did not like to do that. One trustee supporting the idea of including the study in the regular sequence said, "I think the method we are addressing is how we can be most effective in getting out the message. I think we should make it as difficult as possible for churches to avoid the issue."[24] Such methods, now common in SBC life, were a drastic departure from traditional Baptist positions.

The Board placed the study in the regular sequence of lessons and a wave of protest went up over the country. There was not much disagreement about the evils of abortion; there was a lot of protest of the method involved.

---

[21]Ibid.

[22]In January of 1993, Simmons resigned his position at Southern Seminary.

[23]Baptist Press, 22 June 1987.

[24]Baptist Press, 18 February 1988.

By 1990, abortion had become a code word and test of orthodoxy. Baptist Press reported that abortion had become the "litmus test" for speakers at meetings sponsored by the Christian Life Commission. The Commission voted 12-11 to "respectfully request our executive director to refrain in the future from inviting speakers who support the so-called pro- choice position on abortion." Harry A. Lane, pastor of West Side Baptist Church in Greenwood, South Carolina, said, "There are more important issues than abortion we ought to agree on. The issue of salvation is far more important, yet we work with people who have different theological views."

Liz Minnick, a homemaker from Austin, Texas, disagreed. "Abortion is the benchmark issue . . . because this is life. The way you look at abortion colors how you look at all issues, from creationism to pornography."

The original form of the motion would have precluded the appearance of Glenn Stassen, professor of ethics at Southern Seminary. He had once signed a petition that targeted the removal of abortion from the criminal law codes and warned against an absolutist position. Stassen represented the kind of person who should not be on CLC platforms according to Skeet Workman, a homemaker from Lubbock, Texas. Stassen replied,

> Our blind son, David, is extensively handicapped as a result of the German measles Dot got in the first three months of pregnancy. We did not get an abortion. Instead, we have tried to help David cope with the suffering of 14 operations, including heart surgery twice, and struggle against heavy odds to grow into a bright linguist who speaks German without an accent.[25]

Free choice of Baptist consciences promised to reap a heavy harvest from reactionary non-Baptist fundamentalism.

In March, 1990, the Southwestern Baptist Theological Seminary trustees went on record as being "pro life." The motion by Lee Weaver from Birchman Baptist Church, Fort Worth said that the trustees

fully support actions and efforts to bring the people of this nation to an

---

[25]Baptist Press, 5 March 1990.

> understanding that all life is God-given from conception. . . . This
> seminary wishes to be known as a Christian institution standing for the
> God-given rights of all humans and therefore takes its stand as pro life
> and condemns any act of abortion, euthanasia or any other act against
> God or against man who is created in God's image.

The motion originally sought to include the faculty and administration,
but that portion was deleted after pleas by President Dilday and new
board chairman James Draper.[26]

In May, 1990, The Southern Baptist Theological Seminary trustees in
executive session, asked President Honeycutt to express to Paul Simmons
their disapproval of "the harm done to this seminary" by Simmons'
public activities related to abortion, adding that "his continued activities
in this area may be considered sufficient grounds for dismissal." The
board also voted to express "deep concern for intemperate comments
about controversial issues which negatively affect the public perceptions
of Southern Seminary" to Glenn Hinson, professor of Church History. He
had criticized the conservative leaders of the denomination.[27]

Letters to the editors of the state papers decried the "gagging" of the
professors as trampling their rights and Baptist tradition. The *Western
Recorder* called the action "mind control."

In the spring of 1991, Midwestern Seminary trustees discussed
instructing the faculty on the subject of abortion. The board finally agreed
to refrain after appeals from seasoned trustees.

An issue on which there was little true difference of opinion among
Southern Baptists was being pushed by fundamentalists to the point of
divisiveness.

Prayer in the Public Schools

On several occasions—in 1964, 1971, and 1980—the Southern Baptist
Convention had passed resolutions supporting the Supreme Court
decisions in 1962 and 1963 banning state-mandated prayer and Bible
reading in public schools. The Baptist position historically was in

---

[26]Baptist Press, 14 March 1990.
[27]Baptist Press, 1 May 1990.

opposition to any form of government interference in or sponsoring of religious activities. It was held traditionally that state-sponsored prayer in the public schools would inevitably interfere with the rights of minorities who were not powerful in the political group that would make the decisions about school prayer.

Many felt that the prayers in the South would be Baptist or Methodist prayers; the prayers in Utah would be Mormon prayers; in New Orleans, Catholic prayers; and in Harlem, perhaps Muslim prayers. While all these groups had the same rights under the Constitution, many were unable to protect their rights in the context of the public schools.

The Baptist Joint Committee on Public Affairs had often reiterated this position held by Baptists generally. This body represented eight Baptist groups in Washington.[28] Proposals were in Congress in the spring of 1982 to call a constitutional convention to deal with school prayer and other issues. Thirty one state legislatures of the required required two-thirds of 34 had already called for such a convention for a variety of reasons.

There was also a proposal in the Congress to strip the federal courts of jurisdiction to hear challenges to state and local laws related to prayer in the schools. This would have removed the issue to the states where it could become the political football of the politicians.

The fundamentalists—Baptist and otherwise—were calling for the "restoration of God" to the classrooms of America. Reagan was their ally and Jesse Helms their standard bearer. It was common to hear that God had been banished from the school system and that when He was restored, the nation would be once again on the right track. All kinds of good things were attributed to "a minute of silent prayer" by those who were sometimes downright belligerent about the matter.

Baptist Press reported that in May, 1982, James M. Dunn, Executive Director of the Baptist Joint Committee—Baptists' chief church-state spokesman—"condemned President Reagan's call for a constitutional amendment on public school prayer as 'despicable demagoguery.'" He said the president was playing politics with prayer. "He knows that the Supreme Court has never banned prayer in schools. It can't. Real prayer is always free." He said that in spite of public misunderstandings about the court decision, Reagan knows better. "He knows that the court in

---

[28]Baptist Press, 4 April 1982.

those prayer rulings affirmed and encouraged studies about religion in public school classrooms. What the court has done is protect religious liberty."

He pointed out that the ruling was supported by most religious bodies in the country, including the National Council of Churches, encompassing 40 million Christians and that every national Jewish organization has consistently opposed "compelled ritual." He pledged that the Joint Committee would lead the fight against the constitutional amendment.[29]

The declaration did nothing to endear Dunn to the fundamentalists in the convention. He had already crossed swords with them on several issues, and this effort would cost him dearly.

On May 6, 1982, President Reagan announced that he would shortly submit a constitutional amendment on prayer in the public schools. Pressler, Ed McAteer, and Dorothy Patterson (wife of Paige Patterson), were invited to a related White House ceremony. Pressler was asked if this issue was on his agenda in the convention in June in New Orleans. He replied, "I have no agenda—I never have."

Two church-state specialists joined other national religious leaders in denouncing the proposal at a Capitol Hill press conference. John Baker, general counsel for the Baptist Joint Committee on Public Affairs, stated that involving government in prayer would "trivialize and secularize it." He said that true prayer has never been and could not be banned from public schools. "What was banned was the use of the coercive power of the state to promote the religion of whichever religious group was dominant in a particular school district."

R. G. Puckett, Executive Director of Americans United for Separation of Church and State, said that his organization opposed the school prayer amendment since it would violate the spirit and intent of the first amendment. He denied that the Supreme Court ruling had thrown God out of the class rooms. He said it is "rather faulty theology" to assume that God could be removed from the classroom by the Supreme Court or restored to it by Congress.[30]

On May 17, 1982, President Reagan sent his proposed amendment to Capitol Hill. It read, "Nothing in this Constitution shall be construed to prohibit individual or group prayer in public schools or other public insti-

---

[29]Baptist Press, 6 May 1982.
[30]Baptist Press, 10 May 1982.

tutions. No person shall be required by the United States or by any state to participate in prayer."

Immediate reaction was forthcoming from Southern Baptist leaders. Harold Bennett, executive secretary-treasurer of the SBC Executive Committee said that he is happy with the resolutions on school prayer passed at annual meetings of the convention during the past 20 years since the Supreme Court struck down state-required prayer. The last convention resolution was passed in 1980.

My own reaction was that the amendment was unnecessary since it

> makes no provision for anything not now possible. As desirable as prayer in public schools may be, mandatory or supervised prayer is antithetical to our Baptist free faith. To make public prayer a political football is to deny the meaning of real prayer. To give this issue to each local community is to guarantee political confusion over a sacred, personal, religious act.

James Dunn of the Joint Committee joined us in this opinion.

Jimmy Draper, pastor of First Baptist Church, Euless, Texas, favored passage.

> I would not be unhappy with the wording of the president's amendment. I do not agree with those who suddenly say we cannot acknowledge God in the classroom. We acknowledge him in the Constitution itself and in other national documents.[31]

Fundamentalist leader Paul Pressler and Norris Sydnor, chairman of the SBC Resolutions Committee, assured the convention that the prayer amendment would not be pushed in the 1982 New Orleans convention meeting. Sydnor said that he would work for passage of the amendment but he would not ask the convention to endorse it.[32]

In June, 1982, in New Orleans, the convention was asked to approve a resolution that declared, "our support of the...proposed constitutional amendment." In July, an aide to President Reagan confirmed that New Right leader Edward McAteer received White House encouragement to

---

[31]Baptist Press, 21 May 1982.
[32]Baptist Press, 10 May 1982.

work for SBC support of the constitutional amendment on school prayer. Morton C. Blackwell, special assistant to the president, told Baptist Press that he and McAteer conferred regularly and consulted before the New Orleans meeting. "McAteer played a major role," he said, in shepherding the resolution through the committee and advised committee chairman Sydnor, a Religious Roundtable leader in Maryland, and advised on the matter during the floor debate. He repeatedly offered suggestions on the platform to Sydnor and other committee members.[33]

The resolution received the strong support of Morris Chapman of First Baptist Church, Wichita Falls, Texas, and Charles Stanley of the First Baptist Church in Atlanta. Both were subsequently elected president of the convention.

The resolution passed by a three to one margin, an about face for the body from the 1980 position.

Many Southern Baptists were of the opinion that if the White House would interfere directly with the functions of the convention, church-state issues were already of great importance.

Jimmy Allen, a past president of the SBC, spoke at a breakfast sponsored by the Campaign for Religious Liberty, a coalition of more than 50 religious, political, and educational organizations on the eve of the first Senate hearing on the prayer amendment. He declared, "We are not here because we don't believe in the need for prayer but because we believe in the need for authentic prayer." Opposing coerced prayer is essential, he said. "Once you decide that prayer is a free and voluntary expression to God." He roundly criticized the politicizing of a sacred matter.[34]

The battle was joined as the Senate Judiciary Committee opened hearings of the constitutional amendment. Ed McAteer and Jesse Helms urged the passage, while Jimmy Allen, president of the Radio and Television Commission of the convention, and Senator Mark Hatfield urged rejection.

In the second hearing of the Senate committee, Deputy Attorney General Edward Schmults and television evangelist "Pat" Robertson voiced strong support for the controversial amendment, while Southern Baptist minister and former congressman John Buchanan joined other

---

[33]Baptist Press, 1 July 1982. (It was subsequently reported by Baptist Press on 8 July 1982 that Sydnor had never attended a Southern Baptist Convention before.)
[34]Baptist Press, 28 July 1982.

educational and religious leaders in denouncing it.

This battle would go on for years, though both the amendment proposal and Jesse Helms' bill that would strip the Supreme Court of the power to review such cases finally lost in the Congress.

Southern Baptists—and doubtless other religious bodies—lost much in fellowship and trust.

Creeping Creedalism

A creed is a brief authoritative statement of religious beliefs. "Authoritative" is the operative word for Baptists.

From the beginning in 1845, Southern Baptists declared that they had no creed but the scriptures. For eighty years, the convention refused to adopt even a statement of faith. Under the pressures of the evolution and other controversies, the convention in 1925 adopted the first Baptist Faith and Message statement. The 1963 statement was essentially the same as the 1925 version, with minor variations. E. Y. Mullins of Southern Seminary was the leader in the forming of the 1925 statement. The statement itself denied that the statement should be creedal, and the 1963 statement reiterated the same position.

W. W. Barnes, Southwestern Baptist Theological Seminary historian, declared in 1934 that the 1925 statement was the first step toward creedalism and that it would be easier in the future to become creedal. With the adoption of the 1963 statement, there came to the convention from time to time attempts to interpret the confessional accord to fit the desires of various messengers. Most of these attempts would have to do with the article on the nature of scripture.

With the advent of the inerrancy argument, it gradually came to be understood by the party faithful that the official position of the convention was inerrancy. Increasingly, also, there were calls for formalizing some statement of beliefs that would be the official definition of what a Southern Baptist should believe to be called a "good Southern Baptist." As has been noted before, there had never been an official definition.

In November of 1983, Jimmy Draper Jr., president of the Southern Baptist Convention, suggested the denomination establish "guidelines" to detail what Baptists should believe. He suggested that a committee be appointed to draw up "some minimum things Baptists believe." He said after the establishment of limits to what Southern Baptists could believe, "moderates" and "liberals" who could not accept them could leave. The implication that these beliefs would be in keeping with the fundamentalist desire was clear.

Draper asserted, "No matter what they say, Baptists have got a creed—everyone's got a creed. . . . We do believe in something. We have a statement of faith and a confession of faith. They are creedal in a sense." Draper cited four things that should be in any guideline of belief: "They are bedrock. If there are leaders or teachers who find they cannot accept these four things, they ought to leave. Anyone who cannot accept them is not a true Southern Baptist and ought to have the integrity to leave."

The four include a belief in the full humanity and deity of Christ, substitutionary atonement by Christ for the sins of mankind, justification by God's grace through faith, and belief in the bodily resurrection of Christ. He said that he would not want a statement on inerrancy since it would create controversy about definitions.[35]

This was probably the first time in our history that any such suggestion was made. Almost all Southern Baptists would readily accept his four "bedrocks." Yet, for many it was far too simple. It was not inclusive enough for some. There were too many things left out that are important to the nature of the faith. Some thought that the propositions should be differently phrased. Some wanted interpretation of a word of two. That it was attempted at all was an affront to many. He stated that he wanted such a movement to come from "a groundswell" of opinion. If there was a groundswell at all, it was in opposition to his proposal.

Draper, who previously had said Baptists should have some kind of limits "of how far you can go and still be a Southern Baptist," called in October for unity around certain guidelines. He added: "We have to set some kind of parameters for Baptist belief. If we don't, people will end up believing anything they want."[36]

Immediately, Draper's suggestion stirred up a theological hornet's nest. John M. Lewis, pastor of first Baptist Church of Raleigh, North Carolina, called it a horrible idea in the light of Baptist history and theology. He thought that it would be further divisive. Even Paige

---

[35]Baptist Press, 17 November 1983.
[36]Baptist Press, 17 November 1983.

Patterson was "lukewarm" to the idea. Cecil Sherman of the moderates thought the idea would come to nothing. Kenneth Chafin of South Main Baptist Church in Houston, a moderate, termed the suggestion "a subtle attack on the integrity of the institutions and agencies" of the denomination. He thought the suggestion poured gasoline on the fire. Robert Tenery, soon to be editor of the the inflammatory *The Advocate*, a fundamentalist paper, said that a lot of neo-orthodox folk could sign the document, that it did not go far enough. He also said, "The question is will they (signers) honestly stand by what they have signed. . . . Do they have the integrity to stand by that?"[37]

Baptists historically have believed that what they believe is a matter between them and God. Their priesthood allows them to "end up believing anything they want" so long as God alone approves. The concept of setting "parameters" of Baptist belief requires some official document, with official interpreters, a system of judgment and judges. It involves the idea of excommunication as well as voluntary departure. All of this is foreign to historic Baptist principles.

It seemed necessary to me to comment on these goings on in my final address to the state convention leadership that convened in Nashville in December of 1983. In part, I commented,

> Any Baptist who thinks he knows what another Baptist ought to be is in danger of not being a Baptist. . . . Believe or depart is not the prerogative of any single Baptist or group of Baptists. The assumption of authority over others by any group of Baptists is to cease to be Baptists.[38]

The SBC across the years prior to the fundamentalist take-over had consistently rejected actions appearing to be creedal in intent. In June, 1969, at the height of the *Broadman Commentary* controversy, the SBC rejected a motion to have all writers and seminary professors sign doctrinal statements. All the seminaries had conservative statements of doctrinal beliefs that furnished the basis of decision making and faculty contracts.

Instead of the proposed statement, however, the convention adopted

---

[37]Baptist Press, 1 December 1983.
[38]Baptist Press, 9 December 1983.

a statement that

> call[ed] the attention of agencies to the doctrinal statement framed after
> careful discussion in 1963 and vigorously urge elected trustees to be
> diligent in seeing that programs assigned them are carried out consistent
> with that statement, and not contrary to it.[39]

This statement itself bound the agencies to the confessional statement in
the daily practice of their ministry.

It was a first step down a long trail.

As the take-over gathered strength, contests and conflict often
developed over incidents and incidentals. Too often, these side excursions
seemed to sap the vitality of constructive debate. Most leaders of agencies
and institutions, as well as state convention executives, were often silent
on the truly important issues that we confronted. Some, seeing the
problems from the perspective of the scholar's seclusion, were vocal on
important matters.

One of these was Walter Shurden, by then chairman of Mercer
University's Department of Christianity. In an article in the summer issue,
1985, of *Baptist Heritage Update,* he compared fundamentalism and
creedalism. He said that three dangers of fundamentalism are that it
rationalizes faith, erodes denominationalism, and minimizes freedom. In
his comparison of liberalism and fundamentalism, he said, "Both interpret
the Christian faith primarily in terms of intellectual propositions about
God. Their propositions differ, but their method is the same."

He continued: "Fundamentalism transforms the Christian faith into
theological ideas to be believed rather than a person to be loved and
obeyed," It results in "the loss of the intensely personal nature of the
faith," and reduces Christianity "to a set of doctrines to which one must
give assent."

"Creedalism is the first cousin of fundamentalism." Southern Baptists
historically have resisted creedalism. They "did not want human
statements about the Christian faith to be equated with the essence of
personal faith."[40]

When the Peace Committee (discussed at length later) made its report

---

[39] Baptist Press, 12 June 1969.
[40] Baptist Press, 15 May 1985.

to the convention in June 1987, it included in its findings its interpretation of *The Baptist Faith and Message* statement. The committee said in part,

We, as a Peace Committee, have found that most Southern Baptists see "truth without any mixture of error for its matter," as meaning, for example, that:

(1) They believe in direct creation of mankind and therefore they believe Adam and Eve were real persons.

(2) They believe the named authors did indeed write the biblical books attributed to them by those books.

(3) They believe the miracles described in Scripture did indeed occur as supernatural events in history.

(4) They believe that the historical narratives given by biblical authors are indeed accurate and reliable as given by those authors.

We call upon Southern Baptist institutions to recognize the great number of Southern Baptists who believe this interpretation of our confessional statement and, in the future, to build their professional staffs and faculties from those who clearly reflect such dominant convictions and beliefs held by Southern Baptists at large.

The committee also acknowledged, "However, some members of the Peace Committee differ from this viewpoint."[41]

The convention adopted this report by an overwhelming vote, after the body had had only minutes to see the complicated document. It was obviously a document approved by the fundamentalist leadership, and the faithful supported it.

In July, at a meeting of the trustees of the Home Mission Board, policies governing the employment of elected staff members and missionaries were established according to the guidelines of the Peace Committee report. The directors instructed

our administration to assure that in the future we only employ professional staff and appoint missionaries whose theological positions "clearly reflect the dominant convictions and beliefs held by Southern Baptists at large" as illustrated in the findings section of the committee report.[42]

---

[41]*SBC Annual* (1987) 237.
[42]Baptist Press, 31 July 1987.

This board had already approved guidelines precluding the appointment of divorced persons as missionaries, refused to employ persons who led churches to ordain women as deacons, and refused to give pastoral support to churches with women pastors. The board now added at least four other dicta from the Peace Committee about who could serve.

The trustees of Southern Seminary passed the same regulations as those in the Peace Committee report about future employees. The trustees predicated employment, tenure and promotion on the four criteria of the committee report. Only after a prompt review by the Association of Theological Schools, their professional accrediting agency, did they relent.

Reaction to such creedal procedures was not long in coming. Charles Fuller, pastor of the First Baptist Church of Roanoke, Virginia, thought it wise to say, "The Southern Baptist Convention Peace Committee did not draft a creedal statement, nor is it a watchdog."[43] All agencies were expected to draft a reply to the Peace Committee's report by the next meeting of the convention. Whether the Committee thought the report was creedal or not did not affect the response expected of the agencies. Some began immediately to fashion their future theological decisions according to the report.

Widespread protests did little to stem the tide of regulations imposed by implication in the votes of the convention about one matter or another.

The list of criteria to be met by the agencies and presumably by "good Southern Baptists" continued to increase. A partial list follows.

The tenets of *The Baptist Faith and Message.*
The Peace Committee Report, with its four doctrinal declarations.
The correct position on abortion.
The correct position on ordination of women to ministry
    or the diaconate.
The correct position on divorce.
Adherence to the correct position on inerrancy.
The correct position on school prayer.
All of these doctrinal declarations claimed basis in scripture.

For a denomination that had long held scripture to be its only rule of faith and practice, it was gathering a considerable list of creedal man-

---

[43]Baptist Press, 25 September 1987.

dates.

Chauncey Daley, Editor Emeritus of the *Western Recorder*, wrote a guest editorial entitled "A New and Different Convention." In it, he summed up the situation in the SBC rather well. He said,

> As the old convention died, a new organization which had been developing in the womb of fundamentalism for a decade was born. And the tragedy is that the new convention has little resemblance, except the name, to the denomination God and our Baptist forefathers built from 1845 to 1979. . . . The old was characterized by freedom and soul liberty; the new is characterized by repression and forced conformity. The old was inclusive; the new is exclusive. The old found unity in diversity; the new coerces conformity with creedalism.
>
> Creedalism is the death blow to freedom and the priesthood of every believer. Creedalism exists when particular interpretations of scripture are made the standard and are used to judge the orthodoxy of all Southern Baptists. . . .
>
> The new convention is totalitarian. If this word sounds too strong, consider Webster's New Collegiate Dictionary definition of totalitarian: "Of or pertaining to a highly-centralized government under the control of a political group which allows no recognition of or a representation to other political parties."
>
> Baptist historians are now faced with compiling a new list of Southern Baptist distinctives. Soul freedom, the priesthood of every believer, separation of Church and State, and other distinctives precious to Baptists of other days died with the old convention. Creedalism, totalitarianism and a controlled press will head the new list.[44]

B. H. Carroll, An Unacceptable Giant

By the standards of the modern Southern Baptist leadership, the "John Wayne of Texas Baptists" could not serve on any board of any agency or be employed by the Southwestern Baptist Theological Seminary that he founded!

B. H. Carroll was divorced from his first wife whom he married as

---

[44]*The Religious Herald* (Virginia) 9 August 1990.

a fifteen-year-old girl. A jury gave him a divorce on grounds of her infidelity.[45]

B. H. Carroll was the long-time pastor of the First Baptist Church in Waco, Texas, where he had women deacons! In his discussion of 1 Timothy 2:8 to 3:13, he questioned that the word we usually translate "wives" (meaning wives of deacons) meant that at all. The context, according to Carroll, "required the rendering: 'women deacons.'" He also said, "The Waco church of which I was pastor for so many years, had, by my suggestion and approval, a corps of spiritually minded, judicious female deacons who were very helpful, and in some delicate cases indispensable."[46]

It was said also that he smoked big, black cigars.

---

[45]James Spivey, "Benajah Harvey Carroll," in *Baptist Theologians*, ed. Timothy George and David Dockery (Nashville: Broadman, 1990) 307.

[46]B. H. Carroll, *The Pastoral Epistles of Paul, 1 and 2 Peter, Jude, and 1, 2, 3 John* (Grand Rapids: Baker Book House, Grand Rapids, n.d.) 45.

Chapter Eight

Is There a Way Out?

"Peace, Peace. . . . There Is No Peace."[1]

"Southern Baptists are in an identity crisis of major proportions," Harold Cole, recently retired chief executive of the South Carolina Baptist Convention, told a meeting of the Historical Society of South Carolina in March 1982.

> We are being told by some that we have been what we really never have been and that we are who we really are not. We have at this time no more urgent need than to grasp afresh who we are and what we are to do in the world. Behind the battle over labels, competing leadership styles and the struggle for institutional control, lies an agonizing effort to decide what and who we really are.
>
> Perhaps the major problem is fundamentalism with its new code word of inerrancy. This time it is more sophisticated and has a master strategy to take over the Southern Baptist Convention by seizing control of its institutions.[2]

Cole summed up well some of the growing confusion about the state of the denomination. People were, in fact, beginning to hear of "historic Baptist positions" that were neither historic nor Baptist positions. Diversity that had been there for a century was being addressed as though it was a new heresy. Denominational machinery was being seized for the promotion of narrow and reactionary purposes. This was a new phenomenon for Southern Baptists. No one could remember or find in history books anything like it. It was obvious by now that this was a "new day" and, to use the vocabulary of pilots and meteorologists, there

---

[1]Jeremiah 6:14 (New International Version).
[2]Baptist Press, 1 March 1982.

was towering cumulus in all quadrants threatening to become cumulo-nimbus storms.

A Survey of the Dilemma

It is not possible to understand the atmosphere and tension without a look at events that transpired during the middle years of the controversy. Roughly, they would range from about 1982 to 1987, when the direction seemed irrevocably fixed. A quick rehearsal of some of these events, as recorded by Baptist Press, will give some impression of the kaleidoscopic events and changes occurring.

1982

The naming of the convention committees in 1982 were withheld from the public until the first day of the convention. This report in the past had been the source of much controversy. The withholding now caused further controversy.[3]

Bailey Smith, retiring president, thought the "new peace" in the Southern Baptist Convention was his greatest contribution. His greatest surprise was the "national exposure" afforded the president. He admitted:

> I had no idea the visibility I would have. The leader of the denom-ination is in a different world. The president of the Southern Baptist Convention is a world leader. My name has been in every major news-paper—not only in America, but in Europe as well. . . . The Los Ange-les convention was a "harmonious convention. Only a man who believes in inerrancy could have brought the harmony. . . . Only a man who believes as I do could have brought the conservative forces together.[4]

One is forced to conclude that Smith had been talking or listening only to a small group of fundamentalist leaders or was singularly insensitive to the turmoil.

The fundamentalists promised not to bring the matter of school prayer

---

[3]Baptist Press, 6 April 1982.
[4]Baptist Press, 3 May 1982.

to the New Orleans convention.[5] As recounted above, no sooner than the announcement was made, a White House aide used right wing politician Ed McAteer to pass a resolution supporting President Reagan's constitutional amendment on school prayer.

In Rome, Georgia, at a press conference that was attended by only one newsperson, Jack Harwell of the *Christian Index*, Adrian Rogers, past president of the convention, said that doctrinal unity and program unity in the SBC rise and fall together. He noted that he was in favor of the denomination's cooperative efforts, but he felt it was "not only illogical, it is immoral to ask a man to support with his money and with his influence . . . things that are theologically repugnant to him." Southern Baptists "have made a golden calf of the program (Cooperative Program). . . . It's almost easier to be against the virgin birth than the program."[6]

Seven former presidents reacted to Rogers' statement by immediately defending the Cooperative Program, the unified mission budget of the convention. They acknowledged that it was not a perfect mechanism, but that it was far superior to the old societal method of financing missions and education.[7]

In his press interview Rogers had supported a change in *The Baptist Faith and Message* statement on scripture, favoring the reading that the Bible "is" truth rather than "has truth without any mixture of error for its matter." Former SBC presidents Herschel Hobbs, Carl E. Bates, Jimmy R. Allen, Owen Cooper, and Franklin Paschall all opposed the change. Paschall commented, "It's a distinction without a difference." Jaroy Weber, president in 1975-1976, said he could accept Roger's suggestion and understood that a motion would be made in the forthcoming convention to accomplish it.[8]

None of the four men who were considered likely to be nominated for the presidency wanted to see the Roger's suggestion adopted. Much press space was taken up with various potential nominees decrying what they thought was Rogers denigration of the Cooperative Program. None of this contributed to Bailey Smith's "new peace."[9]

---

[5]Baptist Press, 10 May 1982.
[6]Baptist Press, 14 May 1982.
[7]Baptist Press, 28 May 1982.
[8]Baptist Press, 4 June 1982.
[9]Baptist Press, 7 June 1982.

In June of 1982, during the opening session of the Southern Baptist Pastors Conference prior to the opening of the convention meeting in New Orleans, Vice President George Bush defended the religious right. He told 42,000 people in the Superdome that the movement represents a "healthy development." He added, "I think wisdom counsels us not to fear it, or to condemn it, but to welcome it, and I embrace the constructive contributions it can make to strengthening the United States as one nation under God."

Bush's remarks were among the most direct of any Reagan administration official on the movement that includes Jerry Falwell's Moral Majority, Christian Voice, and the Roundtable, which is a group headed by Southern Baptist layman Ed McAteer.[10]

McAteer would play a major role with the resolutions committee during this convention, coaching it on the Reagan Amendment resolution.

The SBC evangelists averted "a bitter battle which threatened to divide the 350 member association." They were debating the issue of the authority and duties of the executive director, and voted to transfer them to the elected officers. The conference was also troubled by charges that the president, Freddie Gage of Fort Worth was manipulating the conference as a "political machine" to support conservative causes centering on biblical inerrancy.[11]

James T. Draper, Jr. pastor of the First Baptist Church of Euless, Texas, was elected president of the convention over Duke K. McCall, president of the Baptist World Alliance. Draper was a conservative and the choice of the fundamentalists.

The fundamentalist control was not yet absolute. Gene Garrison, pastor of the First Baptist Church of Oklahoma City and a moderate, was elected over seven other candidates for second vice president of the convention.[12]

After the meeting in New Orleans, the Baptist Press heralded, "Conservatism Sweeps SBC in Resolutions, Election." The story read:

> After electing a conservative president for the third time in five years, the 20,437 messengers intensely debated and then adopted resolutions

---

[10]Baptist Press, 14 June 1982.
[11]Baptist Press, 17 June 1982.
[12]Baptist Press, 17 June 1982.

endorsing a constitutional amendment on prayer in public schools, encouraged the teaching of scientific creationism in public schools, and condemning abortion except when the life of the mother is endangered.

There were two successful challenges of nominees of the Committee on Boards to posts on the trustees of the Sunday School Board and one for a trustee on the Southeastern Seminary Board.

James Draper, newly elected president, in his first news conference rejected any alliance with conservatives who have sought to control the convention. He emphasized a desire to promote communication between conservatives and moderates.[13]

Draper, in a letter sent to 34 state paper editors and to Baptist Press, pledged to consult with the vice presidents during the year. The underlying issue had to do with the nominations to committees that the president by by-law was to make "in consultation with the vice presidents." Their first meeting was cordial.[14]

As the editors of the state papers reviewed the New Orleans meeting, they used terms such as uneasy, hostile, volatile, polarized, uncertain and tug-of-war to describe what went on there.

J. B. Fowler of the *Baptist New Mexican* said the "lack of trust that has developed across the denomination the last three or four years made this the most divisive convention I have attended since 1950 when I went to my first one in Houston."

Presnall Wood of the *Baptist Standard* of Texas wrote that Southern Baptists "left Los Angeles in 1981 thinking they had turned the corner on a wearisome controversy, but they left New Orleans still standing on the corner."

C. R. Daley of the Kentucky *Western Recorder* said that the meeting

is history and we are still together with no formal split in sight. . . . There were no clear winners but there were clearly some losers. They were Bold Mission Thrust, mutual trust among Southern Baptists and the "sweet, sweet spirit in this place" which we often sing about.

Al Shackleford, the editor of the Tennessee *Baptist and Reflector*,

---

[13]Baptist Press, 17 June 1982.
[14]Baptist Press, 1 July 1982.

said, "It is now evident that our convention has evolved into two political parties. . . . It was distressing . . . to see that on almost every issue faced the votes—and the debaters—were predictable, right down the party line." Most of the editors agreed that the struggle was over control.[15]

Soon after the convention meeting, Keith Parks, president of the Foreign Mission Board, told his trustees that he felt compelled to speak out against polarizing issues within the convention that were "not our first priority." "Missions is the spiritual magnet that has held iron-willed Southern Baptists together." Yet, "I came away from this convention with a feeling there had been an unconscious shifting of our focus." Parks said he believes that both he and elected members of the board, as well as staff, have an obligation to speak out against "anything that would hinder the foreign missions expression" of the denomination.[16]

In July, James Dunn, executive director of the Baptist Joint Committee on Public Affairs, told the Christian Life Commission conference that religious freedom, historically advocated by Baptists, is the most fundamental of freedoms and no outside force has the right to dictate another's inner convictions. Dunn said,

> Religious freedom goes back to the purpose of God in creation and is rooted in the very nature of God. God dared to create us free beings. This liberty is so sacred, so basic, so inalienable that God refuses to force his will on us. It is morally wrong to force one person to support another's religion.
>
> Unfortunately, some (Baptists)....have forgotten history, forsaken their identity as church-state separationists and embraced the medieval doctrines that we have so long resisted. They claim from the state both freedom and special privilege.[17]

The newly elected president, James Draper, addressed the trustees of the Sunday School Board in August. I had nominated Duke McCall as Draper's opponent at the June meeting in New Orleans. Draper debunked the idea that he and I were adversaries. He also debunked the idea that he was elected by Judge Paul Pressler. "I am owned by only one person, Jesus Christ." He acknowledged the pressures on him, from left and right,

---

[15]Baptist Press, 8 July 1982.
[16]Baptist Press, 14 July 1982.
[17]Baptist Press, 19 July 1982.

and joked, "I figure if I work it right, I'll have everybody mad at me by Pittsburgh (site of 1983 SBC)."

In a more serious vein, he commented, "There are some theological problems. . . . The blanket charge the seminaries are liberal is not true, nor is the blanket defense that there are no liberals. We do have some problems. We must look at them; deal with them." He commented that the problems would require a great deal of patience and warned, "We do not trust each other."[18]

William Self, pastor of Wieuca Road Baptist Church in Atlanta, told 2000 women at a leadership conference of Woman's Missionary Union at the Ridgecrest Conference Center that Southern Baptists were in danger of being stampeded from their goals of missions and evangelism into a swamp of creedalism. "We have a generation that doesn't know doctrine, and it will be this generation that will decide if we will enter the promised land God has called us to or if we will go back into the wilderness to wander." He also expressed distress over the mood of this year's SBC meeting, saying that there are factions within the convention that would substitute a political agenda for the spiritual mission.[19]

Morton Rose, vice president of the Sunday School Board for Church Programs and Services, invited Fred Wolfe, pastor of Cottage Hill Baptist Church, Mobile, Alabama, to visit the Board to see for himself the work and personnel. Wolfe, president of the SBC pastors conference, had been identified as a critic with growing influence. After his visit, Wolfe said that Southern Baptists needed to put aside philosophical differences, accept diversity that is inevitable, and begin to trust each other again. He said, however, that he did not believe that Pressler and Patterson maneuvered the elections of Adrian Rogers, Bailey Smith, or James Draper as presidents of the convention. (Wolfe went on to become a leader in the fundamentalist movement.)[20]

The Sunday School Board owns and operates Baptist Book Stores all over the country. At the dedication of a new Fort Worth store on the campus of Southwestern Seminary, I took opportunity to speak to the denomination. I commented that belief in the Bible is "paramount" but there are issues on the other side of orthodoxy, including soul competency of

---

[18]Baptist Press, 4 August 1982.
[19]Baptist Press, 18 August 1982.
[20]Baptist Press, 30 August 1982.

the believer, free exercise of religion, and equal participation in a free church in a free state. Commenting on the participation of a White House aide in the work of the resolutions committee at the recent meeting of the SBC, I felt it necessary to say, "I distrust religious decisions by politicians as much as I distrust political decisions by religious professionals." Commenting on the bookstore, I said, "Let there never come a day in Baptist life when we try to tell one another what to read; or come a day when we pile books together and burn them because we're afraid of error." (Little did I dream that the next history of the Sunday School Board, written by a professor of Southwestern Seminary, would be destroyed because the trustees thought it slanted.)[21]

In September, moderates led by Cecil Sherman of Asheville, North Carolina, offered a proposal to depoliticize the denominational presidency. They suggested that instead of the president having sole power to appoint the committee on committees, the source of presidential power, that these nominations be made by state leadership. The suggestions included having the executive secretary, state convention president, and chairman of the state executive board nominate four names for each state's positions on the committee on committees. From this list the SBC president in consultation with the two vice presidents would choose one layman and one ordained person to be appointed to the two positions. Similar provisions would be made for the committee on resolutions.

Draper was asked "voluntarily" to follow the procedure in his appointments and to support changes in the SBC Constitution and bylaws. President Draper rejected the idea. He added that he did not believe Southern Baptists would accept such a change and added he had contacted a "variety of leaders" in the denomination, "none of whom could support this."

Sherman was disappointed and frustrated by the response. The North Carolina pastor said the meeting was "congenial and harmonious," but the bottom line is that Draper, "in essence said 'No' and 'Trust me.' Sherman commented, "Well, I have been there before. Two years ago, I went to breakfast with Bailey Smith (then president of the SBC) and he said 'Trust me.' I had a hard time believing it then, and my misgivings were generously confirmed."[22]

---

[21]Baptist Press, 16 September 1982.
[22]Baptist Press, 17 September 1982.

At the September, 1982, meeting of the SBC Executive Committee, President Draper said that the president should retain "all of the discretion and initiative of the office." After saying "God wanted me to be president of the Southern Baptist Convention," he said the plan to depoliticize the convention's presidency would require that the president give up the only real power a convention president possesses: the power to appoint key denominational committees. He said that he was trying to establish communications within the denomination and told of his efforts to be a peacemaker within the strife-ridden denomination.[23]

This refrain would be heard again and again during his administration. He seemed to really try without dealing with the central issue. Whatever the rhetoric or efforts, the crux of the matter would be his appointments.

In October, President Draper met with eight other leaders to discuss ways to ameliorate the controversy. Seminary presidents Honeycutt of Southern and Dilday of Southwestern; William Hull of First Church, Shreveport; Adrian Rogers; Paige Patterson; Fred Wolfe, president of the SBC pastors conference; and convention vice-presidents John Sullivan and Gene Garrison attended. The group agreed that there were points beyond which they could not go, but there was room for negotiation. Dilday and Patterson were pleased that conversation was possible. Patterson and Draper, however, were not sure the meeting was "productive." Draper announced that he would call a larger group together soon.[24]

A few days before, W. A. Criswell warned that Baptists were in danger of losing their educational institutions to "the liberals." He criticized comments of Keith Parks, who had said that Baptists were straying from their purpose of missions. He criticized William Self, who recently warned of the "swamp of creedalism." He said, "The liberals are taking our institutions away one by one."[25]

The next week, President Draper affirmed Keith Parks and expressed regrets that Criswell, his former pastor, had said things critical of Parks that received wide publicity. Criswell "spoke hastily . . . and not accurately," according to Draper.

---

[23]Baptist Press, 22 September 1982.
[24]Baptist Press, 7 October 1982.
[25]Baptist Press, 4 October 1982.

At Southwestern Seminary, Draper told the faculty that he wanted fair representation of all theological views in the classrooms of the colleges and seminaries. He said, "Most conservatives would be happy with parity in our classrooms. We would be happy with a fair presentation of all views, but we should make a concrete attempt to bring known conservatives to our faculties."[26]

These views would be popular for a time. Parity became the code word of the fundamentalists until the power base was completed. Then, the demand would be for faculties of the "conservative" position—all this in spite of the fact that the vast majority of the seminary faculty members would be classified as conservative by any impartial judge.

During the fall state conventions, many of the controversial issues of the SBC were dealt with by the states. Generally, these debates did not reach the emotional level of the national body. Most had fairly peaceful meetings, often opposing the prayer amendment and supporting the Cooperative Program, the national unified mission budget.

In November, President Draper held his next meeting of leaders to discuss the problems. Forty persons representing all sectors of denominational life met. Most came away from the meeting talking about the depth and seriousness of the differences.

In this meeting, fundamentalist leader Paige Patterson raised six questions that agency heads especially should consider. The first two concerned "parity" or representation of inerrantists on faculties, administrations, and boards of agencies and in the literature and books published by the Sunday School Board. The third concerned coverage of the views of inerrantists in the denominational press. The fourth asked if assurances could be provided that those "theologians and denominational executives who do not adhere to inerrancy can be counted upon to state publicly, clearly and unambiguously precisely what they do believe without hesitancy and without duplicity?" The fifth sought assurances that students who are inerrantists will not be harassed in state or SBC-related institutions. The sixth sought a financial plan that provided for a system in which Southern Baptists could participate without the necessity of supporting that which is morally and theologically repugnant to them.

Don Harbuck, pastor of First Baptist Church, El Dorado, Arkansas, commented at the close of the meeting: "Our differences are probably

---

[26]Baptist Press, 18 October 1982.

wider than they have ever been; our diversity is greater than it has ever been." He felt the denomination could remain intact, "provided that the judgmental spirit and exclusivistic posture of fundamentalism does not insist upon a narrowing of our common faith to the point that many significant segments of Southern Baptist life are excluded."[27]

On the same day the leaders met, the group organized to counter the takeover voted to disband. Kenneth Chafin, pastor of South Main Church in Houston, told the press,

> We found that the state paper editors tried to paint us as part of the problem. They can't even tell the difference between the fellow who sets the house on fire and the fireman who comes to put it out. Well, as far as I am concerned...the firemen have all gone home.
>
> Now there is only one group stirring the waters and that is the group that is trying to convince Southern Baptists that their institutions have been corrupted by people who do not believe the Bible.

Chafin was critical of agency executives for not fighting for themselves and their agencies. He also said that the fundamentalist group was "basically dishonest. They repeatedly deny they are part of any group or that there is any political activity. It is pretty difficult to negotiate with a group that won't even admit they are a group."

Cecil Sherman, another leader of the denominational loyalists, said that the future of the group would not be decided until a steering committee meeting on November 29, 1982. He also criticized denominational executives for vacillating. "It seems that they are so intent on harmony that it has become the end all."[28]

As the year came to an end, the future for the Southern Baptist Convention was far from certain.

Southeastern Seminary president Randall Lolley told Georgia Baptists,

> Your six southern Baptist seminaries are magnificently unalike—just like Baptists are not alike. but they are together. . . . God has not used a cookie cutter at Southern or New Orleans, at Midwestern or Golden Gate. . . . Together but not alike! United through diversity.[29]

---

[27]Baptist Press, 16 November 1982.
[28]Baptist Press, 16 November 1982.
[29]Baptist Press, 6 December 1982.

In my annual address to state leadership in Nashville, I called on the executives to emphasize democracy and soul competency. Acknowledging that we were a diverse group, it seemed necessary to say that not in my lifetime have the agencies of the SBC and the state conventions been so keenly sensitive to the will of Baptists as they were that day.[30]

On the same day, two members of the Sunday School Board presidential search committee reported that their work was progressing harmoniously without pressures from any special interest group. Continued health problems had necessitated an early retirement for me, though I could not be relieved of my responsibilities for another year.

1983

In January of 1983, a new independent journal was born and named *SBC Today*. It was founded by Walker L. Knight, soon to retire from the Home Mission Board. The purpose was to give news and information about the Southern Baptist Convention on a timely and national basis. The fundamentalists thought that it was to be a journal of the "moderates." In the light of the attempts to control the press by the fundamentalists, it was a welcome outlet for opinions other than the party line.

In late January, W. A. Criswell, pastor of the largest Southern Baptist Church (Dallas)in the country, gave a press interview in which he said that the SBC is declining and will be replaced as the major evangelical denomination in the United States. He said, "I think we will erode. . . . I think we will gradually acquiesce. God will raise up somebody else to take our place." His predictions were based on his feeling that "infidels" were taking over the colleges and seminaries and that the denomination was turning away from evangelism.[31]

Russell Dilday, president of Southwestern Seminary, speaking to a group of 170 pastors and denominational leaders in Nashville, said in February 1983,

> It is my firm conviction Southern Baptists are still a Bible-believing, Bible-teaching people. The problem is people are confusing biblical

---

[30]Baptist Press, 13 December 1982.
[31]Baptist Press, 27 January 1983.

authority with biblical interpretation. . . . The Bible has always been the sole authority for faith and practice among Southern Baptists.

In discussing inerrancy, he said that he believed,

The Bible is inerrant and infallible in its function and should therefore be judged on the basis of its purpose. . . . The purpose of the Bible is to lead men to Jesus Christ. We should be concerned with the results and not the process, because God did not choose to reveal his word to us in exact, scientific and technical terms. . . . Once we get away from the technicalities of language we find out there is not all that much difference in what we believe. Southern Baptists are unified in their commitment to the Word of God.[32]

As dissatisfaction grew over the direction of the denomination, various people began to search for ways to contribute to the work of those agencies they approved of and skip the others. A study committee on the Cooperative Program (the unified missions budget) issued a recommendation that included: "that Cooperative Program gifts from churches which by church action elect to exclude certain budgeted causes from their undesignated gifts be considered by the Southern Baptist Convention as Cooperative Program funds."

The recommendation was withdrawn when the report was presented to the Executive Committee in February, 1983. At that juncture in the controversy, the denominational loyalists were trying to protect the unified giving program to insure the income of the mission boards and the seminaries. In the years to come as the fundamentalists tightened their grip on the denomination, the opposite would be true. The loyalists would be clamoring for a way to bypass the Pressler-Patterson-controlled agencies in favor of the more moderate ones.[33]

In May, the Committee on Boards, chaired by Charles Stanley of Atlanta, released its report. This early release followed a request by James Draper, convention president, that the report be released early. Of the report, Stanley said that the committee has been

fair in nominating people who really, truly, represent the full spectrum

---

[32]Baptist Press, 18 February 1983.
[33]Baptist Press, 23 February 1983.

of Southern Baptists. We've not undercut anybody, we've not tried to take a lot of people off, we have been I think, considerate of people who have been there and serving.[34]

Less than a week later, the SBC "moderates" announced that they would make no organized efforts at this year's annual meeting in Pittsburgh to challenge incumbent president Draper or the nominations to the boards of trustees. Cecil Sherman, moderate leader commented,

> This committee on boards has removed the eccentrics, the strange people. It is filled with people who are doctrinaire, narrow. They are one kind of Baptist. They are people who have a low estimate of our schools and publishing house, are basically critical of the denomination but continue to give some kind of support to it.

This committee on boards has surgically excised the kind of Southern Baptists who will not conform (to their kind of fundamentalism). The exclusion is not an accident; it is a very meticulous thing.

David Sapp, pastor of the First Baptist Church of Chamblee, Georgia, added that the report "is pretty right wing . . . representing only one element of the convention. It would be hard to attack, however."[35]

Baptist Press predicted in May, 1983 that the inerrancy faction of the convention was expected to conserve previous gains but launch no new strategies at the June meeting in Pittsburgh. Paige Patterson, inerrantist leader, commented, "We really don't have much agenda for Pittsburgh. We hope Pittsburgh will be a reasonably peaceful convention."

Baptist Press commented that with an incumbent president generally sympathetic to their views, a very conservative slate of nominees to serve on SBC boards, strongly conservative statements on abortion, doctrinal integrity, belief and support of the Constitutional amendment on school prayer already in place, the inerrancy faction is not expected to launch any new battles but merely to react to challenges to these gains.

The Baptist Joint Committee on Public Affairs would come in for its share of criticism. It had continued the former SBC line on the prayer amendment by opposing it. This did not make the inerrantists happy.

---

[34]Baptist Press, 5 May 1983.
[35]Baptist Press, 11 May 1983.

Patterson commented, "If the board of trustees cannot control them (and keep) them from misrepresenting the views of Baptists to the public and the government, then the only alternative is to defund it. . . . [It] has not represented conservative concerns."[36]

The June convention went about as expected. James Draper, who had frequently called for peace, was reelected without opposition—the only incumbent in a dozen years to do so. A spirited argument rose as to whether the convention should meet in Las Vegas in 1989. Some thought a Christian body should not meet in what they felt was the capital of sin. Others argued that the convention should give testimony about the gospel in the city of legalized gambling. The body approved the building of a new SBC building in Nashville to cost about eight million dollars. This action would cause problems for years.

All challenges to persons on the Committee on Boards reports were "brushed aside." This was the end of an era.

One resolution praised the denomination's seminary professors and asked trustees of the six SBC seminaries to be responsible for seeing that professors abide by denominational and institutional statements of faith.[37]

Reaction to the Pittsburgh convention was a little more favorable from some of those threatened by the rightist course of the immediate years past. Wake Forest University professor, E. Glenn Hinson (he would soon return to Southern Seminary) expressed "cautious optimism" over the actions of the convention and felt that the "Baptist idea of voluntariness in religion will survive." He said that from the beginning Baptists have affirmed the idea that "to be authentic, faith must be free; to be authentic, religion must be voluntary religion."[38] He felt that President Draper deserved credit for efforts to bring peace

Samuel T. Currin, a protégé of Senator Jesse Helms of North Carolina, was elected by the convention to a place on the Baptist Joint Committee on Public Affairs and immediately opposed the stance of that group on the public school prayer amendment before the Senate Judiciary Committee. Currin was named chair of the SBC liaison group to the Joint Committee, called the Public Affairs Committee. Before he ever met with or consulted the Joint Committee, Currin stated his support of the prayer

---

[36]Baptist Press, 13 May 1983.
[37]Baptist Press, 16 June 1983.
[38]Baptist Press, 23 June 1983.

amendment to the Senate. His letter indicated that as chairman of the committee, he was speaking in the name of the committee.[39] Currin was at the time United States District Attorney for the Eastern District of North Carolina.

Within days, twelve of the fifteen members of the committee publicly disclaimed the letter and denied that the chairman was speaking for the committee. I felt it necessary to say to the press,

> In my opinion, no Baptist can speak for another Baptist and no committee chairman can speak for a committee without proper authorization. The committee itself needs to meet and authorize any statement that purports for speak for the committee.[40]

In the first meeting that he called, Currin made a series of moves indicating his intent to take charge and move it toward the fundamentalist agenda. The committee, a liaison group, usually did not meet except for specific reasons satisfactory to the members. He attempted to set up a series of regular meetings. The agency executives who were members did not like his ideas and refused to give in to his demands. He did not yet have the votes to get his way. We left the meeting believing that rightwing politicians had an agenda that was not suitable for this body. We were proved to be prophets—without honor in any country.

And the tune went on.

A South Carolina church ordained a woman and called her as pastor.

The appeal of a Clarksdale, Mississippi, Baptist church school to stay an investigation of its tax-exempt status pending the outcome of an appeal was denied.

James L. Sullivan, my predecessor at the Sunday School Board, told the Home Mission Board staff that both groups in the controversy were wrong when they wanted to kick the other out of the convention. He advised some method should be sought to bring all toward the center of the theological spectrum.

President Reagan renewed his pledge to seek enactment of a tuition tax credit law. The announcement was made by a leader of the New Right coalition, Paul Weyrich. His intention would further divide Baptists.

---

[39]Baptist Press, 28 June 1983.
[40]Baptist Press, 1 July 1983.

Professor J. W. MacGorman of Southwestern Baptist Seminary said that there was an answer to the problems of the denomination. He said, "If all of us would listen attentively to the Father and be attentive enough to his leadership, that is the ultimate answer." He was, of course, right. However. . . .

Stan Hastey, director of information services for the Baptist Joint Committee, told the annual conference of Americans United for Separation of Church and State that the Religious Right does not represent the conservative viewpoint on First Amendment issues. Hastey said,

> They espouse in fact a radical view. Those who are the real conservatives on First Amendment question are those . . . who join the late Justice William O. Douglas in contending the the "First Amendment says what it means and means what it says."

Five women Southern Baptist pastors stated in October that they knew they were "bucking the system," but each claimed a strong call from God into a pastoral ministry.

Bill Moyers, then a correspondent and senior news analyst with CBS evening news, told the Religious Liberty Conference that Baptists

> cannot turn away from politics just because it is not the place where souls are saved. . . . For Baptists possessed of a civic self, politics, like tolerance, is desirable because it is necessary. Here is where liberty will be saved or lost, laws deliberated, issues decided, justice mediated and values defended.

In October of 1983, President Draper called again for unity within the denomination on the things that are essential. He said that Baptists must agree to disagree on the things that are not essential to salvation. He commented that one thing that is not essential and on which agreement is not necessary is the question of ordination of women. The spirits of many were willing, but the flesh of others was weak.

The issue of women deacons was providing the occasion for outbreaks on controversy in Oklahoma City and Chicago.

Anthony Campolo, a sociology professor at Eastern College, told a lay renewal conference that Christians must give up their struggle for power and attempt to deliver the world of its evils through love.

Midwestern Seminary trustees approved a report from their instructional committee concerning professor G. Temp Sparkman. He "does not teach or advocate universalism, but rather he teaches in accordance with the seminary's statement of faith with reference to this matter." The survey of his theological views was done after a letter expressing concern was mailed to each trustee in June, 1983, by a Kansas City layman. No evidence existed that he had first talked with Sparkman.

This mode of attacking professors and executives would become almost a standard procedure.

In their fall meeting, the Alabama Baptist Convention passed a resolution asking that funding for the Baptist Joint Committee on Public Affairs be totally withdrawn. The motion on the resolution was divisive in the convention, with a motion to refer failing by 244-213 vote. The campaign of the fundamentalists was gathering momentum and would continue for years.

In December, President Draper's proposal to name a committee to draw up some "irreducible minimums" for Baptist belief, drew replies from a wide range of opinion. Creedalism versus confessionalism formed the framework for the discussion. There was little evidence that this recommendation was going anywhere. Draper was seeking a place where all Baptists could stand. Many thought this was not the way to stake out the territory. The argument was to gain more momentum.

In my annual address to state convention leaders, I named four issues which were creating confusion in the denomination. They were (1) charges of liberalism in institutions, (2) debates about creeds, (3) election of trustees, (4) efforts to make peripheral issues a test of faith. I suggested that the charges of liberalism had been heard for forty years and thought the time had come to say "Who is it? We need specifics. If they are here, name them and we'll help you get rid of them. If they exist only in some one's imagination, let us prove it and get on with the work of the Lord."[41]

On the positive side, I said, Southern Baptists enjoy many strengths, including freedom, a common heritage, common bonds of interdependence, and great resources. "Our freedom allows for differences without rupture of fellowship." The speech was reported at length by Baptist Press and sent to all the state papers, some of which reported it.

---

[41]Baptist Press, 9 December 1983.

So 1983 ended with much stirring among the brethren with more to come. By now, everyone had an opinion, and it seemed that no one was listening.

1984

Beginning in January of 1984, there was more of the same. James Dunn, executive director of the Baptist Joint Committee, declined renomination to a second term on the board of directors of People for the American Way. His membership on this board had caused a lot of controversy. This did little to quiet his opposition. Albert Lee Smith, one term congressman from Alabama, said that the only way to stop the opposition was for Dunn to resign.

The frequently vocal Sam Currin was glad that Dunn refused further service. He said, "I feel that PAW is antagonistic to everything we stand for," adding that he had refused to attend a BJCPA-sponsored religious liberty conference in October "because some representatives from PAW were on the program. I felt if I went, I would have betrayed the SBC."[42]

At the February meeting, the SBC's Executive Committee continued to seek "common ground," pointing to efforts for missions and evangelism and against hunger, pornography, and abortion as areas of agreement.

In evaluating Draper's efforts at peace, he appears to have been the most conciliatory of the presidents elected by the fundamentalist movement. He actually reached out to both sides in an effort to find that common ground he spoke about. The basic problem was that in spite of his efforts, he could not control either side. The only way he could have influenced the outcome would have been with appointments that represented the broad spectrum of the convention. This would have won him friends among the moderates but would have alienated the fundamentalists. It appeared by this time that the die was cast and that there was no way back.

The Executive Committee rejected the Alabama convention's request to withdraw funding of the Baptist Joint Committee. The vote was unanimous. This matter would be raised again and again until the convention defunded the Committee completely in 1991.

---

[42]Baptist Press, 20 January 1984.

President Draper named the Tellers Committee for the forthcoming convention meeting in Kansas City in February. It was balanced and seemed to be a step in the right direction.

Also in February, a group of pastors announced that there would be another pre-convention meeting for pastors and others called "The Forum." The meeting would be an alternative to the Pastor's Conference, which had become a "revivalistic religio-political platform."[43]

James Draper reviewed his presidency in March of 1984. He felt that Southern Baptists were less likely to "kill each other" now than they had been two years ago. He thought that there was more openness now among the SBC executives to "input and inquiry." He thought that there was "an admission" by institutional leadership that Southern Baptists have some "substantive differences." Admission of that fact is "a giant step" toward dealing with it.[44]

The matter of ordained women continued to plague the Home Mission Board. In its meeting in March, 1984, the board reaffirmed its policy of not requiring ordination as a qualification for missionary appointment. Ordination is a matter for the local church according to the action. However, bitter debate surfaced. One member said he "deeply resents" the board's publishing a mission study book, entitled *We Spell Missions AMERICA*, that included the testimony of a woman who had been ordained. He said, "This article is a veiled criticism and condemnation of those of us who take a Bible-centered position on the issue of ordination of women. The gist of the article is pro-ordination of women."[45]

At Southeastern Seminary, three fundamentalist leaders said that they were encouraged by progress they had made in the past five years in getting "equity" for their views in the nation's largest Protestant denomination. The three said they wanted their view that scripture is without error taught at the six Southern Baptist seminaries and reflected by the other 14 agencies. Appearing with Paul Pressler and Russell Kammerling, Paige Patterson said: "We have seen no substantive effort on the part of any institutions or agencies to date to rectify the injustice that presently exists in representation." He did praise the efforts of

---

[43]Baptist Press, 29 February 1984.
[44]Baptist Press, 2 March 1984.
[45]Baptist Press, 15 March 1984.

William Tanner at the Home Mission Board as being sensitive to the desires of the fundamentalists.

Pressler claimed the inerrancy movement had had an impact and "the direction of the convention is irrevocably set. I do not think there will be any reversing of the direction that is now set."

Patterson said, "If I were personally selecting the faculty . . . yes, the whole faculty would be inerrantists."[46]

On March 21, 1984, the Senate defeated President Reagan's proposed constitutional amendment to permit vocal, organized public school prayer. The vote was 44 against and 56 favoring, only 11 votes short of the two-thirds majority required to pass a constitutional amendment.

There was ample evidence by May that the Baptist Joint Committee on Public Affairs would be the center of continuing controversy. In an interview with Bobby Terry, editor of *Word and Way*, news journal of the Missouri Baptist Convention, James Dunn went to the heart of the matter. When asked why the Committee had become the center of controversy, Dunn gave two reasons.

First, he said, religious liberty and church-state separation had never received more national attention than in the last three years. He illustrated by naming school prayer, tuition tax credit, the constitutional convention, court stripping, religious and civil liberty issues, an ambassador to the Roman Catholic Church, tax exemption for church-related schools, and a wide range of government intrusion questions related to the Internal Revenue Service, local zoning ordinances, historical commissions, city councils, and others.

The second thing he mentioned was the apparent erosion, or the illusion of erosion, within Southern Baptist life of their historic commitment to a very dedicated stance on church-state separation. These two major trends had converged.[47]

There were serious problems for the moderates as convention time approached. They had difficulties finding a presidential candidate who had a chance of getting elected. This was a continuing problem. On two occasions, I had been approached by a group of behind-the-scenes denominationalists asking me to stand for president. I could not while I was president of the Sunday School Board. By the time I had retired early in

---

[46]Baptist Press, 15 March 1984.
[47]Baptist Press, 31 May 1984.

1984, the issues were so firmly fixed and the resistance to a denomination-al leader so firm that there was little chance any one of us could suc-ceed. We had been put in the category the judge called "liberals," and of course no review of sermons, addresses, and writings would convince the unconvincable. The need for another sacrificial lamb was so great, how-ever, that I was persuaded to let my name be submitted. Health was a genuine problem, and I had great reluctance to risk what was left. John Sullivan, pastor of Broadmoor Baptist Church, Shreveport, had decided to run for president as a middle-of-the-roader. My supporters and his talked the matter over. He would not withdraw, and because of my commitment to supporters I could not withdraw. The fundamentalists told the press before the election that "Grady Cothen is a representative of the radical left." We felt that Sullivan could not be elected for a variety of reasons. He was sure I couldn't be. In fact, neither of us could have been elected and I was sure of it and I think he was too.

It turned out we were both right; we got beat on the first ballot by a man who was virtually uninvolved in Southern Baptist life—Charles Stanley, pastor of First Baptist Church of Atlanta. He was widely known for his television work but had attended perhaps only one or two meet-ings of the SBC before his election. His church contributed very little to cooperative Baptist causes, (2.1 percent of undesignated receipts, by Stan-ley's admission); he sponsored his own missionaries and had little to do with Georgia Baptists. He was, obviously, the choice of the fundament-alists. Interestingly, in his press conference after the election, he declared,

> I was not elected by any particular group; I can guarantee you that. . .
> . It was not until this morning (Tuesday) that I was willing to say yes
> to the Lord. And I had to say yes to him out of pressure from him and
> not from anybody else in this world.

In that prayer meeting, among others, were former SBC presidents Bailey Smith and Adrian Rogers, and fundamentalist leaders Paul Pressler and Paige Patterson. He said that he did not believe in women exercising authority over men when asked about women's ordination. He favored the prayer amendment of President Reagan. He was a founding member of Moral Majority and remained a director of The Roundtable, a political organization founded by Ed McAteer. His son was a student at an independent Baptist seminary.[48]

The nomination of Paul Pressler to the SBC Executive Committee was sustained over a challenge to substitute a well-known pastor, Bruce McIver, to the post. The convention refused to substitute nominations from the floor for those nominated by the committee on nominations.

The press heralded, "Ultra Conservatives Hold Convention." At last, the fundamentalists passed a resolution opposing women as pastors or deacons. The only vote the moderates won was narrowly turning back an effort to defund the Baptist Joint Committee on Public Affairs.[49]

By now the controversy affected every facet of Baptist life. There seemed to be at this juncture a new direction on the part of some of the chief executives of the denominational agencies.

Russell Dilday, president of Southwestern Seminary, took the offensive. He wrote in the July issue of *Southwestern News*, which was circulated to 35,000 alumni, former students, and friends, that the real issue in the strife did not involve conservative versus liberal theology. An evidence of this, he said, is that "leading conservatives with unquestioned orthodoxy are voicing their opposition to the fundamentalist political machine." He warned that it was not rumor but fact that fundamentalist had put together what he called

a powerful machine, computerized, national in scope and aimed at control of the democratic processes of this convention. . . . The issue divides itself more accurately along the lines of "the spirit of Southern Baptist cooperation" on the one side and "the spirit of independent fundamentalism" on the other.[50]

Dilday would be vocal on the issues for two years to come. He would pay a heavy personal price for his stance.

William Tanner, president of the Home Mission Board lamenting a trend toward "politicization of the Southern Baptist Convention," called for unity within diversity in Baptists' mission efforts. Tanner said that he came away from the convention meeting feeling that both the Home and Foreign Mission Boards' reports to the convention were given "polite but

---

[48]Baptist Press, 13 June 1984.
[49]Baptist Press, 14 June 1984.
[50]Baptist Press, 13 July 1984.

inconsequential hearings. I did not feel the response to either report by our convention indicated a great sense of burden, urgency or expectancy that has been characteristic of our people in days gone by."[51]

President Tanner had grasped the greatest tragedy of the controversy.

In August, President Stanley of the SBC spoke at a political rally in Atlanta where Pat Swindall and Bill Bronson were seeking votes for congressional seats.

Later in the same month, president Charles Stanley and former presidents Draper and Rogers agreed to serve on the executive board of the new American Coalition for Traditional Values (ACTV). Another former president Bailey Smith is a member of ACTV's board of governors.[52] It is true that they acted as individuals, but it is equally true that they could not divorce themselves from the high office of president of the Southern Baptist Convention. Baptists, again, by association at least, seemed to be supporting the right-wing political agenda.

ACTV had identified ten basic concerns by which it planned to measure political candidates. Headed by a constitutional amendment prohibiting abortion, the list included support for a public school prayer amendment, tuition tax credits, and opposition to homosexual rights, pornography, and "misguided" welfare programs.[53]

At the fall convocation at Southern Seminary, President Roy Honeycutt joined his seminary colleague from Southwestern Seminary when he spoke of "holy war" against "unholy forces, which if left unchecked, will destroy essential qualities of both our convention and this seminary." He said the "independent fundamentalists" had a breakfast meeting in Kansas City, in an effort to "enlist campus subversives." He also charged "one of the Texas leaders" had called a student who frequently drives the (seminary) president's car to see if he could provide "anything . . . which might be of help . . . to the independent fundamentalist party."[54]

He was immediately challenged to public debate in at least three locations by Paige Patterson. He called Honeycutt' convocation speech "a demonstration of denominational fascism which is determined to brook

---

[51]Baptist Press, 2 August 1984.
[52]Baptist Press, 30 August 1984.
[53]Ibid.
[54]Ibid.

no criticism and will do whatever is necessary to squelch and suppress it." Paul Pressler, concerning the student driver, said, "I cannot imagine what he is talking about in reference to the student driver. I do not know anyone who drives for him."

On September 14, Stafford Durham, third year student at Southern Seminary and former driver for president Honeycutt, filed a formal complaint with the Federal Communications Commission, alleging that Pressler secretly tape recorded a telephone conversation on September 1. The student said,

> We talked for approximately one hour, during which time the conversation was tape recorded by Judge Paul Pressler without my knowledge . . . and without a beeper to indicate a recorder was in use.
> . . . I had no knowledge the conversation had been taped until I read the article in which Judge Pressler admitted to playing our private conversation to the reporter.

Durham further said that he talked to Pressler in Houston in 1979 and attended a Heart of America Bible Conference in Louisville in November of 1979 and spent about a day with him.[55]

Pressler replied, "No honest person should object to a record being kept of what he says" in response to the filing of a formal Federal Communications Commission complaint against him. He did agree that he had had prior contact with the student on three occasions. He denied that he knew the student had been the president's driver.[56]

While in Nashville for the Executive Committee meeting in September, 1984, SBC president Charles Stanley met with the members of the Southern Baptist Press Association. This group included Baptist Press editors and editors of the state Baptist papers.

Stanley said it was only after God brought him to his knees and caused him to weep that he finally submitted to God's will to be nominated for president. He said he was "not president out of choice, not by a coalition, but because I could not live with myself if I had not said, 'God, if you would like to publicly humiliate me to do something else in my life that's fine.'"

---

[55]Baptist Press, 17 September 1984.
[56]Baptist Press, 18 September 1984.

He told the group that he understood the concern of many over the percentage his church gives to the SBC unified budget (2.1 percent of undesignated receipts) and his lack of prior involvement in the convention. He said that he was trying to improve the contributions to the Cooperative Program. He had been "deeply encouraged" by visits he had made to SBC agencies and institutions in recent months, particularly a visit several weeks ago with SBC Foreign Mission Board personnel. Stanley said, "This emphasis on evangelism is a vital point of view that needs to be conveyed to most Southern Baptists."[57]

In his address to the Executive Committee, Stanley had appealed for the application of the "love principle" in the denomination. He defined it as "the willingness to accept others with whom you might not agree and who might not accept you."

Porter Routh, retired executive of the Executive Committee, called on Stanley in an open letter to use this principle in naming the Committee on Committees. Routh said that he asked himself what a layman with fifty years of experience in Baptist life could do to help a young president who did not have much experience in denominational life. He decided to recommend that the SBC president appoint elected state leadership to the committee. He suggested that Stanley appoint the state convention presidents and the presidents of the state Woman's Missionary Unions. These were popularly elected persons in each state, represented no known political agenda, and would be composed of a broad spectrum of Southern Baptists who were supporters of missions and evangelism.

Routh said that he had made a similar suggestion to Bailey Smith when he was president—this time recommending state presidents only—and that Smith had liked the idea. He did not follow it, saying, "After I had checked it out, it didn't seem as good as it was at first."

Stanley's associate in Atlanta said that Stanley would have no comment "at this time."[58] He did not follow the suggestion. Once again, the rhetoric did not fit the act.

As the differences escalated, W. A. Criswell, a graduate of Southern Seminary, on hearing President Honeycutt's criticism of the fundamentalist movement, demanded that the president resign. He said that

---

[57]Ibid.
[58]Baptist Press, 4 October 1984.

Honeycutt should not criticize the people who pay his salary.[59] This refrain became a rallying cry by the fundamentalists as they demanded that any employee of any institution or agency refrain from differing from any decision of the movement leadership. This call, repeated frequently, would become a major factor in quieting any opposition from traditional professional leadership.

As a rallying cry for opposition, this "he who pays the piper calls the tune" attitude was unprecedented. If it had been applied to most of the new leadership of the convention, they would have had few votes.

The faculty of Southern Seminary adopted a resolution affirming belief "without reservation, in the inspiration and authority of the Bible and all that the Bible affirms about itself." The document, "A Resolution of Gratitude and Commitment to Southern Baptists" expressed thanks to Southern Baptists for 125 years of prayer and financial support of theological education through the seminary and reaffirmed the faculty's commitment to "Jesus Christ as Lord and to the centrality of the Bible for all matters of faith and practice"[60] The olive branch was extended by an harassed faculty.

At Southwestern Seminary, a motion was made in the fall (1984) trustee meeting to instruct President Dilday to stay out of denominational politics. One unnamed trustee said that about seven out of thirty trustees favored the motion. At this juncture in the controversy, trustees were unwilling to silence the president. Two executive sessions were held during the trustee meeting. This is an unusual procedure in Southern Baptist life, usually reserved for matters related to personnel decisions.[61]

In a new moderate publication, *The Call,* among other calls for denominational peace, T. B. Maston, long-time professor at Southwestern Seminary and distinguished ethicist, commented that the conflict was

> the most serious that the convention has faced in my lifetime. . . . It is unfortunate that some well-trained and effective pastors are permitting themselves to be used or manipulated by the relatively few who are in basic control of the (fundamentalist) movement. This, to me personally, is the most serious disappointment in the whole matter.

---

[59]Baptist Press, 10 October 1984.
[60]Baptist Press, 16 October 1984.
[61]Baptist Press, 18 October 1984.

He predicted, "Unless there is a split within the ranks or a change of leadership of the movement to take over the Southern Baptist Convention, the ultimate results of the takeover would be a disaster for and to Southern Baptists."[62]

The fall meetings of the state conventions revealed a wide variety of responses to the conflict. Several states affirmed women in ministry, at least one affirmed women's ordination, and others reacted to the church-state problems pressed on the denomination by the activities of the fundamentalists and the resistance of the moderates.

The issues were rapidly penetrating the state organizations.

In November of 1984, Franklin Paschall, former president of the convention, proposed the formation of a committee to study and recommend actions to end the controversy. He suggested in the meetings in Tennessee and Kentucky that

> the Southern Baptist Convention authorize the appointment of a committee which would include representatives of our agencies and leaders of the conservative group who feel there has been a departure from what is commonly believed among us as expressed in *The Baptist Faith and Message*. This committee would report to the . . . Convention as soon as possible on specific ways to affect reconciliation, strengthen unity, and equip us to meet the awesome challenge of today's world with the glorious gospel of Christ.[63]

The suggestion was to be adopted by the convention in a radically different form and would occupy attention for years to come. Interestingly, no agency executive was to be on the committee and only one former executive.

Groups in a number of states on both sides of the conflict held meetings late in 1984 and 1985 to rally support for their causes. Presidents Honeycutt of Southern Seminary and Dilday of Southwestern Seminary spoke often and vigorously in support of their institutions and traditional Baptist positions.

Missionaries home on furlough acknowledged that the controversy was damaging missions as the growth of gifts declined and budgets were

---

[62]Baptist Press, 14 October 1984.
[63]Baptist Press, 19 November 1984.

held at the level of the previous year or lowered.

Students at Baylor University organized "Informed Baptist Students" to disseminate information about the convention.

Other Baylor students presented to the president a "student manifesto" asking that specific professors "be reproved and instructed in sound doctrine." Listing campus activities that dishonor God, the three-page document said that to call Baylor a Christian university "blasphemes the name of Christ." It also said that the faculty should be required to sign a statement of their personal salvation experience and members of the administration should openly support the pro-life movement or be dismissed.[64]

1985

Paul Pressler addressed a meeting of Oklahoma pastors in Oklahoma City in January, saying he was "in the area" to preach a weekend revival 190 miles to the southeast. He denied that the two-hour luncheon was anything more than a friendly informative get-together. He said about the coming convention meeting in Dallas in June that "God hasn't brought us this far to lose." He said that he updated the participants on "how liberals are organizing to wage Roy Honeycutt's holy war on Southern Baptists with Cooperative Program funds."[65]

In February, Pressler brought "four hours of testimony" and "35 grievances" against Baptist Press to the meeting of the Executive Committee, where he now had official status as a member. He focusd in subcommittee meetings on two press releases in September. In the first, the accusations of the Southern Seminary student were reported. It was issued on September 17. The reply of Pressler to the charges was released on September 18. Pressler was angry that the first story was released without his reply.

In the administrative and convention's arrangements subcommittee, Pressler passed out a seven-point, 65 page stack of documents detailing his complaints against Baptist Press. In his written presentation, Pressler listed 35 objections to the story about the student and the phone recording. He also charged that Baptist Press "gives liberals in the

---

[64]Baptist Press, 19 December 1984.
[65]Baptist Press, 18 January 1985.

convention full and ample opportunity to respond" to accusations, but "conservatives are not always afforded that privilege."[66]

In response to the Pressler charges previously expressed, the Southern Baptist Press Association had commissioned a special inquiry into the incident. The six-page report was prepared by journalism professors John Merril of Louisiana State University, Clifford Christians of the University of Illinois, and John DeMott of Memphis State University. All three were members of the ethics subcommittee of the Association for Education in Journalism's committee on professional freedom and responsibility.

The journalism professors said they found no "evidence of ill will toward Pressler" and no evidence the Baptist Press staff was "motivated by unprofessional intentions to damage the reputations of the principals involved." The issue was that the two reports were released on succeeding days. The professors commented, "Release of the report of Sept. 17, without the response of Pressler, was not unfair under the peculiar circumstances existing." They described Baptist Press's dilemma this way: "Should a reporter report the news immediately, even though the response to some accusation contained in it cannot be included in the first report, . . . or should he suppress the news temporarily while getting the response?" The professors said the Baptist Press stories in question

> show exemplary restraint and discretion in what is admittedly a potentially sensational event. They are both news accounts which refrain from editorializing. They do not speculate regarding motives, editorialize about the ethics involved, or entertain reflections from unattributed sources.

Pressler was not satisfied with their study, saying in an interview afterwards it was done by "hired guns" who were "paid" to say what they did.[67]

Pressler's influence in the deliberations of the Executive Committee would continue to grow. He soon learned that the subcommittees were the place to present his ideas and argue his case. He was protected from much of the unfavorable publicity by this method since the Executive Committee procedures decreed that "background rules" applied to the

---

[66]Baptist Press, 20 February 1985.
[67]Baptist Press, 20 February 1985.

deliberations of the subcommittees and work groups. These rules forbid the attribution of statements to any person, thus, it was impossible to expose much of the behind-the-scenes maneuvering.

As more fundamentalists were elected to the body, his influence grew. Two seasoned members of the Executive Committee who had observed the changes told me that by the time of the discharge of the Baptist Press staff in July of 1990, Pressler was in complete control of the committee. He did not win everything he wanted and sometimes someone opposed him publicly. He had, according to these members, enough votes to get his major programs enacted.

When the members were accused in the press of being rubber stamps for the fundamentalists, the members of the Committee protested vehemently in the press that they were not pawns to be manipulated by Pressler. But the actions kept coming out largely as he wanted them. When his term expired, he insisted on participating in the meetings of a subcommittee on institutions of which he had not been a member. His cause there apparently was to guide the discussions on accreditation of the theological seminaries.

Independent preacher Jerry Falwell felt it necessary to warn that the Southern Baptist Convention would split if Charles Stanley was not reelected as president in Dallas in June of 1985.[68]

Hard on the heels of the Falwell pronouncement, Paige Patterson predicted a showdown but not a split when the convention met in June. He urged that churches send more than the pastor and his wife as messengers to the convention. Failure to do so, he said, could be a sad situation if "Charles Stanley, the only internationally-known television preacher Southern Baptists have ever had, is humiliated (by being defeated)."

The rhetoric was heating up with Bailey Smith, former president saying,

> I believe a man who does not believe all the Bible is the Word of God ought to go sell aluminum siding. I don't know why we are debating the issue. . . . I am grateful to stand with men who are little extreme to the right and extremely committed to Jesus Christ.[69]

---

[68]Baptist Press, 21 February 1985.
[69]Baptist Press, 22 February 1985.

Few of the moderates knew why we were debating the issue either, since no one could find more than a handful of people or any professors who did not believe that the Bible is the Word of God. And they were not debating the issue.

In Wake Forest, the Southeastern Seminary faculty unanimously adopted a statement affirming the ministry of the woman (Debra Griffis-Woodberry of Annapolis, Maryland) who had been ordained as pastor.

Since this did not agree with the interpretation of scripture by the fundamentalists, the faculty was judged by many as not believing the Bible.

In March, Nelson Tilton, church starting specialist for the Home Mission Board, warned that the denomination's infighting was undermining efforts in starting new churches.

In Arkansas near the last of February, six pastors said they had

an insatiable, indefatigable desire to speak. Many groups over the SBC have met to express the opposite view of the trends (within the SBC). We believe it would be a sin against God and our great denomination to remain silent and not voice the point of view represented by the conservatives of the Southern Baptist Convention.[70]

Russell Dilday of Southwestern Seminary said in March, 1985, in Little Rock, Arkansas, "I disagree with the statements, however, that our denomination is 'drifting away from the Bible' and that our seminaries are teaching liberalism." Casting himself as "fundamental" in beliefs, he said, "I don't mind calling my position (on the Bible) inerrancy. I believe in the infallibility, the complete, perfect trustworthiness of Scripture."

Dilday added that if, as Pressler has said, the only issue in the SBC is whether or not

Scripture is entirely God's word and does not make mistakes, then the argument is over, because there is no debate about that in Southern Baptist life. I don't know anybody in the SBC who would not agree the Bible is the inspired, authoritative Word of God.[71]

---

[70]Baptist Press, 12 March 1985.
[71]Ibid.

In March at Southwestern Seminary, the administration and the trustee academic affairs committee recommended the termination of a professor. The charges included lifestyle and behavior, profanity and vulgar language, cursing the dean of theology, poor churchmanship, including no record of active churchmanship, poor quality of work and "no scholarly" approach, insubordination, intentional distortion of truth, lack of response to significant warnings, and other matters.

In an atmosphere charged with political implications and allegations, a "profane" man was being returned to the classroom as the trustees rejected the recommendation. The vote by secret ballot to fire the professor was 19-12, but fell short of the two-thirds majority necessary, as required by seminary bylaws.[72]

The difference among the trustees seemed to fall out along political lines. It was an interesting phenomenon to have some of the most ardent fundamentalists arguing to return a "profane, incompetent, poor churchman" to the classroom. The termination was finally accomplished in a later meeting.

Later in March, Foy Valentine, long-time executive director of the Christian Life Commission, told the Commission's national seminar, that there was "nothing to be gained by dividing up into camps and calling each other names" on the volatile issue of abortion. He urged Southern Baptists "to act with discernment, judgment, compassion, wisdom and courage" in dealing with the issue. He said, if society is to limit unwanted abortions, then it also "must support the prevention of unwanted pregnancies, and the church must work far more responsibly in this arena in the future than we have done in the past."[73]

The Southwestern Seminary faculty responded promptly to a charge in the *Star Telegram* story by reporter Jim Jones. He quoted Paul Pressler as saying in regard to Dilday's recommendation of the dismissal of the professor, "I don't know (the professor). But I think this (firing incident) is another example of the inept administration which has caused Russell Dilday to lose respect and confidence of many at the seminary and many on the board of trustees."

The faculty said in part,

---

[72]Baptist Press, 22 March 1985.
[73]Baptist Press, 28 March 1985.

We, the undersigned members of the faculty of Southwestern Baptist Theological Seminary . . . in the light of recent developments and press reports, wish to affirm our president, Russell Dilday. He stands tall in the line of illustrious presidents of this institution. His administration for the past six years has been distinguished by a theologically conservative stance. He has led this seminary to significant growth at every level. . . . We affirm, contrary to the suggestion that the recent trustees' action has impaired his leadership, that, indeed, he enjoys our full confidence.

This letter has come about spontaneously. It is completely independent of the administration. By this, we underscore our solidarity in support of our president.

One hundred faculty members out of 101 signed the open letter. The one who did not was the professor whom the president tried to fire.

Pressler, when told of the letter, said he believed it was "obvious to anybody with any intelligence at all" that such an action by the faculty would be instigated by Dilday.

In commenting on a petition among students, Pressler said, "A petition among students, which I heard from the Fort Worth *Star Telegram*, had been able to garner less than 300 signatures among the over 5,000 students [*sic*] at Southwestern." According to seminary records, there were 3516 students registered at the school for the 1985 spring semester. One student started the circulation of the mentioned petition and had more than 800 signatures at the time of the press contact. He expected to have more than a thousand by the time he could present it to the president. Other similar petitions were also being circulated.[74]

By the end of March, the conflict had reached such proportions, that former president James Draper warned that the Cooperative Program (unified missions budget) might collapse if Charles Stanley was not elected for a second term. He told the Baptist Public Relations Association in annual meeting that the heads of Southern Baptist institutions are leading a "massive attempt. . . financed by Cooperative Program funds" to deny Stanley a second year as SBC president.

Draper, now a trustee of Southwestern Seminary, said that he would "be speaking in every church I can between now and June" to promote Stanley's reelection. Later he said that Dilday was "reportedly using 50

---

[74]Baptist Press, 29 March 1985.

per cent of his time trying to defeat Stanley . . . and he is not going off salary for that time so he is using Cooperative Program funds."[75]

Similar charges to those made against Dilday were made against Roy Honeycutt, president of Southern Seminary. Both presidents told me privately that Cooperative Program funds were not used for expenses in their efforts. While they did not say so, I am certain that they both felt that their activities were in complete keeping with their responsibilities to defend their institutions' integrity.

At a meeting at Southeastern Seminary, convention President Charles Stanley called "for us to sit down and talk about our beliefs and possible differences" because the situation is so explosive (within the denomination) that something needs to be done.[76]

In April, 1985, former SBC presidents Rogers, Smith, and Draper appeared on the 700 Club hosted by Pat Robertson to explain their positions on the controversy and underline the importance of the re-election of the current president, Charles Stanley. The program contained filmed comments from presidents Dilday and Honeycutt. Robertson urged churches to respond to the "crisis" in the SBC and send properly elected messengers to Dallas next June to support Stanley.[77]

Various persons in many different settings spoke of some facet of the controversy in the first part of 1985. Rallies, associational meetings, and caucus groups met all over the country trying to explain the conflict or trying to gather forces for the Dallas meeting in June.

Randall Lolley, president of Southeastern Seminary, speaking at a meeting of Concerned Southern Baptists, said that president Charles Stanley "ought not be president of the group he doesn't love." Lolley said that Stanley had told him personally that "he had no confidence in the six Southern Baptist seminaries when he became president and therefore had counseled young people, including his own son and daughter not to attend one of the Southern Baptist seminaries." He listed actions taken recently that would make the coming SBC meeting volatile and explosive.[78]

In April, for the first time known in convention history, the presidents of 23 state conventions met on their own initiative to discuss the

---

[75]Ibid.

[76]Baptist Press, 4 April 1985.

[77] Baptist Press, 4 April 1985.

[78]Baptist Press, 12 April 1985.

problems of the denomination. In a prepared statement after their meeting, the presidents declared:

> The manner in which the present controversies are being discussed among Southern Baptists, in many instances, diminishes our ability to reflect Christ's love to the world, limits our ability to carry out the great commission and diverts our attention from the responsibilities God has given us.[79]

The Committee on Boards released its report on April 16. The chairman characterized the report as "very good" and added: "I feel we have a very strong core of people being nominated this year. It is my prayer our work will contribute to a healing in our convention. We tried to rise above the problems and not become a part of the problem."

Jerry Gilmore, a Dallas attorney, was eligible for a second term but was not renominated. The chairman said that William Tanner, Home Mission Board president, considered Gilmore an "outstanding trustee and for the past two years a most effective chairman." The two Texas members of the committee recommended Gilmore for re-nomination.

Questions arose, however, the chairman said, concerning Gilmore's wife, Martha, who was an ordained Methodist minister.[80] The vote not to re-nominate was 25 to 22.

President Stanley and Southwestern Seminary president Dilday met at the seminary with the press. Stanley charged that the problems existed because of liberal teachings in the seminaries, and Dilday said that the problems had to do with strategies to control the boards of SBC agencies.

On April 19, the president of the Foreign Mission Board, Keith Parks, said that he would not support the re-election of Charles Stanley as president of the convention. The mission board administrator said attacks on Southern Baptists' cooperative mission approach and suspicion cast on SBC agencies had erupted into a distrust of Southern Baptist missionaries. He felt that when threats were made to withhold funds, the result was that "the missionaries are the ones becoming hostage to the conflict and the lost of the world are the losers."[81]

---

[79]Baptist Press, 12 April 1985.
[80]Baptist Press, 16 April 1985.
[81]Baptist Press, 22 April 1985.

The response to Park's statement was immediate and spirited. The fundamentalist leadership was "grieved." The moderate leadership was supportive.

Gene Garrison, pastor of the First Baptist Church in Oklahoma City, proposed a meeting of key leaders from various factions in the denomination in an effort to "keep this thing (the SBC) from coming apart." He said that the leaders of the right-wing or inerrancy faction turned down the plan. "They said that it was too late. . . that the missiles are already in the air." Garrison and Adrian Rogers discussed the plan. Baptist Press reported that Rogers had a meeting with Stanley, former presidents Smith and Draper, Paul Pressler, Paige Patterson, Russell Kammerling, and Fred Powell, senior associate pastor at First Baptist Church in Atlanta.[82]

On April 26, SBC Vice-President Donald V. Wideman said that he was "not given opportunity or asked to give input to the list of names from which President Charles Stanley made his appointments" to key committees for the 1985 annual meeting of the SBC.[83] Stanley said on the same day that he provided lists to vice-presidents Zig Ziglar . . . and Don Wideman . . . for suggestions and input. "We did not sit down and discuss the whole thing, but I told them to provide me with suggestions and I would consider them."[84]

In the midst of all the talk and confusion, moderates found a candidate whom they could support who was thought to have a chance to be elected. Winfred Moore, pastor of First Baptist Church in Amarillo, Texas, had not been active in the controversy and was a well-known conservative. His participation in the denominational processes, by his own admission, had been limited, but he was a loyal supporter of the SBC and his church regularly contributed large sums of money to the Cooperative Program. He, as president of the Baptist General Convention of Texas, had been thrust into various discussions about the national controversy.

Late in April, Russell Dilday endorsed Moore for the presidency and predicted that he would be elected. The meeting was to be in Dallas, and Moore was prominent in Texas Baptist affairs.[85]

---

[82]Baptist Press, 26 April 1985.
[83]Baptist Press, 26 April 1985.
[84]Ibid.
[85]Baptist Press, 1 May 1985.

At about the same time, more than 1200 Tennessee Baptists attended a "Confronting the Issues" rally in Knoxville. Speakers at the meeting, which lasted more than three hours, were past SBC president Adrian Rogers and Paul Pressler, leader of the fundamentalists.[86]

President Honeycutt of Southern Seminary issued a statement on May 3 decrying the "distortion of my writings" by three former presidents of the SBC: Rogers, Smith, and Draper. He also charged that Stanley, incumbent president, misrepresented his theological position. Paige Patterson, he said, misquoted his comments on Old Testament passages. "By innuendo and misrepresentation my commitment to the inspiration and authority of the Bible has been questioned by mass assault of every convention president elected since 1979." Until the last few weeks, Honeycutt said, his 22 years of writing had elicited only one critical letter, "a positive suggestion concerning the translation of a Hebrew word in Amos."[87]

In May, the Executive Committee of the Home Mission Board voted to affirm recent public statements by the presidents of the SBC's two mission boards and urged the re-election of the board's former chairman (Jerry Gilmore who had been bumped by the Committee on Boards) to the agency's board of directors.[88] This committee of the Board had not yet passed under the control of the fundamentalists.

A survey of state convention presidents revealed that president Charles Stanley had largely disregarded suggestions by state leadership in the appointment of two key committees of the SBC. In announcing the appointments, Stanley said that 62 were selected from a list of more than 500 names submitted by "state convention executive directors, presidents . . . and individuals." Following vice-president Wideman's comments on the appointments, Baptist Press contacted the presidents of 21 of the 26 states eligible for representation on SBC committees. With one exception—Alabama—each of the presidents reported none of the persons they nominated for the two committees were named.[89]

As the convention neared, the drumbeat of debate quickened.

On May 14, a seven-member task force of state convention presidents met and drew up a plan to create a special committee of the SBC to study

---

[86]Baptist Press, 3 May 1985.
[87]Ibid.
[88]Baptist Press, 8 May 1985.
[89]Ibid.

means of resolving the crisis. Their recommendation was to be presented to the other state presidents on June 10 before the Dallas convention meeting and recommended to the convention the next day. Winfred Moore, moderate candidate, and president Stanley were joined by former president W. A. Criswell in approving the idea.[90] Former president Franklin Paschall of Tennessee (who made the first proposal for a peace committee) disassociated himself from the efforts of the presidents. But he said, "I will vote for any peace proposal if it makes sense."[91]

In their May meeting, the Foreign Mission Board of trustees voted to affirm President Keith Parks with only one dissenting vote, but tabled another motion that would have affirmed SBC president Charles Stanley by name. The vote to table was 29 to 19.[92]

Missionary Norman Coad from Mali wrote that facing the grim reality of famine in Mali was difficult enough without having to worry about squabbles among Southern Baptist supporters at home. "You have no idea how deeply grieved we are here over the insanity of our good friends who are on both sides of the issues in the present Southern Baptist Convention political crisis." Speaking of praying over the problems, he commented, "We do this looking over our shoulders, depleting our energies, interceding for our base of support while the battle rages hot and heavy all around us. It doesn't seem right, but that's the way it is."[93]

The committee charged with local arrangements in Dallas was struggling with how to fit the anticipated 30,000 into the Grand Hall, which would seat only 20,000.

The pastor of the First Baptist Church in Dallas, W. A. Criswell, sent letters to 36,000 ministers in the convention urging them to reelect "God's prophet" (Charles Stanley) as president of the convention.[94]

On May 29, Baptist Press headlined, "Dallas SBC '85 Might Be Predicted 'Big Shootout.'" At issue was the presidency, resolutions on a variety of issues, the continuing controversy over the Baptist Joint Committee on Public Affairs, the challenges to committee reports, and the

---

[90]Baptist Press, 17 May 1985.
[91]Ibid.
[92]Baptist Press, 23 May 1985.
[93]Baptist Press, 24 May 1985.
[94]Ibid.

general direction of the SBC and the creation of a "Peace Committee."[95]

Paige Patterson said of Winfred Moore, the probable nominee of the moderates, that he "was a tool for the liberal faction within the SBC." The deacons and the congregation of Moore's church both pledged "unreserved support of him through our prayers, influence and resources."[96]

"Shootout in Dallas"

In June, 1985, a record 45,431 messengers crowded into three halls to face a "showdown" on the future of the denomination. The unprecedented attendance almost doubled the record number of messengers present in Atlanta in 1978. (22,872) The record throng elected Charles Stanley to a second term after a hot contest with Winfred Moore. The vote was 24,453 for Stanley to Moore's 19,795. Even in defeat, Moore received more votes than any previously elected president.

In a shift toward good will, Moore was nominated as first vice president without his consent and beat the incumbent fundamentalist vice president, Zig Ziglar, by 22,791 votes to 10,957. Moderate Henry Huff, a Louisville attorney, beat fundamentalist nominee W. O. Vaught.

Evangelist Billy Graham endorsed Stanley at the last minute, alienating many of his friends, but perhaps producing some votes for Stanley.

At his news conference, Stanley continued to talk of reconciliation but refused to say if he would consult more fully with the vice-presidents than he had previously done.

Moderates led by James Slatton of Richmond, Virginia, tried to replace the Committee on Committees' nominees to the Committee on Boards. Stanley ruled that persons nominated from the floor must be considered one by one. Messengers overturned the ruling in the convention's closest vote, 12,576-11,801. This was a frontal assault on the president's primary prerogative.

This surprise came at the end of the Wednesday morning session. The evening session saw a bitter, extended debate when Stanley announced his three parliamentarians had decided the only way to challenge the

---

[95]Baptist Press, 29 May 1985.
[96]Baptist Press, 31 May 1985.

Committee on Committee's report was to reject it outright. For parliamentarians to overrule the vote of the body was unprecedented and would bring a lot more conflict. The messengers then voted to approve the report of the committee. The vote raised new questions when registration secretary Lee Porter said he had received "numerous" reports that surplus ballots were distributed outside the convention center before the session began.[97]

Frustration and anger carried over to Thursday's final-day deliberations. Moderates repeatedly challenged what they considered Stanley's heavy-handed tactics.

Almost lost in the heat of battle was the recommendation to form the "Peace Committee." The convention agreed to form the panel to consist of 22 persons, 20 men, and 2 women. The committee would occupy the attention of the denomination for two years to come.

An Editor Speaks

Julian Pentecost of the *Virginia Religious Herald* wrote this account of the fundamentalist takeover.

We make no claim to fully understand the principals of the takeover movement or their lieutenants but there are some things we do know. Their "talk" and their "walk" are often separate and distinct. There is little correlation between their profession and practice, their belief and behavior, their creed and conduct.

At times there is an eerie schizophrenic dimension characteristic of them which is disturbing and even frightening. They are comfortable with power, prestige and privilege. . . .

They insist on an inerrant and infallible Bible, as they interpret the words without biblical support, but frequently give no evidence of so much as an elementary understanding of Jesus' emphasis on the primacy of love of neighbor as the fulfillment of the law and prophets.

As long as the fundamental-conservatives maintain their control of the convention they will strive in direct and indirect ways to superimpose their doctrinal stance on all others or make life miserable

---

[97]Baptist Press, 17 June 1985.

for those who are resistive. Committed and competent denominational servants will continue to be accused, harassed and sacrificed in order to keep the passions of the "faithful" inflamed.[98]

---

[98]Julian H. Pentecost, *Religious Herald* (Virginia) 21 June 1990.

Chapter Nine

One Last Try

"We Hoped For Peace . . . ."[1]

Many thoughtful Southern Baptists were frightened at the possiblity of schism. By the time the convention convened in June, 1985, several suggestions had been advanced that led to the formation of the committee to study the problems.

The Peace Committee

The committee chairman elected by the convention was Charles Fuller, pastor of the First Baptist Church, Roanoke, Virginia. He was considered uncommitted to the battle, though he said that he was an inerrantist but had not been a part of the inerrantist movement.

Generally believed to represent traditional Baptist values were: William E. Hull; Cecil Sherman; William Poe, a North Carolina attorney; Winfred Moore; Robert E. Cuttino, a South Carolina pastor; Mrs. Harrison Gregory, a former president of WMU; and Albert McClellan, former Associate Executive Secretary of the SBC Executive Committee.

Leaders of the rightist side were Adrian Rogers and Jerry Vines, co-pastor of First Baptist Church, Jacksonville, Florida. Also believed to be representing this view were Charles Stanley; Jim Henry of First Baptist Church in Orlando; Ray Roberts, retired Executive Director of the Ohio Convention; Edwin Young, pastor of Second Baptist Church in Houston; William Crews, pastor in Riverside, California; and Mrs. Morris Chapman, wife of pastor of the First Baptist Church, Wichita Falls, Texas.

---

[1]Jermiah 8:15, New International Version.

Between the two sides, according to two of the members, were John Sullivan; Doyle Carleton, layman from Florida; Charles Pickering, attorney from Mississippi; Herman Born; and Charles Fuller.

Two members, Herschel Hobbs and Daniel Vestal, strongly supported traditional values but sometimes voted with moderates and sometimes with the other side. On crucial issues, they stood on the moderate side.[2]

The committee was authorized for the following two years with the provision it bring at least an interim report next year to the Atlanta (1986) convention. The convention action stated the purpose of the committee as follows:

> That this committee seek to determine the sources of the controversies in our Convention, and make findings and recommendations regarding these controversies, so that Southern Baptists might effect reconciliation and effectively discharge their responsibilities to God by cooperating together to accomplish evangelism, missions, Christian education, and other causes authorized by our Constitution, all to the glory of God.

Note that the instructions related to the purpose of the convention —missions and education.

Further the committee was instructed to recognize the role of trustees and report its progress at each meeting of the Executive Committee. The agencies should cooperate with the committee, which was to adhere to certain other technical matters and make a report in 1986 or a final report in 1987. Southern Baptists were urged to exercise restraint, to refrain from divisive action and comments, and to reflect Christian love while this committee was doing its work.[3]

The committee met 14 times during the two years. Early in its meetings, it decided that it would tape-record its deliberations and seal the tapes for ten years. This was done, it was said, to protect the persons who appeared before the committee and its members. Chairman Fuller told me that he felt that this freed everyone who appeared to speak their minds without fear of recrimination.[4]

---

[2]Albert McClellan, "Theses Concerning the Great Fundamentalist Takeover Controversy of the 1980s, A Traditional Baptist View." (1990) Unpublished.

[3]*SBC Annual*, (1987) 232–33.

[4]From transcribed notes of a personal conversation with Charles Fuller, 4 June 1991.

Charles Fuller, commented on the composition of the committee:

> There was distinct representation on the moderate side, distinct representation on the conservative side. . . . I think there was an effort to give representation left, representation right, and representation center, and position in between.[5]

When asked if these people on the committee were liberals and conservatives, he commented:

> I think in the classical sense of a liberal or the classical sense of a conservative, you are really hard-pressed to make those distinctions . . . to say that we had anti-supernaturalists on the committee and so on, no. But to say by comparison to what the committee itself would refer to as the center of Southern Baptist life, there were definitely those that were left and those who were right.

The committee invited Southern Baptists to write to them and let them be a repository of complaints, questions, and observations. When asked if those communications were available for research, he said that they were not. They were a part of the sealed material. The committee agreed that anything that was made a matter of press releases would be available in the office of the Executive Committee.

When asked about the agenda, Fuller said the first meeting was an organizational and a "get acquainted" session. At first, the discussion centered on whether the conflict was theological or political. He said, "I think that the whole committee early on came to the conclusion that we needed to address the theological issues because that was the pressure that was being placed. We knew we were dealing with political issues as well."[6] When asked what the theological issues were, Fuller replied,

> The reference that was made from the start was, is there a drift, how much of a drift is there theologically, where is the drift, where can it be identified, and the term drift you may remember was one of the early terms that was used to described what was happening. There is a drift.[7]

---

[5]Ibid.
[6]Ibid.
[7]Ibid.

The seminaries were the center of the focus on theological matters. The committee decided to form teams of four from the group to visit with the seminaries and other agencies. A list of common questions was devised to be asked in each seminary so that there would be comparable data received by the committee. Teams could ask any other questions that seemed pertinent.

It was agreed that the teams would interview the presidents, the chairpersons of the executive committees of the trustees, and the academic deans. Fuller said that he made a careful attempt in naming the teams to have two from each point of view to have balance. Issues raised were to be referred back to the boards of trustees so that the trustee system would be in proper perspective and responsibility for any response or correction made.

The teams made their visits and reported back to the full committee. The general nature of their reports indicated that in three of the seminaries—New Orleans, Golden Gate and Southwestern—there were relatively few if any problems. It seems clear, however, that the committee discussed all of the seminaries. Questions were raised about three or four faculty members at Southern and at least one at Midwestern.

At Southeastern, the ground rules of the visit were made clear to the president. The interviews were to be with the president, the dean, and the chairman of the trustees.

In reporting on the meeting, President Randall Lolley of Southeastern Seminary commented as follows.

> They, the visiting team, were to arrive on our campus in the late afternoon of a certain day. We were to have dinner at our house, and the next morning we were to have our meeting. All day had been set aside. When we finished our meal, Dr. Henry (the chairman of their group) advised that they had to go back to the motel and have a meeting, which he inferred was an organizational meeting. Which I assumed was an organizational meeting of their own committee.
>
> But as it turned out, they had prearranged without my knowing it or anybody communicating it to anybody, they had prearranged a meeting with representatives of the radical student group. They let the CEF (Conservative Evangelical Fellowship) meet with them before they ever met officially with the dean, the president, or the chairman of trustees. By my calculation, they had less than six specific things to inquire about when they got to the campus that afternoon or evening.

But on meeting with those radical students, they ended up with up in the teens—14, 15, 16. And the concerns were written out on fragments of paper, focused on some professor, but written out on little bitty fragments of paper. And the investigating team came with those very fragments of paper the next morning. . . .

At the lunch break I heard some conversation to the effect that the team had met with students, and I inquired about it and was told, yes, they had met with some students. . . . If I had it to do over again I would have canceled the afternoon session and declared the whole thing null and void, because these students brought these radical, rigid, weird charges, with no focus at all—it was just broad charges.

One, for example, that I remember so vividly, levied against John Steely who was one of the greatest guys I ever knew . . . the students said that he supported women in ministry. That's the only thing they said about him—supports women in ministry. . . . The Peace Committee spent a good bit of time wanting to explore what it meant on our campus to support women in ministry—as if that were a mortal sin.[8]

According to President Lolley, the committee asked about eighteen or twenty faculty persons. Many months later, they sent further inquiries to the seminary about seven faculty members.[9] The teams visiting the other seminaries apparently stayed with the plans related to who would be interviewed.

When asked about the total number of professors the committee was concerned about, chairman Fuller said that there were a total of five or six about which there was real concern.

And I'm sure that there would be some others that would fall into the marginal area or the area that some of these committee members would like to pursue a little further, but as far as identifiable names and issues and materials gathered and so on about those persons and so on, a half a dozen.[10]

When I asked whether there was a theological trend discernible in this group, he replied,

---

[8]From transcribed notes of a personal conversation, 19 May 1991.
[9]Ibid.
[10]From transcrbed notes of a personal conversation with Charles Fuller.

No, I wouldn't say a trend. I think that there were certainly some things which were similar or common, but it was not like here are a half dozen, and I really would not want to be held to the half dozen, (nor say) here are six people alike, all of them teaching the same thing, all of them dealing with the same area. No, no.[11]

There was some concern expressed about the possibility of belief in universalism by one or more professors. According to McClellan, this issue was mentioned only once.

Another issue according to Fuller, was that faculty should be examined

> by looking at employees of denominational agencies and institutions, [and asking] what is their churchmanship? What is their position about salvation? Are these people exemplary in terms of their involvement of church life and in terms of their church conduct, behavior and so on?
>
> Now I must confess that the constantly repeated issue that arose again and again, what about the Bible? What is their position on Scripture.[12]

Some of the Peace Committee felt some questions about Southern and Southeastern never got answers that were satisfactory to them.

Matters of problem were referred back to the trustees.

Visits were made not only to the seminaries, but to the Foreign Mission Board, the Home Mission Board, the Sunday School Board, Historical Commission, and the Christian Life Commission. All agencies were asked to reply to the concerns of the Committee.

In retrospect, and with limited data available from the committee and with the records sealed, it seems that the investigations of the committee paralleled the problems in the denomination. The questions related to inerrancy seemed to dominate the deliberations and investigations of the committee. It seems equally clear that there was not a solid scholarly examination of the issues of inerrancy.

Chairman Fuller said that the committee said in its report (to be discussed later) that

---

[11]Ibid.

[12]Ibid. (McClellan noted in conversation that the matter of church involvement was not discussed in most of the interviews.)

We believe that most Southern Baptists when asked the question, what do you think this means, "the Bible is truth without mixture of error" (from *The Baptist Faith and Message*) they would reply saying, it means that Adam and Eve were real persons, that a miracle is a miracle, that if the Bible says John wrote the book, John wrote the book.[13]

While this is not a precise quote of the report, it illustrates the kind of definition of inerrancy that the committee apparently was dealing with as it examined the faith of the faculties and denominational employees. Chairman Fuller was aware of several different definitions of inerrancy.

This understanding of the committee came from their opinion that if the ordinary Southern Baptist were asked what "without error" meant, the above understanding would be given.[14] No survey of Southern Baptist opinion was made. This raises, of course, questions about evaluative criteria.

One of the more significant events during the work of the committee was a meeting of the committee and agency executives including seminary presidents at the conference center at Glorieta, New Mexico. During that meeting, the seminary presidents issued a statement of their intentions that became known as the "Glorieta Statement." In this statement they made significant statements related to their faith and the direction they would lead the seminaries. The statement included: an affirmation of the miracles of the Old and New Testaments, an affirmation of the full inspiration of scripture and its binding authority, and the assertion that "The sixty six books of the Bible are not errant in any area of reality."

They recognized that there were legitimate concerns on the part of some about the seminaries; they would address them. They stated: "We commit ourselves . . . to the resolution of the problems which beset our beloved denomination. We are ready and eager to be partners in the peace process."

They then specifically: reaffirmed the seminary confessional statements; pledged to foster in classrooms a balanced, scholarly frame of reference for presenting fairly the entire spectrum of scriptural interpretations represented by the constituency; repudiated any caricature

---

[13]Ibid.
[14]Ibid.

and intimidation of persons for their theological beliefs; committed themselves to fairness in selection of faculty, lecturers, and chapel speakers across the spectrum of the constituency; pledged to lead the seminary communities in spiritual revival, personal discipleship, Christian lifestyle, and active churchmanship; and pledged to deepen and strengthen the spirit of evangelism and missions and to emphasize afresh the distinctive doctrines of our Baptist heritage.[15]

The Peace Committee affirmed the Glorieta Statement and ceased its official inquiry into the affairs of the seminaries, referring unanswered questions and unresolved issues back to the administrators and trustees of Southern Seminary, Southeastern Seminary, and Midwestern Seminary.

Cecil Sherman, long-time leader of the moderate cause, promptly resigned from the committee. He told Baptist Press in a written statement:

> The statement made by the six seminary presidents sets a course for theological education in the Southern Baptist Convention for years to come. . . . Fundamentalists began with the premise theological education was "drifting into/toward liberalism." The Peace Committee bought this premise. . . . The seminaries have taken a long step toward their critics. . . . What they have done will satisfy for a season, but Fundamentalism will ask for more concessions from our educators. In the end, serious theological education will wither.[16]

President Adrian Rogers called the action of the seminary presidents "a courageous action." He proposed a list of things that Southern Baptists could do that would help the process. One of them went to the heart of the matter: "We can pray and work for fairness in all appointments so that we have the best Baptists cooperatively and theologically to represent us."[17]

The moderates responded quickly. They were led this time by James Slatton, pastor of River Road Baptist Church, Richmond, and Winfred Moore of Amarillo. The statement said,

---

[15]Peace Committee Report, *SBC Annual,* (1987) 235.
[16]Baptist Press, 24 October 1986.
[17]Baptist Press, 24 October 1986.

We feel the Peace Committee has addressed itself to the concerns of the fundamentalists. Moderates until now pretty much have been dealt out of the picture. . . . The seminary presidents have bent over backwards in an attempt to find authentic peace, a way in which we can have inclusion of all our people and all our sincerely held views. . . . This now will be the most revealing moment in our long and tragic controversy, for the ball is now in the court of the fundamentalists.

The moderates called on President Rogers to appoint as the SBC Committee on Committees the sitting presidents of the eligible state conventions and the sitting presidents of the Woman's Missionary Union. They also requested the fundamentalists to stand down on political organizing and that each side refrain from sending an emissary around the country to organize politically and to promote a partisan agenda for the annual meeting. Among several other proposals, they suggested representatives of both groups get together to select a candidate for president that both could support.[18]

A Window of Opportunity

At this point, the possibilities for peace probably were greater than they had ever been before or would be again. Moderates had made substantial overtures and seemed to be in a conciliatory mood. The principal demands of the fundamentalists were met by the seminary presidents. The moderates made reasonable requests related to nominations to the Committee on Committees.

The crux of the matter now was the nominations. As in the past, no mutually acceptable nominations were forthcoming. In spite of the fact that three presidents in a row had vowed to represent all Baptists, no one of them did so in the appointments.

At Southern Seminary, President Honeycutt told the faculty that nothing had changed and that the seminary would proceed as normally as possible. Adrian Rogers was unhappy with this statement, interpreting the press release to mean that Honeycutt was turning back from the Glorieta statement. Honeycutt said that was not his intent at all but that he was

---

[18]Baptist Press, 29 October 1986.

saying in effect that the seminary was already proceeding according to the terms of the agreement. The press coverage did not help either side.

It should be said that faculties at some of the seminaries did not like the Glorieta Statement. Some moderates, including Cecil Sherman, felt that the presidents had "caved in" to the fundamentalists.

The presidents felt it necessary to reply to the publicity, especially the public press. They denied "capitulation" and repudiated all "victory claims" and "capitulation" allegations. They urged broad support of the statement and expressed hope for progress in solving the controversy.[19]

Two or three seminary boards of trustees would subsequently affirm the Glorieta Statement.

The Beat Goes On

One description of the balance in the Peace Committee went as follows.

> As it turned out, the Peace Committee was a battle of leaders, with Rogers and Vines on one side and Sherman and Hull on the other side. . . . In time, as one issue after another was confronted, Adrian Rogers proved to be the superior debater. His articulation, simplicity, timing, use of language, well-planned strategy, persistence, and winsome appeal proved too much for the opposition. In spite of his advantage, the moderates were still in the battle until Cecil Sherman resigned. . . . After his resignation, several of the seven unknown or non-committed votes appeared to begin gradually shifting to the (fundamentalist) side.[20]

Albert McClellan said that the inerrancy issue would have made a difference if it had ever been publicly debated by the Peace Committee.

> If debated by competent debaters, new understanding would have emerged, giving the traditional side enough votes at least to launch a minority report. But it was never debated. . . . The committee spent two years dealing with symptoms. . . . The talk did not deal with the broader, deeper and wider subject of Biblical authority but always with

---

[19]Baptist Press, 7 November 1986.
[20]Name withheld. Information from written information submitted.

alleged infractions of limited detailed inerrancy.[21]

McClellan said that the work of the committee is best perceived not in stages, but in climaxes. Each climax was a turning point in the committee's lack of progress. His list and comments on them follows.

[1] December, 1985–February, 1986—the visits of subcommittees to the agencies.

> Some of the (fundamentalist) members of the subcommittees were unhappy that the visits had not been a witch-hunt. As late as the last meeting of the committee, some were still complaining that "we have not done our job, we have not talked to the professors."

[2] January, 1986—the fruitless excursion into the theological and political aspects of the conflict.

> Meetings and talks did little except relieve general accusations accusing all agency employees and professors of being liberal Unfortunately, it did intensify attacks on individuals. The interviews did not move the denomination closer to reconciliation.

[3] February, 1986—the diversity statement.

> The statement recognized diversity as a fact in Southern Baptist life. The traditional side (moderate) were committed to it because they assumed diversity is good. The (fundamentalist) side was for the statement, because it recognized SBC diversity as a fact, which in their estimation is bad.

When released, the fundamentalists mounted an attack on diversity as divisive, therefore, evil.

[4] June, 1986—the report to the convention that nothing had been done toward the goal of reconciliation.

[5] October, 1986—the Glorieta meeting, which, at first, gave some hope.

[6] October, 1986—Cecil Sherman's dramatic resignation.

[7] February, 1987—Public discussion of the Pressler tape (The

---

[21]Albert McClellan, "Theses," 15.

Firestorm Chat tape), that led to Dan Vestal's aloofness from the committee.

[8] May, 1987—the seminary presidents conference on inerrancy, which was "exceptionally well-planned" and well attended. The conference made little difference in the work of the committee and was "ignored by most of the pastors and churches. It may have even strengthened the fundamentalist side."

[9] June, 1987—The all-night meeting of the committee on the eve of the convention meeting in St. Louis and the subsequent report. The minority failed in an attempt to make a minority report. The committee was continued for one year, but without further developments. It was dismissed in 1988.[22]

These crises listed by McClellan probably highlight the mood within the committee at given times. Much of its inner workings will not be known until the tapes and minutes are unsealed. It is obvious that the conflicts were are times severe. Several committee members, however, have told me that the members developed great respect for each other during their long and sometimes heated sessions. One volunteered that if it had been possible to get all Southern Baptists together for these kinds of meetings, peace may have been possible. It should be observed, however, that the meetings did not resolve the differences between the committee members.

The Committee Report

The Peace Committee brought its report after two years of deliberations to the meeting of the Southern Baptist Convention at St. Louis on June 16, 1987.

The committee had promised that their report would be available four to six weeks before the convention so that there would be adequate time to study it. The messengers received a copy as they entered the meeting hall for the session in which the report was made. The report covers almost ten pages in the Annual. There was obviously no opportunity for it to be thoroughly studied, barely read, before consideration began.

The committee explained that the report simply had not been finished

---

[22]McClellan, "Theses," 15–17.

until four o'clock of the morning of the same day. It was announced that it would be released by noon of that same day but was not, but the chairman explained that was caused by a printing delay. When asked about the late finishing of the report, Chairman Fuller said, "Again and again we would come to the wall and just simply could not—it just simply would not materialize, it would not come together. . . . We were at an impasse."[23]

When the report was presented for approval, three motions to amend were made. All three were defeated. One motion to extend time for discussion for ten minutes passed. A motion to defer action until the messengers had time to study it failed. A motion was made to extend the time for fifteen minutes, it failed.

The report was overwhelmingly adopted. Many attributed that action to the perception that this was a fundamentalist document. Time to study it would have helped that feeling perhaps. Some observers estimate that it passed by 95 percent favorable vote, but it seemed to me that that estimate is much too high.

The document consisted of five major divisions.

The Introduction recited the formation of the committee and the assignment given it by the convention. It included matters of staffing, finance, instructions about reporting, and members of the committee.

Section I. Sources of the Controversy

Theological Sources. Using *The Baptist Faith and Message*, as a yardstick, the committee stated that there was considerable diversity among Southern Baptists in their understanding of the nature of scripture. The principle difference was over the statement that the Bible was "truth without any mixture of error." In the seminaries and agencies, the committee found that some believed that the statement meant in all areas. Some held that truth relates to matters of faith and practice.

The committee reported on the Glorieta meeting and statement of the seminary presidents, and their attempts to implement it.

The report stated at the conclusion of that section on theological sources: "The question for the majority of the Peace Committee, however,

---

[23]From transcribed notes of a personal conversation with Charles Fuller.

remains not whether there is diversity in the Southern Baptist Convention, but how broad that diversity can be while still continuing to cooperate."

Political Sources. The report indicated that

In the opinion of the Peace Committee, the controversy of the last decade began as a theological concern. When people of good intention became frustrated because they felt their convictions on Scripture were not seriously dealt with, they organized politically to make themselves heard. Soon, another group formed to counter the first and the political process intensified.

They studied restructuring the appointment process, the timing of the pre-convention meetings, charges of political malfeasance, and voter irregularity.

Section II. Findings

On Theology. The committee found that in the seminaries, "there was not a theological balance represented in the faculties." The committee adopted two statements on findings on theology, the second of which affirmed the concept of inerrancy without referring to it directly.

1) The Foundational Statement:

It is the conclusion of the majority of the Peace Committee that the cause of peace within the Southern Baptist Convention will be greatly enhanced by the affirmation of the whole Bible as being "not errant in any area of reality." Therefore, we exhort the trustees and administrators of our seminaries and other agencies affiliated with or supported by the Southern Baptist Convention to faithfully discharge their responsibility to carefully preserve the doctrinal integrity of our institutions receiving our support, and only employ professional staff who believe in the divine inspiration of the whole Bible and that the Bible is "truth without any mixture of error."

2) The Statement on Scripture:

The Bible is a book of redemption, not a book of science, psychology, sociology or economics. But, where the Bible speaks, the Bible speaks truth in all realms of reality and to all fields of knowledge. . . . We affirm that the narratives of Scripture are historically and factually accurate.

The committee stated that it understood the Southern Baptist view of scripture to mean:

(1) They believe in direct creation of mankind and therefore they believe Adam and Eve were real persons. (2) They believe the named authors did indeed write the biblical books attributed to them by those books. (3) They believe the miracles described in Scripture did indeed occur as supernatural events in history. (4) They believe that the historical narratives given by biblical authors are indeed accurate and reliable as given by those men.

The report continued:

We call upon Southern Baptist institutions to recognize the great number of Southern Baptists who believe this interpretation of our confessional statement and, in the future, to build their professional staffs and faculties from those who clearly reflect such dominant convictions and beliefs held by Southern Baptists at large,

The report acknowledged that some of the committee did not accept this interpretation.

On Politics. After its investigation, the committee found, "that the extent of political activity . . . at the present time creates distrust, diminishes our ability to do missions and evangelism, is detrimental to our influence, and impeded our ability to serve out Lord." Two statements on politics were also adopted.
1) The Foundational Statement on Politics:

It is the unanimous conclusion of the Peace Committee that fairness in the appointive process will contribute to peace. . . . We exhort the present and future presidents, . . . the Committee on Committees, and the Committee on Boards to select nominees who endorse the Baptist Faith and Message Statement and are drawn in balanced fashion from the broad spectrum of loyal, cooperative Southern Baptists, representative of the diversity of our denomination.

2) The Statement on Politics:

More recently, these groups have developed organized coalitions centered on theological perceptions and individual leaders committed to a defined viewpoint. The coalitions have adopted political strategies for electing officers of the convention, appointing committees, and changing or preserving the character of accepted institutions. These strategies have included extensive travel, numerous informational and ideological meetings, mailouts, network of representatives who share in this common strategy, and sustained efforts to recruit messengers to attend the convention. . . . The extent of political activity within . . . at the present time promotes a party spirit; creates discord, division, and distrust . . . is detrimental to our influence; and impedes our ability to serve our Lord. . . .

We recommend that the Southern Baptist Convention request all political factions to discontinue . . . (1) Organized political activity; (2) Political strategies developed by a group with central control; (3) Holding information—ideological—meetings; (4) Extensive travel on behalf of political objectives within the convention; and (5) Extensive mail-outs to promote political objectives in the Convention.

Section III. Conclusions.

The committee's Conclusions included these statements.

We have kept our differences from creating hostility, until recently, and not only have we lived in peace, but with remarkable harmony and cooperation.

We must never try to impose upon individual Southern Baptists nor local congregations a specific view of how Scripture must be interpreted. . . .

There is but one way for us to survive intact as a denomination. It involves the recognition of some basic facts, among which are these:

(1) Changes are now taking place in the leadership of many Southern Baptist Convention boards.

(2) These changes will impact these boards and agencies for years

to come.

(3) The role of many who have exercised leadership in the past will change as colleagues of different persuasions will fill leadership roles.

(4) This change will mean that some who have been in general agreement with Convention programs in the past will have less involvement, while those who previously have had difficulty in agreement with certain Convention programs will have more involvement.

A further suggestion was made.

Our leaders must have and must demonstrate a view of Baptist life that reaches beyond the limits of their own personal theology. No effort should be made or should be permitted to be made which would seek to eliminate from Baptist life theological beliefs or practices which are consistent with The Baptist Faith and Message Statement and which ave found traditional acceptance by substantial numbers of our people.

Section IV. Recommendations.

The committee made recommendations, which included the reaffirmation of the cónfessional statement—declaring it was not a creed but should be used as "parameters for cooperation." All future presidents and committees should appoint persons from the broad spectrum of loyal Baptists and recognize the right of the churches to give to the agencies of choice without intimidation. Specific recommendations icluded:

We recommend that . . . trustees determine the theological positions of the seminary administrators and faculty members in order to guide them in renewing their determination to stand by the Baptist Faith and Message Statement . . . to the Glorieta Statement. . . . In the future to build their professional staffs and faculties from those who clearly reflect such dominant convictions.

We recommend that Baptist Press, all state Baptist papers, independent autonomous journals and individual Southern Baptists refrain from the use of intemperate and inflammatory language, labeling individuals and impugning motives.

They requested that inflammatory resolutions cease, that the leadership of the Pastor's Conference and the SBC Forum take steps to the end of "getting together."[24]

A Critique of Peace Committee Report

Several elements of the report were on target. The description of the theological controversy did not get to the heart of the matter, as subsequent events would demonstrate. The discussions in the committee centered on "the drift" from an inerrancy position. The practical insistence of the fundamentalists was on a different set of theological problems though they talked about "the drift."

Subsequent events show that the movement was really aimed at a dramatic change in historic Baptist positions related not only to the nature of scripture but to the insistence on interpretations of scripture and the promotion of various social and political programs. The statements of the leaders of the rightist movement support this analysis.

The definition of what "most Southern Baptists" believe about the Bible that contained the four illustrations became a stumbling block to the peace process. The statement is probably true, but here interpretations of scripture became a matter of fellowship and no room was left for anyone to differ and remain in the new Baptist mainstream.

It is probably true that there was not "a theological balance represented in the faculties" if by that the committee meant "parity" of inerrantists. If, however, the Chicago Statement on Inerrancy were the issue with its many qualifications, there would have been more "parity." Trained scholars have a hard time accepting assertions outside the realm of faith when they cannot be demonstrated to be true. The basic premise of inerrancy rests on the original "autographs," which, of course, are not available. The fundamentalists essentially were arguing for inerrancy in the presently available manuscripts, which have "scribal inadvertencies and inconsistent numbers" according to biblical scholars. The faculties and the fundamentalists were often talking about two different ideas. According to Albert McClellan, the Peace Committee did not debate the issue, and so the report reveals.

---

[24]Peace Committee Report, *SBC Annual* (1987) 232–42.

In describing the changes that were taking place in the convention in the section on Conclusions, the committee and, then, the convention virtually read all previous leadership out of the picture for the future. This would not have been so catastrophic had it not been applied also to anyone who disagreed with the fundamentalist leadership.

These actions would furnish discontinuity in many areas of convention life that would suffer from lack of perspective, procedural knowledge, historical understanding, and mature judgment. Many persons coming into responsible positions at every level of convention life were inexperienced in leading and managing multi-million dollar institutions, to say nothing of setting a tone of collegiality and cooperative understanding.

In this regard, the document was internally inconsistent, since in one place it argued for balanced appointments to boards and in this section just referenced said that the only way to survive was in a complete change in leadership.

The committee had argued about whether the illustrations of "truth without any mixture of error" should be in the findings or in the recommendations. Some of the committee felt that they should be in the recommendations section and thus would be more binding on the agencies after the convention adopted them. The chairman insisted that all parts of the report were of equal value and, thus, it did not matter which section they fell in. This view was likely a part of an attempt on his part to get the report before the convention. The convention was told that they were all equally important. H. H. Hobbs told me that he strenuously objected to placing these interpretations in the recommendations. He was operating from the previous stance that only recommendations were binding on agencies.

Within weeks, the interpretations of "truth without mixture of error" were to be used by more than one institution as creedal requirements for employment. The trustees of Southern Seminary enacted them as requirements for hiring, promotion and tenure of faculty. The Association of Theological Schools promptly sent a team to the campus to see what was going on.

It is important to note the instruction of the convention:

We call upon Southern Baptist institutions to recognize the great number of Southern Baptists who believe this interpretation of Article

I of the Baptist Faith and Message Statement of 1963, and in the future, to build their professional staffs and faculties from those who clearly reflect such dominant convictions and beliefs held by Southern Baptists at large.[25]

A non-creedal people now were binding their institutions to an interpretation of a confessional statement adopted in 1963. For a people who historically had said, the scripture is our sole rule of faith and practice, this was a long step.

The call for a cessation of political activity was badly needed. Both sides had stepped up the heat before the Dallas meeting, and things had long ago gotten out of hand. Some saw the problem as two sides fighting for control, and from one view this was accurate. From another view, there was a group taking a convention they did not build from a group who was fighting to protect the integrity of the convention and its institutions.

The committee requested "writers and individual Baptists (to) refrain from characterizing fellow Southern Baptists in terms such as 'fundamentalist,' 'liberal,' 'fundamental-conservative,' 'moderate-conservative.'" The convention approval of this request had little if any effect on either side.

By the fall state convention time, the terms listed above were in use by both sides. In a few places, organizations were disbanded in the hope that there was a better way. There was growing evidence that the fundamentalists did not want anything less than total control.

In January of 1988, in a letter attributed to Paul Pressler, (it bears his name and a signature) the terms "liberal" and "liberals" were used twenty-three times. This letter was addressed to "Dear Friends." The friends apparently circulated the letter widely.

It is certain that the convention action on the Peace Committee report changed little so far as the conflict was concerned. It is also certain that much of the fundamentalist agenda became the formal action of the convention and binding on its institutions.

---

[25]Ibid., 241.

A Columnist Looks At Southern Baptists

Ina Hughes has written this reflection.

The Baptists are so busy fussing with each other, they probably won't mind a comment or two from an outsider. . . . Infighting just gives the doubting Thomases of the world a headful of questions. . . . Could it be that people outside the church are more tolerant, open-minded, forgiving? How does a God of love fit into this kind of push-and-shove theology? . . .

Religious tough guys and well-meaning zealots sometimes win the battle and lose the war. But another, more subtle thing is happening. New Right religious conservatives are not only turning the road to salvation into a mine field of doctrinal traps and checkpoints; they are robbing the English language of some perfectly good words and phrases. . . .

The word now on the auction block is "fundamental." Supposedly, in its religious connotation, the word has to do with the basics of the faith. For Christians, according to the instructions and example of Jesus Christ, these basics are very straightforward. Trust him, love each other and focus all your energy on picking up pieces rather than breaking things. . . .

Today, the word "fundamental"' doesn't conjure up many images of people out to love each other. It's more often applied to people who think God would be offended if a woman got ordained or people who have figured out which of several English translations of Greek and Hebrew words is the inerrant one. . . . It seems to me that the fundamentalists are more into rules, regulations, anger and judgment than the basics of the first four books of the New Testament—in any translation. . . .

And holy wars—in any church or denomination—are a contradiction in terms.[26]

---

[26]Ina Hughes, *The Knoxville News-Sentinel*, 33: 775.

Chapter Ten

An Iron Hand

"Troubled On Every Side"[1]

Another kind of problem had begun with the June, 1985, convention meeting. The president, backed by the parliamentarian, made a ruling that was clearly outside accepted procedure. As previously described, President Charles Stanley ruled that the Committee on Committees report nominating the Committee on Boards could not be amended. The body voted not to sustain the ruling. Usually, in Baptist affairs, whether a matter stood depended on the will of the majority. In this case, after the ruling and the intervening afternoon, the president ruled that the only way any changes could be made was to reject the committee report completely. This was a historic ruling in that it defeated the will of the majority. After debate, the body finally approved the nominations to the committee.

Baptists Sue Baptists

A Birmingham layman, Robert Crowder, indicated that this was a gross violation of the bylaws of the convention and that unless the SBC Executive Committee took steps to remedy the matter, he would file suit in court. Critics of the ruling argued that the nomination of the committee was a report to the convention, thus, it became the property of the body which could deal with it in any fashion it chose. Since the bylaws did not specifically provide for amendments to this item, the ruling was that it was not permitted. Whatever the merit of the ruling, historically the will of the body was the law in a convention meeting. A number of former

---

[1] 2 Corinthians 7:5.

officers of the convention and former parliamentarians were of the opinion that the ruling was wrong and that the vote of the body should have been respected.

Crowder claimed at the September, 1985, meeting of the SBC Executive Committee that his rights were violated and that the current Committee on Boards, commissions and standing committees of the SBC, were illegally elected. His attorney made a ten minute presentation of his claims. The Executive Committee went into executive session—the first time in thirty years—and voted to affirm the action of the convention. From a practical view, the Executive Committee does not have the authority to reverse an action of the SBC. It was reported that 15 to 20 members voted against the action. Crowder gave notice that the only alternative left to him and those supporting him was to file legal action.[2]

In November, Mr. and Mrs. Robert Crowder and the group supporting them, called "Baptists Committed to Fairness," instructed their attorneys to proceed with the filing of a suit to enforce the existing bylaws of the Southern Baptist Convention.[3] Leaders from both right and left felt that this was not a proper way to solve the problems of the convention.

On December 5, 1985, Crowder and his associates filed suit against the SBC in the federal district court in Atlanta. The suit claimed that the plaintiffs were "irreparably harmed" by the rulings and events at the convention meeting. The suit sought to have the election of the SBC Committee on Boards, commissions, and standing committees declared illegal and to prevent the 52 persons elected from serving. The suit claimed that the president made "erroneous rulings" that "violated the rights" of the plaintiffs and denied them the right to vote on matters related to election of the Committee on Boards.

In January, a parallel lawsuit was filed in Superior Court of Fulton County, Georgia, seeking the same relief.[4]

In December, the denomination heard the report that baptisms had declined during the previous year. The projections released by the Research Department of the Sunday School Board showed that the baptisms would make 1985 the third lowest year in baptisms in the last 35 years. The report revealed a decline of six percent from the 1984 level.

---

[2]Baptist Press, 20 September 1985.
[3]Baptist Press, 19 November 1985.
[4]Baptist Press, 24 January 1986.

Nearly a dozen state evangelism directors blamed continuing controversy in the SBC as one of the major reasons for the decline. Bob Hamblin, Vice-President for Evangelism of the Home Mission Board said that one of the major reasons for the decline is "We Southern Baptists have been saying to the nation we are more concerned about our little theological differences than we are about winning people to the Lord Jesus Christ."[5]

In February, James Guenther, attorney for the SBC urged the Executive Committee and the convention not to be diverted from their task of evangelism by the lawsuit filed by the Crowder group. The Executive Committee agreed to recommend a change in the bylaw to allow for additional nominations from the floor but not allow more than one nomination at a time.

Protests of the filing of the lawsuit and responses from the litigants would go on periodically until it was resolved.

The suspect Committee on Boards, commissions, and standing committees met in March and nominated 213 persons to places on SBC boards of trustees.

In preparation for the meeting in June of the convention, President Stanley named former SBC president James Draper—together with a former vice-president and a certified professional parliamentarian—as SBC parliamentarians for the sessions. The certified parliamentarian was C. Barry McCarty, an ordained Church of Christ minister. He was to become a fixture in SBC meetings for years and create considerable controversy with some of his actions.

In May, United States District Judge Robert Hall ruled that the first amendment to the Constitution of the United States prevented the intrusion of secular courts into internal church matters, thus deciding the Crowder lawsuit in favor of the Southern Baptist Convention. An appeal was filed with the Eleventh United States Circuit Court of Appeals.

In September of 1987, the Court of Appeals ruled against the plaintiffs, who promptly appealed to the United States Supreme Court. In February of 1988, the Supreme Court refused to review the decisions, thus upholding the rulings of the lower courts.

In July of 1988, President Harold Bennett of the Executive Committee revealed that the lawsuit cost the SBC $280,000 to defend.

---

[5]Baptist Press, 10 December 1985.

The Problems of the Press and Baptist Press

Soon after the beginning of open conflict, accusations circulated that the press was not being fair in its presentation of the news. In the 1981 meeting of the convention in Los Angeles, a motion was made that recommended giving Baptist Press agency status. This proposal sounded to many like an effort of the fundamentalists, not yet in the majority, to take over the news service.

In February of 1982, the Southern Baptist Press Association, made up of Baptist Press editors and state convention paper editors, agreed with their liaison study committee that the Baptist Press should remain a part of the SBC Executive Committee. The committee said in part, the present arrangement will be "satisfactory as long as we have Baptist Press staff members with the integrity of those now serving. But we need to remember that every establishment is always tempted to control the news and if this happens editors will have to resist."

In a resolution, the SBPA members noted that the "purpose of the news service is to provide accurate and adequate reporting, whereas SBC history indicates resistance to information that is threatening or embarrassing and the result is often attacks on the news service." The resolution continued, "The news service is vital to the democratic processes of the convention . . . and [SBPA] is opposed to attempts to stifle or hinder" it in its duties.[6]

The Executive Committee adopted a recommendation to "continue to operate Baptist Press as a part of the Executive Committee with the assurance that Baptist Press will continue to serve Southern Baptists with the support and freedom necessary to maintain credibility and effectiveness."[7]

The problems of the press would be revealed in many forms. The editor of the *Rocky Mountain Baptist*, James Lee Young, quit, saying he could no longer effectively function under the Colorado Baptist Convention Executive Board because of what he termed "censorship." He said that he had been instructed not to print any story about an upcoming

---

[6]Baptist Press, 22 February 1982.
[7]Baptist Press, 25 February 1982.

meeting of the Executive Board without clearing it first with the chairman of the Board.

Editor Walker Knight announced that the name of the new independent national publication dealing with issues facing the Southern Baptist Convention would be *SBC Today*. The publication would be financed with contributions from individuals. The first issue was due in April 1983.

The problems of the press were multiplied when the story of the taping by Paul Pressler of the telephone conversation with the Southern Seminary student hit the news. The Pressler answer was not available until the next day. The resulting conflagration was described in chapter seven. Pressler's anger was demonstrated by the report on February 20, 1985, that he brought into the subcommittee a suitcase full of materials. Afterward, he complained that the ruling was grossly unfair. "I don't know why these people are suppressing the truth. I had 35 grievances against Baptist Press I wanted to present, but they wouldn't let me speak."[8]

The moderates wanted a different slant on the news reports as well, but for other reasons. Interested moderates in Kentucky published more than 30,000 copies of *The Call* prior to the June convention meeting. Still other publications would be born and die during the ensuing years.

In 1980, as the conflict in the denomination began to heat up, a resolution was presented to the convention condemning the editors of the state papers for "political bias." It was not presented for action, since the committee on resolutions thought it improper.

At the meeting of the Executive Committee in February, 1986, guidelines for the Baptist Press were adopted. The purpose of the news service, as stated in the guidelines, is "to report factually and fairly the news of, about and for Southern Baptists." The guidelines acknowledged that ownership and management of the Baptist Press is vested in the Executive Committee

> to provide the required freedom and responsibility necessary for the benefit of Southern Baptists. . . . The news service will strive to be factual and fair, as objective as possible, staying not only in the bounds of legality but also at a high level of professional and Christian ethics.

---

[8]Baptist Press, 20 February 1985.

The guidelines had been in preparation for a year and were adopted by the committee almost without discussion.[9]

As a precursor of things to come, Floyd Craig, the president of Craig and Associates and a Baptist public relations professional, predicted hard times for Baptist news services in the years to come. He said that increased restrictions on the flow of information may be caused not only because of political considerations, fear, and paranoia, but also from economics. . . . He predicted that there will be more pressure on Baptist communications workers to be "masters of ambiguity."

Craig said that with a more restricted flow of information, Baptist "grapevines" will be more alive than ever with "untrustworthy and slanderous" rumors. "The rumors will favor no group more than others." He also predicted more attempts to stereotype groups and individuals; an increased desire to overreact, coupled with a trend toward more burnouts, retirement syndromes, and cynicism; and a reduced emphasis on the skill of listening to others.[10] None of us knew at the time what a prophet he would turn out to be!

In May, James L. Sullivan, former president of the Sunday School Board, addressed the employees of the Board giving his personal assessment of the controversy raging in the denomination. The Board publication, *Facts and Trends*, published an excerpt. The trustees were very upset by the former president's perspective. One motion would have instructed president Lloyd Elder to apologize in *Facts and Trends* for the publication of the Sullivan article and to prepare and submit for trustee approval guidelines for persons speaking at the board. The motion that prevailed expressed trustees' disapproval of the article and noted that it did not express the position of the trustees.[11] Such an action was unprecedented. The furor caused such unhappiness that the usually jovial and considerate Sullivan for a week carried in his pocket a letter of apology to President Elder and the board in case it should be necessary to issue it to stay the confusion.[12]

In Georgia, controversy over the policies of editor Jack Harwell of the *Christian Index*, caused the *Index* board to appoint a five-member

---

[9]Baptist Press, 21 February 1986.

[10]Baptist Press, 9 April 1986.

[11]Baptist Press, 7 August 1986.

[12]Information given to author in private conversation.

review board to oversee the "editorial policies, practices and personnel." The editor of 20 years had been under fire since 1979. The move followed an effort to fire Harwell at the annual meeting of the Georgia convention. In May, 1986, Harwell wrote an editorial critical of the nominations of the SBC Committee on Boards that was chaired by Lee Roberts, a Marietta business man. Roberts prepared and distributed a 32 page document to the study committee detailing complaints against Harwell. He called for "replacement" of Harwell, "not restrictions." The chairman of the board of the *Index* said that most of the unfavorable mail came from the "fundamental-conservatives."[13] The controversy continued as the board terminated Harwell. The State convention in session asked that he be returned to office. The board refused and his termination stood.

In September of 1987, the Executive Committee of the SBC heard a report from its public relations workgroup that the seven-member panel "is studying the Baptist Press news releases from April 1, 1987 to February 1, 1988, to determine balance in the news releases." Workgroup chairman Julian Motley, pastor from Durham, North Carolina, said the intention of the study "is not to imply any imbalance but to address a concern held by many Southern Baptists."

In another matter related to the news service, Executive Committee members responded to an SBC motion calling for a new study of the Baptist Press structure. Their recommendation noted, "Conclusions derived from a study of the structure of Baptist Press in 1982 are still considered valid, and . . . an additional study should not be made."[14]

At a meeting of the Baptist Public Relations Association in April of 1988, Jack Harwell, former editor of the *Christian Index* said that "a KGB atmosphere created by the SBC holy war" hampers the work of the Baptist communicators. He observed that Baptist communications efforts over the last ten years had developed a "cookie cutter syndrome . . . and are more reactive than proactive. . . . When someone raises his head and gets to be a little bit different, it gets cut off, a la Randall Lolley (past president of Southeastern Seminary), Dale Moody (former professor of Southern Seminary), Jack Harwell and others."

Stan Hastey, Director of Information Services of the Baptist Joint Committee on Public Affairs, predicted the current attitude of "circling

---

[13]Baptist Press, 28 August 1986.
[14]Baptist Press, 25 September 1987.

the wagons" during a time of crisis would continue to be a "plague upon our profession." Both Harwell and Hastey cited attempts to gain control of the media, particularly Baptist Press. "There has been a planned systematic crusade by Southern Baptist extremists to capture and control our communications net work," Harwell said. Hastey concurred: "What the critics of Baptist Press want is not balance. They want a press that parrots the prevailing line."

Hastey further observed that the "magical 10th year of revolution within SBC" is nearing and warned that, as in any revolution, the goal is to control the media. "We Baptist communicators are and will continue to be under intense pressure, not because we individually or together are so important, but because what we do is so important."[15]

Media people were increasingly wary of the war.

At the meeting of the SBC Executive Committee at the June convention in San Antonio in 1988, Paul Pressler showed again his displeasure with Baptist Press. Before the meeting he had mailed a 39-page criticism of Baptist Press to members of the committee and to those who were nominated to be elected at the convention meeting. In the meeting, Pressler made a motion to establish new four-point guidelines for Baptist Press. His recommendations followed existing guidelines, except that he wanted written answers to questions asked by Executive Committee members and wanted Baptist Press to recognize the need for admitting error and apologizing for mistakes.

Frank Ingraham, committee member from Nashville and also an attorney, said that good solid criticism of any press is valid, but he thought "criticism to the point of looking for problems is a very difficult thing to respond to." Pressler, he said, constantly and legitimately stays in touch with BP. "I don't know anybody who has more to say about (the way) Al (Shackleford) runs Baptist Press (than Pressler)." But he said that to adopt another set of principles based upon a single letter "is beyond what we want to do and I plead with you that we not pursue the matter further." He then made a motion to table, which was approved 31-29.[16]

In February, 1988, a subcommittee of the Executive Committee, in response to a motion at the 1987 SBC meeting, declined to investigate the news agency's reporting. The public relations workgroup at that time gen-

---

[15]Baptist Press, 22 April 1988.
[16]Baptist Press, 20 June 1988.

erally affirmed the news service but urged greater restraint in reporting controversial issues in an effort to promote peace and harmony.[17]

This conflict would continue to smolder and erupt from time to time as events displeased Paul Pressler and other fundamentalist leaders.

George Cornell of the Associated Press has been a long-time observer of Southern Baptist Affairs and a respected journalist known for objective and fair reporting. He has unusual knowledge of Southern Baptist organization, structure, and procedures. In June, 1985, Cornell wrote a long article, released through Associated Press, concerning the Baptist Press.

His lead said, "One of the best church news services in the country, Baptist Press, has come under increasing pressures to curb its straight, wide-open reporting amid the turmoil in the big Southern Baptist convention." He quoted W. C. Fields, director of Baptist Press: "The pressures have come 'from all directions' wanting the reporting muzzled or slanted. . . . We won't do that, the purpose is to report the news of and about and for Southern Baptists in a full, factual and fair manner."

Russell Chandler, *Los Angeles Times* religion editor and president of the Religion Newswriters Association of about 200 religion reporters for the secular press, said:

Baptist Press is not afraid to tackle gutsy issues and I've never felt they were trying to twist anything, although they've had pressure to do so. They operate by professional standards of covering the news for its news value. I'd have to rate them No. 1.

Cornell added, "Similar evaluations came from former presidents of the association of journalists covering religion, including Richard Ostling of *Time* magazine and Marjorie Hyer of the *Washington Post*." He concluded by saying,

One drawn-out inquiry on a complaint by a fundamentalist strategist, Houston Judge Paul Pressler, about reporting of his alleged secret taping of a telephone conversation, generally found the stories balanced.

"Hired guns," Pressler termed the professors. He predicts Baptist Press would show a "different attitude" as a result of the inquiry.[18]

---

[17]Baptist Press, 20 June 1988.
[18]George W. Cornell, Associated Press, *The Oregonian,* June 8, 1985.

In the RNA Newsletter in 1988, President Ed Briggs published a copy of a letter he had sent to Charles Sullivan, chairman of the SBC Executive Committee. He commented on the criticism leveled at Baptist Press by fundamentalists. He said,

> We in the Religion Newswriters Association, whose members cover religion for newspapers, news magazines and wire services in the United States and Canada are concerned.
>
> First of all, based on a random survey of RNA members, Baptist Press enjoys high credibility, if not the highest, when compared to news operations of other American denominations. Secondly, RNA members told me they believe Baptist Press's coverage of the Southern Baptist Convention is impartial and fair. . . .
>
> Baptist reporters, in a sense, have two great historic streams that guide them. One flows from the Baptist saints who faced jail rather than bow down to dictated religion. The other—from which we, too, draw our purpose for doing what we do—comes from those men who stood steadfast for a free and unfettered press and the people's right to know.[19]

W. C. Fields, long time director of Baptist Press, said to me in talking about the pressures on the news service:

> One of the characteristics of the fundamentalists, whether it's a fundamentalist in religion or politics . . . is the desire to control . . . and one of the first places . . . is the media. . . . From the very beginning in the early 80s Baptist Press . . . , as (well as) the state papers, we had all kinds of pressure from these fundamentalists.

When asked for illustrations, Fields replied,

> Any time a story came out, Pressler, Patterson, or any of that inner circle, several of whom had been president of the Convention, that held them up in an unfavorable light, I could count on hearing from them. I had calls regularly from Pressler . . . or they would get leading pastors or influential laymen to call and complain, threaten, (or) just partially threaten.

---

[19]Ed Briggs, Letter to the chairman of the SBC Executive Committee, 10 September 1988.

When asked if Paul Pressler came to see him, Fields replied,

Pressler in the early years did not come to see me. It was only after about '84 or '85 when he started coming. Of course, when he became a member of the Executive Committee, he made a path into my office constantly and did until the day Al Shackleford was fired.

On the story about the taping of the telephone conversation with the student, Pressler was very upset that the story and his reply did not get out the same day. Fields said, "He stormed into my office just absolutely livid." In rehearsing other confrontations with Pressler, Fields said

The pattern was to fire a shot at anybody who says anything negative and scare the life out of him, threaten him with his job. . . . They (not just Pressler and Patterson but the inner circle) did their best to make them (especially the state papers) gun-shy and to cause them to be so gun-shy as not to handle controversial matters.[20]

Al Shackleford, Vice-President of the Executive Committee for Public Relations and successor of W. C. Fields, had problems from before his tenure began. When word spread that Shackleford was to be nominated for the post, Harold Bennett, the president began to get calls. One of these calls was from Paul Pressler, according to Shackleford. In his conversation with me—recorded with his permission—he said that Pressler told Bennett that Shackleford would not be elected and if elected, he (Pressler) would make a motion at the first meeting to fire him. When asked why, Shackleford, replied,

Because he felt that I had a history of being against the conservative movement and . . . this was based on his file of my editorials and my coverage, even back to my days of being editor in Indiana. I discovered the Judge has an extensive file. Later in the interrogation, he brought up some of the things that I wrote while I was in Indiana.

This was ten and a half years before.

The election process was difficult for Shackleford. After several meetings with various persons and groups, the administrative committee

---

[20]Transcribed notes of a personal conversation with W. C. Fields, 22 May 1991.

voted 13 to 9 to recommend him for election, over Pressler's protest. When the matter came to the full Committee, one fundamentalist made a motion to postpone the election of a vice president until the next meeting, about four months hence. The vote on the motion was 29 to 29, therefore not passing. A secret ballot vote was taken on Shackleford's election and he was elected by a vote of 32 to 26.

After a night of thought and prayer, Shackleford felt he should accept the post in spite of the problems over his election. According to Shackleford, there was in the succeeding three years a long series of confrontations with Pressler and his friends. Shackleford said to me, "As I look back over the number of conflicts that Paul and I have had over Baptist Press articles, it is amazing that nearly all of them were something that was about him."

As the problems continued, Shackleford said of himself and news editor Dan Martin,

> Anytime there was a story, we made sure we contacted Pressler or Patterson to get comment. I frankly think we bent over backwards to let them be spokesmen on every issue, when normally, journalistically, you wouldn't have involved people other than the people who were actually involved in the specific event.

After Bill Moyers' telecast on the problems in the SBC, the Executive Committee in February of 1989 passed a resolution that basically condemned the broadcast. Moyers asked to appear before the Executive Committee in its next meeting in Las Vegas. The request was denied. Moyers fired off an angry letter to the chairman of the committee which he (Moyers) released to the press.

According to Shackleford and others, Pressler came to the meeting of the administrative subcommittee, although he was not a member, to "bring up the specific issue the Baptist Press should not release Moyers' letter and even pressured them to make a motion instructing me that Baptist Press would not release the letter." The full committee, after discussion, passed a mild motion requesting discretion in handling the matter. The decision was made to release the text of the Moyers' letter. It produced an explosion, causing a statement from Pressler to Martin "that he was going to do some things he felt he had to do."[21]

Numerous differences similar in nature would follow. None would honor God or encourage the dissemination of unbiased news reports.

At the June meeting of the convention in New Orleans in 1990, I saw Shackleford in the hall. He was pale and obviously distraught. When I asked him what was the matter, he told me that he had just run into Paul Pressler. Pressler had told him that he was "the dumbest person I have ever known," and that he could not understand how biased and prejudiced he was, and that it was beyond Pressler's ability to comprehend how anybody could be like (that) and not know it.[22] The story he told me that day in New Orleans coincided precisely with the story he told me in our interview in February 1991.

On Tuesday, June 19, 1990, back in Nashville after the New Orleans meeting, Shackleford went in to see Executive Committee President Bennett on routine matters related to the meeting. Shackleford said,

> So he proceeded to tell me that on the previous Wednesday, June 13 at 3 o'clock, ahead of the Executive Committee meeting he had been asked to . . . convene the six officers. . . . Bennett was told in this meeting that there would be a motion presented at the four o'clock meeting that I be fired, and they had the votes and the only way to stop that was for Harold (Bennett) to agree to ask for my resignation and Dan's (Martin) resignation.

According to Shackleford on June 19, Bennett suggested that Shackleford resign effective September 1 and that he could have September as vacation and be paid until October. In no circumstances was he or Martin to be present at the September meeting of the committee. After some thought, both Shackleford and Martin refused to resign. By Friday of that same week, one or the other of them had heard from 11 different states that they were asked to resign. By the time the day was over, they had heard from 20 different reporters. By Wednesday, June 27, the story was in many of the secular newspapers in the south, including Atlanta, Charlotte, Dallas, Fort Worth, and Houston.

---

[21] Transcribed notes of a personal conversation with Al Shackleford (taped with his permission).

[22] Ibid.

In the melee, Bennett was told by the officers of the committee to get the resignations. No further articles were to be released about the matter without Bennett's permission. Bennett could not get the resignations. He was told, apparently by the officers, to fire the two newsmen. He refused.

The officers promptly called a special meeting of the Executive Committee for July 17. An effort was made to try to keep the call of the meeting a secret, but the word quickly spread across the country. There was multiplied confusion, telephone calls back and forth, and a statement was released by the chairman of the Executive Committee, Sam Pace of Oklahoma, who instructed Baptist Press that it was not to be edited in any fashion.

One member of the Executive Committee called Shackleford just before midnight on a Saturday night urging him to resign so the dismissal would not be necessary. Shackleford recalled,

> He even said in the conversation that he just felt like the brethren would be so grateful that not only would they give us six month's salary but they might choose to divide the $50,000 that it (the meeting) would cost, between Dan and me.[23]

The chairman also called urging the resignations. "He did not talk about dividing up the money they would save by not having a meeting, but he felt they would be very generous with us and appreciative if we would have our resignations in there on Monday."[24]

As a matter of integrity, both journalists stuck with their determination not to resign.

At the special meeting,they were told that they would have five minutes each before the administrative sub-committee and five minutes each before the full committee. Feeling that it was improper to appear in a closed meeting, each submitted a written statement to the sub-committee. After two hours, it adjourned to meet with the full committee. By this time about 300 people had showed up to attend the meeting. They were prohibited from entering the hall by off-duty Nashville police, who were out of uniform but armed. Neither of the journalists were asked into the meeting.

---

[23]Ibid.
[24]Ibid.

The session went on for about three hours in executive session. At the end of the meeting, the members of the committee left without any statement. President Bennett informed the journalists that they had been terminated and that they would be given six months salary and vacation time. Subsequently, it was reported that the vote had been 45 to 15 to terminate.

As the press and public crowded in, a press conference was called in the much larger auditorium where a written statement was handed out. No officer of the committee attended, and the announcement was made by an employee (vice-president) of the committee.

No charges were brought against the journalists either in private or in the committee meeting and action.[25] No official reason has ever been given for their termination.

When I asked Paul Pressler what the basic problem with Baptist Press was he replied:

Unfairness. Unfairness towards conservatives. Failure to report things that were good for conservatives, reporting many things that were bad for conservatives in a very unfair light. (They) could extend toward the liberals in the articles the details at great length over a period of several years to the ones in Baptist Press. Nothing was ever done about it. They knew what was wrong. The knew what the problems were. They never accommodated them at all.

When asked why the Executive Committee called a special meeting just two months before the regular meeting and at great expense, Pressler replied:

First of all, there was going to be a motion made on Wednesday afternoon at the convention to fire both of Al Shackleford and Dan Martin. . . . It would have passed by a substantial margin. We felt it was much better for their reputation and everything to handle it quietly. Harold Bennett indicated to the officers that he would handle it quietly and work out generous retirement with them and everything would be smooth. So, we talked to people who were going to make the motion, urged them not to do it, and they acquiesced at the urging of the officers. And then instead of working to alleviate the situation, Al and

---

[25]Ibid. Reported by Baptist Press, 18 July 1990.

Dan wrote their own press releases about their situation, tried to make it, blow it up into a big issue. I was in Europe, I left on the ninth, I think it was, of July. Wasn't here for the meeting. I certainly would have voted to terminate them if I had been there. But in July when the meeting was coming up in September, it had become a big issue in the press and on something like that, the more quickly it's dealt with the better. And I think that was the rationale. I was here to vote to call the meeting and I did and that was the rationale to call the meeting to get the issue over with and behind us because you had some people who were trying to make political hay and to hurt the convention by their unfair and unkind comments.[26]

The Southern Baptist Press Association immediately endorsed the concept of a new press service to ensure a free flow of Baptist news and information.[27] President Bennett said that Baptist Press would continue to function.

The *Knoxville News-Sentinel* on July 18 headlined, "Fundamentalist Baptist Leaders Fire Top Editors." Editorially, the paper called Shackleford and Martin "Pros to the bitter end." The *Nashville Banner* headlined, "Baptist Editors Barred From Vote. " An Associated Press article by George Cornell said that the "Baptist crackdown on its press [was] seen as [a] power play." Cornell commented further: "In early America, Baptists had a catalytic role in securing freedoms, including a free press. Freedom of religion itself first was planted by Baptist Roger Williams in the colony of Rhode Island." "It is ironic that Baptists, with their great contributions to freedom, would now be trying to control the press and do away with its freedom," said Jack Brymer of Jacksonville, editor of the *Baptist Witness*."[28]

In its July 27, 1990, edition, the *United Methodist Reporter* commented:

The recent firing by Southern Baptist officials of their denomination's two highest-ranking journalists is a hard blow to all Christians. . . . Despite being considered expendable by present Southern Baptist

---

[26]Transcribed notes of a taped personal conversation with Paul Pressler, 20 February 1991.

[27]Baptist Press, 20 July 1990.

[28]*The Miami Herald*, 6 July 1990.

Leadership, these men and their agency were respected widely for integrity and competence as Christian journalists.

Their "sin" was to cover with scrupulous objectivity the continuing struggle between Southern Baptist "conservatives" and "moderates" for control of the denomination.[29]

Most state papers editorialized against the firing, and some must have felt the hot breath of the fundamentalists in their states.

One month after the firing of the journalists, the trustees of the Baptist Sunday School Board voted not to publish its centennial history written by Leon McBeth, church historian from Southwestern Seminary. The chairman of the general publishing committee said, "The book was unbalanced."[30]

The termination of the two journalists had various effects in the denomination. Editors generally were horrified. Secular publications commented adversely and sometimes at length. Many felt that the fundamentalists now had complete control of the SBC and its functions. Little news adverse to fundamentalists and the Pressler-Patterson coalition would be published in Baptist Press. Perhaps most tragically, some of the state papers trimmed their sails to the prevailing winds of fundamentalism.

Pastoral Authority and Priesthood

W. A. Criswell said in a session of "The School of the Prophets" at the then Criswell Bible College that "the pastor is the ruler of the church." He continued,

Lay leadership of the church is unbiblical when it weakens the pastor's authority as ruler of the church. . . . A laity-led, deacon-led church will be a weak church anywhere on God's earth. The pastor is the ruler of the church. There is no other thing than that in the Bible.

This declaration came in answer to a criticism of an emphasis of the Sunday School Board on Shared Ministry. Joe Stacker of the board said that shared ministry

---

[29]*The United Methodist Reporter*, 27 July 1990.
[30]Baptist Press, 17 August 1990.

promotes on a biblical basis the development of healthy relationships between pastors, church staff, deacons and church members. The emphasis affirms the pastor as the overseer/leader of the church who equips the saints for ministry. This multiplies the ministry of Christ through persons who lead by example as taught in 1 Peter 5:1-4.[31]

In some ways, this was the opening gun in another battle that would confuse and bother the denomination for years.

A number of thoughtful observers felt that the denomination was being led away from the concept of the priesthood of all believers toward the concept of high priesthood for a few believers. Addressing this issue, Richard Jackson, the highly successful pastor of the North Phoenix Baptist Church, said, "Southern Baptists are abandoning one of their cherished doctrines—the priesthood of the believer—by surrendering control of their denomination to a handful of 'high priests.'" He said that the conflict was a struggle for priesthood—whether individual, free-thinking Southern Baptists would determine the direction and nature of their denomination or whether those powers would reside in a handful of leaders.[32]

Shortly after this incident, Professor Bill Leonard of Southern Seminary, commented that the 1970s and 1980s had been characterized by a movement toward autocratic leadership by pastors and greater specialization of ministerial duties in churches with multiple staffs. These trends had led to a "clergyification" of the Southern Baptist Convention. Jackson said that these trends made "the laity second-class citizens. It undermines the most basic biblical understanding of the church as the whole people of God."[33]

The issue would get white hot in the forthcoming meeting of the convention in San Antonio in June 1988.

A resolution was introduced and passed in the convention meeting on the priesthood of the believer. A series of "whereas's" noted the high profile of the emphasis on the doctrine, that the doctrine was subject to abuse, and that it could be used to justify the undermining of pastoral authority in the local church. Then the resolution continued.

---

[31]Baptist Press, 21 February 1986.

[32]Baptist Press, 12 May 1988.

[33]Baptist Press, 3 June 1988.

> Be it therefore resolved . . . that the convention affirm its belief in the . . . doctrine, . . . Be it further resolved, that we affirm that this doctrine in no way gives license to misinterpret, explain away, demythologize, or extrapolate out elements of the supernatural from the Bible; and Be it further resolved, that the doctrine of the priesthood of the believer in no way contradicts the biblical understanding of the role, responsibility, and authority of the pastor which is seen in the command to the local church in Hebrews 13:17, "obey your leaders and submit to them; for they keep watch over your souls, as those who will give an account"; and be it finally resolved, that we affirm the truth that elders, or pastors, are called of God to lead the local church (Acts 20:28).[34]

Efforts to change some of the strong language in the resolution failed. No amendments were accepted.

About a hundred messengers in protest of the resolution turned in their ballots. Led by Randall Lolley, past president of Southeastern Seminary, about 200 gathered at the Alamo. Standing in front of the site where Americans died for the cause of freedom more than 150 years ago, Lolley declared that the resolution on priesthood was "the most non-Baptistic, most heretical, from the Baptist free church point of view, statement ever made." He wrote the word "heresy" across the resolution and tore it up.[35]

In the fall, twelve state conventions ratified resolutions on the priesthood of the believer generally affirming the traditional stance.[36] Twenty four conventions dealt with the matter.

The issue of pastoral authority would torment many churches for years to come. As the incidence of pastoral terminations rose, the evidence mounted that many Baptists did not care for "pastoral authority." Priesthood would be defended and debated many times.

Higher Education and Fundamentalism

The longer the conflict went on, the more nervous educators became with the problems that developed and those that were feared. Campuses

---

[34]*SBC Annual* (1988) 69.
[35]Baptist Press, 16 June 1988.
[36]Baptist Press, 23 November 1988.

tended to divide along the lines of the denominational division, with students in the main causing the problems. Some student groups seemed to be coached, and some tried to coach the administration and faculty. Trustee groups became restive as the fundamentalist take-over seemed to aim at institutions next. To some of the educators, trouble with a capital "T" seemed eminent.

In Texas, Baylor University, the largest of the Baptist schools, took a dramatic and drastic step. Baptist Press reported,

> Moving to free the school from the perceived threat of a conservative takeover, Baylor University's trustees voted September 21, 1990 to change its charter to put distance between the university and control by the Baptist General Convention of Texas.
>
> By a vote of 30 to 7 with one abstention...the trustees moved to change the university charter to replace the current 48 member board of trustees with a 24 member board of regents who will have "sole governance" of the institution.

The charter change by the trustees without approval of the convention of Texas was in violation of the convention constitution.[37] The university charter had been granted by the Republic of Texas and predates the BGCT charter. Under that charter and Texas law, the university trustees have the exclusive right to amend the charter.

Fundamentalists and many others were outraged. No notice of the change had been given to the state convention. The state convention Executive Director was not told of the change until after it was accomplished. The university officials told state Baptists that it intended to maintain a close relationship with the convention. They cited the threat of a conservative takeover of the university board of trustees, such as has happened to Southern Baptist seminaries, as having prompted the action. The university had been mentioned frequently, according to president Herbert Reynolds, as a takeover target of conservatives.

The chairman of the trustees, Winfred Moore, said,

> I think taking Baylor out of the eye of the political storm, not only in Texas but also in the SBC, will make it much easier for us to get on

---

[37]Baptist Press, 24 September 1990.

with our missions involvement in the state and other places. Baylor will not be there to be shot at or defended. We don't have to expend the energy or defend a takeover of Baylor University.

In the announcement to the press, President Reynolds said, "This is an historic and courageous initiative by the board of trustees. This action will maintain Baylor's academic excellence and continue its worldwide Christian example."[38]

Immediate and sustained conflict broke out over the Baylor decision. Claims of stealing a university and betraying Baptists were heard all over the country. Plans for action to stay the decision were laid, and a committee was appointed to begin the process to see if the decision could be reversed. This conflict would go on with charges and counter-charges until the meeting of the Baptist General Convention of Texas in the fall of 1991. A compromise agreement would put Baylor in charge of its own affairs. A complicated change would allow the Texas convention to elect one-fourth of the regents. Three-fourths of the regents would be elected by the regents themselves.

The campaign of the fundamentalists and others to reverse this compromise agreement is interesting. A personal correspondence revealed these items:

—Vast expenditures were incurred by the fundamentalist group.

—A video cassette of a sermon by the pastor of the First Baptist Church, Dallas was produced and sent to every pastor in the state (over 5000 pastors).

—A professional political consulting firm was employed to give direction . . . and parliamentary expert. . . . was flown in to direct the floor fight at the convention in Waco.

—Professionally written political campaign letters were sent out to every pastor in the state over signatures of fundamentalist leaders.

—A professionally directed 600-unit telephone bank was paid for by the fundamentalist leaders the week before the Waco convention, utilizing carefully scripted telephone messages.

—A major ad campaign in the Baptist state paper . . . was organized and funded by the fundamentalist leaders.[39]

---

[38]Ibid.

[39]From a personal letter, name withheld, 10 December 1991.

Long before the Texas convention met, all hotel rooms in the city of Waco were reserved by fundamentalist forces. So much for the "non-political" nature of the fundamentalist movement! The compromise agreement with Baylor was accepted at the meeting of the Texas convention by a vote of about two to one. The moderates were winners for once. Baylor remained (and remains) in charge of its own destiny.

In April, 1990, Baylor regents incorporated the Truett Baptist Theological Seminary. The new seminary was to be named after the legendary pastor of the First Baptist Church in Dallas. The act served notice on the fundamentalists that Texas would have a theological seminary not controlled by them. The fundamentalists now had a solid majority of trustees of Southwestern Seminary.

On October 15, 1990, Furman University, Greenville, South Carolina, trustees voted to change the school's charter so they, not the South Carolina Baptist Convention, elect their successors. John Johns, president of Furman, said the school's trustees took the historic action "to move our governing body out of harm's way, so it can go back to an emphasis on education rather than being a pawn in the political field." Johns commented that the action "clears up any doubt about who governs the university."[40] This action was, according to some, a violation of its own charter. In November, 1991, the state convention voted by a narrow margin to sue the university in an attempt to change the decision.

In November of 1990, Florida Baptists and Stetson University reached an agreement "that gradually eliminates Florida Baptist Convention funding of the DeLand school by the year 2000 in exchange for granting Stetson more autonomy in the election of its trustees.[41]

On February 27, 1991, the trustees of Meredith College in North Carolina voted to amend the charter so that trustees would elect their successors. The press statement said:

> This decision to amend the charter of Meredith College represents an important move by the trustees to assure that Meredith College can continue its commitment to intellectual freedom and academic excellence as it has for the past one hundred years.[42]

---

[40]*SBC Today*, 2 November 19, 17.
[41]Baptist Press, 16 November 1990.
[42]*Biblical Recorder*, 2 March 1991, 1.

Almost simultaneously—December, 1990—the Baptist Health Care System Board took action that would separate The Baptist Hospital in Nashville from the control of the Tennessee Baptist Convention. The board voted to amend its charter to allow the board to elect its own trustees. After some negotiation and the payment of a considerable sum of money to the Tennessee convention, the action stood.[43]

In reviewing these dramatic actions, R. G. Puckett, editor of *The Biblical Recorder* of North Carolina commented editorially, "The details may vary from situation to situation but the intention is the same in each case; remove the institution from the arena of Baptist conflict and safeguard its continuation as it has been throughout its history."[44]

Some in each state saw these actions as being unethical and a betrayal of the intention of the denomination in their formation. A strong case could be made for this view in some of the actions. From the other side of the argument, the view was held that the fundamentalists had just as unethically stolen an entire denomination. From this view, the decisions of trustees of the separating institutions were simply salvaging what could be saved from the catastrophic changes being made in the denomination.

These decisions by trustees would be contested in each state but almost all would remain firm in so far as the effect was concerned. Baptists were witnessing the disintegration of a substantial part of an enormous educational and missionary enterprise that had been built over the more than one hundred forty year history of the denomination.

A Comedian Comments on Tragedy

Grand Ole Opry star Jerry Clower used his humor to comment on the conflict in the SBC in a New Orleans speech to a conference of Associational Directors of Missions. He said that he had been asked to comment on the woes of television evangelist Jim Bakker. He replied, "I ain't got a dog in that fight."

"When it comes to the SBC," Clower said, "I've got a dog in that fight. . . . I love ya'll. Not just anyone can say that. I can because I've

---

[43]Baptist Press, 7 January 1991.
[44]Baptist Press, 9 March 1991.

paid my dues." He has been a Southern Baptist for fifty years.
When quizzed about his views on scripture, he said,

> I didn't know you could be a Baptist and not believe the Bible. Watch
> my lips: I do not worship the Bible. I had a personal experience with
> Jesus Christ when I was 13 years of age. . . . Let's don't take our focus
> off Jesus. Folks are going to die and go to hell while we decide who
> believes the Bible.

He implied that he had had a problem that others experienced. He
said, (apparently because he had made fun of the inerrancy issue,) "I
done been called to Dallas." The implication was that the fundamentalists
wanted an explanation.

(A demand made of a private Baptist citizen to explain to "authority"
a comment on any subject is unconscionable.)

Chapter Eleven

The Human Cost

"The Blood of Prophets . . ."[1]

As the political skills of the fundamentalists were honed and their control grew more complete, the moderates grew more restive. Repeatedly groups were organized by the moderates among the clergy and laity to try to stay the march of the fundamentalists. Nothing seemed to work to change the direction of the denomination.

From 1985, strong pastors became involved in the presidential elections. In 1985 and 1986, Winfred Moore, pastor of the big and strong First Baptist Church of Amarillo, was the moderate candidate. He had come late to the conflict but furnished moderates good and competent leadership. He was supported by his congregation and by many Texans, as well as moderates all over the nation. In 1986, Adrian Rogers beat Moore by 54.22 percent to 45.78 percent.

The next to emerge in the moderate cause was Richard Jackson, pastor of the North Phoenix Baptist Church in Phoenix, Arizona. Jackson had led his church to contribute a million dollars a year to the Cooperative Program. He was a strong preacher and abhorred what was happening to the denomination. He sometimes confronted Paul Pressler in public concerning Pressler's conduct. On one occasion, he offered to withdraw from the fray if Pressler would.

In 1987, Adrian Rogers beat Jackson for the presidency by 59.91 percent to 40.03 percent. In 1988, Jerry Vines beat Jackson by 50.53 percent to 48.32 percent. The actual vote that year was 15,804 for Vines to Jackson's 15,112. Less than 700 votes out of 31,291 votes cast separated the two. (That year a few votes went to other candidates.) The moderates would not come as close to winning again.

---

[1] Revelation 18:24.

In 1989, Daniel Vestal, pastor of the First Baptist Church of Midland, Texas, emerged as a leader of the moderates. Vestal had been unhappy with the controversy but had taken little part until he heard the infamous Firestorm Chat tape of Pressler's interview with Gary North. He came away from that experience believing that the fundamentalist effort was a travesty against the faith and the denomination. Vestal's church was widely known for its contributions to the mission causes of the convention. At the convention in 1989, Jerry Vines, incumbent president won over Vestal by 56.58 percent to 43.39 percent.

An intense campaign was waged by both sides before the 1990 meeting in New Orleans. Morris Chapman, pastor of the First Baptist Church, Wichita Falls, Texas, was the fundamentalist candidate. Daniel Vestal was again the moderate candidate. Both acknowledged extensive speaking schedules in an effort to win the presidency. This kind of campaigning still did not please many Southern Baptists.

Moderates felt that they had an excellent candidate and that New Orleans furnished the best opportunity to win that they had had for years. The feeling seemed to grow that this was the true water-shed meeting. If they did not win at this meeting, the moderates would face a bleak future in the denomination. There was no evidence that the fundamentalists would ever become inclusive in their complete control of the denominational machinery. If they continued to exclude everyone who did not agree with their agenda, little hope lay of returning to a time when there was peace in the midst of diversity. The fundamentalist decision that diversity of the historic type in the convention was wrong left no ground for participation of moderates. This convention meeting was crucial.

To turn the tide even more strongly toward the fundamentalists, the organization secured the endorsement of Chapman by a half dozen heavy weight pastors. Several of these were pastors of "super-churches" and had considerable influence. Joel Gregory, pastor of Travis Avenue Church in Fort Worth, joined the endorsers. He was accused later of doing so in order to be considered as the next pastor of First Baptist Church, Dallas. Whatever his motivation, he was elected as the pastor ultimately to succeed the legendary W. A. Criswell. When he was elected pastor, he told the press that his friends knew that his heart had always been in the fundamentalist cause.

Morris Chapman, the fundamentalist candidate, won over Vestal by 57.68 percent to 42.32 percent in the New Orleans meeting of the convention in 1990.[2]

The atmosphere for moderates was funereal. Anger seemed to give way to sorrow. It was a common sight to see tears on the face of strong men and women. Everywhere around the Super Dome, moderates could be seen embracing and saying good bye to friends. Many declared that they would not be back to meetings where they were not wanted. Still others felt that the only reason they were not excluded from the meetings was that the money from their churches was wanted by the fundamentalists to pay for their programs.

In forty years of attending meetings of the Southern Baptist Convention, I have never witnessed such sadness and grief.

The fundamentalists celebrated their great victory. All around the hotels and Super Dome, they congratulated each other with many pats on the back, shouts of joy, embraces, and victory signs.

On Wednesday night, Paige Patterson and Paul Pressler, returned to the place where they met many years before—Cafe du Monde—for their celebration. They were met there by a large crowd of friends of the movement. Barry McCarty, convention parliamentarian, called the meeting to order. Patterson and Pressler were presented with framed certificates of appreciation for their work in gaining control of the Southern Baptist Convention.

They celebrated amid the ashes of a great denomination. All over America, millions of Southern Baptists were disfranchised with no representation on the trustee boards of their institutions and no voice in their affairs. The shouts and jeers of the fundamentalists were mixed with the tears and heartbreak of the moderates.

Barry McCarty, whose presence at the celebration was challenged by a disillusioned messenger, said that "I was just passing by, waiting on an order of donuts." A trusted former state executive director and his wife witnessed the arrival of McCarty in a limousine with the president of the convention. He explained that he was "on twenty-four hour call" and had to accompany the president wherever he went. For the first time, the SBC had a parliamentarian who conducted business outside the meeting hall. In 1989, he was paid $14,500 for his services.[3]

The disillusioned messenger tried four times the next day to tell the

---

[2]*SBC Annual* (1990) 56.
[3]Baptist Press, 21 June 1990.

messengers of the convention what had happened. Twice he was not recognized, and twice his microphone was cut off.[4]

For the foreseeable future, the New Orleans meeting in June, 1990, saw the end of organized opposition to the fundamentalists in the election of officers.

Fragmentation Accelerates

The fragmentation of the Southern Baptist Convention had been gaining momentum for months, and the New Orleans meeting gave new impetus.

New institutions were being born, creating new problems for the seminaries. Wake Forest University announced the guidelines for the opening of a new divinity school. Samford University had recently opened a new divinity school. Baylor University had incorporated a new seminary. The Southern Baptist Alliance opened discussions that would result in a new seminary in Richmond, Virginia.

In late August of 1990, almost 3000 moderate Southern Baptists met in Atlanta to consider ways to carry on the work they believed in. A wide variety of persons were present. Many were simply disillusioned with the fundamentalist leadership of the SBC. Many were seeking fellowship with like-minded Christians. Still others were seeking ways to gain support for causes they sponsored.

One observer described the meeting as "euphoric." The spirits of many were high, and all enjoyed the sense of openness and freedom. Many took great care not to be judgmental or critical and not to import from the New Orleans meeting of the convention the feeling of exclusiveness. Great stress was put on inclusiveness and freedom of discussion. Sadness was somewhat ameliorated by the sense of joy that there may be a future for disfranchised Southern Baptists.

The new gathering immediately ran into a plethora of questions. What was this gathering? Was this the first step toward a split in the SBC? Was this the first meeting of a new convention? What was the purpose of the gathering? Was an organization to be formed and structure adopted? Who was in charge? What kind of representation was intended?

---

[4]Ibid.

Was this a one-time meeting? Who would decide the answers to all these and many other questions?

The "causes" were there in strength. Women interested in the plight of women in the SBC and those interested in the problems of women in ministry and interested in the recognition of the ordination of women were there in strength. The representatives of Baptists Committed, a coalition of moderates, were there. The members of the Southern Baptist Alliance, a coalition of perhaps less conservative Baptists, were there. Persons interested in the welfare of the divorced and and pro-choice advocates and opponents were there. The young, tired of the influence and leadership of "the good ole boys," were there and vocal.

The "cause" was threatened by "causes."

The meeting had been called by Baptists Committed (and others) and was presided over by Daniel Vestal, defeated SBC presidential candidate. It was obvious that many churches would be looking for ways to support the missionary and educational causes they loved without the interference of the SBC Executive Committee. There were actually already in place mechanisms by which this could be accomplished. The group were intent on setting up new ways of doing these things.

Some wanted to start a new denomination immediately.

Some wanted to stay in the SBC but conduct education and missions in new ways.

Some wanted new institutions and mission activities.

Many seemed to understand little of the implications of the proposals that were made.

Some of the "good ole boys" had prepared ahead of time a method of funding for such causes as the body, and specifically the churches represented, desired. The Baptist Cooperative Missions Program, Inc. had been formed under the leadership of Duke McCall, former president of Southern Seminary. On the board of directors were five former agency heads of the SBC: McCall; Randall Lolley, former president of Southeastern Seminary; Darryl Morgan, former president of the Annuity Board; Carolyn Weatherford Crumpler, former Executive Director of the WMU; and I, former president of the Sunday School Board. We were joined by a number of leading pastors and laymen.

The corporation was formed simply to facilitate the desires of the churches that would be sending their money by routes that bypassed the Executive Committee. It was our desire that the seminaries and mission boards be funded as fully as possible with the funds of those still interested in them. Many of us felt that we had appointed and sent missionaries in good faith and that they had gone in good faith. We could not desert them, whatever the attitude of the fundamentalists. We had established seminaries and felt that as long as they stayed in the middle of traditional Baptist views, they needed our support. We knew that this was a stop-gap measure and raised questions that could not then be answered. When these institutions became the mirror of fundamentalist thought, then the problems would be different.

The Consultation of Concerned Baptists adopted the corporation as the funding mechanism of the group. We were asked to have it active and functioning by October 1, 1990. We had six weeks to set up a new funding mechanism, solve the legal problems,secure an office, banking arrangements, secure staff, set up procedures to process and transfer funds, and other such matters. Mrs. Hettie Johnson, former executive of the Home Mission Board, gave her time and considerable expertise to help make this happen. Duke McCall and I spent a lot of time and money organizing and getting ready to receive funds. The office was opened and began to receive funds from churches on October 1. By the first of 1991, the funds were flowing through this mechanism at the annual rate of about four million dollars. This was accomplished with no promotion, no firm organization, and no professional leadership.

By the beginning of 1991 in the SBC, the missionary enterprise was showing signs of serious inroads by the controversy. Between 1987 and 1989, the Foreign Mission Board had to appoint 49 missionaries to have a net gain of one. In contrast, between 1980 and 1986, every 49 appointments resulted in a net gain of 12 overseas missionaries. (Thirty-seven of the 49 replaced those who retired, resigned, completed service, or died.) The problem was caused by a combination of fewer missionary appointments and higher rates of resignations and retirements.

In the 1980s the Board lost an average of 38 missionaries annually for every 1000 in service. In 1989, the loss rate reached 47 per 1,000. The 1989 rate sustained a four-year trend in rising missionary losses. In 1989, there were 174 resignations. More than 50 percent of those resigned before completing two four-year terms.

In the fall of 1990, the North Carolina convention General Board adopted a plan to designate 15 percent of its Cooperative Program funds for chosen SBC causes. This would have been a change from the 35 percent that had gone undesignated to the SBC.[5]

The plan narrowly failed in the convention meeting, but the right of the church to designate funds was recognized. A number of North Carolina churches would send funds through the new organization of the Cooperative Baptist Fellowship that grew out of the August meeting in Atlanta. Still others would designate funds to specific causes through the state convention office.

In Virginia in November, 1990 more than 4700 messengers registered. This exceeded the previous high by nearly 2000. The body voted to designate one-half of its 34.5 percent Cooperative Program that formerly had been sent to the SBC undesignated. This meant that the Association (Virginia's name for the state convention) would be designating to causes of their choosing one-half of what had formerly been sent to the SBC to be used according to the national body's distribution formula. The point of the designations was to bypass some SBC causes. This appeared to include the Christian Life Commission and the Executive Committee and changed markedly their support of SBC seminaries.

By August, in Kentucky, numerous churches were escrowing funds formerly given to the SBC Cooperative Program. The people were unhappy with the fundamentalist agenda and expressed themselves in the one way that would register most quickly. By 1991, the Kentucky convention would not meet its budget and would have serious need to reconsider its commitments.

In Arkansas, Missouri, and Texas, groups would form to consider alternate ways to finance missions and education apart from the traditional means. In Texas, the Executive Board would recommend in November of 1991 a plan that would allow churches to designate contributions to the Cooperative Program to eliminate at least five causes in the SBC budget and still call the contributions a part of the Cooperative Program.

The cooperative missions budget had been in place for more than a half century. Churches were accustomed to this channel of giving that allowed them to participate by the one contribution in all that the SBC was doing. The fundamentalist control of the denominational machinery placed this unified giving program in great jeopardy. The training had been so intense and the causes represented were so at the heart of what

---

[5]Baptist Press, 8 October 1990.

a Southern Baptist was that it would take a long time before the method was compromised completely.

Within a matter of weeks of the establishment of the Baptist Cooperative Mission Program in Atlanta by the Concerned Baptists (which became the Cooperative Baptist Fellowship), the verbal support of the national missions program grew dramatically.

The fundamentalist establishment, who had said they could not support that which offended their conscience, now cried foul. The moderates' conscience was another matter altogether. The "liberals," it was said, were trying to destroy the Cooperative Program. Widespread verbal support of the Cooperative Program rose over night. People and churches that had done relatively little for the national effort began talking about raising their gifts. People who had said little in years gone by now were making speeches in behalf of larger gifts to the Cooperative Program. Without doubt, some gifts increased. Little evidence existed that they would replace all the funds lost by the problems of the SBC. It seemed unlikely that the giving would match the rhetoric.

The full story of funds lost by the conflict will not be told for a generation. Many who had included Baptist causes in their wills changed them. More that twenty people voluntarily talked to me about the changes they were making in their bequests.

Two Baptist schools lost more than $14,000,000 in a single bequest.

More than $30,000,000 for a mission cause has been deleted from another will.

Several persons have changed their wills that contained property, money, and stocks for Baptist causes.

At last account, several million had been withdrawn from another Baptist school. These are simply diversions that individuals told me about. No one knows how extensive this trend is.

Changing of The Guard

The late years of the controversy had seen a radical shift in the leadership of the agencies and institutions. One source of stability and continuity in the denomination was seriously disrupted.

Lloyd Elder, president of the Sunday School Board was forced out of office.

William Tanner, president of the Home Mission Board had departed for Oklahoma.

Larry Baker, executive director of the Christian Life Commission, feeling harassed took a pastorate.

Randall Lolley, president of Southeastern Seminary, resigned in protest to the actions of the board of trustees.

Frank Pollard had left the presidency of Golden Gate Seminary to return to the pastorate.

Jimmy Allen, president of the Radio and Television Commission, left the job in frustration.

Carolyn Weatherford left Woman's Missionary Union to become Mrs. Joe Crumpler.

All Shackleford and Dan Martin were discharged from Baptist Press.

At the 1991 convention meeting, Harold Bennett, president of the SBC Executive Committee, announced his forthcoming retirement.

James Smith, president of the Brotherhood Commission, announced his retirement.

Serious challenges have been launched to the leadership of other executives. Almost none have been challenged because of "liberalism," but they have been severely criticized for differing with members of their trustees. The spirit now prevailed in the SBC that the one who paid the piper would call the tune. However, large segments of the financial support came from churches believed to be moderate in their orientation.

Several other executives will shortly reach retirement age. At least three want to continue past the traditional 65 years. They have stated privately that they would like to attempt to maintain the programs of their agency for as long as possible. Whether they will be allowed to do so remains to be seen.

The Trickle Down Syndrome

Serious efforts had been made across the years to prevent the national conflict from affecting the state conventions, the local associations, and the individual churches. Some thought that they were not affected by the problems, and, in some places, asked visiting speakers to refrain from discussing it. I was warned in one state not to speak to the press about the problems. Another visiting leader was told that the problems did not affect the state: "Please don't refer to them publicly and do not mention them in conversation."

The very nature of the body called Southern Baptists was in transition. New definitions of what it meant to be a Southern Baptist were being spelled out. Radical departures from traditional procedures and emphases were shaping up. The lines of communication that had existed between the churches, associations, state conventions, and the SBC were changing. Pastors and other staff members were constantly moving from place to place, taking with them whatever stance was meaningful. Publications were full of the news of the conflict. Every meeting at almost every level was influenced in one way or many by the controversy.

These changes were not new confrontations with modernity; these were confrontations with history, tradition, and polity changes.

Lines were drawn between friends and even families that demanded that sides be taken. Friends of a generation found themselves in different camps. The excessive verbiage caused bad feelings in many places. Almost no one had the luxury of remaining neutral, even though many were steadfastly clinging to the belief that they were not affected.

Churches without pastors were regularly called by fundamentalist leaders—and sometimes moderate leaders—urging the selection of someone favorable to one side or the other. Pastor's selection committees began to ask prospective pastors which side of the controversy they were on. Some churches began to look for "conservative" pastors, and others wanted only "moderate" ones. One common device used by some selection committees was to question the candidate on the matter of inerrancy and matters of literal interpretation of scripture. Others asked in detail about views on a variety of subjects including divorce, abortion, and women in ministry.

Interestingly, pastors were for many years called by votes that were almost always unanimous or nearly so. Many would not accept the call of a congregation if the vote was not overwhelmingly favorable. Now, votes were often seriously divided, frequently over the issues involving the denomination. A friend told me on the phone today of one church that rejected the nominee of its search committee by a vote of 60 to 40 percent.

The churches themselves were frequently badly uninformed about the nature of the controversy. Many pastors simply did not talk to the people about the problems. If they did, the people were likely to receive only the information from the side represented by the pastor. In some cases, the pastor led the people to consider the issues and tried to give a good education in the problems. In the main, it seems fair to say that in the majority of the congregations, the people were largely uninformed about the conflict. They knew there was one but did not understand it.

By the time of the New Orleans convention meeting in 1990, many associations of churches were badly divided over the problems. Many local pastors' meetings became the parade ground for different opinions. In some places, the division was so great that the meetings stopped altogether. Neighboring pastors frequently no longer had fellowship together. In some associations, a predominately fundamentalist or moderate group gradually took control. Evidence of these conditions can be seen in the number of associations withdrawing fellowship from a church for having women deacons or pastor, or having a pastor who had been divorced. When abortion became the litmus test of orthodoxy, further divisions were created, and some fundamentalist pastors became ardent activists on the side of pro-life. A sizable number were arrested for blocking the entrance to abortion clinics.

Churches were divided over these matters. Some could not agree over how to fund missions and education. One voted about 65 to 35 percent to fund missions through the traditional method of the Cooperative Program. After some trauma, the congregation decided to allow the 35 percent of the congregation to fund missions in their own fashion. This was a good Baptist decision!

In a number of cases, moderate pastors could not lead congregations to follow them in finding new ways of funding missions. The churches had had fifty years of training in the cooperative method of doing missions and education and simply could not break from the traditional way. In one case known to me, the pastor is sure that he can lead the church to recognize the problems created by fundamentalist control and redirect mission funds. He has not done so because he knows that he will lose the support of a number of families and that the cost of victory is too high. This seems to be a common problem.

A common question has been, why don't these churches that are dissatisfied leave the convention and form a new denomination. In discussing this matter with seasoned observers, I have concluded that many of these churches simply will not leave the SBC. I could not help but remember the problems of the dissenters in the Missouri Synod Lutheran Church who thought that thousands of churches would join them. Only a few hundred did. In the case of Southern Baptists, many of the churches would not follow even if the pastor wanted to do so. It seems fair to say that only a relatively small number of churches will leave the SBC, even if a move to organize a new denomination begins. It now seems likely that some leading and "bell-weather" churches may be prepared to take the plunge.

Southern Baptists have always been, in the main, a following people in denominational affairs. It will be many years before this strength and weakness will find solutions that are viable.

The Blood of the Prophets

One of the greatest tragedies in the conflict is little noticed and not long remembered. This is the effect of the controversy in the lives of individuals, particularly the pastors, professors, and denominational executives.

A long line of personal tragedies are left in the wake of the fundamentalist purges. Many of the departed left under the cloud of "liberalism." Few, if any—even by Southern Baptist standards—deserve the label.

It should be noted that after 12 years, no professor has been fired for liberalism.

In the Southeastern Seminary conflict, however, a total of at least seventeen professors and a half-dozen administrators have been forced out, have left, or say they are leaving in protest of their treatment. Families have been disrupted and displaced, careers have been shortened or ruined, and some have departed to other fellowships more friendly. The faculty is in shambles and each discipline suffers from either the loss of its faculty or internal turmoil. The faculty members have been discredited in the denomination by innuendo and rumor. Formal charges have been filed against no one. Due process often has been ignored, and no one has been convicted of anything. The implied or stated threat of trustees and administration to examine the theology of faculty members was enough to cause several to give up in disgust. No amount of protest by fundamentalists that they were simply doing their job will erase their responsibility for traumatizing so many fellow servants of the Lord.

At Southern Seminary, the situation has been a little better. The seminary has lost about eight or nine faculty members. Some directly attribute their departure to the controversy. Others say that they were definitely influenced by it. Several who remain at the seminary have been harassed over something the fundamentalists do not like. At least two of the faculty members have departed to non-Southern Baptist posts. The recitation of the resignations does not do justice to the trauma in the lives of the individuals and their families. The suffering in private caused by public embarrassment and false labels cannot be known or detailed by commenting on its reality.

The arbitrary termination of the Baptist Press leaders has been catastrophic in their lives. While they were given six months terminal pay, they will in all likelihood never recover financially or emotionally from the experience. Al Shackleford had every right to expect that some other post in Baptist life would open to a man of his experience and competence. As I write nearly a year and a half since his termination, no one has employed him in the field of his expertise. It seems that many potential employers are intimidated by the vociferous actions of the fundamentalists and do not feel that they can afford to offend them. At the last word available, Shackleford has sold his home and is working in a grocery store to feed his family. The situation with Dan Martin is not much better, though he is serving as bi-vocational pastor of a small church. The press reported that the reason he was not employed as a press representative was that he had commented too vigorously on his treatment by the SBC Executive Committee. His considerable talents languish for lack of opportunity.

Lloyd Elder, former president of the Sunday School Board, said that the first time the board tried to fire him, he felt deserted. His metaphor was that it was as though he had been abandoned. When he was forced out as president of the board, he was publicly humiliated and his family suffered great trauma. Sue Elder, Lloyd's wife, underwent heart surgery. More will be said about him and his situation in the chapter on the agencies.

Larry Baker, the former executive of the Christian Life Commission, was forced out as its leader. While he is a successful pastor, the pain and suffering of his pilgrimage remains.

Public attacks on remaining executives by the circulation of reams of accusations have produced an almost unending series of problems for them and their families. Open conflict with various members of the boards of trustees have not been caused by "liberalism." These problems seem to have been caused by the zealous fundamentalists who want a change of administrative leadership.

One pastor wrote concerning such problems:

> The most shocking and upsetting recent development for me occurred at the most recent trustees meeting at Southern Baptist Theological Seminary in Louisville. In that meeting, Jerry Johnson, a first-year, 25 year old trustee from Aurora, Colorado, delivered an unprincipled, 16-page attack on Southern Seminary, concluding that "One would have to be blind as a mole not to see that (Seminary president) Dr. Honeycutt does not believe the Bible." As a graduate of Southern Seminary, I cannot imagine such a vicious attack being leveled at one of the premier Bible scholars of our denomination. In fact, Dr. Roy Honeycutt was a biblical scholar long before trustee Jerry Johnson was born![6]

Numerous faculty members have been attacked publicly over some interpretation or their view of Scripture. Proof does not seem necessary and due process often does not exist. Staff members of the Foreign Mission Board, the Sunday School Board, and Woman's Missionary Union have been the victims of questionable criticism.

President Russell Dilday of Southwestern Seminary has often been the victim of verbal assault by members of his board and other fundamentalists. He is certainly not a liberal but has often spoken his mind—a hallmark of a Baptist—on the issues confronting him, the seminary and the denomination. Amid the stress of his persecution, he was forced to undergo heart surgery.

President Roy Honeycutt of Southern Seminary, experiencing similar personal attacks, also underwent heart surgery.

This rehearsal of personal trauma caused by the conflict could go on and on.

The problems of the pastors are similar but not quite so public. One pastor told me that though he had not been vocal in his church about the problems, a small group of fundamentalists were intent on getting him fired. His sin is that he does not publicly support the fundamentalist cause. Most of the members are happy with his leadership. He said, "They (the fundamentalists) are like bulldogs, they just won't quit. Every

---

[6]Larry S Burcham, *The Sentinel*, 7 June 1990.

day there is a new confrontation and they will not stop until I am gone."
He is seeking another place to go. His family remains in a state of
turmoil over the uncertainties and unkindness in which they must live.

His name is legion. The evidence grows that the number of pastors
in similar problems is large. No one knows, of course, how many there
are. As information and misinformation about the conflict is disseminated,
increasing numbers of churches are divided over the issue. Often they do
not have enough information to assess the situation rightly. Prejudice or
misunderstanding or outright ill will is dividing more and more
congregations. The pastors and other staff persons are in the vortex of the
whirlwind. A number of pastors known to me personally have departed
to other denominations.

On the other side of the argument, fundamentalist pastors eager to
defend their understanding of the faith sometimes find themselves in an
explosive situation. Moderate parishioners, accustomed to free expression,
servant-ministers, equality in the church, and democratic procedures are
impatient and unhappy with pastors of another genre. Often the pastors,
having learned fundamentalism from peers, don't know what the
problems are until it is too late to salvage relationships with the
congregation.

It should be noted that many of the younger pastors have never
known the Southern Baptist Convention as it used to be. Their entire
denominational careers have been in the shadow of the conflict.

Many of the moderates find themselves without a denominational
home. They have little hope of ever serving in a leadership role beyond
the local church. The invitations that the competent would have gotten a
few years ago to exercise their talents in a state setting or a national
setting are not going to come. The professional relationships that would
have promoted growth and expanded horizons are now limited to their
own kind. Opportunities for larger responsibilities will be slower in
coming if they come at all. Membership on boards and committees that
enlarge understanding and extend service are now reserved for the group
in power.

One young pastor in Georgia summed up this aspect of modern SBC
life in this manner:

One of the hidden stories of the SBC controversy is the anguished
uncertainty of thousands of young seminary-trained pastors, staff

members and missionaries. Thousands of young leaders are just now considering the major directions of their lives. The future in ministry among Baptists appears cloudy. Reports of forced terminations, church splits and institutional turmoil breed discouragement and cynicism.[7]

The processes by which leadership is now chosen are closed to nearly half (if not more) of all ministers, except with their own kind. One mistake in speech, vote, or luncheon companion can spell the end of a promising career.

Fear of just such events is wide spread. The power of "recommendation" is great among Southern Baptists. This simple mechanism is the means of most pastoral changes. Now a moderate pastor can expect to be recommended only by his kind. He can expect to be opposed by others as he anticipates a change in pulpit or ministry. Denominational posts at all levels will be beyond his reach, not because of his lack of competency but because of his lack of support from those in power.

Concerning fear, it is rampant at all levels of the denomination. The executives still in office after years of conflict are afraid of undermining their leadership and support. The employees don't know which way to jump pending the revealing of the direction of the new fundamentalist board of trustees. The pastors are afraid of being displaced and having no place to serve. Such simple things as health insurance, enormously expensive, give pause to one considering a change. To vote wrong on a business matter in the local association or state convention may set the course of a person's ministry. It is not uncommon for a pastor or leader to talk in no uncertain terms in private about what is going on in the denomination and then a few minutes later see that person be totally silent in the face of a public debate. The problem of fear cannot be over estimated in the present situation.

Another pastor wrote concerning the meeting of the convention in 1990 in New Orleans:

> Thursday morning I saw a friend of mine at the Superdome. He had experienced a dramatic conversion during his college years and had surrendered himself to full-time Christian service. I asked him how he felt about the events of the last few days.

---

[7]Gary Furr, *Baptists Today*, 6 September 1991, 4.

He said, "I left the church because I was Catholic. I felt that the hierarchy was oppressive in the way that it forced you to believe exactly the way they did or you got the boot. Now I'm back in a church with the same oppressive hierarchy. I'm back to square one. Now I don't know who I am or where I need to go."[8]

One veteran missionary couple wrote a letter to *SBC Today* commenting on the reaction of former journeymen (short-term missionaries) to the conflict. They said:

All five of these journeymen had completed their journeyman service, returned to the United States, and under conviction God was calling them to foreign mission service, had completed their seminary and/or university studies. They were in our city, not as a group but as individuals and couples, searching for ways and means to respond to God's call to missions.

Each of these fine young men and women told us they could not be appointed by "our" SBC Foreign Mission Board because they were not willing to compromise their integrity by deliberately using words which would make them appear to endorse and, hence, be "acceptable" to the political fundamentalist faction controlling our Foreign Mission Board. All of of these young people are as conservative as anyone could wish or hope to have on our foreign mission fields.

The spiritual depth and evangelistic concerns of each of them was an inspiration to us both, as was their commitment to foreign mission service.

We, personally, have hosted at least eight other former journeymen who felt the same impasse concerning their futures as missionaries. Most of these will somehow find a way to fulfill their callings, but it will probably not be through Southern Baptist channels.[9]

I quizzed at length a veteran observer of missions and missionaries who was in a position to know what was going on. When I asked what the effect of the controversy on the missionaries was, she replied, "totally devastating." The following incidents are her report of different problems and events. She is a person of impeccable integrity and is careful not to accuse or blame without first-hand observation or bona fide proof.

---

[8]James R. Barnette, "Mommy, What's A Messenger?" 2.
[9]Name withheld, *SBC Today,* 3 May 1991.

She told me of a home missionary who was confronted by a trustee of the Home Mission Board. The missionary was told that if he became involved with Baptists Committed (moderate organization) that he would not receive any support from the Home Mission board.

Then there was the missionary couple who were home on emergency leave. He was finishing his doctorate at Southern Seminary. He was advised by fundamentalist mission leaders in his country of service to break away from his doctoral advisor, who was under fire. In his mission, a missionary had been sent to teach the children of missionaries. His comment was that the teacher was not functionally literate and his grammar was so bad that parents were upset at what the children were hearing. He was a graduate of a fundamentalist seminary. Their reaction to the problems made them feel that the mission would not allow them to return. If their colleagues voted for them to return, they were not sure they could do so because of the division in the mission.

Another couple from a mission controlled by fundamentalists were not allowed to return to their work by vote of their colleagues. They were sure it was because of their relationship to a church whose pastor was a prominent moderate.

One missionary went to the convention in Atlanta. Her report was that she was so discouraged by the attitudes and atmosphere she was not sure how long she could be associated with the fundamentalist cause and leadership. The younger missionaries were so discouraged that they were very uncertain of their future as missionaries. None could be considered "liberal" in any sense.

Numerous missionaries have given my informant similar testimonies. A recurring theme has been that they are uncertain how long they can continue in service because they do not know how long they will be "approvable" by either their colleagues or the board.

They are feeling the pressure from a variety of sources. They feel it from their colleagues, from area managers, the board of trustees and senior staff. Their concerns reach all "the way up to Keith" (Parks), the FMB president. He is taking the heat from the professional missionaries because of the actions of the trustees, many of whom have been misinterpreted. More on this in the chapter on the agencies.

The toll on Christian workers has been enormous. Not only have many been terminated or resigned, many other have suffered greatly at the turmoil. Uncertainty and doubt about future directions have taken their toll in the institutions where fundamentalists have elected chief executive officers. By their own testimony, many are seeking other opportunities for service.

The blood of the prophets is spread across the nation. A flood flows unseen and unmourned.

An Illustration

Recently, one of Southern Baptist's stronger churches in a large city experienced what seemed to be a not uncommon loss of its pastor. Because of the prominence of the church and pastor, considerable interest was demonstrated by Baptists generally over why he left.

A church member, deacon and leader in other aspects of church life, wrote a letter to his fellow church members. In it, he laments the state of the church and the departure of the leader:

> Just what forced this superb Christian leader, and his wife, to resign? Just what caused (the pastor) to declare, "The events of the past eighteen months have been extremely stressful and detrimental to the health of my family and to my dearly loved church family?"
>
> For approximately two years there has been within our congregation a small but well-organized group of dissidents who have made it their mission to have their will prevail in our church. I'm not speaking of a theological will, but clearly a will of Power and Control. . . . There is a core element whose mission was to initially get rid of our pastor and thereafter put controls and restraints on our staff. . . .
>
> Even despicable anonymous hate mail and anonymous telephone calls, the dissimulation of forged information, rumors and innuendoes have been used to erode the main line leadership in our church. . . .
>
> Like water dripping on a rock, we have experienced the slow but certain erosion of our fellowship and Christ-centered focus. Political issues of power and control by this small group under carefully contrived "higher purpose" posturing have replaced our unity in Christ.
>
> So what are we to do? We have no focus as a Christian body. We are adrift in a sea of confusion, indecision and grief.[10]

---

[10]Letter to church members. Church name and writer's name withheld. Used by permission.

While the conflict in the church was not over the larger controversy according to the above quoted source, it is a paradigm of the same kind of conflict in many places.

Chapter Twelve

The Seminaries

"Teaching Them To Observe All Things. . . ."[1]

From the earliest days of the Southern Baptist Convention there was a manifest desire among many for an educated ministry. There was also another segment that was suspicious of education and particularly theological education. These groups existed in sometimes constructive and sometimes destructive tension for more than a hundred years. Since the supporters of education were in leadership for most of this time, the seminaries were prominent in the interests of the denomination. Along with the mission boards, they drew a lion's share of the funds. They have also been involved in a lion's share of our controversies.

One astute observer of our history commented that Southern Baptists were in many ways not truly educated theologically for a long time. Given the early anti-education stance of a sizable portion of the constituency, it is remarkable that the problems were so few. Those with what came to be called the fundamentalist mind-set were present from the beginning and seemed genuinely to fear the investigation of problems of religion and revelation. A spiritual paranoia seemed to grip some when complicated issues were aired and discussed.

Many young ministers heard the advice that they were going to do well if they did not go to a seminary and "get ruined." This mind-set had gradually diminished over the years until the beginning of the revolution in the convention. Suspicion of the seminaries was and is a fact that has influenced many aspects of denominational life.

---

[1]Matthew 28:20.

Faculties

The theological seminaries have been on the cutting edge of denominational life. The nature of the educational process makes it essential for faculties to deal with whatever ideas are current in theology. Thus, academics tend to play with ideas like others play with financial speculation or sports statistics. Faculty persons are apt to bring to class their latest readings or discussions. For students schooled in rigid orthodox ideas this can be an unsettling experience. If the teacher scoffs at the pet ideas of the student who is already uncomfortable with the opening world of ideas, the problems are multiplied. Some professors have gotten into difficulty simply because they have not been clear as to whether they were voicing their own opinions or whether they were introducing some radical idea to provoke discussion or thought.

Some younger faculty members are tempted to impress their colleagues or students with their understanding of their discipline. Some incur problems while trying to "make a contribution." As one study concluded, higher education breeds "liberalism," while years of experience in service breeds conservatism.

Another sort of problem experienced by our seminaries is that they are believed by many to lose touch with the thought of the constituency. Many of our professors regularly preach in the churches, and a considerable number act as interim pastors. By these activities, they try to stay in touch with the people and what they are thinking. In some instances, of course, they are. In others, they tend to hear what the people think they want to hear. It takes a strong intellectual constitution for a church member to cross theological swords with a seminary professor. Further, the professors are not apt to be invited to the churches with the more reactionary pastors and people. They may work for years and not hear more than isolated criticisms of the constituency related to the problems of the seminary as they are perceived by the people.

Faculties sometimes have a tendency to become so involved in what they are doing and teaching that they fail to reiterate the fundamentals of the faith in certain settings where it is needful. The nature of scholarship tends to cause the professor to talk in public about the ideas he is presently processing intellectually. It is possible and probable to hear from a professor those ideas that are occupying his time and thought and to conclude from them that he is not really concerned about the basics of the faith. I used to encourage our faculty to stop occasionally and state again their commitment to the faith in such terms that the ordinary Baptist could understand and appreciate. This simple procedure reduces the number of incidents in which the professor is accused of not supporting biblical faith. The sending up of intellectual trial balloons is an exercise in learning for a faculty but often a poor public relations experience for the general church membership.

Faculty members are subjected to unending attempts by the students to educate the faculty. This is sometimes amusing and often exasperating. They hear the same kind of thing year after year. When challenged by ignorance or narrowness, professors sometimes over-react. It is easy in this context to criticize the unsophisticated. When faculty faith or fidelity is questioned, they react as any other human being. The process of teaching theology and biblical studies to the uninitiated is filled with mine fields. To be misunderstood is fraught with hazards. To create understanding, while at the same time educating, takes careful procedures and infinite patience.

Students

The problems are intensified when it is realized that the students come to theological school at many different levels of preparation and intellectual sophistication. Many of them have already been to a Baptist college with a strong religion department. Some have college majors in Bible. Still others have the basic Bible courses required of all graduates. Some of these students are ready for second level courses in seminary.

Many come from state colleges and universities with no preliminary preparation for acquiring a professional degree in theology. Sometimes they have degrees in science or mathematics or some other unrelated discipline. The students start the first year of theological training at seriously different levels of preparation. Years of study and negotiation between the seminaries and colleges have not yet produced a satisfactory solution to the problems. This uneven undergraduate education of the students contributes greatly to the seminary faculty's problems.

In trying to understand the problems of the seminaries, it is necessary to mention "the mystique of academia." I have noticed across the years the exaggerated response of many people to the persons involved in higher education. Those with less education sometimes respond with suspicion and criticism of the school and its faculty. It is an area of life in which they have little experience and naturally are troubled by the unknown. The better educated, appreciating the nature of the experience, sometimes react with respect, admiration, and support. Both may be uncritical in their analysis. But there is something about the presence of scholarship and learning that elicits response.

Trustees

The trustee system in the Southern Baptist Convention has had some characteristics that contribute to the present set of problems. The rotation system for trustees has been good and bad. Usually a trustee can serve for two terms totaling eight to ten years. The system has allowed more persons to have the opportunity for service than a self-perpetuating system allows. This feature provides for an educational experience for the trustees and has probably contributed to the overall welfare of the schools. As the knowledge of the functioning of the school has grown, the support has grown also.

The other result has been that a person often requires several years to learn to function effectively as a trustee. In our system, almost by the time the trustee knows the school and its procedures, the rotation system removes him. This aspect of the system has many drawbacks. For example, the planning process for the school must be done almost exclusively by the staff. Often, there is little involvement of trustees except at the meetings of the board. Committee meetings are often short and hurried. In-depth involvement in the development of the institution is often impossible. To speak frankly, some seminary presidents have liked the system.

Trustees elected under our system frequently have little experience with an academic institution. In the last few years, since the controversy developed, an increasing number of trustees have been named that do not have any professional education. It is difficult to participate meaningfully in running a graduate level educational institution without having experienced graduate education in some dimension. A number of clergy trustees without any seminary education—and sometimes without a college degree—have been elected in recent years. Lay members are being elected without any advanced training. This lack is compensated for when the trustee has expertise in some related field such as finance.

Such trustees are frequently uncomfortable in the presence of those who have made a profession of higher education. They are apt to adopt one of two stances. They may be unduly impressed with the personnel with whom they deal, or they may adopt an adversarial role that creates unnecessary conflict. There are exceptions, of course, but these kinds of problems do arise.

Some moderates have long believed that some unequipped and some very astute trustees have been elected to the various boards as "hit men" whose mission is to cause problems for the administrations. If this is true, the apparent objective seems to be to "make this school conservative." Several events would seem to validate this charge as some of the schools have had unusual attacks made repeatedly by one or more persons.

Whether these assertions are true or not is difficult to prove, and perhaps no real purpose is to be gained by pursuing the matter. It is certain that a number of trustees have been elected that have little background to equip them for the task. Prior to the present difficulties, some trustees were elected that were not particularly effective. The generally good relationship between the administrations and the trustees, however, ameliorated the situation substantially. These trustees often became effective in the discharge of their responsibilities. With the rise of the conflict between the administrators and the trustees elected to change the direction of the institutions, the problems of trustee selection and training have multiplied and become aggravated.

Overall, the trustee system for the theological schools has produced more deeply entrenched administrators. The nature of the trustee experience has left the planning, staffing, financing, and future direction of the school in the hands of the paid staff. In some cases, the trustees met only once a year and then for two or three days. Some of the trustees had little orientation to the task after election. If the administrative recommendations made any sense, they were usually adopted. There was often little background for dissenting from a recommendation. The nature and direction of the school, thus, has been set by the president and his staff.

The other side of the coin is now clearly visible. Trustees elected under the present direction of the fundamentalists often show a different bent. In some schools, the administrations and faculty have flatly said that the substantial numbers of current trustees do not know the difference between administration and policy making. After reading the materials related to the schools and the reports coming out of the meetings, I would conclude that this is true.

It seems to be clear that some of the new trustees have come onto the board with the avowed purpose of changing the nature of the institution. When this is attempted without proper planning or complete knowledge of the documents of the school or the procedures related to accreditation, the result is apt to be chaos. When it is attempted without the prior knowledge of the president, dean, and other staff and faculty, the entire organization is threatened and processes break down.

Two actual incidents will illustrate the kind of problems we have faced.

Several years ago, a new trustee came into a meeting of a committee dealing with student affairs. He said in his first meeting, "I have been elected to straighten out this seminary. How do I go about it?"

In another seminary an almost identical situation occurred. The new trustee approached the president and dean and said, "I have been elected to make this seminary conservative. What do I do first?"

One of the prime problems of Southern Baptist seminaries as this volume is written is the different visions of theological education held by trustees and administrations. A seminary that has been headed in the direction of academic excellence within the framework of a doctrinal statement led by competent educators is in great peril if the trustees hold a different view of its purpose and direction. Trustee efforts to change the direction drastically, for whatever reason, will injure the institution seriously if the task is not undertaken with the interests of all parties in mind. Careful planning for change is essential if the integrity of the school is to be preserved. Careful evaluation of the needed change is the basis for constructive progress. The lack of this careful and cooperative study will result in tumult and conflict.

The eager determination of fundamentalists to change the direction of theological education has led to serious damage to at least two of our schools. In the case of Southeastern Seminary, the lack of knowledge of the school documents and the understanding of due process caused an almost mortal blow to the seminary. The man who was chairman of the trustees when the storm struck the school recently acknowledged that much trauma would have been spared if "we had gotten our act together" in 1987.[2] Trustees that seize leadership of institutions of higher learning without knowledge of the controlling documents of the school and an understanding of due process as employed in higher education will put the institution in harm's way.

Knowledge of accreditation procedures is also essential to the effective leadership of an institution. Few trustees in our system have had training in accreditation processes. In recent history, trustee boards have been shocked that accrediting agencies have looked askance at their actions. Some trustees have attempted to attribute the problems to the theological bias of the accrediting agency rather than to ineptitude in decision making.

The Southern Baptist Convention's handling of the affairs of its seminaries in the last decade is a graduate study in educational problems.

Southeastern Baptist Theological Seminary

The seminary was born out of the need for additional educational opportunities in the southeastern part of the United States. It came at a time of explosive growth in the SBC after World War II. The old campus of Wake Forest University was made available for the the new school.

The seminary was hardly born before theological controversy emerged in 1960. Serious differences between faculty members about New Testament interpretation caused conflict that disturbed the school for a number of years. In 1965, the trustees, acting carefully and with the excellent counsel of Olin Binkley, the president, allowed a professor (one record says two) to resign with generous provision for him for an extended period. The matter was dealt with at length, following prescribed procedures, and culminating in a solution that did not jeopardize the integrity of the institution. Proper procedures, academic freedom, doctrinal integrity, and accreditation standards were all protected.[3] While the matter was painful and required long and careful attention, the school remained strong and education went on.

For twenty years, the seminary continued its relatively quiet process of education. From time to time, small ripples disturbed the smooth

---

[2]Associated Baptist Press, 17 October 1991.
[3]Baptist Press, 20 February 1965.

waters. By the time of the SBC revolution, Southeastern had earned the reputation among many conservatives of "liberalism" and among much of the convention as a good strong school. By SBC standards, it was probably slightly to the left of our center but by no means liberal by usual theological standards. A few faculty members were suspect by some, but no serious problems had erupted. The quiet steady hand of President Olin Binkley had held the school in the middle of the road.

The successor of Binkley, former president Randall Lolley, commented at length on his ideas of administration in describing for me his pilgrimage as a new president. He said,

> I read everything I knew to read on participatory management, because that basically resonated, that was my chemistry. . . . I began to believe that you could take the principles of management by objectives and the principle of participatory decision-making and that you could apply those to a school like that. And I went public early; that was what I was going to do. And I did a lot of things to make that happen. . . . I think in those five years (1974–1979) we came about as far as a seminary could come implementing our decision-making by partnership, shared governance, in which the various publics—basically the administration, the faculty, the trustees, the alumni, the students—the publics of the seminary. Those five components really were woven together into a massive planning process which included physical plant development as well as curriculum development and school design.[4]

This dream of the new president was to lead the seminary to its greatest achievements and contribute to its downfall.

As the pressures grew within the denomination and accusations were made of liberalism in the seminaries, Southeastern became more and more prominent. Professors were accused by the fundamentalist leaders but rarely named in public. It became increasingly clear that when the purge came, Southeastern would be close to the top of the list.

I had been concerned for years about the blanket accusations against the seminaries. When I began this project, I asked Judge Paul Pressler to send me the document that had been widely circulated with the specifics of the charges of theological liberalism. He did so, and I have carefully

---

[4]From a transcript of a taped, personal conversation with Randall Lolley, 19 March 1991.

read the charges. They consist of quotes taken from writings and speeches of various professors and others. There are almost fifty pages of various quotes and/or comments about quotes. I believe that some are taken out of the context intended and, thus, are difficult to analyze. Some are clearly outside usual Baptist thought. Further discussion of the material is contained elsewhere.

In studying the comments related to faculty at Southeastern Seminary, I found four references in these materials. The first had to do with Robert Bratcher, who was terminated at the American Bible Society for comments on inerrancy (previously referred to). Pressler commented that he was subsequently used as a summer teacher at Southeastern.[5]

The second comment mentioned related to a Sunday School lesson written by John I. Durham, professor of Hebrew and Old Testament. Durham held that the Satan of Job was God's servant not his enemy (Job 1:6). He said that the word for Satan was not a personal name but a description of his duty—the word was *hassatan*—literally "*the* Satan" or "the one who accuses." He then asserted that in the Old Testament there was no concept of an empire of evil opposed to God.[6]

The statement caused a storm of protest when printed in the Sunday School quarterly. The Sunday School Board trustees reacted vigorously to this statement by Durham.

The third reference to Southeastern was a copy of a liturgy on women used in a service at the seminary. The liturgy was a clear expression of freedom provided by Christ for all, including women. It contained the phrase, "Jesus broke the law and tradition in his treatment of women." The reply said, "Jesus was a feminist." The remainder of the liturgy was similar in vein.[7]

The fourth reference was to an article in a state paper report of remarks made by John E. Steely, professor of historical theology at Southeastern. Commenting on 1 Timothy 2:11-15, Steely said the logic of Paul did not persuade him. A conferee said that Paul was wrong. "I would never use the language 'wrong' referring to scripture," said Steely. "He is just not coming through with the pure, undiluted strain of the gospel. Paul was not perfect. One reason Paul is my hero is that he was

---

[5]Bratcher statement at Christian Life Commission Seminar, 1981.

[6]*Adult Bible Study* (7 July 1985) 6, 7.

[7]Litany, Southeastern Seminary Chapel, 17 March 1983.

fallible. There is none perfect but our Lord Himself." Steely said that there are "hard sayings" in the scripture (about the role of women) and "we cannot pretend they do not exist," but observed that some of these words of Paul "are in direct conflict with Paul's own words . . . and in conflict with what I think is his (Paul's) overall conception of the gospel."[8]

While these are the specific accusations of Pressler related to Southeastern, there were other unspecified charges made against the school. These were not clear or specific and are not in print so far as I have been able to discover. Then there were the complaints of the students discussed in the section on the Peace Committee.

When the Home Mission Board aroused controversy with its policy on the financial support of an ordained woman pastor, the Southeastern faculty unanimously adopted a statement of affirmation of her. She had earned two degrees at the seminary. This did not sit any better with some fundamentalists than the Home Mission Board support of the woman. This issue was discussed at length when the Peace Committee visited the seminary. (See section on Peace Committee.)

By June of 1987, the convention had elected a majority of trustees who supported the fundamentalist agenda. This fact would shortly change the entire nature of the seminary.

The Peace Committee meeting with the small group of students from the Conservative Evangelical Fellowship (CEF) aroused a storm on and off campus. The controversy spilled over onto the floor of the SBC Executive Committee and into a meeting of the Southern Baptist Press Association. The student body organization decried the fact that no elected representative of the student group had the opportunity to meet with the committee. The student council organization criticized the CEF students for the meeting, saying,

> We . . . feel betrayed in that guidelines were violated, that a hidden agenda was carried out and that no single elected representative of our student body was given the opportunity to present genuine concerns of the entire student population.

---

[8]*Religious Herald*, 28 March 1985, 11.

The CEF group issued a statement of apology.[9] The problem was larger than the student disagreement. It did not settle the furor.

In March 1987, in a closed door session, the trustees of the seminary elected their first woman theology professor. Elizabeth Barnes was elected assistant professor of systematic theology. The vote was 14-13. Baptist Press reported that

> Some fundamental-conservative trustees said they opposed Barnes because she is a woman and not an inerrantist. . . . A pastor trustee . . . told reporters: "She is not an inerrantist. And I do object to a woman teaching theology. I don't think it is biblical." Another professor, considered conservative, was elected by a vote of 25-2.[10]

Of more importance to the future of the school, was that in the same meeting of the trustees, President Randall Lolley presented "A Plan of Action." This document was an effort to satisfy the demands of the fundamentalists on his board and on the Peace Committee, as well as those in the SBC at large.

Former president Randall Lolley, in discussing the plan with me, gave the following account.

> I had formulated a plan of action that would touch what I considered from the Peace Committee conversation the areas of concern that were legitimate. There were about eight or nine of them. To acquire teachers, either elected or adjunctive, who would present experientially the inerrantist point of view. To open chapel to speakers of that perspective. To open the lectureships to speakers of that perspective. To do several other things—it was an eight-point plan of action that the faculty had already endorsed—pretty strongly. I took it to the trustees, sent it to them in advance, told them "This is a document of commitment on my part and the faculty's part to see if we can't partner with you the trustees and get ourselves through this problem."
>
> The trustees first of all tinkered with the statement. They would not accept it the way it was. One trustee fought for the ultimate power, (the) authority of the trustees. That brought up this whole matter of control of the board. I'll never forget trying to point up the difference

---

[9]Baptist Press, 21 February 1986.
[10]Baptist Press, 13 March 1987.

between ultimate and penultimate authority. . . . We wrangled with it. . . . They made some slight changes. And then with (an overwhelming) vote, they voted to embrace it. (The vote was 18–4.)

Lolley continued, "It became our plan of action, and I truly meant to implement that."[11]

For the next trustee meeting (October 1987), the agenda was formulated as usual. Lolley told me that the way the seminary developed its agenda for a trustee meeting was to send letters to members of the board asking for their suggestions related to the agenda of the forthcoming meeting. The agenda was then formulated and mailed to the board about two weeks before the meeting. If they had any questions, they should communicate with the president.

According to Lolley,

The rumor mill had it that some of the trustees were not going to fill in their full agenda items. They were going to "spring them'" on the board. As it turned out, the new 16 (trustees) caucused on Sunday evening before our board meetings began on Monday. . . . I guess at that meeting (they) formulated and finalized their agenda, knowing that they (now) . . . had a one-vote majority. And their agenda was this: (1) to go after the chairmanship, . . . (2) to go after the process by which faculty were elected. . . . The faculty election process had been a process put into our operations manual by joint decision of trustees, administration, faculty and students. Everybody had a role in it. And they were going to go after that unilaterally. And they did. (3) They were to conduct their business that was controversial behind closed doors.

The last thing that apparently they decided upon in that caucus was to begin to structure through their standing committees a kind of oversight of a lot of the features of the everyday operation of the school. For example, the oversight of the chapel speakers, the oversight of the lecture people, the oversight of certain details of the campus student organizational life—to give the CEF certain prerogatives that they felt the CEF deserved over and above any other campus organization. So they intruded themselves into specific areas of the day by day operation of the school—none of which (plans) I knew about.

---

[11]From a transcript of a taped personal conversation, 19 March 1991.

None of this had been communicated to me until the board began to meet.[12]

The next move by the board was unilaterally to change the method by which faculty was selected. Previously, the trustees had not elected visiting and adjunctive faculty. These appointments had been left to the dean, president, and area faculty. The trustees now decided to control such appointments. At this and other meetings, the control of the entire faculty election process passed from Lolley's shared governance concept to one in which the president and the trustees were in control of the "pool" from which a selection was made.

The unilateral action on the selection of faculty rescinded the previous plan that had been adopted as an official document of the seminary by trustees, administration, faculty, and students. This unilateral action without consultation would cause serious problems with the accrediting agencies. None of these actions had been discussed with the president before the trustee action.

After these actions, the board declared itself in executive session. Lolley said,

> They chased over a hundred people out of the room. And for one hour and fifteen minutes I sat in the room, doors closed, people outside singing songs, standing with hands held, totally surrounding the building in which we were meeting. The most weird situation you ever heard in your life. And inside I heard repeatedly these themes. First of all . . . a trustee . . . read a very lengthy document . . . in which he put forward in precise terms the expectation of the board of trustees as regards the school, and he put forward in very precise terms the fact that he and the board wanted me to administer that vision.[13]

I asked if the document was available. Lolley said, "I don't know. It was never made available to me. I never saw it, I just heard it." He added that while they made their expectations very clear, "they didn't give the slightest indication they were going to ask for my resignation or force my resignation."

Concerning the end of the executive session, Lolley commented,

---

[12]Ibid.
[13]Ibid.

Those folks were still out there—mad, sad, singing, praying, holding hands. . . . They (the trustees) began to think about that. One of those trustees made the suggestion—God is my witness—that the best way in the world to open the doors and let the folks come back in the room . . . was for me to go into the middle of the room and kneel down, and for the board of trustees to have their hand on my head or shoulder, showing their love, admiration, and support of their president, and for the board to be praying over the president when these 'bad' people came back into the room.

Lolley refused this "hypocritical" subterfuge and the trustees opened the door. He added,

A couple or three of the students came in—bound, gagged, blindfolded and got right in the middle of where the board had been meeting in executive session. Just went down there and knelt. . . . Some member of the board instructed me to remove the students. But I told them, "This is a free country, and these students are expressing their deep-felt feelings; and I don't intend to ask them to leave.". . . Some trustee threatened to go back into executive session and do all the rest of their work behind closed doors if the students didn't show respect.

The students left of their own initiative. During the two-day session, Lolley came to the conclusion that

their agenda was set. They would have a new leader (fundamentalist chairman). They would elect faculty by a new process. They would engage in the selection of adjunctive faculty. They would intrude themselves into certain day-by-day operations through their standing committees, well beyond any bounds of trustee reasoning.[14]

The faculty had organized a chapter of the American Association of University Professors on campus. They were united in their support of the president and were determined to protect themselves. The trustees through a representative said that they would not relate to the AAUP chapter and would not reply to any communication from them. Lolley told me,

---

[14]Ibid.

I resigned within a week. . . . I wrote a brief statement. The trustees had a new vision, they were my superiors, and I could not work to implement that vision. . . . Given that scenario, it appeared to me . . . the most Christian thing for me to do, and Baptistic thing for me to do would be to resign. And so I did.

Along with Lolley, Morris Ashcraft (academic dean), and three other top administrators also resigned.

Lolloy continued,

Very soon after all of this in October of '87—my resignation— three things happened. First, ATS (Association of Theological Schools) sent a team. Second, the Southern Association of Colleges and Schools sent a team. And third, the trustees appointed a search committee.

After a previous agreement that Lolley would stay on until the end of the academic year or until a successor was elected, he was asked to terminate immediately. He refused, and the trustees elected his successor in March and gave Lolley a two-weeks notice. Lolley observed, "There was no transfer, or transition of leadership."[15]

When asked how important theological issues were in all the problems, Lolley commented,

There weren't any theological issues. Inerrancy is not in my judgment basically a theological issue. . . . I do not believe theology as such had a great deal to do with what went on at Southeastern. They did want some inerrantists on the faculty. But we in that Plan of Action had committed ourselves to (add some).

It was the opinion of Lolley that the new trustees were not knowledgeable about the documents of the seminary or did not understand how fragile such institutions are. He was also of the opinion that they knew little about accreditation processes. It seemed to him that the trustees finally were not interested in accreditation since some of them (not all) felt they were "hostage" to the accrediting agencies and the faculty.

The problem of theology, however, was much on the mind of the trustees. They obviously had an agenda that related to securing a faculty

---

[15]Ibid.

that was conservative by fundamentalist standards. The determination to examine the theology of the faculty, together with the problems of finance (which were to become critical), furnished a ready vehicle to rid the seminary of numerous faculty members without the necessity to fire them.

When asked if the trustees were trying to force a constructed fundamentalist theology on the seminary, Lolley responded, "Yes, I know they are."

Again the ghost of whether theology has been the issue rises again. It is clear that long-time leadership of the agencies thought the fundamentalists were talking about a few professors and writers who displeased them. It is equally clear that they were really imposing a new theology on the institutions and agencies.

A new president—Louis Drummond, Billy Graham Professor of Evangelism at Southern Seminary—was elected quickly after much speculation about who would get the post.

Another key ingredient in this mix was the employment of a new dean. The problems related to selecting a new dean hit the press almost immediately. President Drummond announced that he would nominate Russ Bush, professor at Southwestern Seminary, for the post. Trustee Chairman Robert Crowley announced strong trustee support.

In spite of trustee support, Bush was opposed by the faculty according to the spokesman for the AAUP chapter on campus. Ten names were presented to the faculty for comment in November. One withdrew, three were opposed, and six were approved. The AAUP statement said in part,

> This nomination was made in spite of a unanimous vote by the faculty on Nov. 16, 1988, not to support the candidacy of Dr. Bush due to his lack of qualifications. While Professor Bush was not supported for this position, six other candidates submitted by President Drummond were affirmed by the faculty as possible nominees. . . . The nomination of Professor Bush by President Drummond conflicts with the clear counsel of the Southern Association and contributes to conditions leading to the seminary's sharply declining enrollment.[16]

---

[16]Baptist Press, 24 January 1989.

After three hours behind closed doors, the trustees elected Bush by a vote of 22–8. The faculty protested vigorously, having voted no confidence a second time. One member of the trustees protested that they could have elected an inerrantist that had the support of the faculty. The election stood.[17]

Accreditation Problems

In December of 1988, the Association of Theological Schools sent a special visiting committee to Southeastern to study the situation. In its report to the Commission on Accrediting, the committee cited several problems of a severe nature.

> It is the central finding of the visiting committee that the general effectiveness of the school has been radically impaired. This impairment is rooted in several critical and current conditions as found by the committee.
> A. The overriding opinion of the faculty is that its role has been severely limited, that it cannot function according to accepted roles for a faculty and that it has been alienated from those who determine the orientation of the school. . . .
> The committee found that the faculty and the governing board are at an impasse regarding any shared vision concerning the purpose and nature of SEBTS and its orientation. The absence of this shared vision and the sense of collegiality which it should undergird has had a strong negative effect on the functioning of the school.[18]

The committee noted that a dean had been elected that had not had the support of the faculty. Concerning the office of president, the committee commented, "The Board is perceived as infringing on the role of the presidency in creating so strong a presence as to overshadow that office." The report continued:

> B. The governing board also senses itself alienated from the faculty. Trustees see themselves over and against the faculty, a situation which

---

[17]Baptist Press, 16 March 1989.
[18]Report of Special Visiting Committee of the Association of Theological Schools to the Southeastern Baptist Theological Seminary, 5–6 December 1988, 6.

is inevitably inimical to the effectiveness of an educational institution. It is not unusual for faculty and trustees to disagree on issues, but to be alienated from one another as was discerned by the committee and was reflected in all the relevant documentation is extremely serious. . . .

C. The committee cites thirdly the low morale on the part of the student body. Whereas some students do indeed welcome the reorientation which the school is experiencing, the great majority expressed strong views regarding the weakening of their own educational experience at the school and their distress at the lack of a shared sense of purpose among the faculty, administrators and trustees. . . . Several students said that to study at SEBTS was like trying to get an education in a war zone.

In this section, the committee noted that student grades had gone down significantly and there had been a substantial decline in enrollment.[19] The committee also reported,

D. The committee found evidence that the internecine struggles aired both internally and externally not only consume institutional energies but continue as a source of distraction. . . . That the Board recognizes the seriousness of this situation is found in its own words. *Trustees Report*, page 7: "There was some rhetoric which was improper and some public statements which should never have been made." Unfortunately there is ample evidence that these practices have not been discontinued.

Conclusion: By reasons of the foregoing, the committee is moved to conclude that the effectiveness of the institution is seriously jeopardized. The seriousness of this situation cannot be exaggerated and is hopefully recognized by all parties. The breakdown of a requisite spirit of collegiality, the absence of a shared common vision, and the weakening of the trust relationships among the several parts of the seminary community have served to prejudice the integrity of the institution as envisaged in ATS Standard I, Institutional Purpose.[20]

Several specific problems were mentioned by the visiting committee, including an abrupt change in the method of appointing faculty without proper consultation, the procedural change of appointing adjunctive fac-

---

[19]Ibid., 7–8.
[20]Ibid., 9.

ulty, and the approval of a new administrative structure by the trustees without proper consultation. There were problems in the process followed in naming a new dean. The approval by the Board in the spring of 1987 of the previous president's Plan of Action and the total departure from the Plan in the October, 1987, meeting of the board, the board not having rescinded the Plan. The Board, in the opinion of the committee, over-reached the exercise of power and preempted administrative functions.

When reminded again and again by the trustees of the struggles within the SBC, the committee commented,

> Nonetheless, the only concerns of the Association are the structures and provisions internal to the Seminary. It is the conclusion of the visiting committee that those structures and relationships are so compromised by recent Trustee actions that the freedom and integrity of the Seminary are at risk. It finds that SEBTS is currently in violation of Standards I and IV.[21]

The committee recommended that the seminary show cause why it should not be placed on probation.

Robert Crowley of Maryland, chairman of the trustees during this period, declined to be interviewed. (He should not be confused with the Robert Crowley of Georgia who sued the SBC over its president's ruling in the annual meeting.)

The Response of the Board of Trustees of Southeastern Baptist Theological Seminary to the Report of the Visiting Committee of the Association of Theological Schools is the trustee attempt to answer the criticism of the visiting committee. The response of the trustees occupies 72 pages with addenda substantially longer.

Significantly, the reply stated: "The SBC desire for change and Southeastern Seminary's resistance to change collided in the October 1987 Trustee Board meeting." It is clear from their statements, the press reports, the statements of President Lolley, the faculty statements, and their reply to the visiting committee that procedure was a major problem. It seems clear that the same changes could have been made without the devastation of the institution, if the trustees had changed the nature of their own approach and procedures before taking the confusing actions.

---

[21]Ibid., 21.

As late as the fall of 1991, questions were being asked by the trustees and others where the idea of "shared governance" came from. This illustrated the gap between their understanding of their task and the vision of President Lolley who built the idea into the fabric of the seminary.

In their reply to the ATS, the trustees put much emphasis on the context of the problems, i.e., the conflict in the SBC. Of course, this was basic but did not bear on their lack of proper procedure. The accrediting agencies—ATS and SACS—were and are not concerned about the theological foundations of the institution. They were primarily interested to see that the institution was following its own adopted Purpose Statement and procedures and that it was what it claimed to be.

Interestingly the trustees spent several pages defending or explaining why there was no consultation with the president before changing the faculty selection procedures. Whether the desires of the trustees in this matter were legitimate or not is not the point of the accrediting agencies' concern. The point was how the desires of the trustees were to be accomplished as related to the documents of the seminary and its history.

The Association of Theological Schools asked for a new round of reports from Southeastern, due in May 1991. The trustees, the faculty, and the administration prepared individual and separate reports reflecting the perceptions of the group reporting.

The trustee report to the Commission on Accreditation is an entirely different kind of document from their original report made at the beginning of the difficulties with accreditation.

The trustees affirmed a commitment to shared governance. They outlined the functions and duties of the Board, the president, and the faculty. They paid tribute to the efforts of the ATS in helping them understand their responsibilities and their relationships. They traced their efforts at implementing shared governance. They acknowledged their lack of knowledge in managing certain aspects of continuing controversy with the faculty. They pointed out that shared governance concepts were now included in orientation of new trustees. They emphasized their "non-involvement in the administration of the Seminary." They acknowledged that there had been inadequacies in some areas and that there had been improper actions and a failure to use the best judgment in some circumstances.

They acknowledged that they had become a better board as a result of the problems that had arisen. They stated further, "Accordingly, as a

Board we affirm the value that the process of accreditation has played in helping us understand and perform our responsibilities."[22]

The report of the administration to the Commission cited a lengthy account of examples of shared governance from the perspective of the president and his Administrative Council. This report dwelt additionally on special problems encountered during the days of confusion and changing patterns of authority.

The faculty report saw matters from an entirely different perspective. It was a massive document that cited many examples that from the faculty perspective did not represent shared governance. It was obvious that the changing patterns of authority were not to the faculty's liking and that they yielded the old understanding of their role very reluctantly. The new shared governance arrangements did not coincide with the previous practices, and the faculty chafed under the rapid shift of power.

Still in the shadow of accrediting problems, the trustees in October, 1991, began the rewriting of the Purpose Statement of the seminary. This is the foundational document that defines the identity of the institution. They also tentatively approved a "faculty profile" that requires all new teachers to believe inerrancy. They tentatively approved revised guidelines for selecting new faculty, after refusing to reduce their own role in the process. (According to press reports, the trustees were still struggling with this document in March, 1992.) After this time, however, they would send these documents to the faculty for its consideration before final adoption.

After spirited discussion, the trustees included in the Purpose Statement the following sentence: "The seminary is committed to the complete veracity, inerrancy and infallibility of the Bible as an essential foundation for effective Christian ministry and service."

The faculty profile says, in part, that professors hired in the future will "affirm and teach the Bible as the infallible Word of God" and as "truth without any mixture of error."[23]

---

[22]A Report from the Board of TrusteestTo the Commission on Accreditation, 15 May 1991.

[23] 17 October 1991.

Southeastern Seminary Today

In conversation with President Lewis Drummond, I was told that a total of 13 administrators had departed or were departing the seminary. As of the summer of 1992, a total of about 17 faculty members will have departed. This will leave about ten faculty members on campus, if no others are hired.

Trustee and former chairman Robert Crowley of Maryland commented, "Obviously, the faculty has pretty much given up. The question now is not who's leaving, but who's staying. . . . We are well on our way to doing what our goal has been from day one—establishing the greatest conservative seminary in the world." He further asserted that hiring inerrantists will solve the school's enrollment problem since conservative students still are reluctant to attend. He predicted that the transformation of Southeastern will spark "a mighty movement of God unheard of in the history of Christianity."[24]

Former president Lolley said that the school peaked in all ways during the period from 1979–1981:

> It peaked at the point of a sense of shared governance, of partnership and colleagueship with the trustees, the faculty, the administration, the alumni. It peaked in enrollment. A school of well over 1500 accumulated head count during those three years (and) . . . over 1200 FTEs (Full Time Equivalents), which was about double the number of FTEs we had in 1974 when I arrived there.[25]

The latest report of student enrollment indicates another drop, down 11 percent from 489 full time students last year to 434 in the fall of 1991.[26]

The short-term prospects for the recovery of the seminary are not good. The wounds are deep, trust has been destroyed, and the vision of the trustees will be difficult to attain in the context of the present

---

[24]*Western Recorder*, 30 July 1991.

[25]Ibid., 3–4. (FTE figures vary in different accounts and it is difficult to determine them precisely.)

[26]Associated Baptist Press, 17 October 1991.

problems. The vision of former president Lolley and the faculty he had assembled are now gone.

On December 5, 1991, the Southern Association of Colleges and Schools placed Southeastern Seminary on probation. James Rogers, Executive Director of SACS' commission on colleges said, "This is the final and most severe of our three sanctions. If (the violations) are not corrected, they are removed from the association."[27]

In thinking of the tragic plight of Southeastern, there is enough sorrow to go around. It seems to many that the major responsibility for the decimation of a strong seminary rests with its masters. Responsibility for building a new one in a different image rests there as well.

Afterword

President Drummond, after lengthy controversy with the trustees, accepted a position with the Samford University faculty.

In the fall of 1992, the Association of Theological Schools continued the probationary status of the seminary for another year.

In October, 1992, the seminary inaugurated Paige Patterson, long-time fundamentalist leader, as president. The system of rewards was still functioning.

The Southern Baptist Theological Seminary

Southern Seminary is the "mother" seminary of the SBC. It was first conceived and founded just prior to the war between the states. As soon after the end of the war as possible, the founding fathers gathered again and set in motion the school that would become one of the premier seminaries in the country. They were theologically conservative but not fundamentalist in attitude. They built well with meager financial resources. The principal resource was the character, scholarship, and dedication of the original faculty.

James Petigru Boyce was a moving force behind the foundation of Southern Seminary. In his inaugural address as a member of the faculty of Furman University, he had set forth three ideals that should be basic

---

[27]Associated Baptist Press, 12 December 1991.

in the formation of a theological school for Southern Baptists. His prescription included openness—a call for the admission of any person called of God regardless of educational background. His second requirement was excellence. He was concerned that the minister should have the best possible academic preparation. His third ideal was that the school should have a confessional identity. This provision for doctrinal continuity would insure the direction of the future.

Basis Manly, Jr. drafted the Abstract of Principles that has been signed by every professor at Southern since 1859. He used the Philadelphia Confession of Faith as the basis for the document. It has furnished and now furnishes the basis for faculty contracts and is the measure of orthodoxy at the seminary.

Before the turn of the century, the school and the denomination were confronted with controversy. Crawford H. Toy came to the seminary as a faculty member in 1869. His affirmation of scripture at the beginning was strong. After a number of years, his views changed, apparently influenced by evolutionary teaching and the German scholar Wellhausen. He finally denied the historicity of parts of the Old Testament together with questions about the christological implications of certain prophecies. He was admonished by President Boyce by "a gentle remonstrance and earnest entreaty."[28] Toy, acknowledging that his views of scripture differed significantly from those of his colleagues, resigned in 1879. The matter would be referred to subsequently as the "Toy Controversy."

The second major conflict at Southern was over the views of William H. Whitsitt, a professor of church history. Whitsitt did not accept the Landmark concept of Baptist succession. He felt that the continuity of Baptists could not be demonstrated historically. He based his conclusion on what he considered to be the fact that the first historical record of baptism by immersion occurred in 1641. As he contended for his position, pressure intensified, resulting in his resignation in 1898.

During the administration of E. Y. Mullins, the discussions swirled around the issues raised by the fundamentalist-modernist confrontations. Tension would be ongoing, with a variety of results in the life of the seminary and the denomination. The results were minimized in that the SBC did not become deeply involved in the controversy that swirled in

---

[28]A. T. Robertson, *The Life and Letters of John A. Broadus*, (Philadelphia: American Baptist Publication Society, 1901) 301.

the rest of the Christian community.

All of this is to illustrate that the history of the seminary has not always been tranquil. Other seminaries had their troubles as well, though not usually as dramatic or well-known. A point of great significance is that they usually went through a period of turmoil. As patience or tolerance wore thin and recalcitrant offending parties refused to come back to the theological fold, action was taken to discipline or terminate. After a period of settling down, the institution would go on with its task. These aberrations were usually handled within the framework of due process or quiet discussions behind the scenes.

In the present climate, the Southern Seminary problems could not be so managed. The school became the target of the fundamentalists, particularly their leadership. In the minds of some, the seminary was the locus of all that plagued the denomination. It was singled out as the parent of disorder and improper theology. The attitude of some of its constituencies did not help. They were seen as being arrogant about the superiority of the school as compared to the other SBC institutions. A number of the persons that had been the target of arch-conservatives across the years received their theological education at Southern.

As the Pressler-Patterson coalition gathered power, charges against Southern came to prominence. Various faculty members and President Honeycutt were accused of heresy. The materials circulated by Pressler contained several accusations against both the president and faculty. Eight specific citations were given as evidence of liberalism in the seminary. An examination of those charges revealed that several of them related to interpretation of various passages. For example, one professor was accused because he interpreted the Genesis record to mean that Adam was a representative man rather than one historical person. One was accused of being a universalist because of statements he made on a national television program. He later admitted that he did not properly represent himself or others on that occasion. Five of the charges dealt with more substantive matters.

President Honeycutt was accused of heresy because of his writings, especially his contribution to *The Broadman Commentary*. This volume was published in the early seventies. He addressed the textual problems of the Old Testament that are dealt with by scholars. He called attention to the problems of Mosaic authorship of Deuteronomy and the possible assembling of material by a redactor (compiler). He used other technical terms such as "wonder story" (to him a synonym for miracle), saga (events and achievements in the history of a family or person), legend (the story of the life of a saint, particularly one regarded as historical), and other such terms that commonly are used in scholarly study.

He referred to the story of the "ax head floating" as recorded in 2 Kings. He said in his commentary that this incident was "an example of the manner in which historical events were elaborated across successive generations until the narrative becomes a combination of saga and legend, inextricably interwoven."[29] Professor Emeritus, Eric Rust, was attacked for a statement he made in an article in *The Review and Expositor* in which he stated that from the view of history, the scripture was not inerrant. In an address he made to a pastor's conference at the University of Richmond, he questioned the historicity of the Genesis record of the Garden of Eden and the creation of Eve.

Professor Glenn Hinson was cited for two problems. He suggested in one article published in *Consortium* that some of the words of Jesus in the New Testament were somewhat embellished by the recorders of those words. He raised the question whether the Lord's Supper was actually commanded by Jesus as suggested by Paul. His second problem was that he suggested that God may have revealed himself in other cultures and religions than to Israel and the church.

Clyde Francisco, now deceased, was cited for suggesting that the serpent story in Genesis might be explained: "The Genesis writer used an old story that explained why serpents crawl on their bellies to teach the role of the demonic in the fall of man."[30]

Frank Stagg, professor of New Testament, was cited for his interpretation of the atoning work of Christ. These questions arose from a book Stagg published in 1962.

Taken on the basis of the presentation by Pressler and others, some of these statements sound outside the bounds of acceptable Southern Baptist theology. Some of them probably are. Of those authored by professors, it is important to note that one is dead, two are retired, and only two remain at the seminary. The Honeycutt citations can be

---

[29]"Commentary on 2 Kings," *The Broadman Bible Commentary*, vol. 3 (Nashville: Broadman Press, 1972) 242,

[30]"Commentary on Genesis," *The Broadman Bible Commentary*, vol. 1 revised (Nashville: Broadman Press, 1973) 129.

explained by proper understanding of the technical language of scholars. Further, he, like other Old Testament scholars, struggles with the real problems of the text, trying to make the matters intelligible to modern understanding. It is his view that in the Old Testament the differing accounts of the same event require a serious student at least to try to find solutions. Intellectual honesty requires the struggle. He admits that after the maturing experience of the intervening twenty years that he would use less technical language and phrase some of his discussion differently.

The work and teachings of the other remaining professor, Glenn Hinson, have been carefully examined by the trustees; and it was concluded that he had not taught outside the Abstract of Principles.

These were the kinds of things that came to the fore as the controversy grew and accusations became rampant.

After the meeting of the SBC in 1984, several denominational leaders, including President Honeycutt, took the initiative in defending their institutions against the attacks. Honeycutt, President Dilday of Southwestern, and Keith Parks of the Foreign Mission Board led the way. Honeycutt and Dilday acknowledge that they traveled extensively and made numerous addresses to interested alumni and others. They were accused of using seminary funds for their travels. Both had funds provided from outside the institutions to avoid the charges that inevitably were made.

The meeting with the Peace Committee that resulted in the Glorieta Statement produced as much heat as light in spite of the intention of the presidents. The Glorieta Statement was ratified by the Executive Committee of the trustees of Southern.[31] President Honeycutt declared his intention to follow the terms of the Statement. In May, the full Board affirmed the Statement.

Before the Peace Committee visit to Southern, the president called a group of trustees and advisors together. They were taking the forthcoming visit seriously. They agreed in that meeting that if the seminary had someone teaching outside the Abstract of Principals, formal charges would be filed against him and he would be terminated.

When the subcommittee of the Peace Committee visited Southern, they had thirteen "concerns." Some were less than earth-shaking. One professor, while in college some forty or so years before, had taken a course in yoga.

---

[31]Baptist Press, 12 February 1987.

When Adrian Rogers, representing the committee, rose to present his charges against the seminary, he acknowledged to the participants that he had not read them before the meeting. One report says that they were sent to him the day before. The charges were apparently similar, if not identical, to those circulated by Paul Pressler.

After a day and a half, one trustee said that they were tired of the seminary being attacked. This matter should be settled once for all. If there were teachers out of bounds, the trustees were prepared to dismiss them. If not, the committee was expected to close the case, and the trustees were there to settle the issue.

On the departure of the subcommittee, the president of the seminary called in the professors who had been attacked. They were informed of the procedure to be followed. The group meeting was to be followed by individual meetings with the president, the provost, and the dean of the appropriate school. There was a total of 43 meetings with the six interviewed. The president, since he was under indictment, asked to be interviewed by the same process.

Out of this exhaustive procedure, there came a report of the seminary to the Peace Committee of about 160 pages. It was never acknowledged. It had been agreed that the reports would be sealed by the Peace Committee for a period of ten years. The Southern group decided that, since it was their report, it should be publicized so that the seminary reply would be a matter of public record. They sent the report to all of the state Baptist papers. This procedure did not make the Peace Committee happy. Because of confusion in the mail system, one paper editor got his report before a member of the subcommittee got his.

When the Peace Committee's report became the norm for the seminaries, the Southern Seminary trustee Executive Committee affirmed the document and requested the president to proceed according to Recommendation 5 of the report. They authorized Honeycutt to "proceed to determine the positions of the executive staff and faculty members with regard to Recommendation 5 of the Peace Committee Report." That article instructed the schools to be true to *The Baptist Faith and Message* statement and their own doctrinal guidelines.

The problem area for the seminaries was the passage that instructed the seminaries to "build their professional staffs and faculties from those who clearly reflect such dominant convictions and beliefs held by Southern Baptists at large." This was basically a demand that only believers in the fundamentalist understanding of the nature of scripture be elected.

The press announced on April 26, 1990: "Conservatives Take Control of Southern Seminary Board." The board elected three fundamentalist candidates to board leadership. They requested all seminary employees to "desist from publicly espousing the right of a woman to have an abortion except where the physical life of the mother is in danger" and encouraged them to join trustees in working for anti-abortion legislation.

They established a policy to allow students to use tape recorders in seminary classes.[32] They expressed disapproval of professor Paul Simmons' activities related to abortion. They expressed their "deep concern" over professor Glenn Hinson's "intemperate remarks about controversial issues." They rejected the nominating committee's nomination of three members for the Executive Committee.

The major item of business at that meeting was consideration of an intemperate attack on the president and other faculty members by new trustee Jerry Johnson of Aurora, Colorado. A few days before the meeting, Johnson had circulated a 16-page, single-spaced, paper called "The Cover-up At Southern Seminary." During the meeting, it was published by the fundamentalist journal, The Advocate.

The paper featured an attack on president Honeycutt, using essentially the same kind of charges mentioned above as circulated by Pressler. He summed up his diatribe with the statement, "One would have to be as blind as a mole not to see that Dr. Honeycutt just does not believe the Bible." He accused the president of "playing games" when he signed T*he Baptist Faith and Message* statement and the Glorieta Statement. He accused him of "political demagoguery and whining."

He leveled a broadside at Glenn Hinson and criticized the doctoral dissertation of Molly Marshall-Green. Frank Tupper was accused of using profanity. Paul Simmons was criticized, "not to mention that as an employee of the Southern Baptist Convention he opposes the official position of the convention (on abortion)."

The paper was filled with such words as "denominational insensitivity," 'insolent," "gross embarrassment," "blanket of shame," "hostile forces," "Honeycutt's duplicity," "neo-gnosticism," "aberrant Abstract," and several others of similar type.

---

[32]Baptist Press, 16 April 1990.

The document is a curious one. It was bears the name of a man who was a college graduate but not a seminary graduate. In it there are quotes from a dozen or more sources that one would think could hardly have been available to the young pastor. There are extensive quotations from seminary documents, Baptist state papers, journals, books, and several newspapers from Los Angeles, Louisville, Charlotte, Houston, Atlanta, and Chattanooga. He quotes from speeches made in far-flung places. He quotes from Christopher Marlowe's play *Faustus*. He uses the phrase "neo-gnosticism" and defines it. He cites Hippolytus, mystery religions, and religious syncretism. He discusses for most of a long paragraph what judges do when they apply a statute, contract, will, or opinion of the court. He wrote that they have

> one and only one key interpretive task. It is to determine what those who originally wrote the document intended by the words they used as understood in their day. . . . In the discipline of interpretation in law, this is called the doctrine of The Original Understanding.[33]

One wit paraphrased Johnson saying, "One would have to be as blind as a mole not to see that Jerry Johnson did not write the document."

Trustees had dealt with the issues raised by Johnson before and had closed the cases. Some of the more conservative trustees were appalled that such an attack should be made by such a new trustee with no experience in the field. They were upset that he had had no conversation in keeping with the New Testament imperative with President Honeycutt. They were disturbed that the issues were raised and aired again causing still further damage to the institution and to the faculty and staff.

Southern Seminary's faculty promptly publicly asked Johnson to resign. He did not. Subsequently, at the urging of his trustee colleagues, he did apologize but stated that he had not changed his mind.

About two weeks after the release of the publicity of the incident, I was at Southern for their commencement address. The walls of Norton Hall were papered with letters of support for Honeycutt and the seminary. More than 2000 people wrote of their support and concern.

President Honeycutt prepared a detailed response to the charges made in the document by Johnson. He answered in detail the charges and

---

[33]Jerry Johnson, "The Cover-Up at Southern Seminary," 13.

evidenced his sorrow at being accused of not believing the Bible.

In a called meeting of the trustees in September, 1990, the Johnson matter was the heart of the agenda. After an executive session of about five hours, the trustees dealt with the Johnson matter in two parts. They accepted his apology. The second part of the agenda dealt with his charges. They decided that "the action of the 1986 board of trustees concerning the trustee report to the SBC Peace Committee not be revisited." Almost all of his charges had been dealt with at that time. Trustee Vice Chairman Wayne Allen told reporters that trustees had "drawn a line" regarding the old matters and did not intend to consider them again.

The bomb-shell that came out of that meeting had to do with another action that added to the existing guidelines in seminary documents the findings and recommendations of the Peace Committee report. This would require the school to consider these binding in all employment, tenure. and promotion decisions.[34] (The four points of problem were: the report said that Adam and Eve were real persons, the named authors wrote the books attributed to them, the miracles did occur as supernatural events in history, and the historical narratives given by biblical authors were accurate and reliable.)

Perhaps even more important to the future was the closing paragraph of this section in the Peace Committee Report. It said in part:

> We call upon SB institutions to recognize the great number of Southern Baptists who believe this interpretation of our confessional statement and, in the future, to build their professional staffs and faculties from those who clearly reflect such dominant convictions and beliefs held by Southern Baptists at large.[35]

In effect, this statement democratizes the future course of the seminaries. Right or wrong, methodology, choices, guiding documents, and the future staffs and faculties of all the institutions were put in the hands of someone's understanding of "dominant convictions and beliefs held by Southern Baptists." Freedom was now to be limited to a majority vote on the floor of the convention.

---

[34]Baptist Press, 28 September 1990.
[35]Peace Committee Report, *SBC Annual* (1987) 237.

The SBC creed had acquired a new tenet.

The faculty promptly voted unanimously to ask the school's trustees to rescind their action establishing new employment guidelines for teachers.[36]

A few months later, the Association of Theological Schools, one of the principal accrediting agencies, announced that it would send a visiting committee to Southern to determine whether the actions of the trustees threatened the quality of the institution.

President Honeycutt and the seminary faced a difficult situation. It was a matter of deep concern to the school that the accrediting agency felt the need to examine its decisions. This was the school that had sought academic excellence from its beginning. It had succeeded. Now, because of the decisions of the fundamentalist trustees, that secure position as an educational leader was threatened. The Association was not concerned about the theology but was concerned about the change of the rules concerning employment, promotion, and tenure. These were matters affecting every person on the staff and faculty. Their natural question was "What is going on here?"

No sooner had the problems of the charges against the faculty and the president been ameliorated than a new crisis faced the school. Several facts had to be faced by the institution and particularly its president. The seminary was under the control of a duly constituted board of trustees that was determined to steer the course of the school toward what they considered a more conservative stance. They had the authority and the power to make their edicts stick.

The issue then became, Shall we abandon the ship or shall we stay on board and try to save the ship? President Honeycutt had, and has, an almost unshakeable commitment to the seminary. He decided that his mission at this juncture was to try damage-control. After months of negotiation with trustees, faculty, and staff, a decision was made to make a covenant between the school and its trustees that would accommodate the needs of both, insofar as this was possible. The president's position was that he should help the trustees achieve their vision, if he could maintain the integrity and quality of the institution

A document emerged that they named, "Covenant Renewal Between Trustees, Faculty, and Administration." It was adopted by the faculty

---

[36]Baptist Press, 5 November 1990.

March 28, 1991, and the trustees April 8, 1991.

The Covenant deals with the basic issues of the conflict. The introduction says that the document

> is a spiritual and theological affirmation of our covenantal intentions as trustees, administrators and faculty of. . . . the Seminary. . . . Through this covenant renewal document we renew our vows to God and one another in a fresh spirit of mutual respect, cooperation, and effort to move toward common processes which will maintain the vitality, integrity and mission of the seminary.

The Covenant pledges to respect the policy making function of the trustees, the administrative role of the seminary staff, the and implementing/teaching role of the faculty. It includes a pledge to operate within the seminary Charter and Bylaws, Faculty contracts, and the Faculty Staff Manual. It affirms the desire to be sensitive to the conservative viewpoints and respect the convictions of all. The section on "Intention" affirms academic freedom and responsibility.

The faculty selection section promises to elect faculty members to achieve balance "through intentional employment of conservative evangelical scholars." It affirms the basic positions of the SBC conservative constituents on the matters of scripture. The administration and trustees committed themselves to elect faculty members who sign the Abstract of Principles and affirm the Covenant until such time as the trustees in consultation with the administration and faculty determine that balance has been accomplished. Accountability by all parties to the Covenant is pledged. Any change can be made with the concurrence of the parties. Unilateral changes nullify the agreement.[37]

The Association of Theological Schools appears to have accepted this Covenant as a good faith effort to solve the problems of the seminary. Administrators and faculty seem to feel that this is the best that can be done at this time. It appears to some of them to be a time-buying, honest device that will allow education to progress for the foreseeable future.

About half a dozen faculty members have departed for other places of service. Enrollment is slowly declining. One testimony says that some

---

[37]Covenant Renewal between Trustees, Faculty, and Administration, Southern Baptist Theological Seminary, 1991.

of the strongest doctoral candidates have gone elsewhere. Financial support from the denomination has not provided a merit raise for faculty and staff in a number of years. Faculty morale varies from day to day and depends on the one to whom you talk.

An important factor in the Southern situation was noted by one leader. It was his analysis that the most powerful impact on the seminary is a diversion from the dynamic direction put in motion at the beginning of the last decade. The focus and intensity of direction has slowed and has been pointed away from the purpose of the school. Enormous energy has been drained away from the mission of the seminary and has been expended on controversial matters.

Afterword

In late 1992,serious attacks continued to be made against professor Paul Simmons. His views on abortion had long been a thorn in the side of the fundamentalists. An attempt was made to settle the issue peacefully by buying out his contract. This recommendation was soundly defeated by the trustees. President Honeycutt commented, "We are back to ground zero." The alternative seems to be a trial for heresy. Informants close to the situation believe that such a proceeding is being planned to occur early in 1993.

In October, 1992, President Roy Honeycutt announced that he would retire at the end of 1993. He had previously said that he would like to continue in the post for several more years. Conventional wisdom suggests that he decided on this time frame because he felt that the present Board of Trustees might make a better selection than one not so familiar with recent history. Another scenario suggests that he simply recognized that accomodation to the trustee agenda was no longer possible.

Predictably, the announcement produced profound shock on the campus and throughout the interested constituency. The dreaded day of the inevitable transition was near. In February, 1993, Al Mohler, the editor of the Georgia Baptist newspaper, was selected as Honeycutt's successor.

A great school stirs uneasily in the fundamentalist wind.

Southwestern Baptist Theological Seminary

Southwestern Seminary—founded by Texans, supported by Texans, and serving the world—is a study in contrasts during the current controversy. The spirit of the school in some ways has been parallel to the spirit of Texas Baptists. The school has been vibrant, dynamic, and progressive. It has grown to be the largest of the Southern Baptist schools and is said by many to be the largest such school in the world. Born early in the century, Southwestern has led the way in numbers of students, alumni who are missionaries, pastors who are evangelistic, and pride in its size, numbers, and heritage. As it has grown in size, academic excellence has also grown. The School of Religious Education, as it was long known, pioneered the academic base of Christian education as it is now known in the SBC. Ministers of education all over the country owe their moorings to Southwestern. The school has long been known for its missionary and evangelistic concerns. Its dynamic character and increasing influence has made it a factor in the nature of the Southern Baptist Convention for half a century or more.

Considering the nature of the dynamic Baptist life in Texas and the wide differences in point of view of its leaders, the seminary at Fort Worth has led a charmed life. It has escaped most of the theological trauma that has accompanied its sister seminary in Louisville. While, like most theological seminaries, it has had its share of relatively minor theological spasms, it has not had the paralyzing controversies.

Curiously, the materials presented by Paul Pressler to various people contain only one reference to Southwestern Seminary. That reference quotes a statement attributed to the *Denver Post*. It says in part: "Whether the Bible is inerrant is of little concern to the Southern Baptist in the pew. . . . *The Bible never misleads us in its message but maybe in technicalities.*"[38] (The emphasis is apparently Pressler's.) The remark was attributed to President Russell Dilday. Dilday says that he was misquoted.

Interestingly, the major problems at Southwestern during the revolution have revolved around President Dilday. Few, if any, have accused him of theological liberalism. His problem is that he acts like a

---

[38]*Denver Post* as reported in *SBC—House on the Sand*, 56.

Baptist. If attacks are made, he answers. When asked, he expresses his opinion. He "calls the shots" as he sees them. He has vigorously defended the seminary, attacked despotism, and spoken freely about his understanding of the nature of being a Baptist.

Dilday's stance on the SBC controversy is in keeping with that of his predecessors and other SBC leaders. Traditionally, the denomination turned to its elected leadership for guidance in all kinds of matters. Agency executives who were in a position to know what was going on were regularly consulted about any matter in their realm of competence and sometimes beyond it. Their leadership in the denomination was a strong and continuous factor from the beginning until the beginning of the controversy. Few, if any, thought they were out of line if they expressed their opinion on any subject pertinent to the denomination. No one thought they should be silent on matters related to their institution.

It was not long before President Dilday was under pressure from the fundamentalist faction that had won a place on his trustees. In October, 1984, the first public attempt to silence him occurred. Dilday had asserted in speeches and in writing that the fundamentalist forces were attempting to dominate the denomination and were a threat to Baptist colleges and seminaries. In a trustee meeting held behind closed doors, an attempt was made to get him to stop his comments.

James Draper, a new trustee and immediate past president of the SBC, said later: "I think he's (Dilday) gotten into an area of controversy and polarization that we don't need....I just regret the inclusion of his voice to be a polarizing factor."

A motion was made that would have instructed President Dilday to stay out of denominational politics. An unnamed trustee reported that of the 30 trustees, seven voted for the motion.[39]

At this point, the principal of freedom for Baptists came into conflict with the fundamentalist notion that no institutional leader or employee should disagree with the ruling faction. This aberration would subsequently grow into the widely stated position that any employee of the denomination should not disagree with the fundamentalist leadership or a resolution voted by the convention. With this kind of rationale, unceasing pressure was brought to bear on all denominational employees, especially agency heads and editors.

---

[39]Baptist Press, 18 October 1984.

In March of 1985, speaking in Little Rock, Dilday asserted that the charges that the SBC had drifted toward liberalism were wholly unfounded. He stated that his own theology could be called fundamentalist and that he believed in the total reliability of the Bible and said that he accepted the inerrancy and infallibility of Holy Scripture.

Recognizing the attack on the historical-critical approach to Bible study, Dilday said that conservative scholars "ought to use every legitimate method available to us to better understand the Word of God." He said that in many cases, some tools of higher criticism may be used "to help us understand the text and the cultural and historical settings and know what the Lord is saying to us from his Word."[40]

Few could find fault with his theology, but his stated position on methodology and on the controversy would trouble him for years to come.

As the outcome of the controversy became clearer and pressure mounted, President Dilday tempered his comments on the political situation but did not surrender the right to speak on the subject. In the July/August, 1986, issue of the *Southwestern News*, Dilday commented on a leadership vacuum in the SBC. In the October trustee meeting, another attempt to silence the president was made. It was defeated by a vote of 19-11, commending Dilday for restrained and judicious leadership.[41]

Notwithstanding the president's conservative theology and the traditional orthodoxy of the seminary, repeated assaults were made on the school and personnel. Most were not very specific and seemed to be designed to intimidate the president and faculty. In February of 1987, a group of laity got together to call for arbitration in the defense of the seminary. The meeting also aimed at an effort to redefine the powers of the SBC president.[42] The meeting vented some frustrations but produced no viable results.

The true nature of Southwestern's problems were probably highlighted in an incident in April of 1987. President Dilday recommended the election of prominent pastor James Carter to a post as a professor of preaching. In the academic affairs committee—in executive session—the committee went beyond the usual form of questions about

---

[40]Baptist Press, 12 March 1985.
[41]Baptist Press, 17 October 1986.
[42]Baptist Press, 6 February 1987.

a prospective faculty member. Subsequent reports showed that in addition to the usual kind of questions, the trustees seemed to be interested in the style of worship at his church, the women deacons, the number of preaching professors in the church, the church's evangelism record, and the fact that he was considered a "moderate."

President Dilday commented afterward that Carter is "solidly conservative." But it boiled down to just the practical matter of which side of this controversy Dr. Carter was on. It has become more and more clear that the issues before us are no longer—if they ever were—basically theological. They are indeed political.[43]

In March of 1988, the trustees replied to the Peace Committee report in glowing terms. The trustee committee led by James Draper affirmed that the faculty had shown a "tremendously strong commitment" to the kind of teaching that characterized the school in the past. Draper said that "the administration has been very meticulous in dealing with concerns that have been expressed." He explained that only "four or five" questions had ever been raised about Southwestern.[44]

By August of 1989, Dilday was under pressure again. The trustee chairman, Ken Lilly, met with the president to discuss questions regarding Baptists Committed (a moderate organization) and to seek clarification of another article in *Southwestern News*. The problem was the president's "political activities." A called meeting of the board was considered but rejected. Lilly predicted that the matters would come up at the next regular meeting of the board in October.

He made certain that it would. He mailed an 85-page memorandum to the trustees in late September. Baptist Press reported that

> The memo includes minutes from the Aug. 15 meeting; a copy of the statement issued to the media about the meeting; both the manuscript and a transcript of the May 2 speech; nine pages of quotes from Dilday, ranging to 1984 and citing 55 entries from newspapers, magazines and newsletters; 56 photocopied news articles; and programs of the Baptists Committed meeting. The cover letter notes trustees "will want to hear his (Dilday's) fascinating explanation as to how his political speech was not political."

---

[43]Baptist Press, 8 April 1987.
[44]Baptist Press, 17 March 1988.

Dilday did not receive a copy of the memorandum.[45]

When the trustees met in October of 1989, a large crowd of visitors had assembled. Rumors were wide-spread that the trustees would try to fire Dilday. The meeting room was filled with friends of Dilday and the seminary. The trustees voted 22 to 11 to go into closed session, in spite of the protests of the visitors. The visitors remained in the building and sang and prayed. After nearly five hours, the trustees emerged to be greeted by a crowd that had grown to about 250 people.

The trustees and president issued a joint statement that said in part:

> Our executive session consisted of healthy dialogue in which we all acknowledged our differences and failings. We, the trustees and Mr. President hereby affirm one another and pledge our mutual support. Because of the sensitivity of the issues involved, we covenant together as trustees and president to cease and desist from making any statements, or writings, or engaging in any activities that could reasonably be interpreted as being intentionally political in nature, all the while seeking to deal with each other and the institution we serve in truth and love.

In the debate over the executive session, one trustee opposing the closed meeting noted that the discussion had nothing to do with moral or fiscal matters but dealt strictly with political issues. After the meeting, another trustee told the press that trustees were not critical of Dilday's operation of the seminary but were unhappy with his political activities.[46]

Many moderates were confident that the trustees had "muzzled and gagged" President Dilday. This was a common phenomenon as attempts were made to stop comments by Lloyd Elder at the Sunday School Board, Keith Parks at the Foreign Mission Board, Roy Honeycutt at Southern, Larry Baker at the Christian Life Commission, James Dunn at the Baptist Joint Committee, and others.

As Dilday faced the strong opposition of his trustees to public statements concerning the controversy, he apparently decided, as did his colleague Roy Honeycutt at Southern, that the welfare of the institution came before any other consideration.

---

[45]Baptist Press, 29 September 1989.
[46]Baptist Press, 18 October 1989.

The aggressive and intrusive nature of the fundamentalist drive showed up in other ways at Southwestern. For example, in March, 1990, the trustees passed a "pro-life" statement putting the seminary on record. The original motion tried to commit the administration and faculty. The same attempt would be made at Midwestern Seminary and Southern Seminary.

At the March meeting, Dilday was again on the carpet for comments made to SBC president Jerry Vines.[47] These attempts to silence presidents of seminaries are apparently unparalleled in Southern Baptist History.

Southwestern Seminary Today

Southwestern goes on with its educational task. Its president and faculty have been traumatized by the conflict. Its enrollment has leveled off and on occasion declines.

President Dilday insists that the quality and general nature of instruction at the seminary continues. It is his firm belief that institutional integrity has not been compromised. Outsiders looking at the school wonder about its future when Dilday retires.

Baylor University is in process of implementing the Truett Theological Seminary a short distance down the road. Many think that this is in preparation for the fundamentalist takeover of Southwestern. Another great school with its face set toward its mission awaits its fate.

Midwestern Baptist Theological Seminary

The Pressler materials singled out one professor of Midwestern Seminary for criticism. Professor Temp Sparkman had been a target for some years concerning his views on the nature of the salvation experience. He was also criticized from time to time about his views on the nature of discipleship in a modern world. After careful review, the trustees felt that Sparkman was teaching within the framework of the Articles of Faith. The vote on this motion was 22 to 11.

Midwestern Seminary has been spared the most traumatic results of the controversy. It has not been spared unrest, accusation, intimidation,

---

[47]Baptist Press, 14 March 1990.

and confusion. Illustrative of its problems was the trustee meeting in the fall of 1990.

The trustees passed unanimously a resolution of affirmation that the faculty was teaching within the provisions of *The Baptist Faith and Message* statement. They immediately spent an hour listening to criticism of the faculty and their teaching.

One trustee told the board:

> In view of the discussion we've had here, I'd like to make one observation. I've sat here and heard discussions of students' complaints about faculty, about imbalance of faculty, about trustee input concerning faculty selection, and then I pulled out this resolution of affirmation . . . and read it again. If the majority of the board feels anywhere near like the discussion that has been going on here this morning, then we are grossly hypocritical in sending the faculty a piece of paper with this resolution.

Another trustee said that he had approached 15 or 16 students who said they were "intimidated in classes" and "threatened with being thrown out." He continued,

> When I came on as a trustee there was not one, to my knowledge, not one of the faculty who had a higher view of scripture. We do not have many today I am sure. So if that's the case, the school is in an imbalance. I feel there are some things we need to do to correct that, where students who do have a higher view of scripture can come in and feel comfortable.

President Milton Ferguson said that the trustee's criticism

> is not an accurate representation of the quality, commitment or performance of our faculty in general. I take exception to your presupposition regarding a "higher view" of scripture. I challenge you to charge that these professors don't have a high view of scripture. I understand you to be saying, "they don't have my view of scripture.". . . I would lay their view of scripture alongside yours, mine and others.[48]

---

[48]Baptist Press, 16 November 1990.

Observers of Midwestern have felt that some of the remaining strong moderate trustees, together with President Ferguson's lack of "political activity," have protected the Seminary from some of the more vocal critics. Others have felt that Midwestern has not dealt properly with its problems and are anxious for some stronger actions to be taken.

A controversial new trustee for Midwestern Seminary was proposed at the 1991 convention meeting. He was apparently the choice of fundamentalist leaders. A number of conservative leaders in the state of Missouri opposed his nomination. There appeared to be serious difference between factions of the rightists on whether the nomination should stand.

Greg Warner has reported,

> Some conservatives are upset that new trustees they have sent to Midwestern have failed to bring about certain reforms at the seminary, trustees say. They point to the persistent criticism of Southern Seminary by trustee Jerry Johnston and of the Sunday School Board by trustee Larry Holly and fear that (the new trustee) will be asked to play the same role at Midwestern.   Such fears were fueled by a report that nominations chairman Richards, in defending (the new trustee's) selection, told the committee in March that (the new trustee) would "throw down the gauntlet and cause the trouble necessary to make the changes" at Midwestern.

Some conservatives felt that the layman had a history of attacks on the seminary. Warner said, "Midwestern trustees predict their new colleague eventually will renew his attacks against the school, now from close range."[49] The trustee was elected. The convention messengers were not given the criticisms of the nominee.

It may well be that Midwestern's most difficult days are ahead.

New Orleans Baptist Theological Seminary

New Orleans Seminary had its own difficulties about orthodoxy in the 1950s and 1960s. One professor was terminated for teaching outside the Articles of Faith. Several other professors departed after controversy

---

[49]Greg Warner, *Illinois Baptist*, 19 June 1991, 1,7.

internally. President Leo Eddleman, my predecessor at the seminary, had led in a direction that angered many alumni and divided the faculty. His stand for theological conservatism was overdone in the opinion of many of the alumni.

New Orleans has escaped the worst of the fundamentalist takeover controversy. Perhaps this was due to the conservative reputation of the school. The trustee board has now come under the control of the new rulers. The faculty has been spared in the main. The administration has walked a careful line and has not generally engaged in public criticism of the take-over movement. From time to time, according to some moderate trustees, challenges have been made to President Landrum Leavell's leadership on some issues. To this point they do not seem to impair the seminary.

One challenge to a faculty member came to professor Fisher Humphreys over his book, *The Death of Christ*, published by Broadman Press (owned by the Sunday School Board). Paul Pressler cited two passages from the work with which he did not agree. Humphreys was attempting to cast the atoning work of Christ in modern terms so that it could be intelligible to present-day believers. At the time of publication and the first attacks, I read the book carefully, as did President Leavell. While I did not agree with some of the characterizations of Humphreys, I did not find it heretical. Leavell expressed to me the same reaction. We agreed that from the view of the publisher and the seminary no action against Humphreys or the book was justified.

New Orleans Seminary has fared better than its four sister seminaries. In part this has been because of its president and faculty and in part because of its friends.

Golden Gate Baptist Theological Seminary

The Pressler materials cited only one professor at Golden Gate. Professor Robert L. Cate, an Old Testament scholar, dealt with the nature of the authorship of Exodus in the *Laymen's Bible Book Commentary* . The treatment was about like that of other scholarly discussion. It probably did not fit the requirements of the Peace Committee report. Cate has subsequently departed from Golden Gate.

The seminary, in a magnificent physical location and in one of the highest cost-of-living areas in America, suffers perhaps more than the other schools because of the financial problems the controversy has brought to them all. With the leveling of the Cooperative Program and subsequent decline, the entire matter of seminary finance must be restudied.

Summary

The seminaries of the Southern Baptist Convention were carefully and laboriously built over a hundred year span. They were at last achieving good to excellent standing in the world of theological education. They educated a disproportionate percentage of the theological students in America. They had their problems and successes.

Occasionally a teacher departed from the mainstream of Southern Baptist thought. As a result, they suffered from various levels of distrust. It is the opinion of knowledgeable educators that the seminaries were probably more sensitive to the wishes of the people in 1979 than in a generation. It is almost certain that the schools had had as few theological problems as any comparable group of schools. There were probably fewer true problems in 1979 than there had been in many years.

The fundamentalist political victory and theological recidivism will continue to take its toll on the system for the foreseeable future.

A Professor Speaks

Thomas J. Delaughter was for a generation a professor at New Orleans Seminary. When the controversy over the seminaries began to develope, he wrote an extensive article entitled, "I Have Investigated Those Professors." He cited four lines of investigation.

> The first (line) has been made as a student. . . . I have learned in the passing of time that my disagreements generally were out of ignorance or prejudice on my part. I never knew a professor or colleague who did not believe the Bible to be the inspired word of God.
> . . . .
> My second sphere of investigation of seminary professors was when I served as a trustee. . . . In this relationship I sensed an uncommon

desire among faculty members to serve the Lord, to be true to what we believe as is set forth in the doctrinal propositions or articles of belief formulated by the Seminary and by the convention. . . .

My third investigation of Seminary professors was in the category of church membership. When I was pastor. . . . professors of the seminary and their families were faithful, loyal and supportive members of those churches. . . . The professors whom I have known have been faithful in attendance, prayer, participation in active leadership, in some cases serving as deacons, and supportive in the financial programs of the churches, giving a tithe and more. . . .

A fourth area of investigation of seminary professors was as a professor, a colleague on the faculty. . . . Here I was on the inside. It was in this experience that I learned that teaching was just one phase of the professor's work. Writing books, articles, . . . lesson materials . . . claim their attention. Committee work, counseling students . . . sharing in their family, financial, and pastoral responsibilities are sometimes more than a full time job. . . . As a faculty member I saw family life, financial struggles, social relationships, sin and suffering as inescapable facts among us. It was in these matters that I saw professors stand tall and walk with sure steps. [50]

---

[50]Thomas J. Delaughter, *Baptist Record*, 10 October 1980.

Chapter Thirteen

The Agencies

"Full of Troubles. . . ."[1]

For more than a hundred years Southern Baptists had carefully fashioned a system of agencies, controlled by trustees, to achieve various missionary and educational purposes. Each was designed to carry out some aspect of the commands of the Lord. Across the years, a balanced and extensive group of entities came into existence. Their programs were assigned by the convention and responsibility was fixed with their trustees.

These entities reported in writing (and usually orally) to the annual meeting of the SBC. The reports were regularly available for anyone to see in the *SBC Annual.* The agencies were constantly under the scrutiny of the religious press and sometimes the secular press. Any Baptist could request and receive any financial data and a wide variety of other information. Usually, the only matters not available to the public were those related to personnel matters or some other item involving legal liability.

Denominational leaders commented publicly from time to time on the various items of public interest. Information was available on nearly all of the activities of the many entities related to the convention.

Central to the operation of the denomination were the Foreign Mission Board (FMB), the Home Mission Board (HMB), the Sunday School Board (SSB), and the Annuity Board. The commissions included the Historical, Christian Life, Stewardship, Education, Radio and Television, the American Baptist Seminary Commission, and the Brotherhood. The Baptist Foundation rounded out the list of servant agencies.

The convention related to the Baptist Joint Committee on Public Affairs through its own Public Affairs Committee. The denomination relates as a cooperating body to the Baptist World Alliance. Woman's

---

[1]Psalm 88:3.

Missionary Union is an independent but cooperative auxiliary to the convention.

The conflict had not been under way long before the focus of the power struggle clearly was on the agency trustees. One aspect of the announced agenda of the fundamentalist movement was to capture the trusteeship of the agencies. By 1986–1987 most, if not all, of the trustee bodies were under the control of the fundamentalist coalition.

It should be noted that not all of these new trustees were there to unseat the administration. Many were fine people elected because the nominator thought they were of the right persuasion. It seems certain that a substantial number, especially in the early days of the controversy, were unaware of any specific reason why they had been elected. Various executives have said that when some of them learned of the work of the agency, they became solid trustees with the welfare of the institution at heart. It is also clear that some of them were reminded at some point of why they were there.

Later in the conflict, nominees were chosen from "those who have been with us in the struggle." Pressure to vote the party line was sometimes exerted. Some did and some did not. One president said that one of his trustees assured him of his sympathy with the president's position, but that he had promised in the caucus to vote for the party line. He felt honor-bound to keep his promise. The principal interest of the fundamentalists concerning the agencies (after the seminaries) was in the mission boards and the Sunday School Board.

The Sunday School Board

The Sunday School Board as a title today is a misnomer. It began in 1891 as a board to promote Sunday School. Its beginning was surrounded with vigorous differences of opinion. Some wanted to continue to buy materials from the northern Baptist publication board. Some were afraid of a Board that would be preparing material for independent Baptist churches. Some feared coercion, some heresy, and some just feared.

The SSB was given no money to begin and was instructed to turn its profits—at that point imaginary—into the work of the denomination. In the hundred years of its existence, it has received no mission contributions but, on the contrary, has contributed many millions to various other denominational projects.

Given the wide diversity of the churches and pastors, it was inevitable that there should be periodic disagreement about some material published by the SSB. The range of possible disagreements is phenomenal. Most of them have been visited at some time or the other. James L. Sullivan, president of the SSB for 22 years, used to comment that if the left was shooting at him and the right was shooting at him, he was about in the place he should be theologically.

From time to time in the publishing of millions of pages of materials every year, someone would make a mistake. Consider that the SSB published about 125 to 140 periodicals. These included Sunday School quarterlies for all ages, discipleship materials of many kinds, music publications, church administration materials, pastoral aids, recreation suggestions and methods, and almost anything else needed by the churches or individuals.

Editors combed the materials for errors in syntax, doctrine, style, grammar, and quotations. At any given time, about 1800 people were writing something for the SSB. These writers were a cross-section of the Southern Baptist constituency. The SSB publishes about 100 books in a given year. It operates more than 60 bookstores around the country and two national conference centers with year round programs.

In this complex of writers, editors, speakers, books and services, it seems likely that someone would write or say something that someone would not like. It is not only likely, but inevitable. The history of the SSB is filled with such instances. Two of the more serious ones have already been mentioned—*The Broadman Bible Commentary* and the book by Elliot, *The Message of Genesis*. These two matters had been dealt with by both the convention and the board of trustees before 1974 when I was elected president of the Board.

Between 1974, and my retirement in 1984, there were no serious theological incidents that caused national concern. We undoubtedly made our share of human errors, but they were acknowledged and corrected so that there were no serious problems.

By 1984, there were a number of newly elected members of the trustees that would subsequently cross swords with the newly elected president, Lloyd Elder of Texas. Elder was a member of a large family and accustomed to defending himself. He came to one of the most complex jobs in Baptist life. He had been Assistant Executive Director of the Baptist General Convention of Texas and Executive Vice-President of the Southwestern Baptist Theological Seminary. Both were responsible posts and gave him wide acquaintance with Baptist life. His experience had not included the responsibilities of a chief executive officer. During a denominational crisis, the Sunday School Board was to prove a tough place to become one. Elder was well educated and bright and approached the job with enthusiasm and dedication. He was conservative in his theology and committed to the denomination and its ministries. He spent nearly a year becoming oriented and acquainted with the organization and its programs before his inauguration. He attended all the meetings and planning sessions during my last year and participated in decision making that would affect his administration.

He was hardly in place and under way before the problems began. The writer of a Sunday School lesson on Job, mentioned earlier, departed from what was considered by many to be a conservative position. When quizzed on the incident, the responsible official told the press what he thought happened. Later, Elder discovered that he had not had complete information and reported again. A third attempt was necessary before the matter was satisfactorily explained. Members of the trustees were unhappy with the incident and some wanted to rewrite the guidelines to reflect a more stringent policy theologically.

Early in his administration, Elder commented on various matters that he felt affected him and his institution. He was by virtue of office a member of the liaison committee, the Public Affairs Committee, and thus a member of the Baptist Joint Committee. He affirmed his support of the BJCPA and decried on more than one occasion the efforts of the funda-mentalists to defund or alter the relationship of the SBC to it. This did not set well with the increasing number of arch-conservatives on his board. Various attempts were made to get him to remain silent on such matters.

In the trustee meeting in May, 1986, Larry Holly, a physician from Texas, introduced a motion that to require the administration to send infor-mation to all trustees on the top five to ten candidates for any vacant post requiring trustee approval. This motion, if it had been approved, would have caused endless confusion and could have resulted in serious prob-lems for some potential nominees. It was referred to a committee after Holly used language that he later apologized for as "intemperate."[2] Holly

---

[2]Baptist Press, 7 August 1986.

would be a source of concern for the president for years to come. He was not the only one, but he was a catalyst for introducing problems.

These actions signaled a tightening of the reins on the administration, with frequent intrusions into matters usually beyond the purview of trustees. It seemed obvious that there was a new spirit of judgment and control in a system that had worked remarkably well for generations.

When Paul Pressler circulated his list of violations of Southern Baptist theology, several examples of "error" by the SSB were contained in it. Of the total of 50 items, 19 related to the Sunday School Board, covering the period from 1962 to 1985. Eight items cited concerns with Broadman Press books. Five items concerned the *Broadman Bible Commentary*. Six items concerned the SSB curriculum materials.

Of the 19 SSB problems, which are a part of the total of 50 mentioned above, 12 concerned matters that occurred before 1975. Eleven of them were resolved or considered to have been. Eight of them were both before 1975 and considered resolved. This means that of the 19 charges, 14 of the 19 were either pre-1975 or resolved.

These data mean that five issues needed to be considered. Careful study indicated that four of the 5 relate to differences of interpretation. One issue remained to be considered. No one with experience in the vast publishing operation of the SSB would say that there were no errors made in the materials. There were occasional errors, when measured by the usual conservative theology of Southern Baptists. When they occurred, usually a few letters or phone calls were received. My own policy was that if we received as many as five or six complaints on a given item, out of the millions of pieces distributed, we studied the matter carefully. When we discovered that we had made an error, we acknowledged it and corrected it, if we could. Of course, we could not recall millions of Sunday School quarterlies. Most respondents simply wanted us to acknowledge our mistakes and try to do better. We tried.

Interestingly, the fundamentalist movers and shakers were particularly sensitive to discussions of authorship of the biblical books. Scholars are divided on such matters as to how much of the first five books of the Bible Moses wrote. They are divided on whether parts of the books were gathered by later redactors and bear the name of Moses because he authored parts of them. The problem of authorship is of concern because conservatives often feel that if there is any question about the authorship of a book that bears the name of a writer, inerrancy is questioned.

Scholars struggle with such problems as the Deuteronomy 34 record of Moses' death and burial. The book is attributed to him, and he obviously authored the addresses that are prominent in the book. Scholars question how he could have written of his own death and burial and the mourning of Israel.

No less than six of Pressler's citations deal with problems of authorship. The questioned SSB writers do not deny the inspiration of the passages in question. Their questions have to do with whether the book bearing a certain name in fact was totally authored by the one named. The *Florida Baptist Witness* reported that the Peace Committee, after reviewing the board's stewardship, "saw no need for further dialogue with . . . the Sunday School Board."[3]
The problems that finally resulted in the termination of President Elder did not have to do with theology.

In 1985, in the Dallas convention meeting, a messenger made a motion that the SSB publish a conservative commentary on the Bible. The administration of the Board studied the matter and recommended that no commentary be published, citing extensive research that revealed a lack of demand for such a commentary. When the matter was reported to the board through one of its committees,one member favored the commentary as being a response to unhappy people in the denomination. A motion was made that the board proceed "with haste" to produce a commentary. Two amendments were voted. One called for the commentary "to reflect a strong, scholarly defense of the traditional authorship of the biblical books, the Mosaic authorship of the Pentateuch and a presentation of an apologetic for creationism in the introduction to Genesis."

A second amendment specified that all writers who contribute to the commentary "hold to the position of inerrancy." The substitute motion and the two amendments passed by a wide majority. The project was estimated to cost about $1.5 million. The board agreed to employ the advice of the past presidents of the convention, representatives of the six SBC seminaries, the Criswell Center for Biblical Studies in Dallas, and the Mid-America Seminary in Memphis.[4]

In their next meeting, the trustees named the first consulting editor for the new commentary—Paige Patterson, one of the leaders of the

---

[3]*Florida Baptist Witness*, 26 June 1986.
[4]Baptist Press, 6 February 1987.

fundamentalist faction in the SBC. The trustees further voted to reserve the right to approve all editors of the commentary.[5] This was a further departure from established procedure.

In this meeting, one trustee wanted to have a trustee committee prepare a quarter's Sunday School lessons as a demonstration. He also wanted to include in the minutes a letter from six Sunday School workers expressing concern about literature for preschool children.

Another action required the inclusion of sanctity of human life and opposition to abortion in the list of social and moral concerns referenced in literature. The action included the promotion by the board of a Sanctity of Human Life Sunday and consideration of an annual lesson on sanctity of life.

As the aggressive trustees pushed for more and more of the fundamentalist agenda at the board, tension grew with President Elder. Some trustees felt that he was biased against the conservatives. His discussion with numerous persons at different times was considered political activity, particularly as he dealt with official matters related to the Baptist Joint Committee. It was obvious from press releases and public criticisms of the president that some trustees wanted him to cease and desist any activity that could be interpreted by anyone as being political. Since he was involved in matters that related to the denomination in general, it was difficult to keep some fundamentalists from calling his activities political. It seems obvious, in retrospect, that the attempt was the same as with other leaders, they wanted to silence him.

By late 1988, SBC financial matters were pressing. The Cooperative Program contributions were not meeting the constantly escalating budget, and capital needs were not being met. The new SBC building in Nashville still carried a mortgage amounting to more than 2 million dollars. The SBC Executive Committee requested the Inter-Agency Council to review agency capital needs and make suggestions about possible solutions. President Elder was a member of the Council as were the other agency heads.

Elder questioned what the board could do to help in the matter. The SSB had given the land valued at about $400,000 on which the building had been built and had given the land and building used by the SBC for

---

[5]Baptist Press, 21 August 1987.

many years. With reserve funds in hand, Elder suggested to the trustees that the Board give another $400,000 to the convention to help with the debt and alleviate the budget reductions for the agencies that depended on the Cooperative Program. The trustees were willing to do so, with the proviso that the funds would be spent on the building indebtedness.

At the meeting of the SBC Executive Committee sub-committee that dealt with budget in January, 1989, the proposal was made to make the contribution. In the same meeting, there was a proposal in a sub-committee to reduce the funds allocated to the Baptist Joint Committee and distribute them to the mission boards or a new church-state agency. This was one of many such moves.

There was anxiety among the Executive Committee trustees that the contributed funds from the SSB not be used to restore any potential cut from the Baptist Joint Committee. The president assured the board that the funds could only be used for debt retirement. When the budget came out of the sub-committee to the SBC Executive Committee, the Joint Committee budget had been cut only a few thousand dollars. Paul Pressler made a motion to cut the BJCPA to $71,704 from about $400,000 and give the remainder to the Public Affairs Committee (which he saw as having its own program). The motion lost by a vote of 34 to 35.[6]

The scenario becomes cloudy at this point. During the meeting of the Executive Committee in February, Elder conferred with Harold Bennett, the president of the Executive Committee, apparently in sight of the body. The outcome of the entire matter was a charge made against Elder that he and Bennett had made a deal that if the SSB gave the $400,000, the EC would not cut the funds of the Joint Committee. Others charged that Elder told Bennett that the board might reconsider the gift if the BJC funds were cut. Elder denied any such conversation. So did Bennett.

The budget was finally approved for recommendation to the convention, with the amount for the Joint Committee of nearly $400,000, as originally planned by the sub-committee.

In a later plenary session of the Executive Committee, a member raised the question as to whether Elder threatened to withdraw the funds if the BJC budget allocation was reduced. The Executive Committee minutes reveal that Harold Bennett denied publicly that he and the committee had been threatened. Elder stated to the committee that if the

---

[6]Baptist Press, 24 February 1989.

budget changed from the earlier one he had used to request the funds from the Board, he would have to take the information to them, since it represented a change from the rationale and budget he had used. The earlier budget had treated the debt as a priority emergency need.

While the matter is confusing and reports vary, the results were startlingly clear. It should be noted that the more aggressive fundamentalists on the Sunday School Board were in support of the Pressler effort in the Executive Committee to defund the Joint Committee.

A member of the Executive Committee sent a letter to all members of the Executive Committee charging Elder with manipulating the committee to maintain the support of the Joint Committee. He complained about being held hostage by anyone and that Elder did not answer the questions in the meeting of the Executive Committee. This letter promptly showed up in at least some SSB trustee mail boxes. It apparently had been widely circulated. The matter was reported in March in the fundamentalist journal, *Southern Baptist Advocate.* A three-column headline announced, "Executive Committee Member denounces Elder." The Committee member's letter was quoted, and Holly's concerns were reported.

This tedious story is told without some important details not available. The reason for the story is that it had horrendous results for Elder. Larry Holly seemed to intensify his conflict with Elder. He distributed to SSB trustees the Executive Committee member's letter and other materials that apparently included a transcript of the statement of Elder made to the Executive Committee. He suggested that the trustees review Elder's activities at the Executive Committee meeting with a view of determining whether the president violated the trust of the board.

It is evident from the bits and pieces of information available and conversation with various trustees, former trustees, and observers of the affairs of the Board that Holly was dissatisfied with Elder's performance. Apparently, he saw Elder resisting the efforts of the trustees to sponsor new initiatives and to bring the board into line with the new direction of the convention. According to others, Holly sent quantities of materials to the trustees in preparation for the August meeting in 1989 at Glorieta. They apparently dealt at length with the matter of the SSB contribution to the convention for debt retirement.

Additionally, in July, Holly sent to all trustees a "history of the presidency" of Lloyd Elder. It contained an extensive discussion of the meaning of speaking the truth in love. Apparently he thought he was smoothing the way for his accusations against Elder.

He discussed at some length: his perception that Elder did not tell the truth about the Job incident; the president's discontent with the conservative resurgence; Dr. Sullivan's chapel address, published in *Facts and Trends;* his perception of Elder's personal political agenda in which he ignored trustee instructions to be inactive politically; an Elder statement related to his "discouragement of the events of the past ten years"; Elder's resistance to the new conservative commentary; Elder's opposition to a dated sanctity of life lesson in the Sunday School materials; and Elder allegedly withholding materials wanted by trustees. He dealt long with the problems of the gift to the SBC for the building indebtedness.

Holly intimated that the president lacked integrity and that the board needed a man of integrity who devoted all of his time to the matters of the board. He called for a discussion to review the performance of the president.[7]

The trustees met at Glorieta, New Mexico, on August 7. A motion was made by Joseph T. Knott III, an attorney from Raleigh, North Carolina, to declare the office of president vacant. After almost an hour of discussion and parliamentary maneuvers, the motion was withdrawn. Elder's friends thought the motion should have been voted on to assess properly the situation. His opponents were reported to have discovered that they did not have enough votes to succeed in the effort to oust Elder. A vote to table the motion failed 47 to 31, which may have been an index to the sentiment of the board.

After the withdrawal of the motion, the board approved a six-point statement prompted by the issues raised by Holly. The statement came from a committee with one amendment and was approved by the Board.

The statement: expressed regret for Elder's "judgment and timing" related to the $400,000 gift to the debt retirement but did not question his integrity; requested Elder to give a documented explanation of his actions related to the gift; instructed Elder to seek a "balance" in denominational political views in speakers, writers, and authors enlisted by the board; recommended that a committee be appointed to draft an instrument to use in the evaluation of the performance of the president; and encouraged

---

[7]Information from letter of Larry Holly to trustees, 21 July 1989. This material, with others, was given to the press at Glorieta, 7 August 1989.

trustees with grievances against Elder to take them to the general administration committee for consideration in his annual performance review.[8]

Elder was devastated. Verbal reports from the meeting indicate that in the heat of the discussion, Elder charged that Holly had betrayed the trust of the board. Combat was joined, and the end was not yet.

Along with routine matters at that meeting of the board, the board approved a motion to give administrative control of one of its publications to a non-employee. After unhappiness with student publications, the board created a new publication and gave control of it to the director of the Baptist Student Union at the University of Oklahoma. This was unprecedented. None of the guidelines set up by trustees for control of the affairs of the board were mentioned or followed.[9] Once again, trustees had intruded into administration.

The news of the attempt to fire Elder was reported nationally. In his report to the employees at the end of the week, Elder told of his great distress.

> I have not felt so abandoned since our daughter died in an automobile accident. . . . After the motion was withdrawn—which I consider the depth of cowardice on the part of the trustee who withdrew it—I felt as if I had been laid out on a table for surgery and cut wide open, and left there to see if I would live.
>
> Eighteen able, fine trustees have the perception that I have engaged in political activity and I must take that very seriously. I will not ignore it.

He added that he operated on two principles: "never, never be involved in political activity and never, never be quiet when the environment has a direct effect on the well-being of the Baptist Sunday School Board."[10]

In this last sentence, there is a clue to some of the differences between some of the more reserved of the trustees and the president. Many of his official activities as president related to various affairs of the denomination. His membership on the board of the Baptist Joint Committee and his relationships to the Inter Agency Council and the SBC Executive

---

[8]Baptist Press, 11 August 1989.
[9]Ibid.
[10]Baptist Press, 16 August 1989.

Committee are examples. Any word spoken in behalf of a point of view unacceptable to the fundamentalist majority on the board was interpreted as political activity. Any speaker or writer that differed from the party line constituted a political statement, according to some of his board.

This type of pressure, by now being exerted in all major agencies with the possible exception of the Annuity Board, was unprecedented in Southern Baptist life. The suppression of free speech in religious matters and in denominational life was alien to the spirit of being a Southern Baptist.

Before the month was out, Holly was reported to be circularizing the board and staff in protest of the speech Elder made to the employees.

Whether Holly had been appointed to the board of trustees to be the "point man" is debatable. That he focused the fundamentalist effort to unseat Elder is not. It has been verified by a number of trustees and public records that there was a veritable barrage of mail back and forth related to some item that made Holly unhappy. That he had sympathetic support from a substantial number of the other trustees is also evident from the reports in the press and by trustees of various votes on issues related to Elder.

When I inquired of Bill Anderson, the chairman of the trustees, about the relationship of the Pressler-Patterson coalition to the trustees, he gave me his opinion. He felt that the coalition had no "determinative influence. They had influence with Holly who admires Pressler and Patterson and perhaps with some of the others."[11]

Subsequent events demonstrated that, by the summer of 1990, the relationship of president Elder and the board of trustees was at best tenuous. Demands were made by various trustees for all correspondence, memoranda, and notes related to various items. The attorney for the board apparently had told the president that the trustees were entitled to whatever material they wished to have. There had been votes in the board, according to outside sources, to require the president to send to trustees whatever records were requested. While these were probably labeled "confidential" or "for your eyes only" or some other such designation, they were sometimes circulated among the faithful and some not so faithful.

As a result, matters that should have been in private files in the

---

[11]Notes from a personal conversation with Bill Anderson, 28 February 1991.

Board were circulated to any persons the individual trustees desired. While this release of files to trustees may have been legally necessary, it created many problems for all concerned.

It should be noted that not all trustees participated in these activities. It should also be noted that the fundamentalist majority had the votes to do what they wished. They sometimes appeared to have fallen under the influence of forces that were determined to rid the SSB of Elder.

One pastor commented, "They were not so much after Elder as they were after his job."

The trustees had commissioned the writing of a history of the board, to be published in connection with the celebration of the centennial year in 1991. Leon McBeth, church historian from Southwestern Seminary, accepted the contract to write the book. According to McBeth, he was to write "an interpretive" history. He was apparently given access to any material that he felt he needed to do the job competently. He proceeded with the task for many months, searching records and interviewing appropriate persons.

At some point late in the process, trustees became concerned about the nature of the forthcoming book. According to Bill Anderson, then chairman of the trustees, Larry Holly asked for all the documents related to the book, including the internal memoranda, letters, and other materials. These were soon to be circulated to trustees and others.

According to Anderson, there were several problems with the manuscript. The general tenor of the book was displeasing to the trustees. It was said to be biased against the "conservative resurgence." The second problem had to do with the treatment in the book of the Glorieta experience and the motion to dismiss Elder. The third problem was that McBeth did not "talk to but one trustee" about the matter.[12]

By the summer of 1989, various other persons related in one way or the other to the history had concerns about some aspect of it, according to the materials circulated. Elder was accused of not telling the trustees that there were problems with the book. In a letter to Anderson, Elder said, "Accordingly, the administration responded to but did not initiate concerns about the book." Anderson said that this did not conform to the facts revealed in the file material. My interpretation of this incident was that Elder was saying that the administration (he) did not initiate the

---

[12]Ibid.

concerns. Anderson heard him saying that the administration (general staff) of the board had initiated the concerns. According to Anderson, this sentence was a key factor with some trustees.

A crucial factor in the manuscript controversy apparently was a letter from the board's legal counsel to the board's internal counsel. In it, the lawyer suggested that references to certain personnel matters should not be used because they contributed little and were a source of potential problems. The lawyer further suggested that, in his opinion, the book contained bias and in spots should reflect a more objective tone. The opinion apparently was written prior to considerable editing of the manuscript.

As the controversy escalated over the history, feelings ran high, and a lot of correspondence went back and forth between a number of participants. The trustees were upset by the material distributed by Larry Holly, much of which he had obtained from SSB files. Some of his charges did not conform to the facts. He raised the issue of an employee lawsuit against the board. He charged that a federal court (it was a state court) found the president and the board guilty of various charges and that the board had never dealt with the matter. It should be noted that I was then president but was not even a defendant in the case, and that the judge dismissed all of the charges but one before the case went to the jury. The one remaining charge was defamation of the character of the plaintiff, which constisted of praying for him in chapel without mentioning his name. The board dealt with the matter so often that one member asked publicly that the reports cease. It is not possible to verify all of the other charges related to the book since information is not available.

By now, the president was understandably upset over the entire matter. The staff was trying to protect the president and produce a publishable manuscript, and they were surely upset, the trustees were upset, and problems loomed.

The appropriate committee of the board at the August, 1990, meeting recommended to the trustees that the board counsel the administration not to proceed with the publishing of the book, *Celebrating Heritage and Hope* by Leon McBeth. The Board voted to concur with the recommendation.

Baptist Press headlined the story and said the decision was made because "This board has not wanted to fan the flames of the controversy." Donald Moore, chair of the board's general publishing committee added,

"The book was unbalanced."

Chairman Anderson said, "Any history of the convention or its agencies and institutions is going to offend people on either side. We don't think that is wise. . . . It is a good book, well written, by a fine author, but why risk offending." McBeth responded,

I stand by the book. . . . It is a balanced interpretive history of the first 100 years of the Baptist Sunday School Board. . . . What the trustees did will hurt the board more than me. I feel a deep sense of disappointment. But I feel for the board if the people feel there is no freedom to express views except one set of views.[13]

President Elder refused to comment to the media.

Rather than settling the issue, the flames were fanned. The faculties of Southwestern and Southern seminaries protested the refusal of the board to publish the history. At some point, copies of the manuscript were sent to trustee commmittee members. Later, copies of the most controversial chapters were sent to all trustees. At some point all copies were recalled to be destroyed, except for a copy for the archives. One wonders how many copies were made of those distributed to various persons.

Larry Holly figured again in the circulation of numerous materials to trustees and perhaps others. There was a rising tide of opposition to the president. Anderson and others of the leadership of the board had tried to ameliorate the situation over a period of months. Elder had told me in June, 1990, that Anderson was trying to help him in the solution of some of the problems between some trustees and the administration.

By the fall of 1990, that attitude seemed to have shifted. When asked about it, Anderson replied that he knew that the situation was unsolvable. He told me that the board had reached "a managerial impasse" with the president. Elder and Anderson visited in Florida before the called meeting of the Board in January, 1991. Anderson refused to intervene in Elder's behalf. He said that he told Elder, "If I got up and made a speech in the order of Cicero or Demosthenes, I could not save your job." He added, "You cannot lead this congregation."[14]

Early in January, negotiations were underway to secure the resig-

---

[13]Baptist Press, 17 August 1990.
[14]Anderson conversation.

nation of the president. He refused to go quietly. A special meeting of the board was called for January 17, 1991. Baptist Press reported that in the meeting, President Elder and the trustees mutually agreed to end Elder's tenure as head of the board. In the presence of about 400 people, the charges against Elder centered around three items: financial misman-agement, taping of phone calls without second party consent, and editorial bias in the centennial history.[15] (Bill Anderson told me that the taping charge had nothing to do with the termination. His comment to me was, "It was the book that got him.")

The terms of the termination were generous. Elder agreed to early retirement as president with full pay serving as a consultant until April 1, 1993. After that time, he would receive retirement benefits as agreed upon at his election. He was given the staff car and legal expenses. He agreed to do nothing in competition with the board and to do nothing not in the best interest of the board. He was to continue as president until his successor was elected.

On July 19, 1991, James T. Draper, Jr. was elected president of the Sunday School Board.

During the years of the conflict, the board circulation of materials had dropped from about 54 million annually to about 50 million. The gains in sales were accounted for by price increases. At least one new publishing board had been organized by moderate forces and began to produce literature. Fundamentalists complained about the SSB literature— it was not evangelistic enough. Moderates complained about the literature —it was so bland as to be dull.

The financial problems were attributed to Elder by the trustees. The problems were attributed to the fundamentalist board by the moderates. It was inevitable, with the bad publicity coming from the trustee activity and the convention controversy, that the circulation would decline. The wonder of it is that it did not decline more.

A great institution's trustees had spent half a decade battling with its chief executive officer. It was weakened in many ways. The enormous financial contributions were threatened, and its denominationalizing influence was paralyzed. It may well be that it can never return to the force for good that it had been for nearly a century.

President James Draper was the choice of the fundamentalists and

---

[15]Baptist Press, 21 January 1991.

will have opportunity to continue the ministry of the board to a sizable portion of the denomination. He announced that the board will serve all Baptists and will publish materials for all segments of the SBC. Whether he will be permitted to do so by the trustees remains to be seen. If he cannot accomplish this goal, financial disaster surely lies ahead, not only for the SSB but for many of those SBC and state entities who receive large sums of money from the board.

An Afterword

The situation at the Sunday School Board has followed the scenario of the fundamentalist agenda. Two radical reorganizations of the structure and personnel of the board occurred during Draper's first year.

In June, 1992, President Draper announced drastic additional changes in the personnel of the board. He abruptly "retired" eight long-tenured upper and middle level management employees. The incident immediately was termed the "Black Tuesday Massacre." The "underground newspaper" on Friday of that week asked,

> Did you know that at least six of the executive staff members who are "opting" for retirement were given NO other option? ("No one is being fired????") Did you know that each was told to vacate his office by Tuesday of next week? . . . Did you know that our President, James Draper, would not meet with them personally or discuss their plight at his hands? . . . Did you know that there are NO fewer levels of management, NO fewer administrative positions, and only ONE less Vice-President, and only TWO fewer "boxes" under the new structure than there were under the previous administration??

In making the announcement, President Draper had said to the employees, "Pray for yourselves." The paper asked, "Indeed . . . who will be next??"

The answer was not long in coming. Financial settlements for the "retired" executives were made within the framework of the board's retirement plan. By law, the same provisions must be made for all employees who have the same qualifications with reference to tenure and age.

Study revealed that 191 employees were eligible for the special retirement window. By October, 83 percent (159 employees) chose to take advantage of the opportunity. It is widely reported that some of them were "encouraged" to accept this opportunity since their jobs could be declared surplus.

One long-term senior executive analyzed the list of those who were leaving. He considered that 19 of these should be considered "top management." Middle management lost 22 employees. Thirty-four key professional employees left and 21 were in key positions that current leadership would have difficulty replacing.

Many long-time employees are of the opinion that the purge was intended to eliminate those employees who actively supported former president Elder and those who had serious questions about the new trustee leadership. Draper said the changes were made to reduce overhead and streamline the organization. Interestingly, within weeks advertisements appeared in the state papers asking for applicants for many of the positions just vacated.

In September, Draper made it clear that he felt the reorganization and new directions of the board would serve all Baptists and made an indirect appeal to moderates to consider the materials of the board.

The Foreign Mission Board

From the beginning, the SBC had as its purpose the great commission—missions. The convention actually was organized to furnish a mechanism for doing missions. The two mission boards—home and foreign—were the first agencies founded. They became the "glue" that held us together. When disagreements arose, they were often settled or ignored because we agreed on the major business of the convention.

Two special offerings annually were taken—Annie Armstrong for home missions and Lottie Moon for foreign missions. Together with the Cooperative Program they were the financial foundation of the missions effort. These two offerings became an important part of the calendar of most SBC churches.

Much of the following story will be sparsely documented because much of it came from people vitally involved in the foreign mission enterprise. It should be noted that the information represents the opinions of persons who were in a position to know. It should also be noted that according to these persons, the press did not always give the funda-mentalists a fair break. They charge that the press interpreted events in the light of the experience with other facets of the work instead of the actual motivation and actions of the participants.

Voting control of the FMB by the trustees elected by fundamentalists came about 1986. Mark Corts, a two-year chairman of the board, told me that many thought he was elected as the "hit man" to bring the board into conformity with the fundamentalist plans. He was actually nominated for the board by one of the moderate leaders, Cecil Sherman.[16]

The new members who were being elected from 1980 on were considered to be on the side of the fundamentalist movement. As they came aboard, they were evaluated by both the staff and the board members. They were usually classified by both groups as being on one side or the other, and the tension heightened. Often a we/they situation developed between older members and the newly elected.

Some of the new trustees were accustomed to doing "independent missions" and thus were not accustomed to or did not want to use the board procedures. These were people who, when they heard of a need, were eager to act upon it immediately. The board, for more than a hundred years, had worked in cooperation with the SBC missions organization in a given country usually called the Mission. In addition, there was usually consultation with the Baptist union or convention in the area. Usually a careful investigation of a situation was done before funds were appropriated or personnel sent. Since the needs were so great, the board routinely evaluated them, compared them with other needs, prioritized them, and met those related to the purpose of the FMB.

According to the testimony of Corts, many of these members had not served previously on boards of trustees. They had a tendency, being "conservative activists," to come into the board telling everyone what to do. As in the case of the other boards, some of these new trustees did not seem to know the difference between policy and administration. Evidence from several sources indicates that some trustee leaders and staff members frequently had to emphasize the policy role of trustees.

The board experienced a phenomenon than others had noted. The new trustees had less sense of denominational identity that those serving previously. It was almost as if a new denomination had been born out of an evangelical coalition. The work was being influenced by such outsiders as Jerry Falwell and Pat Robertson and had a flavor of

---

[16]References to Mark Corts from transcripts of taped personal conversation, 19 March 1991.

independent missions or non-denominationalism.

The problems, thus created, intensified the tension within and outside the board. Further, the methods of the FMB were too slow for the sometimes impatient new members. One of their desires, common to new trustees of most any organization, was faster response to the opportunities presented. Evidence indicates that, in fact, the FMB was reacting fairly rapidly to the changing world. There was genuine difference in opinion on how this ought to be done. It was almost a case of fast response versus careful response. These problems intensified as Eastern Europe opened up to a new freedom in the exercise of religion.

A key issue with the grass roots Baptists was the problem of the kind of missionary that the new board would appoint. There was wide-spread apprehension that the time would come when only fundamentalists would be appointed. Some of the new trustees wanted this approach immediately. Their point of view received considerable publicity. Their influence on the actual appointments does not seem to be that great yet.

Corts said that the largest consensus of the board was that the trustees wanted people with hands-on practical and evangelistic experience. It was his contention that the emphasis at the FMB was on evangelism, not on inerrancy. This seems to be corroborated by the statements of President Keith Parks. It is certain that the publicity related to the board took on a new tone of emphasis on evangelism.

Immediately, moderates began to feel that the social and medical ministries of the board overseas were being threatened. Both Corts and President Parks have denied that this is true. Parks has long been an advocate of the evaluation of all institutional ministries (and others) to determine which should be turned over to the national bodies. The changing attitude of many governments toward missionary personnel make such evaluations necessary.

Interestingly, Corts was of the opinion that the insistence of the new trustees created an environment in which the staff of the Board took the initiative in highlighting evangelism. This seems to be a matter of degree since Parks had long insisted that the primary job of the board was evangelism that resulted in churches.

In any case, when the board announced a new emphasis on the field, it created a furor. A program was announced that would require seventy percent of the missionaries to spend at least fifty percent of their time in evangelism. A loud dissent sounded over the nation, with people fearing this meant the death of medical and social ministries. The fundamentalists were blamed with destroying a central facet of the ministry of the board. When I asked whose idea this was, both Corts and Parks replied that it was the staff's.

This confusion highlighted another major problem—the matter of the appointment process and qualifications of missionaries. As just stated, moderates felt that it would not be long before only fundamentalists would be appointed. There was widespread discussion that the process of choosing missionaries had been radically altered. There were frequent statements made that there was a new doctrinal test for appointees. It was also stated that the trustees themselves were interviewing candidates with tests of orthodoxy. The interviewing process had long been a staff matter using trained interviewers. The personnel committee of the trustees was sometimes involved.

President Parks has said that the appointment process is still what it was across the years. It has been a struggle to maintain it, but it is essentially the same. Some trustees want only fundamentalists or inerrantists. However, there have been no more candidates turned down for theological reasons than before the takeover. Corts said that in the last ten years only four people have been turned down for theological reasons. The process of questioning candidates on theology has been to ask more detailed questions than in the past. When asked if the question of inerrancy had been a criterion for appointment, both Corts and Parks said no.

Parks told me that only two things about the appointment process had changed. The board no longer requires a candidate to spend a year in a SBC seminary if they had not attended one. The board also recognizes the endorsing of candidates who have graduated from any accredited seminary. This cleared the way for Mid-America graduates who did not have to spend a year in a SBC seminary. Their numbers have not increased significantly.

One circumstance seems to be changing the kind of applicants. There is a process of self-selection going on that will ultimately affect the missions seriously. Some of those persons who would be seen as "less conservative" are opting not to go through the process. More fundamentalists seem to be applying.

Until recently, the controversy within the convention has not seemed to have been exported extensively to many of the missions. There is great fear among the missionaries that it will be. Some of the national conventions and unions are very concerned that it will be. Occasional outbursts have occurred that seem to be harbingers of things to come.

While the controversy may not have been exported massively,the results of the contoversy are felt in every mission everywhere. Missionaries are aprehensive and sometimes confused about what is going on in the United States.

The problem of resignations must be considered. The record indicates that this is a growing problem. The board has for years had an annual loss rate of about three percent due to resignations and deaths. Twice in the last decade, the rate has been above four percent. Ten to twelve years ago, the average time on the field before resignation was ten to twelve years. Now the average time on the field before a resignation is four to seven years. A serious index of future problems is that the number of missionaries reported has been kept high because of the increased number of short term—two years—people appointed.

When asked about the crises of the FMB, former chairman Mark Corts listed those he considered to be important. He felt the board was in a serious administrative crisis when Parks took over in 1980. Parks addressed old problems, and this caused some new problems. Personnel problems were added by some trustee resentment toward the Executive Vice-President. With Corts, Parks got high marks for administrative ability.

The second crisis had to do with the orienting of new trustees. The orientation session was changed from "one hour to two days." The problems of administration versus policy were dealt with at length. Interestingly, trustees now assume primary responsibility for planning orientation for new ones. Most of the sessions are led by the staff. This planning process is an unusual procedure in the SBC. It will probably accelerate complete control of the board into the hands of those doing the orientation.

Mission strategy has been the subject of considerable difference of opinion. The relationship of the board to other mission organizations in the field has been studied at length, and better solutions sought. Some fundamentalist trustees have pressed for more missionary evaluation in order to "get rid of some dead wood." The process of evaluating individual missions and their effectiveness had been tightened, and the resultant resistance by missionaries has been great.

There was a movement in the FMB to eliminate the organization of the trustees referred to as "local trustees" or "Virginia trustees." This was a holdover from the days when meetings of the whole board were held semi-annually, and someone on the scene was needed to care for interim decisions. Interestingly, the supposed moderates in this Virginia group have been replaced with "conservatives."

A change in the Virginia Association (state convention) budget procedures that directed more funds away from the control of the SBC angered some fundamentalists. They did what had been done before; they suggested moving the board away from Virginia to the mid-west. The rationale given was that the staff was more "moderate" than it should be because of the climate of moderation in Virginia. This alarmed the moderates and probably adversely affected the Lottie Moon Christmas offering.

There were numerous incidents of misunderstanding between the new trustees and the old-line Southern Baptists. Sometimes these resulted from poor handling of news and sometimes from radical departures from traditional procedures. Essentially, the same problems rose that plagued other agencies: women in ministry, ordination of women, divorce, changes in procedure, public pronouncements with inadequate information, changes in emphasis, and others caused their share of confusion.

Probably the worst problem of the new era came over the Baptist Seminary in Ruschlikon, Switzerland. In 1948, the FMB established the international seminary for the training of European leaders. As the years went by, the property became very valuable. The board felt that the school should become more self-supporting and that it should be given to European Baptists. From time to time, the theology of the faculty was criticized. When the fundamentalists came to power on the Foreign Mission Board, the agitation grew. A special study committee was sent to Ruschlikon to consider what should be done. They felt that they were not met with the best of attitudes. Ruschlikon people probably felt they had not brought the best of attitudes.

After a time, a compromise was worked out for the board to continue funding the seminary through 1992. After that time, the funding would be reduced a small percentage each year for a fifteen year period. In the October, 1991, meeting of the trustees, a motion was made to defund the seminary at the end of 1991. This would remove $365,000 from the budget of the seminary, which would be nearly 40 percent of the total.

The reason given was that the seminary showed a continuing "liberal" direction by allowing Glenn Hinson, a professor from Southern Seminary, to teach there during a four-month sabbatical leave. He was viewed as liberal toward scripture. (He had been cleared by the Southern trustees of such charges.) The vote was 35–28 to defund Ruschlikon.

This was a catastrophe for the school. The board had agreed to the support program through 1992 (and declining over 15 years), and the seminary was depending on these funds for the 1992 academic year. President Parks told the trustees that the board's integrity was at stake. The appeal did not deter the vote. A legal contract had been drawn that appears to be legally binding. The trustees ignored the contract.

European leaders were stunned. Their reaction was immediate and vigorous. Baptist leaders from England, France, Italy, Finland, Germany, Scotland, Sweden, Spain, and Norway denounced the decision. The president of the Soviet Baptists joined the protest. The leadership of the confederation of European Baptists said that they would have to reconsider their relationships with Southern Baptists. Some said that it was questionable whether Southern Baptist workers would be admitted to their country, where the relationships were now strained to the breaking point. Missionary John Merritt, who had been elected as president of the European Baptist Federation, offered to resign. The Federation refused.

The faculty of Southern Seminary was joined by the faculty at Southwestern in supporting professor Hinson. The Midwestern Seminary faculty also protested the decision to defund Ruschlikon.

In their meeting on December 9–11, 1991, the trustees voted 54 to 27 to take no further action on the Ruschlikon matter. This pronouncement came after consultations with staff and European guests who came to America to attempt some solution. This left the seminary without nearly 40 per cent of its budget immediately and greatly decreased funds for years to come.

The true state of affairs came to the surface during the meeting: "Trustees insisted they are accountable for the theology taught at overseas seminaries that receive FMB financial support."

Joel Gregory, pastor of the First Baptist Church, Dallas said,

> I have been given a trust by God and the constituency of the Southern Baptist Convention who elected me (as a trustee). That trust was to link fiscal stewardship and theological accounting of money given by the SB constituency. . . . There must be a clear linkage between funds and the

theological integrity of all institutions with which the FMB relates.

Mission leaders were stunned. The FMB had never tried to pass judgment on theological matters in other countries. Keith Parks, president of the board commented, "The vote (by a two to one margin) reflected that our trustees have reduced a missions decision to a theological question. Missions decisions need to be broader than that."[17]

Not only has the controversy been exported overseas now, bonds of trust built over a century have been severed. Theological controversy now will invade more than 70 schools and seminaries all over the world.

Widespread dissent in America has already had a profound effect on the attitudes of many toward the mission board. The Virginia Association voted to set aside $100,000 for the Ruschlikon seminary if the FMB does not restore the funds. Many of the state conventions in November of 1991 voted to ask the board to restore the funds. Churches all over the nation responded with disappointment and dismay. Thousands of individuals expressed themselves in the same vein.

The board decided by roll call vote (54–27) that the defunding would stand. This two to one majority reveals clearly the true state of affairs within the board itself. On the face of it, it seems certain that the board is not interested in reconciliation and that it has no intention of finding solutions that include those who differ from hard-line fundamentalism.

One of the most crucial problems now seems to be that the trustees of the board see no relationship between their actions on such a matter and the future of the mission effort in Europe particularly and the rest of the world generally. Further they seem to see no relationship between their actions and the future support of Southern Baptists generally for the mission effort. There seems to be a defiant and belligerent attitude that says that they have the votes and that makes whatever they do right. Others have a different point of view.

This event signals that Southern Baptists have come full circle. The convention began because of foreign mission problems. It now stands at the point of continued fragmentation over foreign missions. The "glue" of the mission enterprise is being diluted rapidly. It is too early to know the results of these actions, but it is certain that the Cooperative Baptist Fellowship and its mission endeavors will be strengthened.

---

[17]Associated Baptist Press, 12 December 1991.

It is feared that the Lottie Moon Christmas offering for foreign missions will be very adversely effected. It is normally received the first week in December. As this chapter is being written, the news still contains wide-spread reports of anger and disappointment at this abrogation of a contractual agreement. Few issues during the controversy created such widespread and angry reaction.

The reaction to the reaffirmation of breaking the contract will not be long in coming. The trustees seem to feel that when they explain that the seminary had a "liberal" professor teaching Christian Classics for a four-month semester, all will be well. That Southern Seminary trustees cleared Hinson of such charges does not seem to have mattered at all. The very serious disruption of the financial support pipeline of the Lottie Moon Christmas Offering and the Cooperative Program either is not understood by the board or they don't care.

Summary

The future of a leading component of Southern Baptist life is clouded. There is a difference of opinion about the continuation of President Parks beyond the normal retirement time. He stood fast for honoring the contract with Ruschlikon in the face of strenuous opposition from his board. It seems certain that he will be falsely blamed for present problems and his future is uncertain. It seems likely that he will be terminated or will be forced to resign as a matter of principle.

The future of the "convention" way of doing missions is far from certain. The nature of future appointments of missionaries is in the hands of those who have vowed to change the system.

Trustees have destroyed the confidence in the FMB of multitudes of Christians both abroad and in the United States. Cooperative Program support has not kept pace with inflation for years and in 1991, for the first time in many years, fell behind the year before. The problems related to the missionary force continue to grow. Increased resignations, the self-selection process that reduces the number of quality appointments, and low missionary morale all contribute to an uncertain future. The lack of confidence of the missionary force in the staff in Richmond looms as an important factor. Some believe that the staff has succumbed to the blandishments of the fundamentalists. Others are aware of the true situation: the staff is trying to preserve as much of the enterprise as possible.

A key uncertainty haunts the faithful: what happens when Keith Parks retires? It seems certain that a fundamentalist sympathizer will be elected. What then?

Afterword

In January, 1992, Dr. Isam Ballenger, vice-president for Europe, the Middle East, and North Africa, and Dr. Keith Parker, area director for Europe, announced their early retirements due to their unwillingness to carry out the fundamentalist agenda.

In March, 1992, the Foreign Mission Board met with President Parks to discuss his future. The press was excluded. After two days of conversation, it was announced that there had been a "great spiritual experience" and that Parks had been "affirmed." (The difference between a "great spiritual experience" and agreement on policies and strategy did not register on some.) It was immediately obvious that Parks' request for extension of time to carry out his plans had not been "affirmed."

Shortly after, Parks announced his decision to retire in October 1992. On June 10 in his annual and last address to the convention, he asked: "Has the controversy accelerated our purpose of sharing the gospel with the world? I would have to answer no!" An estimated 200 people walked out in apparent protest during Parks' address.

Dellanna O'Brien, Executive Director of Woman's Missionary Union, told members of her organization that they could no longer be silent while "anger and distrust tear the heart out of the denomination. . . . There is no way to calculate the negative effects of the convention controversy on world missions."

Those who thought Parks would go quietly into that dark night were surprised. On October 26, 1992, he sent a letter to 3900 foreign missionaries explaining his retirement. The burden of the letter revolved around the changes that had come to the board during the controversy. A partial list of his reasons follows.

1) Lack of appropriate representation of a "very large percentage of Bible-believing, theologically conservative Southern Baptists" on boards of trustees.

2) Decisions being "increasingly shaped by ultra-conservative theological interpretations rather than tested and adopted mission

principles."

3) An atmosphere of trust and respect for differences of viewpoints has been replaced by suspicion, distrust, criticism, and intimidation.

4) Freedom to disagree being "replaced by expectation of conformity. When issues or problems cannot be discussed honestly, they cannot be dealt with productively or solved."

5) A decline in career missionary appointments and increased emphasis on volunteers that is "bringing an imbalance overseas."

6) Some trustees "without the time, expertise, knowledge, or experience to make administrative decisions" on foreign missions "increasingly doing staff work instead of fulfilling the role of trustees."

7) More pressure on the board's news office, which serves as the Richmond bureau of Baptist Press, "to report only positive news," which Parks said threatens to "destroy the credibility of the press."

8) A new development of asking prospective staff members for expressions of loyalty toward trustees and/or the "conservative resurgence."

9) Increasing emphasis for missionary appointment on the four background statements in the 1987 SBC Peace Committee report, instead of just *The Baptist Faith and Message* statement.

10 The convention controversy atmosphere causing "many fine (missionary) candidates either to believe they cannot be appointed or to decline appointment because they are not comfortable with the present Foreign Mission Board direction."[18]

Trustee chairman John Jackson immediately denounced the Parks letter and disagreed with its intent and direction.

In October, Bettye Law, Vice President for the Americas, resigned, citing the growing tendency toward control and conformity and her inability to support and defend the trustees and their policies. In the same month the board received the resignations of 14 more missionaries from the European area, many as a result of the fallout from the Ruschlikon debacle. Resignations increased significantly from other areas.

In December, after months of conversations with leaders of the Cooperative Baptist Fellowship, Keith Parks accepted the leadership of the mission efforts of the new organization of Southern Baptists seeking alternative ways of doing mission work. Within days, former president

---

[18]Baptist Press, 26 October 1992.

Jimmy Carter met with Parks and pledged his prayers and support of the veteran mission leader and his work.

Parks was roundly excoriated by SBC fundamentalists for going into "competition" with the Foreign Mission Board. He was warmly received by his fellow "old-line" Southern Baptists.

The Home Mission Board

Crucial to the missions emphasis in the SBC is the Home Mission Board, called in the beginning "The Domestic Mission Board". From the earliest days of the convention, the HMB has been of central concern to the people. In the last half century, the board has worked in close relationship to the state conventions in strategy, personnel, and finance. There have been, of course, periodic cries for modernization or reorganization, but generally there has been broad support for it and its programs.

At the outset of the conflict, William Tanner, two-time college president, was the new president. Genial and with great "people skills," Tanner abhorred conflict. As the conflict heated up, his position became distinctly uncomfortable. The issue of ordination of women rose to the fore in the Home Mission Board.

In March, 1984, after sometimes heated discussion, the board affirmed the previous policy that ordination was the responsibility of the local congregation. Ordination was not a requirement for missionary appointment. One member of the board contended that a recent study book was an apologetic for ordaining women as ministers.[19]

In December, the executive committee of the trustees approved Church Pastoral Assistance (pastor's salary aid) to an ordained woman pastoring a church in Maryland. There had been a resolution in the SBC the previous year opposing the ordination of women. When the annual meeting of trustees convened in March, 1985, there was heated discussion of the grant. The board finally affirmed its previous policy by a vote of 39–32. Because of this disagreement, the creation of an effort to help churches and states develop crisis pregnancy centers was almost buried

---

[19]Baptist Press, 15 March 1984.

in the news.[20]

We traveled through Germany with the Tanners during the spring of 1985. He was deeply disturbed about the problems rising in the convention and particularly the issue related to women. From the December action to approve aid to a woman pastor until our travel in May, he had received about 95-98 telephone calls or letters protesting the action. He told me that he had personally called every one of the protesters to discuss the matter.

In July, the issue was back on the front burner. The personnel committee of the trustees voted eight to seven against recommending appointment of an ordained woman to do student work at Yale University. The next day, the board reversed the decision by a vote of 37–34. A committee was appointed to study "ordination."[21] President Tanner urged caution and asked the board to not help polarize the convention.

Nearly a year later, the committee reported. They recommended the affirmation that ordination was not a requirement for appointment but recommended that no pastoral assistance be given to any woman who was pastor of a church.[22]

Almost immediately, the leaders of SBC women in ministry said: "We are deeply grieved to learn of the decision of the board of directors of the Home Mission Board to reject future requests for church pastoral aid from local Baptists congregations with women serving as pastors." The statement called the action an "affront to Christian women and men who understand pastoral leadership as a gift given by the Holy Spirit not according to gender."[23]

In the spring of 1986, President Tanner accepted the post of Executive Director of the Baptist General Convention of Oklahoma.

When the search committee was appointed to find a successor, the conflict broke out into the open. At the first meeting after the selection of the committee, the board refused to hear its interim report. After considerable behind-the-scenes maneuvering, the board voted 40 to 36 to ask for the resignations of the committee. Six subsequently did so. They

---

[20]Baptist Press, 2 August 1984.
[21]Baptist Press, 1 August 1985.
[22]Baptist Press, 9 October 1986.
[23]Baptist Press, 29 October 1986.

said that they had been threatened that if they did not, the board would table every item of business for that session. The reason for the request was that the fundamentalists felt that the committee was stacked in favor of moderates.

The new committee nominated Larry Lewis, president of Hannibal-LeGrange College, as the new president. He was elected by a vote of 52–15.[24] Lewis had been active in the fundamentalist movement before becoming a college president. He told me that he refrained from such activity after assuming the college post. He also said that he had refused to become the contact for the Pressler-Patterson coalition in Missouri.

Under Lewis' administration, the problems of the denomination continued to run their course. As the number of fundamentalist trustees increased on his board, the HMB became quieter. Widespread rumors of poor staff morale and administrative problems continue to surface. Some of these rumors have been verified by various staff members both past and present.

The matter of the appointment of missionaries now seems to be determined by the statement of faith—*The Baptist Faith and Message*—and the resolutions of the convention that relate to personnel qualifications. Lewis subscribes to the notion that the resolutions of the convention are "messages" to the agencies. The Peace Committee report immediately became determinative for the recommendation of missionaries for appointment. The four interpretations of the statement on the Bible—truth without any mixture of error—now furnish a further basis for examining the faith of missionaries.

The problem of ordaining women caused another furor in the board when a pastor who had a woman deacon in his church was hired by the Executive Committee of the Home Mission Board. A trustee threatened to bring the matter to the full board in its next meeting. After consultations, the pastor withdrew.

When the pressure grew within the convention against the Baptist Joint Committee, the HMB canceled its intern plan with the committee. The HMB had funded an intern to work in the program in Washington.

By August, 1989, the HMB, like all the other institutions, was suffering financial problems. In August, the board voted to cut 28 staff

---

[24]Baptist Press, 14 April 1987.

positions in the light of an $8.2 million reduction in its budget.[25] In the same meeting, the trustees accepted recommendations that would have information on nominees for positions from their state sent to the state members. Once again, they followed the national trend, requesting confidential information to be widely distributed.

Support of the Annie Armstrong offering for home missions has been surprisingly good. The Cooperative Program support has been relatively stagnant for a number of years. Missionary numbers have remained high and morale has often registered that of the scene where they work. Some trustees, as in other agencies, try to use independently the power of their office. It sometimes shows up with trustees issuing instructions or warnings to a missionary on their local scene without use of proper procedure. Once again the interpretation of trustee roles was causing distress.

In many ways, the picture of the situation at the HMB parallels that of the other agencies. Support of home missions will be an increasingly difficult problem, while the fundamentalist churches seem to be somewhat more responsive to the Home Mission Board than to other agencies. The reason for the existence of the Southern Baptist Convention is again in distress.

The Christian Life Commission

The Christian Life Commission (CLC) in some ways has been the conscience and the "lightening rod" of the Southern Baptist Convention. It has had as its primary assignment the social and ethical issues of Baptist life. For a generation the commission had prodded the conscience of the leaders and the constituency of the SBC. The commission became prominent during the civil rights controversy. It recommended fairness and rights for minorities at a time when that was not particularly popular.

In June, 1970, a rump session of about 200 fundamentalists denounced the Christian Life Commission for a conference in which situation ethics and black rights had been discussed. One speaker charged that the denominational machinery was in the hands of "liberals" and a housecleaning was needed.

---

[25]Baptist Press, 11 August 1989.

In the convention meeting beginning the next day, two efforts were made to eliminate or withhold funds from the CLC. When that effort failed, two resolutions were offered that would have abolished the agency outright and, that failing, to fire the staff. Three former presidents of the convention counseled restraint, and the resolutions failed.

Skirmishes over one issue or another are common in the relationship between the CLC and the constituency. Usually some moral or ethical issue roiled the waters. But the controversies of the 1980s were not just skirmishes. They represented an entirely different set of problems.

In 1984, a motion was offered in the convention meeting calling for the establishment of a "governmental affairs office" in Washington. In studying the matter, the SBC Executive Committee, not yet controlled by fundamentalists, recommended that this matter be dropped. The recommendation was supported by both the leaders of the Christian Life Commission and the Baptist Joint Committee. This was the first strong effort mounted by the fundamentalist forces to establish an SBC office in Washington that would represent their interests. This effort failed. It was to be the first of many.

With the retirement of long-time leader of the CLC, Foy Valentine, in 1986, the commission was badly divided. The fundamentalists did not yet have complete control. In January, 1987, after considerable maneuvering, Larry Baker, Academic Vice-President of Midwestern Seminary, was elected Executive Director by a vote of 16-13. Fundamentalist leaders announced that he might have only a six-month tenure. At least five seats on the commission would change at the June convention meeting, and Baker was served notice that his tenure might be short. Nine new members had come on the board during the search process. Baker announced that he would spend the early months of his administration trying to build relationships.[26]

True to their promises, in September, 1987, the fundamentalists attempted to unseat Baker. The vote was 15 to 15. Baker was attacked for his positions on abortion, capital punishment, and women in ministry. Baker had stated that abortion may be allowed as an exception in the case of threat to the life of the mother, rape, incest, and "perhaps in the case where traumatic and severe deformity to the fetus is involved." He did

---

[26]Baptist Press, 18 September 1987.

not favor capital punishment. The selection process was also attacked.[27] Two or three commissioners who had voted against Baker's election voted for him in the effort to terminate him.

The fundamentalists swept the election of officers, turning down three nominations of Director Baker. All new officers had supported the termination of Baker. They immediately overturned the long standing action of the CLC and differed with the convention by passing a motion that abortion was justifiable only "when the developing child represents a clear and present danger to the physical life of the mother."[28] Attempts by Baker and others failed to soften the statement to agree with the last SBC action, which denounced abortions but did not mention exceptions. This confrontation expressed the hard line drawn by fundamentalists on the issue and one that would be urged on other agencies.

Another obvious objective of the fundamentalists was to establish an office in Washington. Finally, in October of 1987, the CLC opened the office. It had reallocated funds from other programs and immediately asked the convention for an additional $150,000 to staff the office on a full-time basis. Abortion opposition furnished its immediate agenda.

The program assignment given to the CLC did not cover church-state matters. This did not please the fundamentalist leaders. It was obvious by now that there was a strong desire for a political affairs voice in Washington D. C., and strenuous efforts would be made to get it. They were sure that the Baptist Joint Committee was not what they wanted.

In December, 1987, three members of the commission and four members of the SBC Public Affairs Committee met to discuss the merger of the CLC and the PAC. In October, 1987, the PAC had voted 8–4 to request the SBC to dissolve its ties to the Joint Committee and allocate the BJCPA funds of $485,200 to the PAC. A letter was sent to the commissioners of the CLC, with a ballot, asking them to vote on the merger. These actions were taken without the knowledge of Director Baker.[29]

The consultations between the two groups were taken without the knowledge of all the members of the Public Affairs Committee. Members of both groups not privy to the discussions issued immediate protests. The attorney for the CLC said that the mail ballot may be illegal.

---

[27]Baptist Press, 18 September 1987.
[28]Baptist Press, 18 September 1987.
[29]Baptist Press, 4 January 1988.

Extensive defenses were made by the group who had met to consider merger. The chief executives of the commission, the BJCPA, and the Sunday School Board issued statements of criticism of the behind-closed-doors effort.

In May, 1988, Larry Baker accepted the call of First Baptist Church of Pineville, Loouisiana, the site of Louisiana College. He had a tenure at the commission of 14 months instead of the promised six months.

In September, 1988, the CLC quickly elected Richard Land, Academic Vice-President of Criswell College, to replace Baker. Land had a strong background academically, graduating from Princeton and New Orleans Seminary and having an earned D. Phil. degree from Oxford. Many thought that he was Paul Pressler's choice from the beginning.[30]

Land moved rapidly to put into action the agenda of the fundamentalists. By July, 1989, Land announced the hiring of a full-time employee for the Washington D. C. office. He was an employee of the United States House of Representatives Republican Study Committee. This action was possible because of an increase in the CLC budget. It was one of only three SBC agencies to get a budget increase.[31]

Extensive maneuvering had been taking place, with the Executive Committee recommending a new religious liberty organization. It was withheld from the convention at the request of the president. Subsequently, a proposal was drawn recommending that the CLC be given the assignment of religious liberty issues.

In October, the Public Affairs Committee voted to recommend to the Executive Committee of the SBC that the role of the commission not be expanded to include religious liberty issues. The PAC group was loath to lose its power.

In February, 1990, the Executive Committee voted to recommend to the convention in June in New Orleans to reduce the funding for the Baptist Joint Committee on Public Affairs from $391,796 to $50,000. The funds were to be given to the Christian Life Commission. The commission's program statement was to be rewritten to include responsibility for religious liberty and church-state matters. By April, 1990, the PAC, with seven members absent and three abstentions, voted 4–3 to endorse the proposed changes.

---

[30]Baptist Press, 15 September 1988.
[31]Baptist Press, 19 Juky 1989.

Foes continued a major attack on the BJCPA as being too "liberal" for not supporting school prayer, anti-abortion amendments, and several legislative issues. They ignored the fact that the program statement of the BJCPA did not include ethical issues.

The budget proposal deleting most of the funding for the BJCPA passed in the convention vote in June. Funding was increased for the Commission by about 40 percent. The Public Affairs Committee, now called the Political Action Committee by many, had its budget increased to $25,000. The convention added the responsibility for church-state matters to the commission. Land immediately announced plans for expansion of the Washington office.[32]

Pressler announced in the February, 1991, meeting of the SBC Executive Committee that a complicated arrangement had been worked out so that members of the defunct PAC would be allowed to serve on the board of the CLC until their terms expired. This "deal" was recommended to the SBC and approved. Pressler, at last, had what he had apparently wanted from the beginning: a church-state office in Washington.

Seasoned observers feared that the Baptists would not have a clear unified voice in the Capitol. Their fears were soon justified. The Supreme Court agreed to review a ruling barring invocations and benedictions at public school ceremonies. Richard Land said in part, "We must . . . seek to accommodate religious expression, which is a concomitant part of religious liberty." BJC general counsel, Oliver Thomas countered, "There's a lot more going on in this case than graduation prayers. The court is being asked to begin dismantling Mr. (Thomas) Jefferson's wall separating church and state and to replace it with a picket fence."

The issue was joined more clearly during the hearing of the Supreme Court on the issues. The CLC supported a departure from the "Lemon" test (which follows traditional SBC stands) on separation issues:

> The Lemon test involves three judicial criteria. It considers a law or government action to be constitutional if the law or action has a secular purpose, if its primary effect neither advances nor inhibits religion and if it does not excessively entangle church and state.

---

[32]Baptist Press, 14 June 1990.

The CLC-favored position was called the "coercion test." It proposes two standards for courts to follow. It would

> deem a law or government action to be constitutional if the law or action does not coerce people into participation in religious activity which violates their consciences and if it does not threaten to establish an official church.

This view allows for a much closer relationship between religious and state objectives.

Most religious groups in America oppose the abandoning of the Lemon test. The coercion test follows the general directions of both the Reconstructionist movement and the effort to make America "a Christian nation" by legislative means. Under the Lemon test, the government may: teach about religion in schools; provide students with equal access to school property or the right to meet before and after school for religious reasons; release students from class for off-campus religious instruction; provide textbooks and transportation for parochial students; hire legislative chaplains; and extend construction grants and revenue bond funding to religiously affiliated colleges.

Under the coercion test, the government could: hold or sponsor worship services, as long as attendance is not compulsory; subsidize religious education (parochial schools); erect sectarian displays; sponsor prayer meetings and religious training in public schools; and become involved in church affairs through regulation of schools and day-care centers.[33]

Tragically, the Court and the Congress are now faced with a divided testimony by Baptists on many of the crucial issues facing the country.

It should be noted that the marked differences between the points of view of the BJCPA and the CLC represent two different approaches to matters of church-state. Generally, the BJCPA position on separation of church and state relates to the general position taken by Thomas Jefferson, James Madison, and other framers of the Constitution and the Bill of Rights. This view holds that there is or should be a wall of separation that prevents either from interfering with or more specifically controlling the other. This view was espoused by Baptists from our beginning and clearly articulated by John Leland, Richard Furman, and others.

---

[33]*Western Recorder,* 29 October 1991.

The CLC point of view relates to the hyper-Calvinistic point of view espoused by the Puritans early in this country that basically the state and church are better off closely allied. This view seems to forget or ignore centuries of history filled with persecution, inquisitions, imprisonment of religious leaders, and discrimination against anyone not agreeing with the majority. This view, apparently now espoused by the Chief Justice of the Supreme Court, seems to be the driving force for efforts of the right-wing political forces.

The basic differences between these two approaches seem to be hidden from many contemporary Baptists. The present direction of the SBC is clearly in the direction of the CLC position. It should be noted that this position has been handed to the commission by forces outside it by the election of commissioners who either receive orders or are steeped in this tradition. This view of church-state relationships is not a part of the history of the CLC. The present trend differs dramatically from the historic Southern Baptist position.

The confusion grows and disintegration continues. The Christian Life Commission appears headed toward political activism after the fashion long rejected by fundamentalists and many moderates. The direction of the head-long plunge seems to include much of the agenda of the right-wing political establishment. One must raise the question as to the ethics of making an historically non-political denomination and its agencies the instrument of political forces.

The Baptist Joint Committee on Public Affairs

The Joint Committee is not an agency of the Southern Baptist Convention. It is an organization founded by the principal Baptist groups in the United States to monitor and lobby for separation of church and state, foster religious liberty, and promote the free exercise of religion. It is based on the constitutional right of equality of all before the law and the rights of all citizens to the free exercise of religion. The Southern Baptist participation from the beginning included a large share of membership and strong financial support.

The committee has for more than half a century monitored the governmental scene, alerting the various constituencies to problems related to its mission. It has represented various segments of its constituency in such matters as double taxation of missionaries serving overseas, the problems of ERISA as the law related to the pension systems of the denominations, various equal-access controversies related to students, and a wide variety of other issues requiring expert knowledge and access to public officials. These were not attempts to control government but to make certain legislation or administrative law assured religious liberty and equal treatment to all citizens

The SBC participation in the committee had from time to time been subject to criticism when it had made some decision that did not please someone. These were usually short-term problems, and the denomination at large was pleased with the arrangement. It has been the opinion of many that this was one of the most effective organizations for religious liberty on the national scene.

With the coming of the fundamentalist take-over, the situation changed dramatically. During the preceding years, under the directorship of James Wood, the committee had taken a position that favored pro-choice on abortion. The contention was that abortion was a church-state issue. This was not a serious public issue in the SBC until the fundamentalist coalition took charge.

James Dunn became Executive Director almost at the same time as the take-over. He had an agreement with the search committee that the BJCPA would not publicly fight the abortion issue. They agreed that the assignment for ethical concerns rested elsewhere. The fundamentalists wanted the Joint Committee to take a strong stand against abortion.

A second reason for the dramatic change of atmosphere, according to Dunn, was the succession of President Reagan and his radically different philosophy following immediately after President Carter. Carter had stood for traditional Baptist beliefs. He was against government interference in religion, an ambassador to the Vatican, heavy-handed governmental power in matters related to abortion, government mandated school prayer, and federal funds for parochial schools.

When President Reagan came to office, his position on many of these matters was almost 180 degrees in reverse. This focused the differences between the Joint Committee and the fundamentalists. They followed the party line of the right-wing political structures, which were substantially different from the half-century direction of the committee.

An additional factor heightened the conflict. The right-wing evangelists on radio and television were delivering the party line in the name of religion. Of the most prominent ones, only Pat Robertson was a Southern Baptist, and many thought he was more so in name than in fact. Dunn's predecessor thought the evangelists were doing a lot of talking about issues without very much research and sometimes without checking the facts. The Joint Committee had been critical of the attempt to control the direction of the government by religious fiat. It further was critical of the use of political reforms to promote religious ends.[34]

All of this caused the fundamentalists, even before they had consolidated their power, to launch an effort to take over the Joint Committee. Dunn believes that one of the great longings of the right-wing political coalition was to have a religious voice on Capitol hill for their own political purposes. The effort to establish one would continue for years.

Another factor in the conflict was the personal relationships between James Dunn and Paige Patterson and, to a lesser degree, Paul Pressler. They had crossed swords in Texas on a variety of issues. There was substantial disagreement on Dunn's part with the fundamentalist agenda. His was the traditional Baptist position on many matters, and theirs was, at least in part, the old Puritan position.

Further, Dunn became a member of the board of People for the American Way. One of its purposes was to counter the extremism of the radical right television evangelists. A number of Baptists were members of the organization and members of the board. A film was made that admittedly took some of the evangelist's remarks out of context and ridiculed the religious right. Dunn appeared briefly in the film, commenting that he was a member because he believed in separation of church and state. This was the final straw. It gave the fundamentalists a tool that they were expert in using.

With the Joint Committee following the traditional Baptist line and the fundamentalists following a new but ancient course, the confrontation was inevitable. By 1982, Paige Patterson told a Washington reporter that something would be done to silence him (Dunn). Dunn admits that some of his rhetoric was not suited to the amelioration of the conflict. Pressler attacked Dunn when he served on a committee to survey the BJC for the SBC Executive Committee. He told Dunn, "You know we could change the executive director and that might solve all of our problems."[35]

---

[34]Transcript of a taped personal conversation with James Dunn, 8 February 1991.
[35]Ibid.

He was no kinder to Stan Hastey, an associate of Dunn's. Pressler told the old story of hitting a pony across the nose with a two-by-four to get his attention. He said to Hastey, "Maybe that's what we need to do with the press office of the BJC, get a two-by-four and get his attention."[36] Both men testify that there were plenty of verbal two-by-fours in the ensuing years.

When the Public Affairs Committee of the SBC, liaison group to the Joint Committee, got enough fundamentalists to dominate the PAC (1987), they began the long road to control of the Joint Committee. They gave to the Washington office a series of impossible demands. They demanded: a unilateral (excluding representatives of other Baptist bodies) SBC personnel evaluation of the BJC staff, all correspondence to or from the staff for the last three years, all of the green books of individual personal travel expenses for the last five years, a list of all memberships of the BJC, and a couple of other items. The Joint Committee Executive Committee voted unanimously to refuse access to correspondence and expense accounts and to refuse the demand for the staff to be unilaterally evaluated. The other items were submitted immediately. No agency head of the SBC, several of whom were on the BJC, voted to support the demands of the fundamentalists.

From that point, a long series of efforts was made to shift the responsibilities of church-state matters to the Christian Life Commission or defund the BJC. For years, at almost every meeting of the Executive Committee or the convention, some effort was made to strike at the Joint Committee. In 1990, the fundamentalists finally mounted a strong effort resulting in reduced funding of the BJC to $50,000. In June, 1991, by a motion from the floor, the convention voted to withdraw all financial support. In the September, 1991, meeting of the SBC Executive Committee, a motion passed to disassociate the SBC from the BJC altogether.

Seeing the handwriting on the wall, a small group of Baptists met in Washington early in 1990 to form a parallel organization to give disfranchised Baptists an opportunity to support the BJC. Invitations to participate resulted in several hundred responses. Abner McCall, former president of Baylor and Gardner Taylor, famed black preacher from New York, and I serve as co-chairmen. Substantial funds have been given outside the usual SBC channels, but further assistance is mandatory.

---

[36]Transcript of taped personal conversation with Stan Hastey, 10 may 1991.

The Joint Committee continues to function effectively, but its ministry is hindered by conflicting opinions from the Christian Life Commission office.

Other Agencies

The other commissions of the SBC, with the exception of the Radio and Television, have fared rather better than those discussed above. Apparently all are under the control of the fundamentalists. In most cases, the program assignment has not been subject to public debate or active controversy.

The Radio and Television Commission fell under the control of the fundamentalists early on. Controversy, very much like those described earlier, occupied the attention of the commissioners and other Baptists for years. President Jimmy Allen, former president of the convention, finally gave up in his efforts to market the commission's products on a national level. He was not allowed to sell a major component of the production capacity to a private firm that offered the commission a reasonable price and television time for years. After his departure, the commission bought the cable network of Jerry Falwell, guaranteeing him time for years to come.

The Annuity Board has fared well during the years of controversy. The warning issued by then president Darryl Morgan, that controversy on that board would cause a "run on the bank," apparently had its effect. The new president, Paul Powell, seems on the way to successfully maintaining equilibrium.

Woman's Missionary Union is not an agency of the SBC. It has occupied auxiliary status since its inception more than a hundred years ago. It has been a prime supporter of the mission efforts of the denomination. The controversy has effected it less than other components, since the convention has no control over its activities. Since many of the fundamentalist leaders apparently do not support the organization and have no units in many of their churches, the WMU has continued to support the mission causes. It has been accused of feminism and heresy, since it has systematically supported women in ministry, though it has not been an open advocate of ordination of women.

The present leadership of WMU seems to be looking to the future. Recent announcements intimate that the organization is changing rather rapidly and will participate in an expanded way with Baptists who sponsor missions, whether after the fundamentalist pattern or not. The organization, like most SBC organizations, is having difficulty sustaining its enrollment. Some of this is due to the radical societal changes of the last 25 years, and some of it is undoubtedly due to the controversy.

Few SBC entities have had the profoundly positive effect on the mission enterprise that WMU has had. Approximately one-half of the budgets of the mission boards come from the offerings originated and sponsored by WMU. The fundamentalist leadership has appeared to have little interest in WMU, and some have ridiculed it.

If the support of WMU is lost for the mission boards, the work will suffer catastrophic results.

Summary

With the few exceptions noted above, there is hardly a cause sponsored by the SBC that has not suffered dramatically from the fundamentalist controversy. Not one of them is stronger today than it was before the conflict. All are more poorly funded and have less harmony than before. None is as effective as it was before. Statistics have grown (and will be cited by those who disagree with this analysis), but as the momentum has slowed in almost everything the denomination does, the future appears to hold further problems for the agencies.

Point of View, Different Perspectives

In a meeting of moderate Baptists, searching for light and continuity, I was approached by a veteran foreign missionary. As were many of their kind, this one was searching for answers to the bewildering convolutions of the missionary world. Some were confused by the actions of the trustees and some by what they perceived to be the conduct of the staff. This one came quickly to the point.

"Why is Keith Parks (president of the Foreign Mission Board) such a wimp?" The question startled me, for it did not fit my understanding of Parks. It seems that his attempts to cooperate with a fundamentalist-controlled board made him appear to some to be without proper administrative backbone. The question really had to do with why he did not do something to reassure the mission staff that all was well. The missionaries saw that things were different, and they felt that he should do something to assure that they would return to normal. Under the circumstances, there was little he could say that would not cause more harm than good.

Parks' point of view was that of a man totally dedicated to the foreign mission task. He was intent on doing everything possible to maintain the level and excellence of that work. He tried in every way integrity allowed to guide the program to which he had given his life. Sometimes he differed strongly with the trustees to whom he was responsible. His way and theirs differed, sometimes radically. To those observers who had significant administrative experience, he appeared to be struggling to cooperate when he could and resist when he must.

To me and a host of others, he represented a way of doing missions that has a hazy future under the fundamentalists. His alternate resistance and cooperation said that he is trying to do what he could to protect the mission effort from the inevitable. He obviously intended to do this as long as he could.

These are two views of a continuing struggle to preserve a great institution at great personal cost to the president.

Chapter Fourteen

Past, Present, and Future

"The End Is Not Yet. . . ."[1]

An evaluation of the controversy in the Southern Baptist Convention must begin with the question, "What/who were Southern Baptists?" and then "What/who are Southern Baptists?"

Before 1979, there was a body of theological beliefs usually held by Southern Baptists. There was always an emphasis on basic biblical beliefs. The edges of that body of doctrine were sometimes indistinct, and there were not many sharp definitions. It was by any standard conservative. There were differences in such matters as eschatology and a variety of other debatable positions. It was not so much theology that distinguished Southern Baptists from other evangelical bodies. A number of other evangelical Christians held similar biblical positions.

While the fundamentalists have forced on the SBC certain theological dicta, it was not true theology that suffered most from the conflict. The greatest victims of the controversy have been the distinctives that made us different. A principal distinctive of ours had to do with *polity and the nature of the church.*

One principle that was basic was the idea that all believers are priests with equal standing before God and in the church. This meant absolute freedom of the individual from ecclesiastical control. It also meant that the individual was responsible to God for himself and accountability was inherent in the concept

Ecclesiology was a central idea, with the democratic free church at the center of all our organizations. The local association of churches was

---

[1]Matthew 24:6.

free, independent, and autonomous. So were the state conventions of Baptists and also the Southern Baptist Convention.

These units were interdependent but autonomous. The central building block of this impossible organization was cooperation for common purposes. All of this remarkable unity was possible because it was always voluntary.

For all units, from the individual to the national body, there was the free exercise of religion according to conscience. No cookie-cutter mentality was needed; no ecclesiastical control was possible or desired. Each person was free to pursue his gift or calling.

These simple but profound principles enabled the building of a great denomination.

The rise of convention control in various aspects of denominational life threaten the most basic of our principles. The obvious efforts to control the press, the opinions of executives and professors, the use of speakers and writers, and the effort to enforce the opinions of the leaders are destroying the basis of cooperation.

Another characteristic of the denomination was its unique way of *doing missions and education.*

Across more than a hundred years a carefully integrated system of agencies and institutions was constructed. At every level of denominational life, the people at the association or the convention decided voluntarily which segment of the ministries they wished to sponsor or fund. Agreements were worked out between units, so that after a century certain activities would be carried out at certain levels. These were cooperative decisions, with no unit having authority over any other.

These arrangements could be made and continued because of a common vision of the task of education and missions. This method came to be called the "convention" way and was sharply different from the societal method. The convention method, by common consent, gave integration and efficiency.

The principle component in this awkward and unwieldy system was mutual trust. It is obvious now that the trust necessary for such cooperative effort has disappeared.

Another principal component of our identity related to *church-state matters and free exercise of religion.*

One historian said that the greatest contribution of Baptists to western civilization has been the idea of separation of church and state. Whoever should get the credit must be sorted out by history, but it is certain that the SBC stood firmly for this basic understanding of roles. This concept was inherent in our understanding of the priesthood of the believer and the free exercise of religion.

The official position of the SBC has been altered radically on this central component of our life. We now have an official agency of the denomination calling for a change in the Supreme Court's position on separation of church and state. We have representatives of the denomination lobbying for tax funds for church schools and for religious preference by government. The school prayer issue continues to erupt. The attempt to cripple the Baptist Joint Committee on Public Affairs has put it in jeopardy.

Those people who are involved in all of this do not seem to know that public policy follows public money as the night the day. When the regulatory agencies begin to insist on regulating the pursuits of the churches, a new tune will be played.

Additionally, Southern Baptists were a *non-creedal people.* The idea of freedom from ecclesiastical controls involved the idea of the authority of scripture. Scripture, interpreted by the individual with whatever guidance he or she chose, sometimes tested by the practices of the larger church, was the "sole rule of faith and practice." The resolutions adopted by any body had little effect usually on individuals and churches. All of them could be ignored with no repercussions.

The distinctives that collectively identified us as Southern Baptists suffered most in the controversy.

Polity

The organization of fundamentalists and centrists who joined them, with every convention vote, gradually built a fence around all of the institutions. At every point of dispute, the issue--not only the decision--was to be decided with a majority vote, and that was supposed to end the matter. This volume is filled with illustrations of that principle.

It is apparent that many did not realize that this course of conduct would influence or determine decisions at every level of SBC life. Some intended that this should be so. The pastors, churches, associations, and state conventions are being seriously impacted by this democratization of ethics and polity decisions.

Almost immediately after a decision that related to ethics or theology, agencies began the difficult process of conforming and relating the decision to every employee and policy decision. These decisions often were unrelated to a particular entity, but fundamentalist leadership in that group felt the right or necessity to impose the convention resolution or motion on the institution.

Writers, speakers, teachers, and administrators were now subject to the majority opinion, regardless of the fact that it may have reversed last year's ruling. If a writer or speaker in any one of the hundreds of meetings diverged from the party line, there were immediate repercussions. Administrators began to chose only those who would raise no questions or discuss no convention decisions. There have been repeated occasions when a speech or paper has been reported to Dallas or Houston before the individual got home. On several occasions, trustees have discussed these events in their next meeting.

The convention has become a legislative body, setting standards of belief on any subject discussed and establishing rules and regulations that administrators dare not ignore. The votes in the convention meeting are almost always what the fundamentalist leaders want.

We are rapidly developing *ecclesiastical authoritarianism*. It is not the orderly, carefully articulated, slowly developed, gradually implemented ecclesiological authority of some of the older denominations. The lines of communication that process decision making are often private. The agenda is worked out in unofficial caucuses. The enforcement is placed in the hands of a board of trustees elected by the machine.

The appearance is that of a developing order of "high priests" dictating direction. The shadow cabinet in the background has had great power, but even it seems to be fading.

A system of reward and punishment is functioning. The loyal and faithful get appointed or invited. The opposition, however mild, is not appointed, invited, or recommended.

Blow at the Heart

The basic foundation on which we have stood in our educational and missionary work has been mutual trust. It must be said again, this trust is now gone. Distrust lurks in every level of the work. The institutions and employees are suspect. The radical actions of the trustees at several institutions make them suspect by long-time supporters. Thus, the base of cooperation is crumbling.

Every major institution save the Annuity Board has been thrown into turmoil. Attacks have been launched against most of the old-line chief executive officers. Reams of charges have been circulated against the presidents of several agencies, often without sending the accusations to the presidents.

The public is confused, and the churches are uncertain. The goodwill that had been carefully developed over many years among the rest of the religious and secular communities is suffering. The ability to evangelize around the world has been seriously compromised by the unchristian broadsides that have been thrown by both sides. Our ministry has fallen on hard times because of the events of the last 12 years.

The fundamentalists have *redefined what it means to be a Southern Baptist.*

If the conflict had been about correcting a leftward drift in the agencies and seminaries, the entire affair was totally unnecessary. Since the major thrust was a change of control and introduction of the spirit and mindset of fundamentalism, the result is a radical change in the basic nature of the denomination.

At the beginning, there was little significant difference on truly theological matters. Several rightist leaders have said in recent years that there is little difference in our understanding of the nature of scripture. The differences on social matters--such as abortion--were small. There was little difference of opinion on the nature of the educational and missionary enterprises.

If one assumes that there were a half-dozen problems in the seminaries, these could have been dealt with through procedures already in place. It had been done before.

Out of my dim literary memory there rises the story of a man who burned down his house to roast a pig. The metaphor seems appropriate to what has happened in the SBC.

Prognosis

The tools of Baptist religious communication and decision are similar to those used in education: reason, dialogue, persuasion, logic, and freedom. In the world of Baptist religion, some methodologies are unacceptable: coercion of belief, use of political power to attain religious ends, attempts to force conformity, and regimentation.

It is no wonder that the future of the SBC is shrouded in the fog of misunderstanding, distrust, and outright hostility. Few would claim that these are Christian characteristics. Few would claim that what has happened in the last dozen years was Christian either. If we had really practiced the truth of the Bible we have fought over, none of this would have happened.

Out of this religious miasma, some things seem certain to come.

Fragmentation

Almost every level of denominational life seems to be undergoing important change. Some of it is subtle; some of it is like a freight train in the living room at midnight.

The following list of events illustrates the crumbling structures of the denomination. One of the basic problems with these changes is that each brings with it a set of implications and complications that create yet other breaches.

The state convention of Virginia in November, 1992, set up and entirely new system of supporting missions and education beyond the state. There are now three "tracts" by which churches can fund projects in which they have trust. This compares with one in place for more than half a century. Churches can now chose not to fund the SBC efforts and remain in fellowship in the state. One tract permits the funding of the Cooperative Baptist Fellowship projects directly. This, of course, limits the support of the SBC. The complicated nature of the plan threatens the affiliation of some churches with the national body. Baptist life in Virginia borders on turmoil.

The convention in South Carolina in November, 1992, ended all formal relationships with Furman University, its foremost educational institution.

By April of 1992, the Cooperative Baptist Fellowship reported that its mission gifts had risen by 60 percent.

In 1992, the North Carolina convention ousted two churches on grounds of improper actions concerning homosexuality. The national body followed suit.

During the year, the Christian Life Commission and the Baptist Joint Committee on Public Affairs battled each other in Washington over the issues related to prayer in public functions. The CLC urged the abandonment of the "Lemon Test" by the Supreme Court on church state issues. Confusion grows about who is the "real Baptist."

The Kentucky convention had a tumultuous meeting in 1992, debating the matter of making the support of SBC projects optional for churches while allowing them to remain in fellowship with the state body. Moderates, fearing the rewriting of our history, organized "The William H. Whitsitt Baptist Heritage Society" to preserve the history and memory of the moderate movement. Interestingly, Whitsitt was the central figure in one of the early SBC controversies.

In Virginia, fundamentalists raised the issue of establishing a new state convention since they could not control the present one. Soon, some of their leaders cautioned against it. Division was the name of the game.

The new president of the Executive Committee of the SBC, Morris Chapman, called on moderates related to the Cooperative Baptist Fellowship to either get in the SBC or get out. The problem had to do with the fact that the moderates were sponsoring their own mission efforts and presumably getting money that the SBC wanted. It is of interest that when the fundamentalists did the same thing, no one called on them to get out. It was assumed that they were free and Baptists. H. H. Hobbs, former president of the SBC, joined in Chapman's ill-conceived pronouncement. The statement was widely interpreted as a threat that if they did not leave, they would be thrown out.

SBC leaders in a meeting with WMU leaders implied that if the WMU assisted the Fellowship efforts, it was likely that a new women's organigation would be formed.

Laymen in Texas charged that a move to support the Cooperative Program by fundamentalists was a mask for an attempt to take control of the state convention.

Associated Baptist Press announced plans for a monthly newsletter of Baptist news targeted at the laity.

In Mississippi, a motion was made in the state meeting to defund the *Baptist Record*, the state convention's journal. Unhappiness with its middle-of-the-road approach seemed to be the motive.

The Arkansas convention passed a resolution calling the views of the newly elected President of the United States, Bill Clinton, immoral.

In one state, a messenger said that to vote for Clinton was a sin.

In Oklahoma, the state board of the Convention there passed a new advertizing policy for the state Baptist paper:

> *The Messenger* advertising policy was amended "to exclude advertisements for organizations which compete with BGCO or SBC entities for funding and program loyalty.". . . . The amendment extends the exclusion to cover all such groups, including the Cooperative Baptist Fellowship...The amendment was approved unanimously.[2]

In the spring of 1992, three former fundamentalist presidents of the SBC called for the defeat of fundamentalist leader Paul Pressler for a seat on the Foreign Mission Board. He resisted and won the seat.

In the June meeting of the SBC, Larry Holly, late of Sunday School Board fame, intoduced a resolution that, in effect, declared the Masonic Order an unholy affair. The motion passed that required a reluctant Home Mission Board to do an in-depth study of Masonry, with the obvious view of condemning any who belonged to it. Widespread protest (and support) broke out over the country. The fundamentalist agenda seemed to continue to consist of attacks against abortion, homosexuality, Masonry, and for the creation of a Christian nation by force of law.

The single signal of hope in the states was the fact that the fundamentalists made little headway in most states during the 1992 state convention season in establishing their leadership.

The fragmentation will continue for the foreseeable future. The several states are seriously divided over the issues. Many of the associations of churches are experiencing the same problems. Churches increasingly are becoming involved. Groups of fundamentalists or moderates have formed in many of them. Various levels of conflict exist across the country. Where the conflict does not exist, there has been a marked lack of information or interest in the problems.

Loss of Institutional Support

Institutions are already losing the support of a substantial number of moderates. The financial structures are being weakened. Wills and

---

[2]*The Baptist Messenger*, 24 November 1992, 3.

bequests are being changed. Cooperative Program support has fallen to nil in some churches, has been altered radically in others, and probably will continue to decline. For more than half a century, the entire denomination has pushed the Cooperative Program method of funding missions and education. Now many voices are stilled because of principle. As one board chairman said to me, "The conservatives now have to put their money where their mouth is." Whether this will come remains to be seen. Many of those most vocal about it have done little to this point. It does not seem reasonable that the loss of the support of thousands, if not millions, of Baptists will lend itself to financial stability.

The readjustment of state convention budgets as related to the national budget continues. A few, principally the smaller conventions, have added a fraction of a percent; others have drastically reduced funds that would go to national causes.

The recital of fragmentation fissures is almost unlimited.

Many individual churches have joined the confusion and are looking at other ways to do missions. Various plans have been presented to churches, associations, and state conventions that would seriously alter support to national agencies.

It seems clear that we are rapidly moving back to a societal method of mission sponsorship (rejected in 1845) and away from the convention method.

During fiscal 1992, mission giving through the national Cooperative Program was down again. Inflation also continues to eat away at support in actual dollars.

State executive directors are seriously discussing what to do next with relationship to mission giving.

With the development of new seminaries or divinity schools, the problems will increase. The pool of students is somewhat smaller than normal because of demographics, and now these students have to face the wider choices available. The funding formula for the six SBC seminaries is enrollment driven. It seems inevitable that support will diminish. Duke McCall, fifty-year veteran of denominational and educational leadership, said recently, "The seminaries are headed for the dark ages."

The wide diversity in the society reflected in the denomination almost ensures further division of opinions and actions in the future. As the churches and associations work their way through the confusion, it seems likely that much energy will be wasted and many people alienated. At every level, people and institutions are being required to face the issues and make decisions that will further divide.

Incidentally, a new trend is developing that will further fragment the convention. Now national convention presidents who either do not know the system or do not care to observe it are proposing programs for action that properly belong to the agencies and their trustees. As new initiatives are publicly announced before any or little consultation, new tensions are sure to develop as agencies try to fit these demands into ever tightening budgets. The president gets a lot of what he thinks is favorable press, and the agency gets a new problem.

Add to the confusion the fact that, historically, fundamentalists have been unable to get along among themselves. Every fundamentalist movement sooner or later has divided as the circle is continually narrowed. The more creedal become the demands and the narrower the leadership circle constricts, the more the problems of collegiality. Cracks already seem to be appearing within the fundamentalist circles in the SBC.

Paige Patterson, hero of many fundamentalists, was "dismissed" recently at Criswell College. The council of former presidents of the SBC flew to Dallas to insist on his reinstatement. The press reported that, after seven hours of debate behind closed doors, he was reinstated. One trustee, who did not want to be identified, said that he was not voted back in, but that the trustees simply agreed with the pleas of the faithful "to wait awhile." Their wait was rewarded when he was elected as president of Southeastern Seminary.

Many observers feel that the leadership of the movement has moved out of the hands of the Patterson-Pressler coalition into the hands of the super-church pastors. Some insist that the new group is moving as far away from Pressler-Patterson as possible.

Among the trustees of the agencies, there are already two distinct groups. There are those who seem set on disrupting the agency and getting new leadership. Often, there seems to have been irresponsible or vindictive action that has brought great grief and irreparable damage. These trustees are called by others "loose canons" or by less complimentary names. Some of the more thoughtful and knowledgeable trustees are beginning to see that things are not as bad as they thought and that institutions are not built by destroying them. Which group will have control remains to be seen.

What Remains?

The Southern Baptist Convention will continue. Even weakened, it is still one of the strongest in the nation. To this point, the momentum and loyalty gained over a century of progress have kept the statistics decent. During the twelve years of the conflict, the numbers have continued to grow slowly. That momentum seems to be about exhausted. New motivations and financial support do not seem to have materialized.

More than half of the churches in the convention have less than 300 members. Most of the individuals in these churches do not receive the state Baptist paper. They have little source of information about the problems of the denomination, except from the pastor. Sunday School Board materials that have been a formative influence in the past now can contain no information about the problems.

Many of these pastors have chosen not to deal with the conflict and relate it to their congregations. Add to these the larger churches that have adopted the same stance. Then add the churches led by fundamentalist pastors who will frequently stone the denomination for "liberalism." With all of these churches lacking adequate information, but with generations of training for support of the mission programs, the machinery will grind on for years.

As for the convention's direction, it is difficult to know. The new masters are riding high. There is a new kind of arrogance that puts women down, moderates out, has the answers to the unanswerable, and has not heard that "pride goes before the fall." Whatever the faults of the old system, they certainly did not exceed those produced by the new.

And, the "little" preachers and others who furnished the troops for the new order have lost again. The super-churches are in control.

There is a generation of young preachers and laity who never knew the SBC before the conflict. They have no way of knowing what it used to be. Many of these will accommodate themselves to the new order, not knowing the implications. Some will find themselves completely at home with a new kind of authority. Some will seek other fellowships.

And a large number of former leaders and hosts of supporters are lost to the cause forever. They could furnish a nucleus for a new denomination. Most are not going anywhere because they were born and nurtured in the spirit of Southern Baptists as they used to be.

Somewhere, sometime, I learned a quatrain that epitomizes the feeling of multitudes.

> I'm Southern Baptist born,
> Southern Baptist bred,
> And I'll be a Southern Baptist
> Even when I'm dead!

Prospects for a new denomination fashioned after the old Southern Baptist Convention seem dim. However, support for one is growing.

The old denomination continues to fragment amid tears of the disfranchised and the assurance of the new leadership that all is well.

Ichabod! The glory has departed!

"The Southern Baptist Synthesis"

We came from sophisticated cities like Charleston and from rustic crossroads like Sandy Creek. We came educated and uneducated. We came with evangelism and we came with educational institutions. We came with the local church and the universal church. We came with Calvinistic theology, Arminian theology, and no theology. We came applauding confessional statements, and we came deploring confessional statements. We came affirming culture and rebuking culture. But mostly, I think, we just came together. That togetherness is a marvel to those of us on the inside and a mystery to those on the outside. And it is the togetherness, the diversity, the synthesis, which we must receive and confess and forgive. Above all, we must *know* it. Or there will be no hope for the denomination's future.[3]

---

[3]Walter B. Shurden, "The Southern Baptist Synthesis: Is it Cracking?," *Baptist History and Heritage* 16 (April, 1981): 11.

Index